D.D. Dougherty, Lillie Dougherty and the Early
Years of Appalachian State

Contributions to Southern Appalachian Studies

1. *Memoirs of Grassy Creek: Growing Up in the Mountains on the Virginia–North Carolina Line.* Zetta Barker Hamby. 1998

2. *The Pond Mountain Chronicle: Self-Portrait of a Southern Appalachian Community.* Edited by Leland R. Cooper and Mary Lee Cooper. 1998

3. *Traditional Musicians of the Central Blue Ridge: Old Time, Early Country, Folk and Bluegrass Label Recording Artists, with Discographies.* Marty McGee. 2000

4. *W.R. Trivett, Appalachian Pictureman: Photographs of a Bygone Time.* Ralph E. Lentz II. 2001

5. *The People of the New River: Oral Histories from the Ashe, Alleghany and Watauga Counties of North Carolina.* Edited by Leland R. Cooper and Mary Lee Cooper. 2001

6. *John Fox, Jr., Appalachian Author.* Bill York. 2003

7. *The Thistle and the Brier: Historical Links and Cultural Parallels Between Scotland and Appalachia.* Richard Blaustein. 2003

8. *Tales from Sacred Wind: Coming of Age in Appalachia. The Cratis Williams Chronicles.* Cratis D. Williams. Edited by David Cratis Williams and Patricia D. Beaver. 2003

9. *Willard Gayheart, Appalachian Artist.* Willard Gayheart and Donia S. Eley. 2003

10. *The Forest City Lynching of 1900: Populism, Racism, and White Supremacy in Rutherford County, North Carolina.* J. Timothy Cole. 2003

11. *The Brevard Rosenwald School: Black Education and Community Building in a Southern Appalachian Town, 1920–1966.* Betty J. Reed. 2004

12. *The Bristol Sessions: Writings About the Big Bang of Country Music.* Edited by Charles K. Wolfe and Ted Olson. 2005

13. *Community and Change in the North Carolina Mountains: Oral Histories and Profiles of People from Western Watauga County.* Compiled by Nannie Greene and Catherine Stokes Sheppard. 2006

14. *Ashe County: A History; A New Edition.* Arthur Lloyd Fletcher. 2009 [2006]

15. *The New River Controversy; A New Edition.* Thomas J. Schoenbaum. Epilogue by R. Seth Woodard. 2007

16. *The Blue Ridge Parkway by Foot: A Park Ranger's Memoir.* Tim Pegram. 2007

17. *James Still: Critical Essays on the Dean of Appalachian Literature.* Edited by Ted Olson and Kathy H. Olson. 2008

18. *Owsley County, Kentucky, and the Perpetuation of Poverty.* John R. Burch, Jr. 2008

19. *Asheville: A History.* Nan K. Chase. 2007

20. *Southern Appalachian Poetry: An Anthology of Works by 37 Poets.* Edited by Marita Garin. 2008

21. *Ball, Bat and Bitumen: A History of Coalfield Baseball in the Appalachian South.* L.M. Sutter. 2009

22. *The Frontier Nursing Service: America's First Rural Nurse-Midwife Service and School.* Marie Bartlett. 2009

23. *James Still in Interviews, Oral Histories and Memoirs.* Edited by Ted Olson. 2009

24. *The Millstone Quarries of Powell County, Kentucky.* Charles D. Hockensmith. 2009

25. *The Bibliography of Appalachia: More Than 4,700 Books, Articles, Monographs and Dissertations, Topically Arranged and Indexed.* Compiled by John R. Burch, Jr. 2009

26. *Appalachian Children's Literature: An Annotated Bibliography.* Compiled by Roberta Teague Herrin and Sheila Quinn Oliver. 2010

27. *Southern Appalachian Storytellers: Interviews with Sixteen Keepers of the Oral Tradition.* Edited by Saundra Gerrell Kelley. 2010

28. *Southern West Virginia and the Struggle for Modernity.* Christopher Dorsey. 2011

29. *George Scarbrough, Appalachian Poet: A Biographical and Literary Study with Unpublished Writings.* Randy Mackin. 2011

30. *The Water-Powered Mills of Floyd County, Virginia: Illustrated Histories, 1770–2010.* Franklin F. Webb and Ricky L. Cox. 2012

31. *School Segregation in Western North Carolina: A History, 1860s–1970s.* Betty Jamerson Reed. 2011

32. *The Ravenscroft School in Asheville: A History of the Institution and Its People and Buildings.* Dale Wayne Slusser. 2014

33. *The Ore Knob Mine Murders: The Crimes, the Investigation and the Trials.* Rose M. Haynes. 2013

34. *New Art of Willard Gayheart.* Willard Gayheart and Donia S. Eley. 2014

35. *Public Health in Appalachia: Essays from the Clinic and the Field.* Edited by Wendy Welch. 2014

36. *The Rhetoric of Appalachian Identity.* Todd Snyder. 2014

37. *African American and Cherokee Nurses in Appalachia: A History, 1900–1965.* Phoebe Ann Pollitt. 2016

38. *A Hospital for Ashe County: Four Generations of Appalachian Community Health Care.* Janet C. Pittard. 2016

39. *Dwight Diller: West Virginia Mountain Musician.* Lewis M. Stern. 2016

40. *The Brown Mountain Lights: History, Science and Human Nature Explain an Appalachian Mystery.* Wade Edward Speer. 2017

41. *Richard L. Davis and the Color Line in Ohio Coal: A Hocking Valley Mine Labor Organizer, 1862–1900.* Frans H. Doppen. 2016

42. *The Silent Appalachian: Wordless Mountaineers in Fiction, Film and Television.* Vicki Sigmon Collins. 2017

43. *The Trees of Ashe County, North Carolina.* Doug Munroe. 2017

44. *Melungeon Portraits: Exploring Kinship and Identity.* Tamara L. Stachowicz. 2018

45. *Always Been a Rambler: G.B. Grayson and Henry Whitter, Country Music Pioneers of Southern Appalachia.* Josh Beckworth. 2018

46. *Tommy Thompson: New-Timey String Band Musician.* Lewis M. Stern. 2019

47. *Appalachian Fiddler Albert Hash: The Last Leaf on the Tree.* Malcolm L. Smith with Edwin Lacy. 2020

48. *Junaluska: Oral Histories of a Black Appalachian Community.* Edited by Susan E. Keefe with the Junaluska Heritage Association. 2020

49. *Boone Before Boone: The Archaeological Record of Northwestern North Carolina Through 1769.* Tom Whyte. 2020

50. *From the Front Lines of the Appalachian Addiction Crisis: Healthcare Providers Discuss Opioids, Meth and Recovery.* Edited by Wendy Welch. 2020

51. *Writers by the River: Reflections on 40+ Years of the Highland Summer Conference.* Edited by Donia S. Eley and Grace Toney Edwards. 2021

52. *Wayne Howard: Old Time Music, the Hammons Family and Mountain Lore.* Lewis M. Stern. 2021

53. *Lost Cove, North Carolina: Portrait of a Vanished Appalachian Community, 1864–1957* Christy A. Smith. 2022

54. *LeConte Lodge: A Centennial History of a Smoky Mountain Landmark.* Tom Layton and Mike Hembree. 2024

55. *D.D. Dougherty, Lillie Dougherty and the Early Years of Appalachian State.* Doris Perry Stam. 2024

D.D. Dougherty, Lillie Dougherty and the Early Years of Appalachian State

DORIS PERRY STAM

CONTRIBUTIONS TO
SOUTHERN APPALACHIAN STUDIES, 55

McFarland & Company, Inc., Publishers
Jefferson, North Carolina

ISBN (print) 978 1 4766 9663 8
ISBN (ebook) 978-1-4766-5477-5

LIBRARY OF CONGRESS AND BRITISH LIBRARY
CATALOGUING DATA ARE AVAILABLE

Library of Congress Control Number 2024042766

© 2024 Doris Perry Stam. All rights reserved

*No part of this book may be reproduced or transmitted in any form
or by any means, electronic or mechanical, including photocopying
or recording, or by any information storage and retrieval system,
without permission in writing from the publisher.*

Front cover images: Dauphin Disco and Lillie Shull Dougherty in front of their
new home, circa 1903; campus snapshot panorama, circa 1926 (both images
Doris Stam Collection, University Archives, Special Collections Research Center,
Appalachian State University, Boone, North Carolina).

Printed in the United States of America

*McFarland & Company, Inc., Publishers
Box 611, Jefferson, North Carolina 28640
www.mcfarlandpub.com*

Table of Contents

Acknowledgments   ix
Preface   1

1. Dauphin Disco Dougherty: Life Aspirations at Age 21   3
2. Dougherty Ancestors: Grandfather Elijah Dougherty (1744–1865)   7
3. Ellen Bartlett and Daniel Baker Dougherty (1865–1876)   15
4. Lillie Shull's Family: Pioneers on the Watauga River, Tennessee   22
5. Early Education for the Dougherty Boys (1876–1888)   28
6. Wake Forest College (1888–1892)   35
7. Dauph Becomes a Professor (1892–1894)   46
8. Winning the Love of Lillie Shull (1894–1897)   51
9. Newly Married and Considering a Big Change (1897–1898)   58
10. The Doughertys Return to Boone and Start a High School (Summer 1899)   70
11. Watauga Academy Begins (Fall 1899)   81
12. A Whole New World Opens for Students (1900–1902)   87
13. Poorly Trained and Poorly Paid Teachers: Seeking State Aid (Fall 1902)   99
14. The Fight to Establish State Support: Appalachian Training School (Winter 1903)   111
15. Appalachian Training School Begins (1903–1906)   119
16. Joys and Sorrows, Threats, and Farms (1907–1911)   131
17. More Children, Extended Family, and an Elopement (1912–1915)   144
18. While Appalachian Training School Grows (1915–1916)   161
19. Changes Come with World War, the Flu Pandemic, and Tweetsie Railroad (1917–1919)   176

20. The State Mandates a Major Reorganization: No Longer a Regional
    High School (1920–1924) ... 188
21. From a Normal School to a Four-Year College (1925–1929) ... 202
22. Lillie Shull Dougherty's Last Years (1930–1945) ... 216
23. Dauphin Disco Dougherty: The Dougherty Family Legacy
    and the Brothers Compared ... 228

Chapter Notes ... 243
Bibliography ... 275
Index ... 287

D.D. Dougherty, Lillie Dougherty and the Early Years of Appalachian State

Doris Perry Stam

Contributions to
Southern Appalachian Studies, 55

McFarland & Company, Inc., Publishers
Jefferson, North Carolina

ISBN (print) 978-1-4766-9663-8
ISBN (ebook) 978-1-4766-5477-5

LIBRARY OF CONGRESS AND BRITISH LIBRARY
CATALOGUING DATA ARE AVAILABLE

Library of Congress Control Number 2024042766

© 2024 Doris Perry Stam. All rights reserved

No part of this book may be reproduced or transmitted in any form or by any means, electronic or mechanical, including photocopying or recording, or by any information storage and retrieval system, without permission in writing from the publisher.

Front cover images: Dauphin Disco and Lillie Shull Dougherty in front of their new home, circa 1903; campus snapshot panorama, circa 1926 (both images Doris Stam Collection, University Archives, Special Collections Research Center, Appalachian State University, Boone, North Carolina).

Printed in the United States of America

McFarland & Company, Inc., Publishers
Box 611, Jefferson, North Carolina 28640
www.mcfarlandpub.com

Acknowledgments

For making this book possible, my deep gratitude goes to:

- My mother, Lillie Brown Perry, who deeply respected and adored her parents—Clara and Lester Brown, and her maternal grandparents—Dauph and Lillie Dougherty.
- Chip, my amazing and incredibly gifted husband for 36 years, who pushed me to a higher level. He skillfully and happily edited my first feeble efforts while he was being treated for cancer during 2008-10, and helped me publish my first book, *Mountain Educators: The Dougherty Family and the First Fifty Years of Appalachian* (2010). He died in 2011. His provision for me has enabled me to continue this endeavor. I feel his presence in all I do.
- My siblings: Donna and Henry and Susan, for reading early chapter drafts and cheering me on.
- Former ASU Interim Chancellor Dr. Harvey Durham put wind in my sails when I felt no one cared about Appalachian's history. He cared. And he boosted me back into the project after I taught school overseas for a year (2019–2020).
- Greta Browning and Ross Cooper, from Appalachian State University Special Collections and Research Center, who both helped me in countless ways with kindness and professionalism.
- Cousin Bill Brown, whose generosity during the last decade has made Founders' Plaza, the statues of D.D. and Lillie Dougherty, and Founders' Day celebrations possible.
- Tim McKewon, UNC Professor Emeritus, who respected me when I most needed it, mentored me, and gave extensive and wise counsel, as did his wife, Lou Ann Phelps.
- Michael C. Hardy encouraged me, as did his fine book, *A Short History of Watauga County*.
- Linda Demerest, who out-of-the-blue stepped in to clean up the details in thousands of source notes and bibliography entries, blew more wind in the sails that pushed me toward the finish line. God sent you.
- Dozens of people who helped me edit, track down photographs or other details, notably: Caroline, Ann, Dianne, Laurie, Harvey, Tim, Juanita, Becky, and Eddie.
- Many friends and family who have cared about me and endured my neglect of them as I prioritized this project for the last four years. Donna

and Linda, particularly, consistently recognized the great effort and emotional cost involved in pressing on with this enormous task and expressed their appreciation. I am deeply grateful.
- And, for the time and skill given to masterfully elevate this manuscript, to Lou Ann Phelps, gratias tibi ago.

Preface

This is a story about the evolution of higher education in North Carolina seen through the lives of two people who were devoted to its pursuit in the establishment and expansion of what we know of as Appalachian State University.

The 125-year history of this school rests on the foundation created by Dauphin Disco Dougherty and his wife Lillie Shull Dougherty. This husband-and-wife team, joined by his bachelor brother, Blanford Barnard Dougherty, founded and sustained the school through decades of challenges and hardships. Beginning in 1899 as semi-private Watauga Academy, then, in 1903, as the state-supported Appalachian Training School, with the Doughertys' guidance the school grew through two decades as a regional high school, its transformation into Appalachian Normal School in 1924, and its evolution into Appalachian State Teachers College in 1929.

Dauph (D.D.) was head of the school and taught mathematics and science until 1921, when the ever-enlarging role of business manager demanded his full-time attention. Lillie labored side by side with her husband privately and professionally in her capacities as primary teacher, music teacher, homemaker, hostess, wife, mother, and, after his death, business manager and treasurer of the college. Blan (B.B.) became Watauga County superintendent for 16 years (1899–1915), which included oversight of the school they founded in 1899, and co-principal for the four years of Watauga Academy. In 1921, with the re-organization of all the state teacher training schools, Blan became president of Appalachian, and stayed in that position until 1955, making Appalachian a family led institution for 56 years. Dauph's health began to fail after 1924, and he died in 1929, at which time Lillie took over as business manager. She died in 1945.

The larger educational movement in the South after Reconstruction, the Blair Bill, the Farmers' Alliance, the Populist and Fusionist political alliances in North Carolina, and the Southern Board of Education are part of the backdrop to AppState's story. Democratic party politics in the early 1900s, led by Charles B. Aycock, play a part in the semi-private school becoming a state-supported regional teacher training center "for whites."

Far removed from the government machinery and power-politics of Raleigh, and from the economically thriving and growing cities in North Carolina, the isolated mountain taxpayers also deserved their distribution of state benefits, the Doughertys argued. Advocating for their region, each of the three Doughertys played a major role in advancing the economic opportunities through education that came to the northwestern counties of the state. Interwoven with the Dougherty family story is the development of the village of Boone into a thriving town, finally more accessible by roads and railroads.

Although much of AppState's history was lost due to campus fires, a trail of clues pieced together from family letters, the two biographies of Blanford Barnard Dougherty, the histories of peer institutions, and other research reveal an extensive heretofore unnoticed sub-structure of Dauph Dougherty's decisions and leadership, and the significance of Lillie's many roles. While B.B. Dougherty received two honorary doctorates during his lifetime and is credited with securing the bill which established a state-supported school, Appalachian grew from a regional high school into a four-year college in 1929 largely through the behind the scenes work of Dauph and Lillie Dougherty.

The scope of this book encompasses the family backgrounds and major influences in the lives of the founders, their years of teaching and administration, and the legacy they established at AppState, with a focus on Dauph and Lillie Dougherty and the first three decades of Appalachian. The depth of research and space limitation prevent details of president B.B. Dougherty's leadership past the death of his brother Dauph.

When I inherited Dougherty family photographs and letters, dating back to the 1880s, a weight of responsibility came upon me to preserve and identify the importance of these documents and images. With my parents and extended family all rooted in Watauga County, I had a knowledge of local families that a general researcher could not gain, and which helped me tell the story of Appalachian through the eyes of students who attended (particularly both of my grandfathers), as well as give flesh to the bare facts of the growth of the institution. My first attempt to compile this information, *Mountain Educators: The Dougherty Family and the First Fifty Years of Appalachian* (2010), was quickly out of print and needed a few small corrections and updates. The result of many more years of extensive research, I trust that this greatly expanded and academic biography and history will be valuable and enjoyable for all readers as Appalachian celebrates its 125th anniversary.

1

Dauphin Disco Dougherty

Life Aspirations at Age 21

"..to all who read these lines"[1]

On New Year's Eve, 1890, Dauphin Disco Dougherty, then a junior at Wake Forest College, looked back at the old year and ahead to the new and wrote: "My hope is that the new year will be a happy one to all who read these lines which were written as the old year died on December 31, 1890, at Wake Forest College."[2] As he worked by the light of an oil lamp, Dauph's deep-set eyes, shaded by thick brows, were dark and unflinchingly serious.

Studious and responsible as always, he had completed his lessons for the next day's classes. His roommate, whom he jokingly referred to as "my old lady," had returned from a Christmas visit home with cake and turkey, upon which the two had feasted all week. They had hoped to ring in the new year, literally, from the bell tower, but couldn't find the tower key. Instead, to mark the occasion, they had found Tennyson's poem "The Death of the Old Year" and *recited it in the hall to 80 sleeping boys as the hands of the clock inch[ed] towards 12:00 o'clock.*"[3]

Unable to visit his own

Dauphin Disco Dougherty, Wake Forest College student portrait, c. 1892 (Doris Stam Collection, University Archives, Special Collections Research Center, Appalachian State University, Boone, North Carolina).

family for Christmas, the 21-year-old Dauph marked the onset of the new year by earnest soul-searching and resolution:

> Looking at the old year in a more serious light have we anything to be thankful for or regret? Ought not we to turn back on the out going year and try to remedy the errors that we have made [and] in every way improve the new year which lies before us with its many and varied opportunities of doing good, of making our lives better and of trying to better the conditions of those around us.
>
> New Year's Day is a great day for people to make promises to do better but in less than a week they will all be broken in some way. A good rule is to say I will try to be kinder and consider the rights of others more. How much enjoyment is lost by the neglect of this virtue! How beautiful is the golden rule if correctly followed. What a stream of blessing would come upon the human family if the individuals which compose it would be more considerate.[4]

For the Other Fellow

Dauphin Disco Dougherty wholeheartedly devoted himself to being a man of virtue, of godly character. To care about others was uppermost in Dauph's determined young mind and heart.

Even at the age of 19, he was known as a young man of integrity who had an impact on those around him. In the style of that day, his friend W.R. Cullom reflected, writing in 1930 about their time together at Wake Forest in 1890: "…one of my best-loved classmates. He was from Watauga County—a man simple in his habits as a little child, as honest as the sunshine, as rugged in soul as the great hills whence he came, as tender of heart as the gentlest of women, as strong an intellect as any giant of the mountains. This man was D.D. Dougherty."[5]

Do these flowery words seem like merely veneer? Dauph Dougherty took his manifold duties and responsibilities seriously. He prepared thoroughly for classes that he took and later those he taught. He prepared himself to become a responsible scholar, administrator, citizen, husband, father, and church leader.

At the end of his life, in 1929, many testified to these qualities.

> Every great man possesses some outstanding characteristic that makes him unlike his fellows—some one thing, some another. It was always easy for those who knew his inner life to see these distinguishing characteristics of Professor Dougherty. Here it is: while others thought and moved in the usual tenor of life, he was planning ways and means whereby he could help and encourage those who needed it most—to make life a little happier and sweeter for the other fellow.[6]

Kind words and helpful deeds characterized his life, according to a long-time faculty member who noted that Professor Dauph "always extended a helping hand or dropped a word of cheer."[7]

In the words of his colleague and childhood schoolmate, Emma Horton Moore: "None but close friends really knew the great depth of character that made up the wonderful manhood of Mr. Dougherty, so unassuming was his disposition and yet so far reaching his good works and influence. He was a kind friend to all and was ever ready to give help and advice to those who needed it."[8]

"He was at all times considerate of others," testified his closest friend, the Rev.

William Bradshaw, from Morganton, who also wrote: "Owing to his retiring disposition, few men were privileged to know him as I did. A man of steadfast purpose and high ambition, his life was an unusually busy one. Despite his manifold duties however, he was at all times thoughtful of others, always willing to share the burdens of his fellow man...."[9]

Dauph Dougherty stares out with such seriousness from his formal school poses that it is difficult to imagine the light-heartedness or personal warmth to which people attest. Yet Dauph's son-in-law, Lester Brown, described him thus:

> Although he was a great thinker and often saw oppressing conditions that affected him deeply, Professor Dauph was not an overly serious man. He had a wholesome appreciation for wit and humor and was not at all short on either. ... The antics and sayings of children amused him and brought from him many a hearty laugh. ... In the foibles and frailties of men, including himself, he often saw the "funny" side and laughed about [them]. His sense of humor helped to buoy him up in a world that sometimes seemed contradictory.[10]

"He reminded me of Santa Claus, as he was very jolly and friendly," remarked LeVerne Fox, who grew up around Dauph Dougherty and later worked for him.[11] The enjoyment of family, a delight in the world of plants and animals, and a God-given love for people, seemed to strengthen Dauph as he carried out his duties. The weight of his calling and resulting authority were never easy. He managed a very full load until a heart condition slowed him down in his fifties.

A Servant Throughout His Life

Appalachian professor Vance C. Howell wrote that D.D.D. sought always to serve the people and the state, in a quiet and even unknown way. Describing his service as "devoid of selfish, self-seeking purposes," Howell wrote of his employer:

> To him [D.D.] it mattered not whether the world was aware of his achievements. His rich and ingenious mind made its approach to the solution of every problem in the form of a question. His ever-repeated question was this: Is the state being served nobly and well? Is this action right? Is it wrong? Is it just? Upon his judgement—almost always correct—he acted without hesitation and without fear. He, at all times, put the College first, for it was the very soul of his life's dream.
>
> His keen intellect and powerful initiative constantly brought into the life of the Institution new ideas and principles which were far in advance of his times. His constant fusing, into the life of the Institution, ideals of modern and progressive education has had no small part in the rapid growth of this college.
>
> ... In his service to the state his friends bear testimony that he never said or did anything in private that he would not say or do in public.

His truly was a life dedicated to the educational welfare of the entire state.[12]

Influenced by Family

Dauph's decision to devote himself to the betterment of others came from observing his extended family, who served in their communities, and from the enormous impact of preachers and teachers upon his life, exhorting him to follow in their footsteps. Lillie Shull, future wife to Dauph Dougherty, left a legacy which confirms a similar background and trajectory to that of her husband and life partner. Both Lillie and Dauph came from families who mirrored the American pioneers, enduring the physical hardships which instilled in them an ethic of hard work and self-reliance. From their families Dauph and Lillie learned core values which guided their attitudes and actions, encouraging them to love God and serve others.

2

Dougherty Ancestors
Grandfather Elijah Dougherty (1844–1865)

Dougherty Ancestors: The Lure of Iron Ore

As a boy Dauph Dougherty helped his father in the blacksmith shop. Intensely enterprising, Dauph's father and grandfather Elijah infused in him a mindset of hard work, big dreams, and service to others. Handling iron took a strong body and a quick mind, something which Dauph Dougherty's father, Daniel Baker Dougherty, developed as a young lad under the demanding tutelage of his own father, Elijah. Elijah had learned from his father Jacob and grandfather Thomas.

Generations of Doughertys had already been working the iron ore in America. Dauph's family emigrated from Ireland to America in 1744.[1] The first to be born in America was Thomas, who enlisted as a private in the Revolutionary War from New York. Hearing of the iron ore in the southern mountains, Thomas brought his family down through Virginia to Ashe County in 1806. He had married Margaret DeFoe in 1779 after being discharged from the Colonial Army at age 33. France was Margaret's home country. She had moved to England and then emigrated to America. Her French influence filtered down through the generations, for her great-grandson, Daniel Baker Dougherty was to name his first child "heir to the throne," or Dauphin.

To encourage ironmaking in North Carolina, a legislative act of 1788 offered to everyone who erected a set of iron works a grant of 3000 acres of vacant land certified by the county court as unfit for cultivation. The large acreage of the grant was needed for the hardwood necessary to produce charcoal, so essential for the alternating red-hot heating at a bloomery.[2] A land grant was given to a certain Daniel Daugherty (spelled with "au") in Ashe County around the time that Thomas Dougherty moved to the area. This Daniel may have been a cousin of Thomas, and most likely the namesake for Dauph's father Daniel Baker Dougherty. The mouth of Helton Creek on the North Fork of the New River was the site of Daniel Daugherty's forge.[3]

Thomas Dougherty, great-great-grandfather to Dauph, and his wife Margaret probably passed through their cousin Daniel's Big Helton mining and forge operation in Ashe County, but they kept following the North Fork of the New River and then over to the lower Roan Creek Valley area of east Tennessee where Thomas purchased 600 acres.[4] Large iron deposits allowed Thomas to engage in the manufacture of iron for many years in an area known as Dry Run.

A typical Appalachian family log home ("A Tidy Door-Yard," photograph by Margaret W. Morley, ca. 1900–1915, courtesy North Carolina Museum of History).

Dauph's Grandparents Elijah and Eve Mast Dougherty

Dauph's grandfather, Elijah Dougherty, was born in 1807, grandson of Thomas and Margaret, son of Jacob and Esther Dougherty. Elijah's physical strength grew as he helped in taming the wilderness to establish a farm, digging for ore, and hammering on the anvil. According to his niece, Elijah had "a great ability and energy and a great vision of the possibilities around him. Providence gave him faculties that enabled him to become an all-around leader in a backward area."[5]

Exploring up and over the Stone Mountain ridge, crossing the state line into North Carolina and down to Cove Creek (N.C.), Elijah's excursions gave him familiarity with what became western Watauga County. When he was 21 years old, he chose well in marrying Eve Mast of Cove Creek in 1828. Fairly soon he purchased a considerable acreage of land on Mill Creek, Tennessee, near his extended family.[6] In the 1830s, Elijah began in earnest to master his surroundings, still a frontier settlement, and provide for his wife and their own future family. Twelve children were born to Elijah and Eve Dougherty between the years 1832 and 1856.[7]

Elijah Dougherty was a man of ingenuity and determination. As the pioneer population grew, with high quality iron available, skilled blacksmiths like Elijah set up shops near their homes or at crossroads. These shops functioned as the car service stations of their day, where mule or horse could be shod, and broken hoes and wagons could be repaired. As skill and ability developed, "many of the blacksmiths branched out into the manufacture of plows, hoes, wagon wheels and tires, adzes, axes, mattocks, scythe-blades, shovels, and other tools and equipment," creating little factories all over the area in reach of every farmer.[8]

Every pioneer farmer was dependent on the mining of iron ore for implements. "The blacksmith was a gunsmith, farrier, coppersmith, millwright, machinist, and a 'surgeon general' to all broken tools and implements. His forge was a center of social as well as industrial activity."[9] Generations of Doughertys would prove to have the strength of mind and body for the demanding endeavor, and would serve others well in their communities.[10]

A large, gushing spring on Elijah's property joined the streams coming off the mountains, which Elijah harnessed for many uses.[11] He erected a grist mill and built a sash-saw mill which operated in a perpendicular manner, quite modern for the times. Elijah opened a road down Mill Creek to Roan Creek to encourage traffic to his mill,

A blacksmith shop which may have been similar to that belonging to Elijah Dougherty (Special Collections & Archives, Doris Ulmann Collection, Hutchins Library, Berea College).

which served the community and brought bartered produce or some rare cash. Elijah Dougherty even operated a water-powered carding machine used for separating sheep's wool into rolls, then spinning on a big wood wheel into yarn for weaving and knitting. "Great bags of wool came in from all over the county and were brought from North Carolina across Stone Mountain by horseback to be carded."[12]

Capitalizing on growing community business, Elijah enlarged his well-equipped blacksmith shop with space for making wagons and carriages.[13] Several of Elijah's sons would later establish their own wagon-making businesses, including Dauph's father, Daniel Baker Dougherty. Elijah had a large multi-faceted business on his property, with at least three hired workers for the pottery and tanyard, but probably many other day laborers who worked for pre-war rates of 10 cents a day.[14]

Elijah and Eve's Children: Working Hard

None of Elijah and Eve's sons married as young men—presumably they were consumed with the family work and may have been saving their money.

Elijah and Eve's children were:

1. Louisa, b. 1832 (married John Hagaman)
2. Daniel Baker, b. 1833, married Ellen Bartlett *when he was 34*
3. Thomas, b. 1837, married Polly McBride *when he was 33*
4. Mary, b. 1839 (married Theron Hagaman)
5. Harvey b. 1841, married Nancy Hayes *when he was 29*
6. Elizabeth, b. 1843 (married Sherman Farthing)
7. Isaac, "Ike," b. 1844, married Leah Adams *when he was 30*
8. Adam, b. 1846, remained single
9. Caroline, b. 1849 (married Harrison Farthing)
10. Jacob, "Jake,." b. 1851, married Dora Glen *when he was 32*
11. Jackson, b. 1854, remained single
12. Joseph, b. 1856, married Elizabeth Latham *when he was 28*[15]

The challenge of such intense work in the shops and on the mountains, often near extreme heat, were aspects of the family workload shared by all the Dougherty boys, with an equal amount of energy required of the girls and their mother to tend the animals and gardens, keep the fireplaces going and the woodstove hot, prepare and cook meals, care for the house, and keep the family of 14 in fairly clean and mended clothing. Eight sons and four daughters consumed a great deal of cornbread and milk, butter and eggs—mainstays of the pioneer diet.

Lumbering, required for the extensive amount of wood used in the forge, was dangerous. Elijah's brother died in a lumbering accident, leaving 11 children for his widow to raise.[16] Blacksmithing was also hazardous and dirty work. Smells from

Elijah and Eve Mast Dougherty raised a family of 12 children 35 miles north of Boone. Elijah built a fine home before the Civil War of brick made on his property (from O. Lester Brown's book, *Blanford Barnard Dougherty: A Man to Match His Mountains* [1963]).

the lime pits, used to remove the hair from animal skins, and the disgusting run-off from the washing process, plus the pits of crushed tanning bark,[17] joined with the smithy and pottery operation to create a strong atmosphere on the Dougherty farm that far exceeded the aroma of all the cows, chickens, pigs, and horses they owned. But it was the sounds that first greeted one from afar: ringing anvils, bellows huffing and puffing, hissing heat, saw-mill, gristmill grinding, carding mill machinery, axes chopping, wagons rattling about, harness tinkling.… From sun-up until sun-down, there was *work—lots of noisy and dirty work!*

In 1854 Elijah set up a brick kiln on his land and burned bricks to build a fine colonial style house.[18] Making bricks was a slow process, requiring appropriate clay and sand in large quantities, which came from the Roan Creek. Kilns had to be kept hot—the firing process of the "green" molded clay and sand necessitated high oven temperatures to cure the brick. To have the thousands of bricks needed took many months and was costly. Hired hands must have helped with the laborious task of making thousands of molds, carrying them in and then out of the kilns, piling the baked bricks, and finally bricking the wooden house structure.[19] When Dauph visited his grandparents he took note of the beautiful walnut stairway, special wood carvings for each fireplace, a different kind of wood for each, and classic mullioned windows.[20]

How did Elijah oversee all these projects or even conceive of them? His public education was extremely limited in the backwoods of Tennessee. It must have been his grandfather Thomas and grandmother Margaret, who may have had schooling in New York, that instilled in him a love of learning and the unquenchable spirit and work ethic that enabled Elijah to flourish independently. "A student through life and an assiduous reader, Elijah had a useful library," uncommon and expensive at the time. According to his niece, "Elijah was the only land surveyor for many miles. Interested also in agriculture and all natural resources, he made a report on the wild grasses of his mountain section to a nationally known scientist who published the results."[21]

While tensions between North and South increased and storm clouds gathered, the Dougherty children worked on the farm and in the shops. The Doughertys had donated land for the Pine Grove Baptist Church and sent their children to the one-room log-house school at the church whenever they could spare them from the farm during the few weeks in which the school operated each year.

Siding with the South and the Creation of Watauga County

Prosperity came to Elijah and Eve with all their enterprises, but the Civil War interrupted. When the war seemed imminent, Elijah and his family made plans; some would stay, some would go. All but the older boys stayed on the farm to protect their property. Their neighbor and the wealthiest farmer and landowner in the county, Matthias M. Wagner, sided with the Union, as did most of the county, although he owned slaves.[22] Even though surrounded by Union sympathizers, the Doughertys chose to support the Southern cause. But why?

Dauph's grandmother, Eve Mast Dougherty, wife of Elijah, had uncles who were men of great prominence in Watauga County, N.C.: Benjamin Councill, Dudley Farthing, and Ruben Mast. Her grandmother, Eve Bower Mast, had a sister, Sarah Bower, who was married to the wealthiest land and slave owner in the county, Jordan Councill, Jr.[23] Eve Bower Mast also had brothers in Ashe County, George and Absolum Bower, who had great amounts of land and slaves. George was elected state senator in 1812 and held multiple terms. Eve Dougherty's paternal uncle Reuben Mast lived in Valle Crucis and was state representative in the House at the time of the formation of Watauga County. It was a 35-mile two-day journey on horse-back from Valle Crucis to Jefferson at that time, and two days back home (a 45-minute car drive today).[24]

The eastern part of North Carolina had a long-time opposition to the creation of any new counties in the west. Representative Reuben Mast joined his brother-in-law Dudley Farthing, and his two uncles, Jordan Councill, Jr., and Sen. George Bower, to sway the state government and create Watauga County in 1849.[25] These influential relations, Eve's extended family, sided with the Confederacy to protect their assets, as did her mother's parents, who also lived on Dry Run in Tennessee.[26] Although Elijah and Eve Dougherty did not own slaves themselves, they committed themselves to their extended family and the South.[27]

The Civil War Military Record of Dauph's grandfather, Elijah Dougherty (1807–1892), reads as follows:

> Elijah Dougherty equipped and sent five sons to the Confederate Army and Homeguards. His spacious home was situated on the main way between North Carolina and Tennessee, making headquarters for the soldiers of the Southern Army in this section. Six blocks of wood were fitted in the lower half of the big windows, with portholes to fit the guns, which made this brick house a veritable fort. So famous had this house become that it was named "Little Richmond" by the enemy and this name has gone down in history.
>
> Elijah Dougherty was too old for enlistment in the army, but in countless ways he aided the South. In his blacksmith shop he made horseshoes for the cavalry horses, repaired firearms and made dirks and Bowie knives for the Homeguards. He employed a bootmaker to take leather from his tannery and make it into boots for soldiers. He also furnished a number of horses for the Confederate Cavalry. The use of his home and all his equipment contributed to aid the Confederate cause. This statement signed by Confederate veterans: Captain B.R. Brown, Co. A, 65th Reg., 6th Cavalry, N.C. Robert P. Mast, Co. 2, 6th Cavalry, N.C.[28]

Unidentified Confederate soldier (Library of Congress).

Elijah's son Daniel Baker rode his horse up and over Stone Mountain and down to Boone, where he enlisted in the cavalry on October 10, 1862. Harvey enlisted in Johnson County on November 1 but was moved to the N.C. 65th Cavalry serving as a private under his brother Daniel, who had been appointed a first lieutenant. After enlisting, the boys returned home to the Tennessee family farm to await orders.[29]

Horses were expensive and valuable commodities. Apparently, Elijah Dougherty had a large enough herd to "furnish a number of horses" for the cavalry, and to send two sons out in the cavalry. In 1850 the price for a horse was $150–$200.[30] The value of horses remained the same for decades, as indicated by the census of 1870, when a horse and saddle cost $200, sugar was seven cents a pound, molasses 15 cents a gallon, flour $3 a barrel, and corn 40 cents per bushel.[31] To put these costs in perspective, many day laborers then earned only 10 cents per day.[32]

Cavalry made up some of the elite forces of the armies, with speed and mobility offering helpful advantages.[33] "The American Civil War saw cavalry tactics move largely away from the offensive towards the defensive, with the emphasis on screening, raiding, and reconnaissance."[34] The Dougherty brothers were fortunate to be on horses in the cavalry, and to have their father and brothers to help supply horses and keep them shod, though during their military careers they lost their mounts at some point.

Dauph Dougherty grew up hearing the tales told over and over of the escapades of his aunts as well as his uncles. Isaac, who at 16 was too young to enlist, joined the area Home Guard and led a group who were *not* violent killers, like many notorious Home Guards. Isaac recorded some of the daring Dougherty family escapades:

> During the Civil War my mother and sisters would cook three-day Rations when the Scouts would be in the vicinity. There was always much plotting about getting this food through safely to our cache at the foot of the mountain. Enemy [Union] spies were camped nearby as lookouts to see what was going on at our house which they called "Little Richmond." Of course, it would at once be evident that scouts or soldiers of the Southern army were near if my sisters were caught carrying food; so, baskets and sacks were fashioned on belts and hung under their long, full skirts. The girls apparently walked along empty-handed, nonchalantly gathering a few dried branches for lighting a fire until they reached the concealment of the woods not far away.[35]
>
> The girls would also carry news to the neighbors when they heard of the approach of the enemy, so everything could be put out of the way. Corn and meat and everything had to be kept concealed; only enough for the present meal could be brought out. This food was surreptitiously cooked and eaten without delay. Some members of the family always stood on guard to quickly notify the others of the approach of [Union] marauders.[36]
>
> When the coast was believed to be clear in the neighborhood, Aunt Hiley Dougherty and younger sister Caroline would set out on horseback in search of stolen property. They would recover woven cloth, wearing apparel and soldiers' blankets, and sometimes tanned leather from the leather pits. These had been taken by the men who had plundered and robbed when the home was briefly unprotected. … This was a daring adventure for women in those days.[37]
>
> My small brothers also were busy through these war years. Brother Jake was only 12 years of age at the beginning of this Civil War and Jackson was two years younger. They carried provisions to the soldiers who came our way going across the mountains to the nearby woods. It was never safe for these men to spend the night at the house as they might be surprised anytime and captured by an overwhelming number of the enemy. These two small boys took care of Cavalry horses and were messengers. They carried word through the neighborhood when

a horseman would bring news of the approach of the enemy. They had a little bull wagon and hauled drinking water to soldiers encamped in the nearby mountains.[38]

After the Civil War: An Eye Towards Watauga County

Elijah and Eve Dougherty had many options for refuge with relatives over the Stone Mountain in Watauga County. After the war ended, they took their children for shelter, spending possibly a year or more in North Carolina. It remained unsafe to stay in the predominantly Union supporting area of their Tennessee home because of local hostilities, continued revenge, and violence in the area.[39] "Tragically there were many murders in Johnson County committed by both sides during this terrible war."[40]

The civil war was over. Or was it? It was a very uncivil war in and around Johnson County and many families moved away. Many of the families, like the Doughertys and the Browns, who had left their property, returned later, after the war, and were slowly accepted back into society.[41] Daniel and his brothers had big dreams and plans for their futures, not unlike their parents, Elijah and Eve.

Dauph Dougherty's father and brothers bought and sold land in Johnson (Tennessee), Ashe and Watauga counties (both in North Carolina). Records for Watauga County before 1873 are limited because of two courthouse fires. Union General George Stoneman ordered the Court House and records be destroyed in 1865 when he marched through the village of Boone. After being rebuilt, a mysterious fire destroyed everything in a new Court House in 1873.[42] Persons who had copies could prove ownership with these duplicate deeds, and for that reason some transactions and deeds prior to 1872 are in the current deed books.

For the Dougherty family members there were probably more pre–1873 transactions than are listed in the Watauga County deed books, but it is most interesting that between 1866 and 1906 transactions as the *grantor* of real estate are listed more than 100 times. Daniel Baker, listed as D.B., was also listed as a surveyor and commissioner on many transactions.

Purchases of property as *grantees* in Watauga County begin in 1866 for Daniel Baker Dougherty and list at least 21 transactions before his death in 1902. Transactions for his brothers are listed 39 times, and once for his father. Before the war ever started the brothers had likely made plans to invest in the newly formed Watauga County and its county seat of Boone. Immediately after the war, as soon as Daniel could get to Boone, in 1866 he made a deal with Benjamin Councill concerning a dividing line.[43] The town of Boone would be significantly influenced, in multiple ways, by Daniel Baker Dougherty and his children.

3

Ellen Bartlett and Daniel Baker Dougherty (1865–1876)

Family tree:

Elijah & Eve Dougherty
Daniel Baker Dougherty b. 4 December 1833

Edwin and Caroline Bartlett
Ellen Caroline Bartlett b. 25 March 1845

Daniel and Ellen m. 5 December 1867
Dauphin Disco, b. 11 March 1869
Blanford Barnard, b. 21 October 1870
Lura Etta Mae, b. 11 May 1875

Ellen Caroline Bartlett and Her Father, a Tinner by Trade

Elegant cherry and other shade trees lined the streets of Jefferson in Ashe County, North Carolina, when Ellen Caroline Bartlett was a teenager.

Ellen Bartlett, 16 years old in 1861 at the beginning of the war, longed to be married. Like all the other girls in Jefferson, North Carolina, she was preoccupied with romance, though not a marriageable young man was left in town. Looking pretty and being finely dressed were prized in their social circles. The "society" of Jefferson, including Ellen's father, Edwin Bartlett, thought highly of itself.[1]

Edwin Clinton Bartlett, Dauph Dougherty's maternal grandfather, planted the avenues of cherry trees on Main Street, and locust trees along the sidewalk.[2] With the masses of pale pink blossoms in spring and cherries galore free for the gathering, Jefferson was designed to appear elegant on first sight.[3] By 1900, the town had 250 while Boone had 155 citizens.[4] As tinsmith for much of Ashe County, Edwin Bartlett traveled by wagon, staying in homes throughout the area. He became a familiar and friendly face as he sold his tin buckets, cups, cookie cutters, kitchen utensils and other much needed household items.[5]

Also known as "E.C." or "Squire," Edwin opened a hotel on Main Street, a roomy frame building that was so successful that he moved his family next door to a "splendid home" constructed around an old log house.[6] The Jefferson Bartletts were regarded as being somewhat aristocratic, "but in their home, as in the hotel before, people of many backgrounds found hospitality and friendship."[7]

Jefferson, North Carolina, with cherry trees and hardwoods planted by E.C. Bartlett (courtesy Museum of Ashe County History).

Bartlett was appointed as Register of Deeds for Ashe County, beginning a long side-career of 44 years as a public servant.[8] He was elected Clerk of Superior Court, then High Sheriff, and to the Board of County Commissioners in 1872.[9] According to his granddaughter, Alene, the county sent him as a delegate to the North Carolina Constitutional Convention in Raleigh in 1868.[10] Squire Bartlett operated both his home and his business in an orderly way and on a strict time schedule. He also took pride in keeping his horses well fed and nicely groomed, reflecting

Ellen Caroline Bartlett, from a tintype image, holding her flutina, c. 1865 (Doris Stam Collection, University Archives, Special Collections Research Center, Appalachian State University, Boone, North Carolina).

Tinsmith tools, c. 1875, typical of those used by E.C. Bartlett; the photograph is from a northern city and not from Appalachia (Tinsmiths with Their Work Tools, circa 1875 [Object ID 99.261.3] Image from the Collections of The Henry Ford).

his standing.[11] The Bartlett girls were certainly among the leading ladies of the town.

Daniel Baker Dougherty: Weary Soldier

When the War Between the States ended in May 1865, Daniel Baker Dougherty was discharged from Newbourne (New Bern), near the North Carolina coast. From New Bern he had been walking the 300 miles towards home for probably several weeks, penniless and weary. Daniel was not married and already in his thirties, having worked from childhood with his father Elijah's enterprises.

Daniel entered Jefferson looking for a resting place, and was directed to the large, two-story Bartlett Hotel, near the courthouse. Family lore relates the bedraggled soldier asked Edwin Bartlett, then also serving as High Sheriff, for lodging. Sheriff Bartlett invited his new lodger to attend the revival going on at the Methodist Church. Daniel agreed, with a genuineness noted by his host. "Saving souls" and building up the church membership was a priority for Edwin, a zealous Methodist. Edwin let Daniel know that as long as he was interested in the efforts of the Methodists, he could have a place at his table and a room to live in.[12]

Daniel later confessed that he might have been more interested in the food, the family, and the girls (of whom Ellen was the eldest) than he was in the Methodist revival taking place in Jefferson. He remained a faithful Baptist throughout life. The Bartlett hotel was "lively and more or less the center of things."[13] He thought it wise to stay and take in the social life of Jefferson, although he was surely not as well dressed as he would have liked.

One can imagine the 32-year-old Daniel, weary of war, was anxious to live in peace and move on with his life. Mr. Bartlett spurred him on, encouraged his aspirations and probably helped finance the beginnings of a wagon shop for Daniel in Jefferson. Daniel's wagon shop was established before serious courting began, but the initial spark between him and Ellen, when he was a bedraggled soldier, has been passed down in family stories.[14]

So often did Daniel travel to Boone investigating land and potential business, and so often did he talk about Boone, that his nickname in Jefferson was "Boone." A romance was developing between the young Ellen and this interesting and adventurous "Boone." Letters were exchanged as "Boone" traveled to Watauga County and to his home in Tennessee, but only one survived. Although more than 10 years his junior, Ellen decided "Boone" was the one for her. "Boone" (Daniel) and Ellen were married on December 5, 1867, a little more than two months after the above-mentioned letter. He had turned 34 the previous day. She was 22. They were in love.

The newlyweds stayed in Jefferson for two years, with "Boone" operating his wagon shop and traveling some to Boone in Watauga County. About 25 homes and shops lined Main Street in Jefferson, with life revolving around these shops, the town water well, and the courthouse.

Their first child, Dauphin Disco Dougherty, was born on March 1, 1869. The name the parents chose for their first-born suggests some aspirations and ambition.

Daniel's great-grandmother was from France, where the prince was called the "Dauphin." In Latin, "disco" means "I learn." As Latin was taught in all schools at the time, a basic grasp of the language was common knowledge to any with upper elementary school achievements. No fanciful French accent accompanied the pronunciation of his name in this part of the world; rather his name was shortened to Dauph, although some mistook it for "Dolf," a shortened form of Adolphus. In the mountains all first names seemed to be adapted to one syllable, no matter how long the name, or to one's initials.

Daniel and Ellen Dougherty Purchase Land and Move to Boone

Daniel was known as "Boone" only in Jefferson. In the tiny town of Boone, he was known by his initials, D.B. His many trips to the town of Boone had secured relationships with the town's prominent families.

The Councills were the major landholders in Boone. In fact, the town had been called "Councill's Store" until 1849, when the name was changed to Boone. As quickly as Daniel could get to Boone after the close of the war, he made a deal with Jordan Councill, Jr. Daniel purchased the Councill store structure, which at some point was moved across the street and remodeled as his home with Ellen and their sons.[15] The land which Daniel Dougherty purchased from Jordan Councill, Jr., a distant relative, would become the location of the campus of Appalachian State University.[16]

All the Councill family, who were the major power brokers of the county, and who had owned slaves, were shaken by the results of the war, and must have questioned their own future dominance. Jordan Councill, Jr., feared his land would be confiscated by the federal government because of his ties to the Confederacy, and offered to sell the land to Dougherty for half its value, although Dougherty was said to have had little or no money. John Preston Arthur, whose book *A History of Watauga County* preserves valuable local history, wrote: "on the first day of August 1865, Jordan Councill gave Dougherty his bond for title to all his landed property in and around Boone when Dougherty should pay him $3000 cash. Councill moved away but returned and recovered all the property Dougherty had not sold, the proceeds of that which had been sold having been applied on the bond."[17]

Daniel was able to keep some prime land, one hundred and fifty acres, and to continue to invest in Boone. His hopes were strong for the future of Boone.

Tensions remained high in Boone between Union and Confederacy supporters for many years. The Rivers family, who published the newspaper the *Watauga Democrat*, had fled pro–Union people in eastern Tennessee during the Civil War and settled in Boone. As late as 1889, when Daniel Baker Dougherty purchased and co-edited the newspaper with R.C. Rivers, and into the early 20th century, they kept a loaded shotgun nearby as they set type.[18]

More Children, and the Death of Ellen Dougherty

Ellen and Daniel must have moved to Boone before the birth of their second child, Blanford Barnard Dougherty, a son born on October 21, 1870.[19] In 1870 Jordan Councill, Jr., and his wife Sally sold 132 acres on the north side of Boone to D.B.D.[20] A new mother in a new town, Ellen was consumed with two little boys, 19 months apart. The town was smaller than Jefferson, and not as refined, to be sure. Her husband and sons kept her busy, but "now and then," Ellen was able to visit her parents and participate in the social life of Jefferson.[21]

Daniel built a small post office in Boone soon after the Civil War and served as postmaster, as well as a surveyor.[22] And he kept his blacksmith shop. Daniel read the papers and periodicals that came through the mail. He stayed "in the know." Across the street from Ellen and Daniel was the home of Dr. William Bower (W.B., Sr.) and Alice Councill. Mrs. Councill saved the life of Ellen and Daniel's second son, Blan, who almost died of diphtheria at age 3. She was to play a large role in the boys' lives.[23]

New joy came to the family when Ellen delivered a girl on May 11, 1875. But Ellen was not recovering well after the birth of her third child, Lura Etta Mae (Etta), and needed help with the three children. Daniel sent for the help of a cousin in Tennessee, Sarah Dougherty. "It is said that from her sick bed she [Ellen] taught girls to sew, to crochet and knit," wrote Ellen's niece Alene. "My grandfather's story of her was that she could sit in the window and see a lady ride by on horseback, design and make the riding habit she saw worn" in Jefferson before she was married.[24]

Left: **Daniel Baker Dougherty, c. 1880 (Doris Stam Collection, University Archives, Special Collections Research Center, Appalachian State University, Boone, North Carolina).** *Right:* **Daniel Baker Dougherty, c. 1890 (Doris Stam Collection, University Archives, Special Collections Research Center, Appalachian State University, Boone, North Carolina).**

On September 29, 1876, a year and a half after giving birth and herself only 31 years old, Ellen died. Old enough to have spoken with and remember their mother, Dauph was seven and beginning school, and Blan was nearly six. Etta, at 19 months, was now a toddler. The cause of Ellen's illness is unknown to us now. Genetics could have played a role, as several Bartlett siblings also died young. She was the first in the Dougherty family to be buried in the Boone Cemetery.[25]

Daniel was devastated by Ellen's death. How could he care for a baby girl, and two little boys? He couldn't leave the house to care for the farm animals and gardens, go to his blacksmith shop, travel the county as a surveyor, or do his business at the courthouse. How could he cook for the family? Where would he get the money to pay for helpers?

The decision to honor the request of childless relatives Jacob and Sara Adams Mast to allow little Etta to live with them was difficult. Dauph and Blan grieved over the loss of their mother and their baby sister, "lonely over the separation and all their lives were reluctant to discuss it."[26] More than eight decades later Blan told his nephew that "he could never forget the sadness he felt when he saw Etta placed in the arms of Mr. Mast, who was on his horse, and watched him ride away."[27] A housekeeper and cook sometimes helped. Sarah Dougherty, a cousin from Tennessee, stayed on for a while after Ellen's death, before leaving to care for other sick relatives.

Before the age of five, during his mother's long illness, Dauph took the role of older brother and father's helper very seriously. Little brother Blan, eager to do and be like his older brother, stuck close to Dauph all his life.

Daniel would take the boys to the blacksmith shop, where they gave some assistance, but were also hindrances. Blan was told once by his father to "get out of the way," to which the strong-willed Blan replied, "You get out of my way!"[28] Batching as best they could, the two boys grew up without the tender love of their mother. Daniel did not remarry.

A stern creased brow and heavy, tired eyes seem to dominate the more formal photograph of Daniel. The family has only two photos of him. A rugged frontiersman attitude comes across loud and clear in the casual portrait of Daniel Baker Dougherty.

4

Lillie Shull's Family

Pioneers on the Watauga River, Tennessee

Lillie Shull: Growing Up in Butler, Tennessee

Lillie Belle Shull, born January 6, 1874, in Butler, Tennessee, when Dauph Dougherty was five years old, would become the most important person in his life, and he in hers.[1] Lillie was the fourth of seven children born to David Harrison Shull and Martha Sousanna Lewis Shull.[2]

Lillie possessed a strength, an independence, and a self-reliance that separated her from many college-age girls. Not content to marry immediately, she ventured out and taught school in another county, returned to teach two years in her hometown, all the while being pursued by multiple men, including Dauph Dougherty.

David Shull, Lillie's father, was a farmer who had little schooling but possessed a strong mind and was an engaging conversationalist, with high educational, moral, and religious ideals.[3] The Baptist Church was central to his life, and he made certain his family

Lillie Shull as teenager in a handmade gown. This image was inspiration for her statute in the Founders' Plaza at Appalachian State University (Doris Stam Collection, University Archives, Special Collections Research Center, Appalachian State University, Boone, North Carolina).

Founders' Day 2023 focused on the contributions of women to Appalachian. This collage of Lillie Shull's life was used for that event (Doris Stam Collection, University Archives, Special Collections Research Center, Appalachian State University, Boone, North Carolina).

regularly attended. Friends and strangers were always welcome in the Shull home, where preachers were given special honor. David Shull was noted for having a godly focus and a godly character.[4] David's father had come with the early settlers to the virgin forest of northeastern Tennessee. He had moved from Valle Crucis (Shulls Mill) in the early 1800s to this fertile valley at the convergence of the Watauga River with Roan Creek Valley. Bottomland for farming was limited in Valle Crucis, forcing many sons to move further west to better land opportunities in Tennessee.[5]

David, because he was only 16 in 1860, and the oldest of five children of Sarah Shull, a widow, was not conscripted for the Civil War. Eight children were born to David and Martha Shull between 1866 and 1886, of whom two died in childhood. Having two older living siblings and three younger ones, Lillie helped in managing the household of eight, which she would later find, as a career teacher, was not much different than managing a classroom full of youngsters.

Keeping five girls prim and proper, while running a farm and raising a baby boy, made for a busy life. Since store-bought clothes were not available, all clothing for the family had to be sewn at home, where darning and mending never seemed to end for a big family. The girls' sewing skills, evident from their attire in family photographs, enabled several sisters to profit from an informal tailoring business later in life. Quilt making became an art, not just a necessity, through their adult lives.

When schools were reopened after the war, David and Martha made sure the Shull children attended. The prevailing attitude in the rural South at the time that young people did not need school, that life and vocational skills were learned on the farm or in the craftsman's shop, and civic and moral instruction would occur in church and on court day, was not supported in the Shull family.[6] But David and

Butler was settled on the Watauga River in Tennessee in the middle 1800s (Doris Stam Collection, University Archives, Special Collections Research Center, Appalachian State University, Boone, North Carolina).

Martha Shull strongly supported the broader and literary education of all their children.[7]

Butler was a small, remote crossroads when Lillie was a child.[8] Today it lies under the waters of Watauga Lake, a project of the Tennessee Valley Authority, or TVA, during the 1940s to bring electricity to rural Appalachia. The "town that refused to drown" was relocated nearby, house by house, including the moving of a cemetery. Not to be forgotten, an historical museum honoring Old Butler is currently operating in the new Butler village.[9]

Butler lies some 30 miles northwest of Boone, about an hour's drive by today's roads. Before the roads were built in the 1920s, it was a two-day buggy trip.[10] One route lay south of the current highway 321, another climbed over the steep Stone Mountain ridge, and a third meandered north of Trade, Tennessee. A wagon trip in 1894 from the village of Trade, on the NC-Tennessee state line, took two days by rough wagon winding through the gorge and down Roan Creek to reach the settlement later named Butler.[11] Butler's first store, livery stable and hotel were established in or around 1872. Aenon Seminary, a church-established educational institution, stood on the bluffs overlooking the Watauga River. Named in honor of Union officer Col. Roderick R. Butler, what grew into the town of Butler was built on the Shull farm.[12] Until the 20th century, Butler was a small community isolated by surrounding mountains. (Even so, at that time it was larger than Boone, North Carolina.)

Some 20 years after Lillie's birth, Butler was still just "a small village of about two hundred inhabitants, containing three good stores, a cabinet shop, a fine roller process flouring mill," and other businesses that had grown up around the school. An iron bridge across Watauga River and Roan Creek increased access to the area.[13] Butler began to thrive only when a railroad line, spurred by logging companies' local activities, was extended to the town in 1900.[14] The Virginia and Southwestern Railway Company soon connected Butler with communities and ironworks in western North Carolina. Not until the railroad arrived did Butler have a bank.

Aenon Seminary and Music for Lillie Shull

When Aenon Seminary was founded with Baptist affiliations in 1871, the Shull family began sending their children there for their education.[15] The "seminary" was more akin to an academy, with classes for primary through college, unlike today's use of the designation. Aenon, with its attachment to a wider Baptist audience in Tennessee, drew educators with college degrees—quite unusual at that time in the mountains.[16] As late as 1925 "only a few of the elementary teachers in this northeastern part of Tennessee in Johnson County had more than a few hours of college education, and many had no college training at all."[17]

After the Civil War, taxpayers in this area resented supporting public schools "for the poor," referred to as "pauper schools," and preferred to rely on private schools to educate their children. In the 1870s, when the Shulls began attending Aenon, the negative attitude towards public schools prevailed, which led to sparse financial support and low quality.[18] Growing up so soon after the war, Lillie would have naturally heard stories of opposing family alignments in the fierce division between Northern and Southern loyalties.[19]

One of the few college-educated men in the area, Aenon Seminary founder the Rev. L.L. Maples had served as a young man in the Tennessee Legislature for Mossy Creek (renamed Jefferson City in 1901) and Jefferson County but retired in 1871 to return to his first love, preaching.[20] The Reverend Maples brought a message of reconciliation and healing to the entire county, as well as his belief in the lasting power of education. The Reverend Maples' revivals were attended by former slaves and former soldiers from both sides. "He was well known by Union and Confederate soldier[s], as well as slave owners and underground operators alike. 'One of a kind,' they said of his oratory."[21] This was the Shull family pastor, who surely had a strong influence on each family member, including young Lillie Shull.

The Shulls joined many who viewed education as the pathway towards hope, especially with a man of the Reverend Maples' character as headmaster. His wife, Amanda, taught music at Aenon, having been a full-time voice and piano teacher in Jefferson City, Tennessee. Their four daughters became "well-instructed in voice and piano."[22] Together the Maples brought the gift of classical music and training in it to Butler, so very rare in the mountains. Lillie Shull would eagerly learn and excel at music—Mrs. Maples was her first teacher.[23]

Holly Spring College

When the Reverend Maples left to serve in the state legislature again, enrollment at Aenon Seminary dwindled. In 1882 James Hamilton Smith, the son of a judge, joined the faculty as principal. Smith had distinguished himself as a graduate "with high honors" at Milligan College in Elizabethton, Tennessee.[24] Soon Aenon was thriving under the new management, and grew to over 200 students by 1886, when Smith unveiled his big plans for not only the school, but the town.[25]

David Shull, Lillie's father, joined the leading men in the community to consider Smith's plans and the educational needs of the community. Thomas Dougherty, uncle to Dauph Dougherty, was also present.[26] "By the force of his indomitable personality Smith communicated his enthusiasm to these public-spirited citizens."[27]

The idea of a different school name was raised, to be chosen before classes opened in the fall of 1886. Native Americans had used the large spring ("Holly Spring") and nearby cave, a site for ceremonial burials. The cave, with its skeletons, tools, and weapons, had been closed off out of respect. It was an honored site, and Holly Spring College became the new name for the respected school. The term "college" is misleading, because the Primary Department of younger students was a significant part of the enrollment.[28]

Lillie Shull and her siblings joined other students in studying the subjects and the textbooks of that era: Harvey's *English Grammar*; Davy's *Practical Arithmetic*; McGuffey's readers; Swinton's *Word Book*; Mitchell's *Complete Geography; Physiology and Hygiene; The Bible*; and *Penmanship*.[29] Popular books of that time included *Little Women, Grimm's Fairy Tales,* and *Swiss Family Robinson.*

4. Lillie Shull's Family

Under Smith's presidency, the performing arts at Holly Spring grew. The school boasted an auditorium seating 600. There was room for the entire local community and student families from surrounding areas.[30] Lillie, a poised and polished young lady, gave music and dramatic recitations with the literary society on programs and commencement exercises at the College. Guitar lessons, vocal and instrumental music, as well as piano and organ, were taught at Holly Spring College beginning in 1889.[31] Lillie's musical accomplishments with piano, guitar, and voice, for which she was most highly regarded in Butler, would later be greatly valued in Boone.[32]

In 1890, when Lillie Shull turned 16 and was finishing her high school classes—before her freshman year of college—her sister, Mollie, older by four years, married President Smith. Lillie's college classes commenced in either 1890 or 1891. In the fall of 1892, in her second year of college classes, Lillie had a new teacher for sophomore geometry.[33] This professor would be the most important human being in her life.

5

Early Education for the Dougherty Boys (1876–1888)

A Log School for the Dougherty Boys

A primitive, one-room log structure held the first classes that Dauphin Disco Dougherty attended.[1] Cousin Sarah Dougherty, whose own mother had died when she was young, was about age 12 when she came to live with the Doughertys to help with the children.[2]

Blan showed an interest in learning the alphabet, asking Sarah to tell him the names of letters. When Sarah reported Blan's interest to his father, Daniel carved the letters on a board that Blan studied while following Sarah, and so he learned the alphabet."[3] Late in life Blan told a reporter: "'Dolf' [Blan's pronunciation of his brother's name] was twenty months older than I, and usually about three years ahead in his books."[4]

The primitive log school building that Dauph and Blan attended as children sat beside Boone Creek, somewhere near the present Holmes Convention Center on the campus of Appalachian State.[5] Instead of glass windows, a row of logs was left out at intervals around the schoolhouse to admit light. The yearly school term was only eight weeks in the fall.[6] There was very little interest in public schools,[7] and attendance was not compulsory in North Carolina until 1913.[8]

Raising the boys after the death of his wife could not have been easy for Daniel. Cousin Sarah moved to Bethel/Beaver Dams (Watauga County) to help another family. With no female in the house, a cook was hired at times, and neighbor Mrs. Alice Councill sometimes cared for the boys and helped them with their school lessons.[9]

The two sons worked alongside their father in the fields, at the barn, and in the shop. As they grew older, they grew stronger from the demanding manual labor. Dauph helped drive the wagon until he was strong enough to master the anvil and hammer. Blan then took over driving the wagon and handling the teams, at which he grew to excel.[10] Blan later recalled that he helped his father and brother cut timber and grub roots on the farm, and, with oxen hitched to a cumbersome wagon, hauled wood to town to be sold for 25 cents a load.[11]

Father Daniel: A Public-Spirited Man, Committed to Education

Daniel, like his father Elijah, was known as a public-spirited man. According to family members, Daniel lent his support to any worthwhile movement and was regarded as a leader, "not satisfied to be a mere follower."[12] In addition to farming and operating his wagon shop, Daniel wore other hats: land surveyor, practical engineer, and local politician. Daniel, like the rest of his family, tried to acquire any land that he believed would yield valuable minerals.

On court days people came from all parts of the county on foot, horseback, and in covered wagons to trade in " anything from pocket knives to horses; others came for the news and to renew old acquaintances, but horse trading took the spotlight."[13] It was an important social event. Living near the courthouse, Daniel participated in much of the political talk of the day, often inviting people to continue discussions on his porch or in his home, which became an informal beehive of civic and intellectual activity. He was "a progressive and respected citizen. Known as 'Squire Dougherty,' his judicious counsel was sought after and respected."[14] His sons were in a position to observe and learn from their father's role at the heart of the community's commercial and civic life.

No school beyond the most basic existed after the Civil War in the mountains. There was no high school. The Supreme Court of North Carolina had decided in 1870 that public schools were not a "necessity," and thus that the law imposing local taxes for public education was unconstitutional.[15] Sustaining a school, especially in poorer counties like Watauga, was difficult without local tax money.

In 1871, when Daniel and Ellen had been in Boone for one year, the Three Forks Baptist Association voted to establish a high school for the area.[16] In 1873, when Dauph was age four, Daniel donated two acres of land not far from his home for the school, to be known as Three Forks Baptist Institute. Unfortunately, funds for the construction of the high school were exhausted in 1876,

Dauph Dougherty, c. 1888, as a high school student, from a tin-type image (Doris Stam Collection, University Archives, Special Collections Research Center, Appalachian State University, Boone, North Carolina).

and the contractor for the building had left. It took several more years to complete construction with funds contributed by local area churches. Part of the Institute building was rented to the local public school committee and the income used to "to help keep the building in repair."[17] Two church members raised the money needed to pay off the indebtedness.[18] Daniel took upon himself the contract for completing the upper story, enabling the school to open in 1879, after seven years of community effort.

The first classes were conducted by Joseph F. Spainhour in January 1879 and sessions of eight to 10 weeks were held during 1880, 1881, and part of 1882.[19] Dauph was nearly 10 and Blan was eight when the school opened.

Professor Spainhour had previously founded Oak Hill Academy at Mouth of Wilson, Virginia, in 1878, and though himself not a college graduate at the time, was said to be "very thorough in all the branches he taught. His school had a wide patronage, the northwestern counties of North Carolina being well represented."[20] He continued to teach at Oak Hill while also teaching classes at Three Forks in Boone from 1879 to 1882. Teaching at more than one academy was a common practice, and school terms were set to accommodate the availability of the professor.[21]

Three Forks Institute closed permanently in 1882, and Spainhour went to a teaching post at New River Academy. A proposal was made to hire a new teacher for Three Forks, or to sell the property and open a high school at another location, which did not happen.[22] Boone was without a high school. After Three Forks closed, Daniel struggled to piece together a private-school education for his sons.[23] Professor Spainhour encouraged Daniel to enroll his boys at New River Academy, which he did.

New River Academy and Globe Academy

Dauph, age 13 in 1882, was almost ready for high-school level classes, which his father had hoped to provide for him in Boone by his efforts in establishing Three Forks Institute. Although New River Academy was only a few miles east of Boone on the south fork of the New River, walking daily to attend school there was not an option in the harsh winters, so Dauph and Blan boarded with a local farmer.[24] The boys attended this school a total of four months over two successive years.[25] The sum total of Dauph's classroom education before high school was not much more than eight or ten months.[26]

Although Professor Spainhour and his brother W.R. Spainhour successfully taught a large class of students at New River, the academy, like Three Forks, permanently closed after only a few years.[27] By this time Spainhour had earned the money he needed to enter college.

After graduating from Wake Forest College in 1885, Professor Spainhour accepted a new job in Globe, North Carolina, at Globe Academy, and convinced Daniel to send Dauph, now 16, to attend high school there. Money was extremely limited, but Daniel found the cash for Dauph to attend. Globe Academy was the pride of the Globe community on the banks of the Johns River, a 16-mile walk or

5. Early Education for the Dougherty Boys

Globe Academy is visible behind local farmers, who built the school for their children and hired the already well-known Robert L. Patton to teach (Caldwell Heritage Museum, Lenoir, NC).

wagon trip from Boone.[28] Dauph entered Globe Academy as a boarding high-school student in 1885.[29] Blan was not so fortunate and stayed in Boone.

The town of Globe was situated in the Johns River valley, reached from the Lenoir area by treacherous, winding gravel roads that frequently crossed the river. The entire Globe community was destroyed in a massive flood in 1916, from which it never recovered, causing its history to be practically unknown today.

The Baptist-affiliated Globe Academy had been founded by Robert Logan Patton only a few years earlier, but his renown as a great teacher spread the reputation of the school.[30] Inaccessible as the valley was, the high quality of education offered there won wide acclaim, and students "came from the mountains to the sea in North Carolina, and from adjoining states."[31]

Beyond his reputation as a great teacher, the life of Robert Patton and his relentless pursuit of an education were an inspiration. In 1856, at the age of 17, he had run away from his father's farm 10 miles north of Morganton, in rural Burke County, North Carolina, "with five cents in his pocket, a handmade shawl in a pillowcase, and a dream in his heart."[32] "At a time when a laborer could hardly earn enough for subsistence, he made his way through Tennessee and Kentucky into Indiana and Illinois, where he supported himself while studying privately or attending public schools. At Hillsborough, Illinois, he worked his way through three years at Hillsborough Academy."[33] From Hillsborough he attended Exeter Academy in New Hampshire, then entered Amherst College in Amherst, Massachusetts, and graduated in 1876.[34] Twenty years for a college diploma.

Patton received superior training at these excellent schools, among the finest in the nation. In 1876, he returned to his native state, where "for 43 years he devoted himself with zeal to founding schools, teaching, and preaching, mostly in Burke, Caldwell, and Wilkes counties."[35] His son would later write of him: "The two most amazing things to me were, first, how he and his two brothers got the inspiration to be educated when there were not three college graduates in Burke County; and, second, how he never faltered in his dedication to service above self—even to the end. Money never mattered to him."[36]

Professor Robert L. Patton's Return to Appalachia— a Sacred Calling

Patton could have become a state or national leader in either education or the ministry, but he chose to return to Appalachia to preach, chiefly at rural churches, and to begin schools. "When he returned from Amherst in 1876, he was probably the best educated man in Western North Carolina, and people in different communities urged him to come to them and found academies."[37]

Citizens of Globe engaged Robert Patton to teach at Globe Academy beginning August 1882—Patton's fourth endeavor. He encouraged the local people to "own" their school and invest sweat equity for their children's benefit. Parents downed the trees, dressed the lumber, hauled it to the chosen site, and built the schoolhouse.

From his regular reading of the New Testament, Patton felt he had been sent by God to minister to the mountain children of his childhood home,[38] and he devoted himself to the children of these remote areas.[39] He had also been inspired by the words of Mary Lyon, founder of Mount Holyoke Seminary, whom he

Robert Logan Patton at Amherst College, Massachusetts, from which he graduated in 1876 (Dickinson Class Album, 1876, Amherst College Archives and Special Collections).

regarded as the greatest woman teacher this country had ever produced, and accepted the ideal of service she expressed to the students under her charge: "Young ladies, go where no one else is will[ing] to go, and do what no one else is will[ing] to do!"[40]

Patton saw the profound need for education throughout the mountain counties. The few high schools in the state were set in urban centers, and Patton felt they elevated cultural and patriotic teaching over "weightier matters of righteousness, justice and the love of God."[41] He aspired, instead, to teach values of character and "sacrificial service" within the setting of Christian schools.

It is impossible to appreciate how profound was Patton's influence on his students without acknowledging his belief about the importance of teaching "character." It is also difficult to overstate the extent to which he credited his Christian beliefs with the notions of "character" that he sought to instill in his students—beliefs that may seem foreign to modern, secular educational institutions. Patton believed that students should only be educated by Christians and that Christian character must be taught first and foremost. "He believed the profession of teaching was sacred, and that a person who intended to teach should think first in terms of character-building."[42]

"'If we educate the mind and not the heart we have put dangerous tools in the hands of a person who is not able to handle them.' We must train the heart ahead of the mind, for conduct is shaped by motives from the heart—not the mind."[43] On the first day of classes he declared to students that "he had but one rule, which he turned and wrote on the fresh black boarding in clear bold letters—'DO RIGHT.'"[44]

Order and structure seem to have been integral for Patton in teaching "character." Many of his students were older than typical high school age, and he ensured that not a moment was wasted in his classroom. Time was valuable; there was work to be done and so there was no time for foolishness or loafing. He expected every student to accomplish the most possible. Regarding his strictness, he told his students, "I don't care what you think of me now, but I'll value your opinion 25 years from now."[45]

Patton's methods and high expectations made a deep impression on his students, some of whom—such as Dauph Dougherty and Bob Moore, who later served as president of Mars Hill College—retained those values when they became educators themselves.[46] "His [Patton's] first concern was that his students should *be right* and *do right* and *think right*." And then he yearned and labored in order to train them to express themselves by tongue and pen in such a way as to mold public opinion and move men to noble action. He did not care for literary ornamentation, discounted fine, inane phrases and censored mere word padding. He called upon his students to observe the three C's he had learned in college—Be clear, concise, comprehensive.[47]

An Intense High School Experience for Dauph

Dauph Dougherty began high school in 1885 under Patton, just as Patton assumed a supporting role as the associate principal for the school year. This was

Patton's method, to train his replacement before leaving to help another community open a school. Prof. Joe Spainhour became principal, but for only one year.

When Spainhour entered law school, in 1886, William Furney Marshall was engaged as the new principal of Globe Academy. Marshall was a recent graduate of Wake Forest College who excelled in teaching Latin, Greek, and mathematics. He had a special aptitude for teaching higher math, calculus, and trigonometry, which delighted Dauph Dougherty.[48] Dauph, encouraged by his father and Professor Marshall, aspired to attend Wake Forest, regarded by many Baptists as the best college in the state.[49] A keen student of mathematics, Dauph would later enter Wake Forest, surpass Professor Marshall, and earn Wake Forest College's highest accolades in math.[50]

Patton woke his students at sunrise each school morning. The intensity of communal life and demanding academics, with the expectation that they live godly lives as modeled by their professor, nurtured ability and maturity in Patton's students.

School was intense, and intensely satisfying for one with the aptitude of Dauph Dougherty. He and his friends thrived, matured, and grew in character together. The rigors of logic, rhetoric, and debate sharpened their thinking and prepared their minds not only for college, but for lives of integrity, leadership and influence.[51] Close life-long friendships developed between Dauph and classmates at Globe, notably E.S. Coffey (who became an attorney in Boone), Bob Moore (who became president of Mars Hill College), and another Patton student, William Rufus Bradshaw (who was given an honorary doctorate from Wake Forest College for his preaching and influence in Western North Carolina).

Patton's profound influence "lay in his ability to inspire his students with an intense desire to do and to accomplish. The vision he had seen, the inspiration that had fired him was a contagious thing. ... To his school room came a stream of mountain boys and girls to seek an education. They went away with more than they had sought! Their ambitions had been set afire by this dynamic individual."[52]

Many of Patton's students became ministers, lawyers, and educators: Bruce L. Payne, president of George Peabody College (in Nashville, Tennessee) for 26 years; Robert L. Moore, president of Mars Hill College (in the North Carolina mountains north of Asheville) for 41 years; Arch T. Allen, state superintendent of public instruction (1923–1934); B.B. Dougherty, co-leader at Appalachian beginning in 1899 and then president of Appalachian from 1921 to 1955; and, of course, D.D. (Dauph) Dougherty, principal and leader of Appalachian for 30 years, until his death in 1929. Many of the students regarded Patton as the best teacher they ever had, and confessed a great debt to him for making them who they became.[53]

6

Wake Forest College (1888–1892)

Bob Moore: The Influence of a Peer

Lack of cash nearly ended Dauph Dougherty's dream of attending college, but Professor Patton's exhortations and example encouraged him to press on. Opportunity to earn some money even led Dauph to forgo celebrating with classmates at his high school commencement.[1] Yet Dauph developed many lifelong friendships with his colleagues at Globe Academy, such as his bond with Bob Moore (later president of Mars College). Correspondence between Dauph and Moore reveals a sweet friendship based on mutual fondness, playfulness—in correspondence Moore addressed Dauph as "my dearest darlingest Doph"—and shared boarding-school experiences like most adolescents.

"Mr. Dougherty, I'll declare I miss you more than all the rest, for we had such a jolly good time together, and especially with our 'sweethearts' as Prof. styled them," Moore joked in a letter to Dauph later that summer.[2] Moore teased his friend about several girls who showed serious intentions toward Dauph, and begged Dauph to continue to correspond with him. Nevertheless, Moore conceded, "I know you prefer college to girls for the present."[3]

Dauph wrote many letters to his friend Bob Moore, which were not preserved, and only four from Moore to Dauph were saved by the Dougherty family. In one such letter, Moore's reply sheds some light on Dauph's state of mind after graduating from Globe Academy: "Your epistle, saturated it seemed with all things agreeable and pleasant to your humble mate, came to hand and it did me good all over.... Sorry to learn that you have had ill health for some time and worst of all that the 'blues' have taken hold upon you."[4] Worries about finances for college, supporting a potential future wife and family, working himself to the point of exhaustion and illness, missing the liveliness of boarding school, and concern about his father's erratic land speculating seem to have dampened the spirits of Dauph.[5]

Moore admitted to Dauph in August of 1888 that he was considering teaching school during the coming year to earn tuition money for college, yet encouraged Dauph to attend Wake Forest.[6] But Dauph was also considering the University of North Carolina, and even sent a UNC catalog to Moore.[7] Their high school professors—Patton, Spainhour, and Marshall—had encouraged them both to attend the Baptist college. Bob's correspondence encouraged Dauph to attend Wake Forest

Robert Lee Moore, with his wife and daughter in 1912, was a close friend of Dauph during their shared high school and college years. Moore served as president of Mars Hill College for 41 years (Mars Hill College Photography Collection, Southern Appalachian Archives, Mars Hill College).

with him, along with his brother and cousin.[8] Yet apparently Dauph made a convincing case for Chapel Hill, as Moore replied: "Your reasons for attending Chapel Hill were presented so logically and persuasively that I was almost persuaded to go with you, be with you, and struggle with you through college life at Chapel Hill."[9]

Both Dauph and Bob Moore would later lead dignified and serious lives and hold positions of great responsibility, but their correspondence as recent high school graduates, weighing hard decisions about their academic future and finances, reveals a difficult, uncertain time. Although the two friends both considered attending UNC together, ultimately both chose to enter Wake Forest in the freshman class of 1888.

To Wake Forest College

The decision was made, and Wake Forest College was the destination for Dauph Dougherty. As had his friend Bob Moore, Dauph sought and received a loan from the Bostwick Loan Company. The Bostwick endowment to Wake Forest College in 1886 was designated for loans to needy students, established only two years before Bob and Dauph applied for college entrance.[10]

The 1890s were notoriously hard for most Americans, and Daniel Baker Dougherty's financial support of his son during his years at Wake Forest was minimal. In Dauph's first month at college his father (Daniel) wrote that he hoped to borrow money from his brother Ike: "I will write you & try to send you some money. Be careful times were never so hard."[11]

Getting to Wake Forest from Boone required four days of travel, at substantial cost.[12] The first leg was getting to Blowing Rock, then down to Lenoir, which had secured a railroad in 1884, 35 years before a train arrived in Boone. Several transfers were required, and an overnight stay in Salisbury, before the train arrived in Raleigh, where another line took travelers to Wake Forest the following day.[13] But Dauph did not take this daunting step alone. He began his education at Wake Forest not only with Bob Moore, but with fellow Globe Academy graduates Billy and Hight Moore, Ed Coffey, and Rufus Bradshaw—all Patton students who remained lifelong friends.

Dauph soon drew the attention of Professor Charles E. Taylor, who led Wake Forest College as its president from 1884 to 1904. Professor Taylor quickly formed a high opinion of the new student's abilities and encouraged him to study chemistry and civil engineering.[14]

Students at Wake Forest College gather near the archway leading to the campus, Wake Forest, North Carolina, c. 1890 (Original Campus Photographs, Z. Smith Reynolds Library Special Collections & Archives, Wake Forest University, Winston-Salem, NC, USA).

President Charles E. Taylor (seated, center) with the faculty of Wake Forest College, c. 1890 (Original Campus Photographs, Z. Smith Reynolds Library Special Collections & Archives, Wake Forest University, Winston-Salem, NC, USA).

Dauph's younger brother, Blan, remained in Boone, among other things minding the post office, which their father had built after moving to Boone.[15] Both Blan and Daniel wrote to Dauph at Wake Forest; their letters, full of spelling, grammar, and punctuation errors, revealed that they had not enjoyed Dauph's educational advantages.[16] But Daniel expressed pride in Dauph's "first-class" report from Wake Forest.[17]

Daniel Baker Dougherty and the Watauga Democrat

A man with little formal education, Daniel Dougherty, known to some as "Squire," was well established in Boone as a farmer, blacksmith, and grist mill operator. Keeping himself in the middle of town activities, he served as Boone's mayor for two terms, and as justice of the peace from 1890 to 1900, a title that granted him the power to regulate elections, to appoint judges and county commissioners, to approve or veto the commissioners' actions, oversee taxation, try petty cases, and solemnize marriages. Daniel Dougherty is also credited with expanding the postal service in Watauga County during his years as postmaster.[18]

The *Watauga Democrat* was founded in 1888 by Joseph F. Spainhour, Dauph's former teacher, the same year that Dauph began college at Wake Forest. The four-page, six-column paper appeared weekly and, in a style typical of the partisan press of the day, the owners praised their party's candidates and demonized their opponents.[19]

Spainhour sold the *Democrat* in 1889 to Daniel Baker Dougherty and Robert Campbell Rivers. Rivers served as publisher and Dougherty as editor.[20]

Through ten years of editorials, Daniel "expressed his political views and his concern for the growth and development of Watauga County," urged the building of better roads and promoted the building of a railroad to Boone.[21] Dauph wrote articles for the *Watauga Democrat* during college to earn extra money, and sent them to his father, who praised his writing and passed along compliments from the paper's readers.[22]

Although silver was again discovered in the area, and Daniel had also leased an iron vein on Beaver Dams, his frequent land purchases, his industry, and his wide-ranging efforts to produce income never seemed to accumulate much wealth. Blan was so concerned for his brother, whose need must have been urgent at times, that in the spring of 1891 he purchased a money order of his own, $30 of precious hard-earned cash, and had it sent to Dauph.[23]

Blan Dougherty as a teenager, from a family tin-type (Doris Stam Collection, University Archives, Special Collections Research Center, Appalachian State University, Boone, North Carolina).

Dauph worked at home in Boone during the summers of his college years, and resumed tutoring his younger brother as he had when they were children. Letters from Blan in 1888 reveal that his spelling, punctuation, and grammar lagged far behind Dauph's: "We was certainly glad to hear from you & know you was well and harty…. You should let pa know ahead what you kneed."[24]

Not having the same educational opportunities as Dauph was frustrating and deeply disappointing to Blan. He was 18 years old when his brother left for college. Dauph was 19 and a half. In December 1888 Blan attended the short sessions at Boone Academy and New River Academy.[25] "I seem like I can't get in school worth a cent but as soon as moving appears I will start then I am going to be as hard to stop as it was for me to start."[26]

With great persistence, and quite a few starts and stops, Blan would eventually earn two undergraduate degrees and receive two honorary doctorates, from Elon College (1936) and Wake Forest College (1946). But he could not match the academic achievement of his older brother.[27]

Wagons gather around the square in Lenoir, North Carolina, c. 1900. Blan Dougherty became a skilled "teamster" or wagon driver, taking many loads of cabbage down the steep wagon road to Lenoir (Caldwell Heritage Museum, Lenoir, NC).

Gentlemanly Deportment and Academics at Wake Forest College

At Wake Forest College, Dauph again found high standards for not only academics, but personal character. Here, too, the emphasis was on Christian character, but like the "character" taught at Globe Academy, notions of "Christian character" were colored by the cultural context of Old South refinement and political leanings. Many Confederate veterans were among his teachers.

President Taylor hoped to standardize the College's entrance level requirements, but was hampered by the general lack of quality in the academies throughout the state that provided high school and college preparation. With a wide range in ability and accomplishment among freshmen, Wake Forest College was forced to deal with many unprepared students. But Dauph Dougherty and his Globe Academy classmates, having had the advantage and distinction of a high-caliber Patton education, stood out.[28]

The better-educated students coming to Wake Forest "had enough Latin to read Caesar and Virgil; they were well trained in arithmetic, algebra and geometry and in surveying; they could spell and could read selections from many of the masterpieces of English and American literature; they knew Bullion's Grammar and could analyze and parse the most involved sentence in Milton's Paradise Lost. They knew the geography of the world, and the essentials of Greek and Roman and English history and had learned much of the history of the United States. Some of them had brief courses in general science, physics, and astronomy."[29]

Having recovered from the devastating Civil War, the South saw a revitalized interest in education during the 1880s and 1890s, and almost every progressive town wanted a school with a well-trained teacher who could equip their children through all the grades from primary to college preparatory. Wake Forest College made it a priority to prepare students to become the teachers North Carolina so desperately needed.[30]

Dr. William L. Poteat, professor of natural science and biology, was the first person in the South to introduce the laboratory method—as opposed to the recitation method—at Wake Forest in the early 1880s. Dr. Poteat was a popular lecturer on religion, science, temperance, and education. He was also a fierce proponent of academic freedom in supporting the teachings of Darwin's theory of evolution.[31] Dauph so respected Dr. Poteat and his teaching that he chose science and math as the focus for his own future teaching career.

The Philomathesian and Euzelian Literary Societies, in which every student was involved, conducted debates, provided training in diplomacy, and developed students' literary skills.[32] The Societies were regarded as an organic part of the College, functioning more to spur each student to prepare meticulously for competition than for mere "fun." "As with such societies in Ivy League schools, participation had a refining effect on students; the cultural and educational value of this activity was believed to justify the time devoted to it."[33]

Each Society observed solemn traditions; dignity and polish were sources of pride. "Majestic" procedure and decorum were observed. "Vulgar practices such as chewing of gum and tobacco were punished with fines; smoking in the halls was inconceivable; [fines for] boisterousness and slouching in one's seat and sleeping had to be paid."[34]

Students through the years attested to the influence of the two Societies and often claimed that what they got out of the Society was more valuable than what they learned in any department of study.[35] Students who later became governors (W.W. Kitchin), congressmen, doctors, and professors testified to learning the skill of public speaking in these societies.

Baptism at Wake Forest College

According to college historian George W. Paschal, President Taylor, during his tenure from 1884 to 1904, "exemplified the majesty of a well-ordered life," and the regulations and requirements instituted by Taylor—including compulsory attendance at daily chapel services—were seen by Paschal as "a positive rather than a restraining force."[36] Students were "stimulated to lives of moral cleanliness and healthy religious interest," which Paschal says were evident in the personal lives and influence of the faculty, and in the "wholesome surroundings" and the appeal of the religious life of the College.[37]

Paschal recalled that he and other students like himself found "joy in religion and in the worship in chapel and church."[38] "The chief influence" on many, asserted Paschal, "had been the vitalizing religious atmosphere of the College," especially for those who made professions of faith and commitments to baptism following revival sermons held each year. Among these were Bob Moore and Dauph Dougherty, both of whom would describe this as a turning point in their lives.³⁹ Of the 36 students in their graduating class of 1892, 14 became ministers, among them Dauph's close friend, Rufus Bradshaw.

While attending classes and daily chapel at Wake Forest College, and Sunday worship services at Wake Forest Baptist Church, Dauph was influenced and inspired by many fine and godly men. Public baptism was a sober step. Dauph's training in logic and rhetoric had taught him to examine ideas thoroughly, and he did not easily adhere to anything without debating it in his own mind. Attending Baptist churches all his life, he was familiar with the concept, and had witnessed the baptism of his friend Bob Moore while at Wake Forest. But Dauph had not taken it seriously for himself until April 6, 1890, when he was baptized by his college professor, the Rev. W.B. Royall, as a witness to a change in him and his relationship with God.⁴⁰

Dauph later told his wife that "everything brightened up" when he made that great decision.⁴¹ Lester Brown, his son-on-law, wrote that Dauph's baptism was "the great thing ... that gave stability and purpose to Professor Dauph's life."⁴² W.R. Cullom, Dauph Dougherty's classmate, attended Dauph's baptism. Cullom described Dauph as honest, simple, gentle, and "a giant intellect," and valued Dauph, their other classmates, and professors as part of his "good fortune" at Wake Forest.⁴³ There was nothing flashy or vain about Dauph Dougherty. Humility was the habit of his heart. Patterning his life after men such as Professor R.L. Patton, he cared about how to honor God, and did not try to impress other people.

A Senior in College: An Excellent Student

After his junior year at college, Dauph returned home, burdened with the need for funds to return to college and graduate. He had secured the Bostwick Loan Fund for tuition, but room, board, and travel costs amounted to a daunting sum. Contemplating taking a teaching job to earn enough to finish his education, Dauph secured a letter of recommendation from L.R. Mills of Wake Forest College to aid him in finding a teaching post: "Mr. D.D. Dougherty, of Boone, Watauga Co., N.C., completed the School of Pure Mathematics in this college in June 1891. His class standing was excellent [underscore original]. He impressed me as a gifted young man—worthy of the respect and esteem of all good people. I can most heartily recommend him as a teacher of Mathematics."⁴⁴ However, somehow, without having to take a teaching job, Dauph found the necessary funds (probably loans from family and friends) to return in August 1891 to Wake Forest for his final year.

Back home in Boone, Daniel's financial situation in Dauph's last year of college was dire. After boarding at a hotel for a few months while both of his boys were away, Daniel returned to his home and made enough repairs to spend the winter there, but wrote Dauph that he was "sorely pressed" about taxes and "strapped for money."⁴⁵

Blan "Opens School" at Three Watauga County Public Schools

Blan is reported to have finished a high school course at Globe Academy, although it was not on a par with Dauph's high school training.⁴⁶ At that point in time education was not standardized even at Globe. Blan yearned to attend Wake Forest, but the money was simply not available. Public school teachers were in great demand, and the dollar-a-day salary was very appealing. Blan was already a respected master of horses and skillful with wagons and teams, but he could not make that kind of money hauling cabbages. Laborers toiled by the day, from sunup to sundown, at half the wages of a teacher, and often their pay was not in cash form.[47]

Teachers with any amount of high school education were in demand. State Superintendent of Public Instruction Sidney M. Finger complained that many teachers were "school boys and girls without sufficient knowledge in books," and especially lacked training in school government and management.[48] This fact would linger in the minds of the Doughertys and shape their important future decisions.

Blan applied for a teacher's license but initially failed the geography section of the exam. He "opened" his first school at Shull's Mill in the winter of 1890–1891, with students up to fourth grade, but returned to Globe for additional training in March. By September 1891, he was hired by Watauga County again to "open school" in Zionville, close to the Tennessee state line.[49] It was a tough 12-week job, and did not pay well.[50] The school committee in Blowing Rock offered a substantial increase for him to teach their three-month winter term, which he accepted.[51] At age 21, Blan was an experienced teacher, and was acquainted with families in three corners of Watauga County. These many relationships would serve him well in future years, but, for the moment, Blan was discontent.

Dauph Tutors Blan Via Mail: Blan Attends Wake Forest

Blan confided to Dauph that, although he had benefited from teaching and learned a lot, he was tired of teaching, and wanted to return to school himself and become a lawyer, educate whom he liked, and then get married. "I want [won't] be satisfied unless I come to school," Blan insisted in a letter to Dauph that fall of 1891.[52] Blan was anxious about advancing his education, and entreated Dauph to mail him more exercises to do on his own, which he would return to Dauph for review. Blan recognized what was lacking in his skills and pressed himself to learn, aspiring to pass entrance examinations for Wake Forest College. "I never went to school a great deal," Blan later told his nephew. "My final preparation for college was made at home," often with his older brother as his teacher.[53]

Dauph sent Blan more exercises and study material, and urged him to come to Wake Forest.[54] Although he never did attend law school, despite a lifelong interest in law, nor did he marry, Blan did finally get to Wake Forest College in January 1892. Correspondence between Blan and Dauph at the time reveal an almost frantic excitement and inexperience on Blan's part, and Dauph's calmer advice about maintaining good relations with the school where Blan was about to leave his teaching post.[55] Both brothers saw the advantage of Blan attending Wake Forest while Dauph was still there to help him with living and other arrangements.

Blan had never ridden a train when he embarked on his first trip to Wake Forest College and was completely ignorant even of the protocol of surrendering his ticket

On June 4, 1884, the first train arrived in Lenoir, North Carolina. Boone would wait another 34 years for a train depot (courtesy Caldwell Heritage Museum, Lenoir, North Carolina).

to the conductor.[56] His records of school attendance showed he also lacked preparation for entrance as a freshman. Therefore, President Taylor advised him to enter the sub-freshman class. Rather than do this, Blan attended classes with the regular freshman class without registering. After three months, he proved he could do the work and was accepted as a freshman.[57] However, Blan would only have this one semester at Wake Forest College.

High Honors and the Last Weeks of College

Every candidate for a degree from Wake Forest was required to give four original addresses at the "Senior Speakings," or write a thesis.[58] During his senior year, Dauph wrote an honor's thesis on "Polar Lights."[59]

Dauph was preparing to graduate from college with a fine record. But as the school term ended, and while his freshman classmates were cramming for examinations, Blan packed his few belongings, intending to leave without taking final exams. He saw no use in them for securing a good teaching position, and believed he would not be able to pass them anyway. However, encouraged by his professor to sit for the exams, he did so, leading the class in mathematics and tying for first place in Latin. He later regarded this experience as the turning point in his school career and his life.⁶⁰ Had he not taken the examinations, he probably would never have gone to college again.⁶¹

In June the brothers left Wake Forest. Blandford Barnard Dougherty, who had proved himself to be a hard worker in academics, now had one semester of a college transcript. Dauphin Disco Dougherty had his diploma, graduating with high honors, and sought a teaching post to begin his career.

Nothing in the Piedmont would attract Dauph. The mountains were calling him home, after four years outside Raleigh in the center of the state. Desirable positions were few and far between, but a vibrant and growing school near his paternal grandparents was seeking the skills that Dauph could offer, and arrangements were made. Dauph would now be known as Professor Dougherty.

7

Dauph Becomes a Professor (1892–1894)

Professor D.D. Dougherty's First Job: Fall 1892

Dauph Dougherty's four years at Wake Forest College had come to an end. Dampening the elation of graduation was the burden of indebtedness. The note and interest for his college tuition totaled $258.79. Only a few dollars had been paid towards the loan during his four years of college, and the interest was mounting.[1] Paying back what today would be approaching $10,000 was a challenge in the economy of the 1890s when so little cash was in circulation.

Dauph had been unable to attend the funeral of his grandfather Elijah that year—the distance from Raleigh (Wake Forest) and the expense for travel were too great. When he returned to Boone after graduation, Dauph was glad to see extended family again and to receive their congratulations and expressions of pride. The hopes and dreams of his mother and father were carried in his heart. He was about to fulfill the prophecy in his name and make them proud.

As his brother Blan had recommended, Dauph had secured a teaching post in 1892 in Butler, Tennessee, at "Smith's College," so called by Blan because its president was James Hamilton Smith. The school had been founded as Aenon Seminary (1871), and its name later changed to Holly Spring College in 1886. Offering classes from primary through college level, the terms "seminary" and "college" were used in a broad sense with academies at that time.

Dougherty family grandparents, aunts, uncles, and cousins lived on the northern route from Boone to Butler. After spending some weeks in Boone the summer after graduation, Dauph sent his trunk of belongings and books to Butler to begin his new position.

Dauph's new post was as teacher and assistant to Professor James Hamilton Smith. Neatly dressed, with keen blue eyes, a high forehead, and a stubborn jaw, and respected for his professional air and high standards,[2] Smith sought "pupils who desire a thorough discipline and are willing to work hard and do right…."[3] Smith set the tone at his school, stating that "the intellectual and moral culture of the students" would be maintained and directed so as "to make them better, wiser and nobler men and women."[4] The school Catalogue stated the school purpose: "to give boys and girls a thorough preparation for college, and for the practical things of life.

The formation of character, the cultivation of sound principles, and high ideals of what is worth attaining in life are esteemed of first importance. Intellectual development is considered a serious task," central to education, but to be balanced with the pursuit of godly character.[5]

This should have been familiar territory for Dauph, echoing the educational philosophy of Globe Academy and Wake Forest College. Navigating how to work under Smith seemed clear and direct. In addition to mathematics and the sciences, in which Dauph had excelled at Wake Forest, President Smith requested he also teach German. Dauph would be teaching students of all ages, both children and teenagers.[6]

As the school's enrollment grew, so did the need for housing. Owners of the local general store, which was an anchor for the village, built a boarding house where Professor Smith boarded for a few years. The school benefited the local economy in multiple ways.[7] But as the need for student housing increased further, Smith built a 25-room boarding house of his own, where he lived with his family. Here Dauph Dougherty rented a room when he arrived in 1892, and presumably remained for the next five years.

Dauph soon found that Smith demanded a great deal from his staff. There were always extra duties, and a steep learning curve in preparing lessons. Dauph taught the higher mathematics classes, sciences, and German, enabling the school to grant

Holly Spring College in Butler, Tennessee. Lillie Shull, in a dark dress with a rectangular pin at her front collar and wearing white earrings (circled), is standing in the second row directly behind a mustached man seated on the front row right who has a boy in dark pants standing between his knees. Mollie Shull is in black to Lillie's right. Oldest sister Alice stands tall, fourth from right on the second row, bow in hair. Vinnie sits far right on the front row (University Archives, Special Collections Research Center, Appalachian State University, Boone, North Carolina).

Lillie Shull, with the Aenon Star Literary Society of Holly Spring College, stands third from the left with her head held high, gazing out past the camera. One of her sisters is sitting on the ground directly in front of Lillie, and another sister stands third from right with a very large lace collar on her dress (Butler Museum, Butler, Tennessee).

more college diplomas. Before Dauph's arrival, only two students had earned the B.S. degree, in May 1892—the first college diplomas ever awarded by the school since its founding in 1871.[8] Dauph's abilities were needed to help expand the college area of the school.

A first cousin, Eugene (W.E.) Dougherty was among Dauph's students that first year of his teaching. Seven students, including Eugene, were awarded college degrees in 1893.[9] In spite of the fact that the school was co-educational, only one female student received a college degree from Holly Spring.[10] "After the graduating class of 1894, which had six students, no more students are known to have graduated from Holly Spring, but quite a number completed the prescribed course of study and then transferred to Wake Forest College for further study and graduation."[11] That these students attended Wake Forest rather than Carson-Newman, a Baptist college much closer in Tennessee, to which travel would have been much easier, may have been due to Dauph's influence.

Spring of 1893: Dauph Arranges for Blan's Education to Continue

Six months into his career at Holly Spring College, Dauph felt a growing concern for Blan and his yearning to have a college education. Having assisted Blan to attend one semester with him at Wake Forest College, Dauph now invited his brother to come to Butler, where Blan was admitted as a college student for the spring semester, 1893. The boys may have boarded together at New River Academy as teens, and having shared a semester close to each other again at Wake Forest, the brothers were able to reunite at Holly Spring College. Dauph and Blan's little sister, Etta Mae Dougherty, had also been sent to Holly Spring College in 1890 as a 15-year-old and was a classmate of Lillie Shull. Etta Mae and Lillie were friends. The three Dougherty siblings and Lillie all knew each other. Having had only two college graduates from the institution prior to Dauph's arrival, he must have been gratified when seven of his students graduated at the close of his first year of teaching.

The college level curriculum at Holly Spring College, typical for that time, leans heavily into the Classical model. Freshman: algebra, Latin grammar and reader, Greek grammar and reader, rhetoric, English exercises, and history. Sophomore: geometry, Caesar, *Anabasis* (by Xenophon), *Sallust* (Roman history in Latin), New Testament Greek, botany, and English literature. Junior: trigonometry, Cicero's Orations, Ovid, Herodotus, physics, surveying and navigation, Virgil's Aeneid, Homer's Iliad, and astronomy. Seniors: analytic geometry, Tacitus, Horace, Demosthenes, zoology, political economy, government, calculus, Sophocles Antigone, chemistry, logic, psychology.

A description of the closing exercises of 1893 presents a quaint picture of the well-attended ceremony and its importance in the cultural life of the community: "The hall was so crowded that I did not get a comfortable position, but I enjoyed the exercises. It was a mixture of orations, recitations, dialogues, mirth, and music, and was very credible [*sic*; creditable] to the boys and girls of this society. Wednesday noon was taken up by the exercises of the primary department. The little people always please an audience and the children of Butler are no exception to the rule. The music by the little girls, the declamations, recitations and plays were all pleasing to the large crowd present."[12] The 600-seat auditorium of the school was again full to capacity for the actual graduation program. On the platform were President Smith, Professor Dougherty and Professor Baker, and the graduating class of seven.[13]

Blan Goes to Globe to Teach

Pursuit of a college degree had brought Blan to Butler, but after only one semester as a student at Holly Spring College, Blan left to return to North Carolina and accepted the position as Principal of Globe Academy, Dauph's alma mater. At that time he had only one full year of college classes, from two different institutions, but no college degree. Yet, Blan already had teaching experience from three different public schools in Watauga County, and had also taught for one term at Hamilton Institute in Ashe County, for which he was paid generously.[14]

No records survive that explain Blan's decision to abandon his college education, or Globe's decision to hire someone with so little formal education for such an important post, but several reasons are possible. First, Blan may have foreseen that Holly Spring would graduate its last college class in the next year and that he would

Travel was arduous in the mountains, with deeply rutted wagon roads and dangerous river crossings. Walking long distances was common practice. This photograph of a buggy midstream on the Watauga River, was taken near Butler, Tennessee, c. 1900 (Butler Museum, Butler, Tennessee).

be unable to complete his degree there. Second, it is likely he had run out of funds for tuition, and Globe's offer of income may have been irresistible. Third, Blan had also attended Globe Academy, and his native intelligence and determination may have convinced those charged with hiring a new principal that the education Blan had achieved by diligence and teaching experience exceeded his modest formal credentials and qualified him to carry on in the footsteps of Patton, Spainhour, and Marshall. Fourth, perhaps Dauph, who had been an academic star at Globe, recommended him for the position. Whatever the reasons, Blan left Holly Spring for Globe Academy.

In the spring of 1894, Dauph now had two years' experience as a professor at Holly Spring. Lillie Shull, the lovely geometry student who had captured his heart, was two years older than when they had first met and was herself now a teacher in an adjacent county. He bolstered his courage and began writing to her.

8

Winning the Love of Lillie Shull (1894–1897)

Early Love Letters: From Dauph Dougherty to Lillie Shull

Dauph began corresponding with Lillie Shull in the fall of 1894, when he was starting his third year as a professor, and she was teaching in small one-room public schools several hours away.[1]

But he admitted to having been captivated by her two years earlier, when she was a student in his geometry class: "There is a charm and sweetness about you that I can not resist. ... Need I state it again, you have heard it so often, I love you tenderly, devotedly, and truly. The last two years of my life, my inner life, could be written in one line. 'He loved Miss Lillie.'"[2]

Lillie saved many letters from Dauph, which were passed down through the family. In the oldest (October 11, 1894), Dauph wrote to Lillie in Elk Mills, on the North Carolina–Tennessee state line.

At age 16, even before finishing high school, Lillie had already taught school in a neighboring county.[3] Although she completed high school and some college courses at Holly Spring, Lillie did not earn a college degree before leaving Butler in 1894 to resume teaching. With so few students graduating from college at Holly Spring College (only 15), perhaps there were not enough eligible students to offer the necessary courses for the degree

Dauph Dougherty, c. 1895, in Butler, Tennessee, where he taught at Holly Spring College, 1892-1899 (Doris Stam Collection, University Archives, Special Collections Research Center, Appalachian State University, Boone, North Carolina).

Lillie Shull, a lovely young woman, in Butler, Tennessee, c. 1892 (Doris Stam Collection, University Archives, Special Collections Research Center, Appalachian State University, Boone, North Carolina).

programs, and that is why she did not continue.[4] Or perhaps her family lacked the money to continue her education when younger Shull children still needed schooling. It was often the case in these times that the institutions were spotty and short-lived, and students often had to interrupt their education for lack of funds.

Correspondence between Dauph and Lillie reveals a shared interest in church meetings, sermons, newspaper articles, and class preparations. Dauph was eager to share his reflections on many subjects with Lillie. In one letter he focused on the essays he had chosen for his personal reading. Of Henry Drummond's *Essays*, he wrote that he found the "one on Love [to be] grand" and reported that Brother A.C. Sherwood had quoted from it in his Sunday sermon.[5] "Oh, I wish you were here," he wrote, "so that I could give you an outline of the essay. I know you would enjoy it so much." In another letter he wrote: "I saw frost this morning. We have just finished the study of the philosophy of dew and frost in our Physics. Do you know how frost is formed? This puts me in mind of an old speech I used to learn, when a boy, about 'Jack Frost, looking forth one still clear night' etc. Do you have it in your readers?"[6]

They also sent newspaper articles to each other. "There are several pieces you ought to read, and they are not political either," he wrote. Given the different political leanings of their families, politics may have been a subject to avoid between them. "You do, though, have enough to do without reading everything I want you to," he acknowledged.[7]

Dauph and Lillie grew to know each other in the mingling with friends at Butler Baptist Church and at dinners in family homes, as was the common practice. Protocol had not permitted professor-student personal conversations at school, but now that she was no longer his student, he felt free to pursue her romantically. He was handsome, to be sure, seeking friendship, and contemplating a future with a wife.

Early in his letters, Dauph hints at his growing feelings for her. Using the image of an intermittent spring, which, he explains to her, "runs awhile and then does not," Dauph romanticizes about a future with Lillie: "Is not the human heart an intermittent spring which flows for a while a stream of affection for others and then stops til it gathers again and flows for a short time only to stop and flow again? These springs often change their outlets and pour their streams in a different place. Is not the stream of affection often liable to change? Would that the heart which dictates these lines be a bold spring and never change its tide."[8] Was he bemoaning the fact that Lillie does not seem to be as earnest in her affections toward him? Or stating his as "the heart which dictates these lines," exposing his growing boldness towards her? Perhaps both?

Dauph confesses his loneliness during their separation: "Miss Lillie, I often become faint hearted and think the yoke of life is too hard to bear alone...."[9] The letter concludes with a plea for Lillie to "[c]ome back and stay": "I want to see you. Can't you come home? Why not send after you? ... I do wish you were here. I enjoy seeing you so much. ... When you leave it is like a shadow of darkness coming over our village. You are the social light here for me. Come back and stay."

Finally, he hints that he would prefer to sign the letter as something more than her friend.[10] But Lillie either did not feel the same intensity of emotion or did not communicate it to him. In fact, she actually encouraged him to pursue other women.[11]

Mystery Men and Political Divisions

Lillie had other suitors whom her sisters and other family members appear to have preferred.[12]

Lillie's maternal grandfather had voted Republican in the 1867 election, siding with the Union-supported candidates for governor and U.S. Congress.[13] Dauph Dougherty's family, on the other hand, had chosen to align with the South and identify as Democrats. We do not know the intensity of Dauph's political leanings, but his upbringing and school environments leaned heavily toward the Confederacy. One of the suitors who was approved by the Shull family wrote to Lillie a few years after Dauph's 1894 letter to insist she "quit talking to Democrats." Given the context for that request, the particular Democrat to avoid seemed to refer to Dauph Dougherty.[14] It is not clear what drove Lillie's reservations about returning Dauph's affections, but the influence of her family and known political divisions seem likely.[15]

In a long letter, Dauph expressed hope for a meaningful conversation over Christmas break, pressing the idea of marriage, it appears: "Butler may get along without you but I miss you and would be so glad to see you now. Christmas will be here soon, then I hope to see you. Then we will talk our little matters over and come to some decision."[16]

His workload was heavy, and Lillie seemed to be constantly on his mind, as he wrote again the next day: "I dread next spring my work is so hard, but I have managed to get through thus far and have hope for the future. Have you decided to enter school during next term? When will your school be out?"[17]

Later that month, Dauph heard that Lillie was romantically involved elsewhere and may have been considering marriage. No record exists that Dauph and Lillie met that Christmas, as Dauph had hoped, but they did see each other in Butler in February and shared some reading material. But things did not go smoothly.

In a February 9, 1895, letter, written "at home," Lillie addressed "Dear Prof" with only a few enigmatic lines.[18] Then something unpleasant happened between them and Dauph lost his patience with her. He apologized in a letter that has been lost, but Lillie's written response has been saved, in which she extends her forgiveness. But she appears rattled, ending her letter with: "Excuse me Prof. I just can't get anything written to suite me, and again I don't know what would be proper to write. Yes, I do wish our meetings would be more enjoyable. Prof. please get out of that sad state of mind and enjoy yourself."[19]

Demanding days and evenings filled the young professor's days as he faced the possibility that he might not win her heart. He taught many college-level classes, even on Saturdays, and preparation for those classes was demanding. In addition, he had administrative duties as the president's assistant. Sunday alone afforded some quiet. Living in the boarding hall, Dauph's time with faculty and students began at sunrise and extended until bedtime. But he must have continually thought of Lillie.

Faculty Colleagues

Then Lillie Shull reappeared—*daily*—in Dauph's life, as a new faculty member in the Primary Department of Holly Spring College. Now an experienced teacher, Lillie returned to Butler either in the spring or early summer of 1895. *The Annual Catalogue for Holly Spring College 1895–1896* announced that she would teach the Primary classes previously taught by Professor Monroe Baker while he would focus solely on history and literature in the coming year.[20] The school had over 250 students at this time.

President Smith worked his three professors hard, it appears. James Hill, A.M., taught Latin, Greek, and French. Monroe Baker taught history and literature (English), and the Primary Department before Lillie was hired. Smith is listed as teaching mental and moral philosophy, English, and constitutional law. Dauph Dougherty taught all the math and science classes for three levels beyond the primary department. For the pre-college level, he taught Intermediate, First Advance and Second Advance math, plus arithmetic (written, practical, and university), popular science, physiology, geology of Tennessee, and agriculture. In addition, he taught advanced math classes for four levels of college, and German. No wonder he complained that he did not have a moment during the week to write to Lillie.[21] For two years, 1895–1896, and 1896–1897, Lillie was a professional peer of her former professor, D.D. Dougherty.[22]

Lillie had been writing parts for a short musical drama for a Thanksgiving program, which her primary students were to perform. When she wrote to Dauph on November 26, 1895, they appear to have made amends: "Dear Professor Dougherty, I received your little note yesterday. Was very much pleased to receive it. I believe you told me your feelings in that little note. I appreciated your call Sunday so much. And hope you did…. You must make that little speech about the origin of Thanksgiving. I like to hear you talk in the morning class. I am in very good spirits this week. Hope you are. You can think of me sometimes when you have time. Hope you will enjoy the 'supper.' Your little friend forever, Lillie Belle Shull"[23]

The Dougherty Siblings: Family Developments

Blan may not have observed the growing romantic intentions of Dauph towards Lillie, or might have had his own admiration of her, but Blan spent only one semester as a student in Butler.

After attending Holly Spring College for the spring semester of 1893, Blan left Butler and taught at Globe Academy for two years. He then attended Carson-Newman College, a Baptist co-educational school near Knoxville, Tennessee. He registered as a senior, "having been permitted to 'stand-off' by examination in physics and astronomy, subjects which he had been teaching."[24] Blan regarded this institution as "Tennessee's Wake Forest," and "there he found a higher state of culture, he said, than he had ever known."[25]

Carson-Newman president John T. Henderson was a "quiet, dignified, polished Christian gentleman" who influenced Blan significantly. It is Henderson who taught Blan about psychology, which was to be Blan's favorite subject to teach. (In fact, Blan would teach a class in psychology until his retirement in 1956.)[26] Blan earned his Bachelor of Science Degree from Carson-Newman in 1896 after one year at the college.

Dauph and Blan's sister, Etta Mae, had grown up. In 1896 she married Richard Manly Greene, whose father was a beloved Baptist preacher in Watauga County. For some reason the Reverend Greene did not perform the ceremony, but an old family friend, T.P. Adams, tied the knot in the Mast home on Cove Creek where Etta Mae had been raised. Etta and Richard lived at the Greene family farm in Meat Camp for the next four years. T.P. Adams would, in a few years, play a large role in Dauph and Blan's professional lives.

Good friendships from Blan's years at Globe Academy enriched his entire life. It is here that he met his life-long sweetheart, Clara Ellen Powell. She was said to be a tall, slim, attractive, and cultured young lady with deep blue eyes.[27] Although she was described by her family as "quite prim and proper," she also had a sense of humor.[28] Blan spoke of a few dates with girls at Carson-Newman, where he apparently learned some social graces.[29] "Clara was evidently Blan's first serious interest, though as Principal of Globe Academy, the tall, wiry, dark-toned young man with the piercing dark-brown eyes and the quiet manner was supposedly the secret heart-throb of many of the young ladies at the school."[30]

Summer 1896: A Renewed Spark and Competition

Dauph had Lillie on his mind as he left Butler following commencement to spend the month of June 1896 in Boone. By mid–June, he'd already written Lillie five letters. That summer, his letters document that, at least for him, the relationship had progressed and become decidedly romantic. In his fifth letter, dated June 14, 1896, Dauph addressed Lillie "Dear Loved One." In the sixth, he reported finding Boone very dull, "getting worn out by every thing in the place," and promised that he would return to Butler for the remainder of the summer, and planned to celebrate Independence Day with her.[31] He concluded the letter:

Oh, dear Lillie, I'm always thinking of our matters. I feel more and more that I truly love you. It seems that I do not care for other girls. There's all the difference in the way I feel this summer and the way I felt last summer. Oh, I am so thankful you have given me another chance. I would be in a bad fix if I could not write to you and be on intimate terms with you. There is but one Lillie, one made like her. ... Let me write the last word of this letter the feeling of my heart for you. "I love you." D—[32]

His exuberance continued in his next letter two days later, in which he explained that he could not leave yet because his father needed help with urgent farmwork. Dauph signed this letter "in love," and underlined "one particular" subject that he wished to discuss.[33] This surely caught Lillie's attention.

Lillie's feelings, though, were not so clear. In fact, even as Dauph professed his love and hinted at marriage, Lillie was exchanging letters with Mr. Cress, who wrote in September inferring that he preferred Lillie as his "sweetheart." Referring to Lillie's father's faithfulness to the Republican Party, he admonished Lillie, "You must quit talking to Democrats. There are too many good Republicans among whom to choose for you to submit yourself to such. You must obey me in this—will you?"[34]

There is a gap in Dauph and Lillie's preserved letters after June 1896. Soon both were on the faculty at Holly Spring and saw each other at school and church almost daily. Dauph's work was consuming. In addition to teaching many subjects, he was secretary to the faculty, was active in the Baptist Church and the local denominational association, and probably attended state meetings as well as area meetings.

A mysterious discontent on his part is alluded to in letters from both his father and his brother in the spring of 1897. Dauph's father closed a letter to Dauph in late March 1897, "If you could better yourself by leaving Butler you ought to do so. Much better positions are no doubt open hunt them up."[35]

In late April Blan wrote to Dauph from Globe, North Carolina, hinting at problems at Holly Spring: "It is my opinion that a N.C. fellow would help H.S.C. [Holly Spring College] more than anyone else. ... I trust you will make 'wise moves.' I should regret the school's failing. ... I hear nothing from Mars Hill. That is a good place. ... The future seems dank—but we can come yet."[36] Both Blan and Dauph may have anticipated securing teaching positions at Mars Hill College, near Asheville, North Carolina, where their close friend Bob Moore was already president of the school.

Money was still of utmost concern for each of them. In seeking the "cheapest plan," and writing "we should save our money," Blan entreated Dauph to join him for the Globe Academy graduation festivities on May 21, 1897, revealing despondently how his financial circumstances constrained him: "I am not courtin' much—anything to court less—it is nonsense for a poor unsettled fellow to marry...."[37]

Lillie and Dauph Are Married

And then, suddenly, Dauph and Lillie were married. The developments in their romance were private, with no paper trail. Finally, after having his heart set on the talented and attractive Lillie for five years, she accepted his proposal of marriage.

The two were married June 9, 1897, when Lillie was 22 and Dauph was 28. The simple wide gold wedding band Dauph gave to Lillie is inscribed in cursive capital letters: D.D.D. to L.B.S.[38] She called him "Professor" all her life.[39] The announcement in the *Watauga Democrat* of the marriage of "Prof. D.D. Dougherty and Miss Lillie B. Shull of Butler, Tenn." reported, in part:

> Miss Lillie is one of Butler's best girls and holds a great place in the affections of all. For two years past she has taught in the primary department of Holly Spring College, and the children that were under her will certainly regret giving her up.
>
> The day of their married life has just dawned and as the sun gets higher and brighter, may their happiness increase and when the evening shades of life gather around them may they look back over a happy union. The students of Holly Spring College join in with congratulations and good wishes.—A Student.[40]

9

Newly Married and Considering a Big Change (1897–1898)

Newly Wed: Concerns About Holly Spring College

Dauph must have expressed concern to his brother and father about his employment at Holly Spring College in the spring of 1897, before his marriage to Lillie. Daniel encouraged him to seek a better job elsewhere, and Blan likewise encouraged him to leave the school.[1] Whatever the cause of worry about Holly Spring, Dauph stayed the course for another two school years. Instead of leaving Butler to find other employment, he persuaded his brother to join him on the faculty of Holly Spring College for the school year 1897 to 1898.

Even while Blan was teaching at Globe Academy in North Carolina during 1896–1897, he wanted to further his own education. His father did not endorse the

Prof. D.D. Dougherty and Lillie Shull were wed on June 9, 1897, and remained in Butler for two more years. Her wedding ring is visible in this photograph. She called him "Professor" all her life (Doris Stam Collection, University Archives, Special Collections Research Center, Appalachian State University, Boone, North Carolina).

idea. Blan had already earned his B.S. degree at Carson-Newman College, and their father confided to his son Dauph: "Blan is foolish seems to me wanting to go to school again. I have no idea he will go."[2]

Blan did not see a bright future for himself if he remained at Globe, perhaps because of economic strains in the isolated farming community, and without a market to sell produce, there would be no cash to support a school. He wrote to Dauph in April 1897, "I don't know about leaving Globe, nothing has been said about my leaving or staying. I feel that everything is very favorable for me, the great trouble is that Globe can't make a school. If the outside world should fail—which is liable to be the case—all is gone. No friction in school—everything has been very nice." However, he had been sick with grippe (flu) and lung issues, cough and bleeding.[3] Dauph was worried about his little brother. Poor health and a sinus problem would nag Blan for years.[4]

Blan Joins Dauph and Lillie in Tennessee

Blan had appeared despondent, or at least frustrated, about his financial status and romantic prospects (he wrote Dauph that he was too poor to court). At some point during his time as Principal of Globe Academy, he had asked his girlfriend from that area, Clara Powell, to marry him. Clara apparently felt a weight of responsibility for her widowed mother and was unwilling to leave the Globe and Lenoir area.[5] Blan was not ready to remain in Globe.

Something had soured Blan's former optimism about the future of Globe Academy. Times were tough and money was tight in the mountains, making a precarious situation for private schools. A railroad was never extended to Globe, and, unfortunately, the entire community was later destroyed by the Johns River flood of 1916.[6]

Blan, who had described himself to Dauph as "a poor unsettled fellow," accepted Dauph's offer to teach at Holly Spring College, and moved to Butler sometime after Dauph's marriage and before the 1897 fall term began. He was assigned to teach Latin, which included Latin Grammar, Eutropius, Caesar, Virgil, Cicero's Orations, Sallust, Ovid, Horace, and Tacitus.[7]

Lillie had become pregnant almost immediately after their wedding—perhaps on their honeymoon trip to Nashville. She made the adjustment to morning sickness and marriage in her hometown, with the help of her mother and sisters. Dauph and Blan were busy with teaching and schoolwork. She gave birth to a baby girl on March 9, 1898. They named her Clara[8] on Blan's suggestion, according to family lore—perhaps after Clara Powell, Blan's lost sweetheart in Globe; perhaps after Clara Barton, a prominent figure at that time for her nursing work during the Civil War and her promotion of medical relief through the Red Cross; perhaps after Clara Schumann, wife of Robert Schumann and a composer in her own right, whose music Lillie knew. Baby Clara was given the middle name Bartlett in honor of Dauph's mother Ellen Bartlett Dougherty, who had died when Dauph was only 7 years old.[9]

Surrounded by the Shull family, with the extended Dougherty clan not far away in Tennessee, Lillie stayed home to care for baby Clara, cook, and keep house while Dauph and Blan taught. They were all involved with Butler Baptist Church and the Watauga Baptist Association of area churches. Little Clara brought delight to all those around her. Now that Dauph had a family to provide for, and despite Lillie's attachment to her extended family in Butler, he began to ponder more and more about a future somewhere else.

Blan at Chapel Hill; Dauph Prepares to Leave Butler

Blan remained at Holly Spring teaching with Dauph for only one year before enrolling at the University of North Carolina at Chapel Hill, where he encountered a new educational movement in the University and in the South. He continued to struggle financially.[10]

An "educational crusade" had been underway in North Carolina, and many of its leaders had ties to Chapel Hill. A new program in the field of education, known as pedagogy, had commenced at the University in the fall of 1895,[11] headed by Dr. Marcus C.S. Noble. Blan would be in Dr. Noble's first class of graduates in 1899.

Concerns about Holly Spring College had been simmering in the Dougherty family since before Dauph's wedding in 1897. Two years later, as Blan was leaving Holly Spring to attend UNC, Daniel began to encourage his son Dauph to move back to Boone.[12] With the deteriorating situation at the Butler school, Dauph began to consider Daniel's suggestion, which proved timely. By 1901, Smith was forced to retire for health reasons and to enter negotiations with the Tennessee Watauga Baptist Association about selling Holly Spring College.[13]

Dauph took stock of his finances and his ability to support a family. He had experience with some of his father's business, and knew that he would be inheriting a portion of the large family farm in Boone when his father died.

During their honeymoon Dauph and Lillie had attended the Centennial exhibits and displays in Nashville, filling their

Blanford Barnard Dougherty, c. 1898 (from O. Lester Brown's book, *Blanford Barnard Dougherty: A Man to Match His Mountains* [1963]).

9. Newly Married and Considering a Big Change

Blan Dougherty attended the University of North Carolina at Chapel Hill for the school year 1888–1889, staying in Old East beside the Old Well, pictured here (North Carolina Collection Photographic Archives, Wilson Library, The University of North Carolina at Chapel Hill).

minds with new ideas. Newspapers buzzed with the news of advancements in technologies like the telephone, the expansion of transportation through new railroads, and the growth of industries in the South. Even in remote Butler, Tennessee, plans for a railroad to the town's new logging industry were being discussed. Hopes for recovery from the financial recession of the 1890s abounded with the growing industrial revolution reaching down to the South.

A life-long reader, Dauph kept abreast of events in the public, academic, and religious realms, and was regarded as a "well-informed" man.[14] Although the world was changing in many ways, including the threat of conflict in the Spanish American War and Cuba—these seemed far away from the remote mountain areas of Tennessee and North Carolina.

The Blair Bill, the Peabody Fund, and Tax Inequities

While Dauph was contemplating his future at Holly Spring College, the national discussion about new federal legislation and the developments in education promoted by the Farmers' Alliance were often in the newspapers.[15] Dauph's professors at Wake Forest, as well as his father, had often mentioned the "Blair Bill." Henry William Blair, a moderate from New Hampshire who served as chairman of the U.S. Congressional Committee on Education and Labor from 1881 to 1891, introduced legislation to move control of education from the local level to the federal level. His "Blair Education Bill" proposed to establish federal aid for education;

it passed the Senate on three occasions, was endorsed by presidents, but never passed the House.[16]

Education in America was in shambles after the Civil War and the need for improvement was great, but opinion was divided about whether centralization under federal control was the solution. Dauph doubted the wisdom of transferring too much authority from the local people to the federal government.[17] Local taxes for local schools, under local control, appealed to him. North Carolina sided with Dauph's views and made steps to improve their schools without federal aid.

Dauph also knew about the philanthropic efforts of George Peabody, who had helped the South "recover from the ravages of the Civil War."[18] The Peabody Education Fund distributed millions of dollars to public schools before being dissolved in 1914. It stimulated local school support and teacher training for both whites and blacks, making some headway in "breaking down Southern hatred for the North."[19] But the Fund was only a drop in the bucket of need. "Although North Carolina received $87,000 [from the Peabody Fund], it went to only a few diligent towns where schools were already well maintained."[20] Blan would later seek aid from the Peabody Fund for Watauga County schools, but received none.[21]

Although Dauph was teaching and living in Tennessee, he retained an interest in the state of schools in North Carolina, staying informed through newspapers and through his father and brother. The future of private academies as well as public high schools, which were almost non-existent in the mountain areas, was uncertain.

The response to the Blair Bill in North Carolina proved to be significant: "The diagnosis of public education during the debate over federal aid was seen as a significant factor in setting the stage for the successful educational crusade" between 1889 and 1891, led by Charles D. McIver (president of the school which became UNC-Greensboro) and Edward A. Alderman (president of UNC). "Under the impetus of various forces, the school ideal ultimately became integrated in a public opinion that expressed itself in increased [state] taxation for educational purposes."[22]

However, even with the modest increase in state property and poll tax apportioned for education, Watauga County, like the other "pauper counties," whose local tax bases were significantly less than the industrial centers of the state, was left behind. The state tax for public education basically remained within each county, creating an unequal distribution of state taxes that plagued the poorer counties until the 1930s. The system became, in effect, a county instead of a state system, which enabled the wealthy counties to benefit, while the less wealthy areas of the state, such as Watauga County, continued to struggle.[23]

The Farmers' Alliance

Dauph's father, Daniel Dougherty, like most people in the mountains, was a farmer, although that was not his only endeavor. During the 1880s, when Dauph was in school, farmers had seen a worsening of an agricultural depression, with declining prices and a heavier dependence on the credit system, which resulted in an outcry from farmers across the nation.[24] The Farmers' Alliance grew out of this crisis.

When Daniel Dougherty and R.C. Rivers had purchased the *Watauga Democrat* in 1889, Daniel began writing editorials endorsing the Farmers' Alliance.[25] Having had little opportunity for schooling himself, he advocated for education and saw its importance and value. He discussed these developments with Dauph when they were together and wrote to him about them when they were apart. The Farmers' Alliance wished to encourage more efficient methods of farm production by providing farmers with scientific agricultural information. "A typical meeting of a local alliance often included the reading of papers on such topics as 'contagious diseases of livestock' or 'how to restore fertility to the soil.'"[26]

The Farmers' Alliance played a role in the rise of education, particularly public education, as it mounted a campaign that eventually resulted in the establishment of new colleges to serve the needs of the "producing classes."[27] A group of young professionals in Raleigh called the Watauga Club pushed legislators for the establishment of an industrial school in North Carolina. The club (which, although named Watauga, had no association with Watauga County) called for improved roads and schools, modern agricultural methods, and farmers' institutes. According to one member, the club "was always on the lookout for a chance to extend the opportunities of the common man."[28]

"Legislators had responded and established an agricultural college in North Carolina in 1877—the State Agricultural and Mechanical College in Raleigh later known as State College (now the North Carolina State University in Raleigh)."[29] The state also sponsored the first "normal school" (for training elementary school teachers) in the South for any race, when a school founded by the Freedmen's Bureau for black students, now Fayetteville State University, came under state funding in 1877.[30]

A "normal school" was an institution created to train teachers by educating them in the "norms" or standards of pedagogy and curriculum. "The term 'normal school' was derived from the French term *école normale*, which means 'standard' or 'model school.' One of the first normal schools established was in Paris in 1794."[31]

Teacher training institutes were initiated in 1889–1891, and property tax and poll tax were raised in support of education. The General Assembly also improved teacher training programs for both white and Black schools.[32]

North Carolina's Leonidas L. Polk began a newspaper in 1874 which

…gave advice to farmers, arguing that they should diversify their farms (plant a variety of crops rather than just one cash crop) and raise crops and animals they could use rather than focusing on cash crops such as cotton. In 1877, Zebulon Vance again became governor, and he appointed Polk the first commissioner of North Carolina's new Department of Agriculture.

Polk resigned from the Department of Agriculture after only three years, unhappy with the lack of support he received from the legislature. In 1886, he founded the *Progressive Farmer* magazine and used it to advocate improvements in agriculture, farmers' organizations, and the establishment of a state agricultural college—the North Carolina College of Agricultural and Mechanic Arts, later North Carolina State University, which was established in 1887.

Polk also became active in the National Farmers' Alliance, which had 100,000 members in North Carolina and had moved its headquarters there. He served as the Alliance's president from 1889 to 1891. The Democratic Party showed little interest in the reforms he wanted, and he joined the new People's Party (or Populist Party). Polk may well have become the party's nominee for President in 1892, but he died suddenly that June.[33]

The Farmers' Legislature of 1891 and McIver's School in Greensboro

The Farmers' Alliance was so well represented in the North Carolina General Assembly of 1891 that historians have customarily termed that body "the Farmers' Legislature." This group carried out extensive reforms that had been sought for a decade by the agrarians.[34] They also set up the North Carolina Agricultural and Mechanical College for the Colored Race (now known as the North Carolina State Agricultural and Technological University at Greensboro, or "A & T").[35] A & T was established in 1891 with the intention "to teach practical agriculture and mechanic [sic] arts and such branches of learning as relate there to [sic], not excluding academic and classical instruction" to African American citizens of North Carolina.[36]

The Farmers' Alliance rallied the support of the farmers who "wanted this same practical emphasis in the curriculum of the public schools.... [I]t was the public schools that held the key to improving educational opportunity for the agricultural masses of North Carolina...."[37] As the Farmers' Alliance grew in numbers and political influence, so did the insistence on improvement of public education.

Charles H. Mebane, a Populist, chosen state superintendent of public instruction in 1896, stressed that public schools should be removed from partisan politics. In Mebane's report to the Legislature in 1900, he sought to move the politicians to vote for an increase in the Public School Fund by raising taxes. A common interest in the instruction of the young must be cultivated—focusing on "the future happiness and welfare of children."[38] He argued that universal education could come only if the wealthy saw that paying higher taxes for education would benefit their own children, help poorer sections of the state, and society as a whole. Mebane sought to do "away with the false idea that has been prevalent in the minds of many that the children of the man of means are better than the poor man's children."[39] Mebane and other Populists envisioned a time where the great gulf between the college man/woman and the man/woman of the community was eliminated.[40]

Unfortunately, Mebane was not successful. State supported ("free") public education was not adopted in North Carolina until 1933.[41]

Dauph had been a junior at Wake Forest College in 1891 when he eagerly read about the Farmers' Legislature and the establishment of the State Normal and Industrial School at Greensboro (now UNC Greensboro). The moving spirit in the founding of this institution was Charles D. McIver, a man of intense earnestness, energy, and common sense, who believed that the state should provide for its young women "an institution of higher learning, adequate for every need, and within reach of all." McIver believed that North Carolina could not have an effective school system without well-trained teachers. In this view, he had the endorsement of the Teachers' Assembly and of the Farmers' Alliance.[42]

The act establishing the "normal" school aimed "to give instruction to young women in drawing, telegraphy, typewriting, stenography, and such other industrial arts as may be suitable to their sex and conducive to their support and usefulness." It also intended to keep charges low "so that the daughters of poor farmers might have access to higher education."[43] Yet no daughters of "poor farmers" in the mountains could ever hope to attend the State Normal and Industrial School in Greensboro—it was beyond their reach geographically and economically.

Christian Missions to the Mountain Schools

As politicians established these state-supported colleges, the issue of how to fund them was widely debated. Fiscal conservatives opposed generous appropriations of state money for higher education, and the Baptists in the state, a considerable number, joined their dissent. The Baptists felt that the poor, who most needed state help, would not see any benefit if state money were denied to children and given to young adults at the college level.

Dauph had read about the controversy from the Baptist perspective in 1894, two years after graduating from Wake Forest College. A pamphlet by Wake Forest College president Taylor, and an ensuing article in the Baptist periodical, *The Biblical Recorder*, had stirred opposition. The historian for the Baptist-supported Mars Hill College, John Angus McLeod, felt that this controversy inadvertently pushed the cause of *public* education at a time when the Baptists were hoping to strengthen their *private* Christian schools, to provide Christian influence through a system of private academies throughout the state where public high schools had not been established.[44]

The private school vs. public school debate was not just a political issue for Dauph. It would affect his professional future if Holly Spring College failed, or if he chose to seek another position elsewhere.

Christian private schools were scattered throughout the mountains. After the Civil War, Christian denominations had sent workers to help the impoverished South, most notably the Southern Baptists and the Northern Presbyterians. At times jealousies and competition surfaced between them.[45]

The Southern Highlands lacked means of commerce and communication with the world beyond the mountains. Roads were extremely poor.[46] Those who lived deep within the remote mountain ranges experienced intense isolation, suffered from primitive communication and transportation, and daily faced cultural and educational deprivation. Poverty was pervasive.[47] To meet the need for educational opportunities, churches established private schools, ambitiously called "academies," "institutes," and even "colleges," that functioned primarily as high schools.[48]

Various Protestant denominations were determined to do something about this vacuum of education. In establishing schools in needy areas, they had five basic purposes: (1) to educate students; (2) to improve their social conditions; (3) to convert them; (4) to make denomination allies of them, and (5) to train ministers.[49]

The most extensive missionary work in the field of education in the mountains of the South was begun by the Women's Board of Home Missions of the Presbyterian Church, USA, which was founded for the express purpose of educating and evangelizing the "exceptional populations" of America.[50] This Northern denomination found funding from wealthy congregants in the prosperous cities of the North to fund their work in the ravaged South. But the weakness of their system was in the often condescending attitudes toward the poor in the Appalachian Mountains.[51]

Dorland-Bell School, which merged with Asheville Farm School to become Warren Wilson College, was an effort of the Presbyterian Board of National Missions in New York and typifies "the larger story of the Southern Appalachians' mixed history of cultural wealth and economic poverty."[52] Although overcoming significant barriers to education in isolated areas, "there was always the challenge of balancing the well-intentioned good works of lending a helping hand to a mountain people, while at the same time respecting a rich and old culture that was not always receptive to the interventions of outsiders."[53]

Lees-McRae College, established in 1900 with one dormitory for 12 girls and two teachers, grew at the request of local people out of a reading circle in the Banner Elk home of Presbyterian minister Edgar Tufts and his wife, Bessie, who invited young people to join them in reading around their fireside.[54]

Lenoir College was founded by four Lutheran pastors and educators in 1891 as Highland Academy. After various name changes it was later renamed Lenoir-Rhyne College to honor a donor.[55] Davenport Female College in Lenoir was Methodist-affiliated and offered a Normal Course, a Collegiate Course, and a Model School for primary and intermediate grades.[56]

One historian asserted that the most potent social influence in the mountains of North Carolina during most of the 19th century was the clergy. Not politicians or financiers, but preachers—in particular, Baptist preachers—exercised dominant control of the people.[57] A fundamental difference between the Baptist educational efforts and those of other denominations was the Baptist urging for local school people to depend upon their own resources, not outside sources.[58] Prideful mountaineers did not want a hand-out.

Monroe Dodd, who became the major force for the Southern Baptists' efforts with mountain schools from the late 1890s until the 1920s, described the Baptists' school movement thus: "To evangelize without educating is to make possible useless fanatics; To educate without evangelizing is to make scoffers and skeptics."[59]

Historian George W. Paschal characterized the Baptist system of high schools as the most important development in the field of secondary education in North Carolina during the 19th century.[60] Dauph Dougherty read that the Southern Baptist State Convention of 1898 was encouraging the establishment of more secondary schools, hoping to establish one in every association in the state.[61] It was generally recognized, however, that while the Baptists in the western mountain section of the state were numerous and eager for education, they were too weak financially to maintain good high schools.[62]

Dauph Dougherty deeply felt a religious calling to teach for the betterment of others, but not to preach.[63] Professor Patton, who had been such a strong influence in Dauph's high school years, believed that teaching was a sacred calling, and Dauph chose to follow in his steps—but *without* denominational ties. The risk of another Baptist supported school endeavor failing was a reality, given the economic conditions which had so recently crippled the area.

During the depression of the 1890s it is estimated that 20 percent of the national workforce was unemployed at one time or the other, and that 50 percent of all businesses failed.[64] Regional poverty, and fallout from the national Cleveland Panic of 1893, had made for desperate times in much of the mountains.[65]

Dauph's close high-school friend from Globe Academy, Robert L. "Bob" Moore, faced a dire financial situation when in 1897 he accepted the presidency of Mars Hill College, a Baptist Institution located north of Asheville, North Carolina. Closure seemed almost certain, but a wealthy Northern donor saved the school.[66] The financial stability of Holly Spring College, the Baptist school where Dauph was employed from 1892 to 1899, was similarly threatened, with no wealthy donor in sight.[67]

Factors in Dauph's Decision: Pivotal Letters

In early 1899, Daniel Baker Dougherty, who longed to have his sons near him in his declining years, wrote to both of his sons suggesting that they return to Boone and help start a school. The educational landscape was changing in Boone, and in North Carolina. Dauph and Blan corresponded with each other about starting a school in Boone together. In February of 1899 Blan wrote to Dauph, "I think a school in Boone might do very well," but was willing to join Dauph in starting a school "*anywhere*." The state was giving money for public schools for the first time,[68] and both Daniel and Blan felt this was a significant opportunity for Watauga County and their personal futures.[69]

The aging Daniel, now in his mid–60s, persisted in urging his two sons to return to Boone and set up a school. In March 1899, he again wrote to Dauph:

> There is an impression among our people that you will return to Watauga and build up a school at Boone with B [Blan]. It is taken for granted by the people ... and I am often asked about it, but I can't tell them anything for I know nothing.
>
> Dr. Adams was here a few days ago and requested me to write to you and B. both as he wants his bd. [school board] to elect either of you Co. Supt. Says the people desire this and he is for either of you and for you and B. to decide the matter whether either will accept the Supt. place. Of course I have no choice but would be pleased for either of you to have the place. Dr. says it will pay from $2 to $4 per day....
>
> A school here conducted by you and B. would be well sustained in my opinion the finest opening I think any where. Now consider this and let us know your desires. ... Write to me at once about matters, especially of the Tenn [Tennessee] Boom, & of your school ideas....[70]

A month later, Daniel, apparently pressed by Boone citizens to get an answer from his son, wrote a third letter to Dauph about founding a new school in Boone, and asked for an immediate response.[71] Soon after receiving his father's letter, Dauph apparently resolved to move to Boone and accept the offer from the school board to start a new school.

Dauph then wrote Blan asking him to join in the new Boone undertaking, and sending him money.[72] Dauph's letter was lost but Blan's response was preserved:

> Chapel Hill NC April 21st, 1899,
>
> Dear D. Your letter came last night ... that helps me wonderfully. I need $40 yet—where I am to get it.... I do not know. Tell Prof. S. if he can send me any amount to do so. If I ever needed money I need

A letter from Daniel Baker Dougherty to Dauph Dougherty, 20 March 1899, strongly urging his sons to return to Boone and start a school (Doris Stam Collection, University Archives, Special Collections Research Center, Appalachian State University, Boone, North Carolina).

it now—if Mr. Shull can send any—tell him please to do so. Is certainly embarrassing to be here without money.

As to school matters, I really haven't studied much about it. I can't see anything big enough for two men at Boone. Pa has been writing me about it, but I can't decide to go there till I go and survey the field. I will be home early in June—about 2 or 3—you meet me at Boone, and we will decide then about the matters—you can't depend upon what Pa writes—he doesn't know much about a school. ... I'm anxious for you to leave Butler.... Write again soon[73]

Dauph needed a dependable way to provide for his wife and child, and hopefully more children in the future, and Holly Spring College was floundering. With national efforts by the Farmers' Alliance to promote education, and the prospect of state tax funds to fund improvements, the future of education was looking brighter in North Carolina. The need was substantial in Watauga County, and the call to teach rang in Dauph's ears. With his father aging, oversight of the family farm was also needed.

From Dauph's perspective, the continued pleading of Boone citizens for a new school and the need to fill the county superintendent position promised plenty of work for two men in Boone.

10

The Doughertys Return to Boone and Start a High School (Summer 1899)

Rumor: Opening a High School in Boone

In January 1899 Dauph paid a visit to his father in Boone.[1] After that visit, and at least three months before any definite commitment by Dauph, Daniel began spreading the word that his sons were seriously thinking about starting a new school in Boone.[2] The *Watauga Democrat* printed: "It is rumored that two educators of no small worth are thinking of opening a high school in Boone. This, if it is true, is indeed encouraging, for there is nothing we need worse. The gentlemen are pushers and if they undertake it, they are sure to succeed. We trust they may."[3]

Considering that Daniel was still co-owner and editor of the newspaper, and that the "rumor" likely started with him, the story is a tip-off that he has persuaded his sons to return to Boone. Within the week, Daniel sold his interest in the *Watauga Democrat* to R.C. Rivers, who then became the sole owner and proprietor.[4] Daniel and his brother Harvey had both served on the Watauga County Board of Education in 1874, when their children were quite young. Back in Tennessee, the extended Dougherty family was likewise invested in local education, and many would choose teaching as their profession.[5]

Daniel had been disappointed with the failure of Three Forks Baptist Institute and his efforts to secure a high school in Boone for when his boys were older. There was no high school in Watauga County when his children were teenagers, and he had to send Dauph and Blan away for school.[6] His daughter, Etta Mae, was raised in nearby Cove Creek by Jacob and Sarah Mast, who sent her to Butler, Tennessee, for high school.[7]

In 1899, as Dauph and Blan both faced difficult decisions about their employment as teachers, there was still no high school in the county.[8] Through editorials in the *Watauga Democrat* Daniel Baker Dougherty expressed "concern with the lack of adequate support for the public schools, and wrote that unless the county changed in its attitude toward the schools, the system would remain a failure. 'Neither academies nor free schools can prosper among people who are dead to their interest,' he declared."[9] Soon after endorsing local taxation for longer school terms, he began his "campaign to persuade his sons to establish a school in Boone."[10]

This 1885 stereo image is taken looking northeast toward the village of Boone. The original Boone Baptist Church is centered. Distance right: home and property of Daniel Baker Dougherty (courtesy Historic Boone Collection, Digital Watauga Project).

Faced with a bleak educational situation, Watauga County leaders sought a way to educate their young people and train their teachers.[11] They lacked both an adequate facility and qualified teachers to meet the growing need. As a witness of the limited educational opportunities in Boone, Spainhour, the Dougherty boys' teacher who became a lawyer and founder of the *Watauga Democrat* in 1888, moved from Boone in 1895 to Morganton "mainly to get the advantages of school here for his children."[12]

Blan Dougherty looked back on the situation 50 years later and told his biographer:

> There needed to be a central Academy [for Watauga County and the surrounding areas], large and well equipped, that could meet the needs of all who came to its doors seeking knowledge and training. Few people had more than enough money to barely live on. There was no future for a privately owned school, mainly for this reason. The Baptists were stronger in numbers than any other denomination but were in no condition to sponsor another school. In fact, they had not carried through with their plans for the old Boone Academy [which was initially called Three Forks Institute].[13]

Given the history of failed efforts to support a school, and with the lingering economic depression, it is understandable that Blan felt the task of starting a new school was daunting. Years later, in 1956, Blan mentioned to Boone lawyer (and Blan's former student) Wade Brown that a denominational tie was considered and rejected.[14]

Superintendent of Watauga County Public Schools and a Semi-Private Academy

T.P. Adams led the Watauga County School Board, and both he and the other Board members were well-known to Dauph and Blan. "Doc" Adams,[15] as he was called, was a family friend who had taken a great deal of interest in the education of Daniel's two sons.[16] "Doc" was not a medical doctor, but was esteemed for his knowledge and wisdom in many areas.[17] Having served in the Confederate Army at a young age, after the war he had attended school in Boone, taught himself to read Latin, earned a teaching certificate, and taught several years. He was very civic minded, helped to organize the first bank in the county, was a member of the Board of Education of Watauga County for more than 40 years, and was chairman for most of those years.[18]

The School Board and T.P. Adams wanted either Dauph or Blan to take the position of Watauga County superintendent, to travel throughout the county to *all* the public schools. Adams enlisted Daniel to pass the offer along, and Daniel did convey it in a letter to Dauph on March 20, 1899, with his conviction that the school he encouraged them to open would succeed.[19]

Dauph took the lead in deliberations about whether to commit to founding a new school in Boone. Blan seemed less certain. Expectantly, the Board and local citizens awaited the decision of the Dougherty brothers. It was not until June 1899 that rumors of a new school resurfaced in the local newspaper, which promised that the forthcoming issue would bring news "that is of more importance to the welfare of our town and the county at large, than anything that could happen in our midst. But for fear the enterprise should fail we refrain from giving any particulars this week."[20]

As soon as Dauph and Blan could finish their respective school terms, they met in person with the Watauga County Board of Education. The Board must have provided convincing proof of solid financial support, for they contracted with the Dougherty brothers for Dauph and Blan to teach "free school" at the new academy for a combined salary of $25 dollars per month, and for Blan to become the superintendent,[21] a position he held for the next 16 years.[22] Blan would often be away and unable to teach because of this position. After 10 weeks of "free" (public, tax-supported) school ended, the new school would continue for a winter term as a private subscription school for those families who paid a small tuition fee.[23]

The brothers had discussed the superintendent's position, which had been offered to either man.[24] Dauph had a wife and child and was by personality not inclined to "[fill] the office of a public relations man at large."[25] As the unmarried brother, Blan had more flexibility to travel and stay with student families in rural areas, so it was agreed that he would serve as superintendent.

Finally, on July 13, 1899, the *Watauga Democrat* announced:

> We are indeed proud to be able to state that we are to have established here in the near future a school of high grade. The question of erecting a good school building has been agitated here for the past few weeks, and on last Saturday a meeting of those interested was called, and the handsome sum of $1000, which is the principal part of the amount wanted, was raised for its erection, and we can now state positively that this school is a certainty. The building when completed will be the best one by far that has ever been built in the county, and will be a thing of beauty, and we hope, a joy forever.
>
> Trustees have been appointed, and an industrious building committee is at work, and it is hoped that the house will be ready by October 1st. The building will be erected in a grove near D.B. Dougherty's mill and the site is lovely. Professors D.D. and B.B. will have charge of the school, this fact alone being enough to ensure its permanent success. It will not be a local affair, but a boarding school that cannot be surpassed by any county in this section as to educational advantages, etc. and it is the intention of the professors to bring to this school young men, boys and girls, from all the surrounding country.[26]

Not only was high school education to be made available for young women, but some would even prepare to attend college, and they would be housed in a co-educational boarding house.

Moving, Meetings, Commitments, Decisions

Daniel was noticeably aging. Etta Mae, called Etta by the family, had already moved to Boone with her husband Richard Greene to help with the founding of the school. Daniel may have already shown the family trait of heart disease and needed some caretaking, which his daughter could provide. He most definitely needed a cook, and Etta was an excellent one.[27] She would prove herself a very capable manager by later running a popular boarding house and restaurant, the Greene Inn, for decades to come.[28]

A flurry of activity commenced as moving plans proceeded for the brothers. Dauph immediately set about planning a boarding house on the Dougherty farm southeast of King Street, to be situated on a rise above the pasture on land that was either given, or promised, to Dauph. The boarding house would bring a small income and would also house Dauph and his family. Blan would move in with his older brother.

Blan did not intend to remain single; it was his desire to marry. Everyone in the family anticipated that he would marry Clara Powell from Lenoir. When asked about this, Blan would remark: "Ask the other party." It seems she found Boone too remote, too muddy, and too poor at that time.[29] The two were to write and visit regularly for nearly 60 years but never marry.[30]

At the initial meetings for launching the school, monies were promised and land was donated. D.B. Dougherty and J.F. Hardin gave six acres for the building and grounds.[31] According to his descendants, Hardin donated the first acre of land and the first $25 for the building of the new school, and thus encouraged others to follow suit.[32]

"Trustees have been appointed," according to the article, but their names were not given.[33] The "industrious building committee" raised anticipation for the project by advertising that they hoped "the schoolhouse will be ready by Oct. 1."[34] The proclamation that the site was "lovely" was not an exaggeration. Exuberance and passion were communicated with their aim of creating "*a thing of beauty, and we hope, a joy forever.*" Even today, when the school they founded has ballooned into the much larger Appalachian State University, one experiences an intrinsically pleasing topography in this original area with its south facing hill and pine trees.

By casting the net widely and founding a regional rather than local boarding school that would draw students beyond the immediate community, the risks to the initial supporters could be spread. Confidence was growing.

The initial announcement in July 1899 did not report the name of the new school, for one had not yet been chosen. Ultimately the Board agreed to call it Watauga Academy, a name that honored the county and invoked the wider area they expected to serve. From a Cherokee word, whose actual meaning may be lost, "*watauga*" is generally thought to mean "beautiful waters" or "whispering waters."[35]

Watauga Academy was to be privately run by a board of local trustees in cooperation with the Watauga County schools. Not everyone shared the optimism about the new academy. Early in July, apparently responding to correspondence from Blan resigning his teaching position at Globe Academy, Caldwell County Board of Education chairman F.P. Moore expressed his disappointment and considerable doubt about the wisdom of plans for a new school in Boone. Recalling the failure of previous attempts, Moore wrote on July 19, 1899:

> Your favor received some days ago. Very sorry you could not teach for us. Duty may tell you to stay at Boone if so you should. You'll have a hard pull at Boone. You could have made more money at Lenoir.... I hope you are in the right place. Eternity will tell if time don't. I know you and your brother will make a strong train and mighty fine thing you are with the monstrous hard pulling you'll have to do. Boone has good clever people, but its past record in some respects will injure it for generations yet to come May the Lord deliver us from a small town. I know a man of your thinking capacity can see some stumps in your road. You'll likely have a good school, and imagine it will be reported as a Methodist school, and your hands may be tied in a measure. Am I thinking to discourage you? Well, it does look like it. I know you do your own thinking and you are not influenced much by what other folks say.[36]

Despite its discouraging tone, Moore's letter reflects his high opinion of Blan's intelligence, of the independence of his thinking, and of the force that Blan and Dauph's combined efforts could create. If the brothers felt their plan was right, nothing would deter them from it. F.P. Moore was well aware of the longstanding association these brothers had with their Baptist institutions. Moore's assumption that the school would be Methodist may have reflected Blackburn's efforts in building a Methodist church in Boone, or Blan's lukewarm church attendance.[37]

Boone's reputation, "its past record," was known in Globe, where the community was very proud of its own record with Globe Academy. But Moore's prediction of long-term injury, "for generations yet to come," would be turned on its head. Laboring long and hard, the Dougherty brothers would prove Moore to be wrong.

"Eternity will tell..." and "a hard pull"

F.P. Moore's prediction that the school would flounder and his diffident "eternity will tell" did not deter local optimism. On July 20, 1899, the day after his letter from Globe, the *Watauga Democrat* again spoke glowingly of the proposed school:

It is indeed gratifying to see the interest being taken in the school enterprise that is now a certain thing in Boone. The people all over this and adjacent counties are thoroughly aroused on the subject and the funds for the erection of the buildings continue to grow. The bills are now nearly all in the hands of the sawmill men, who are all encouraging the work by donating liberally to the fund. The delivery of the lumber will begin within the next few days.[38]

Events proved Moore wrong. Three years after his discouraging letter to Blan, Moore would become a trustee of the school—no small commitment financially or otherwise. The community of Globe, where Moore was postmaster and merchant, was itself destroyed in 1916 in the Johns River flood. Moore served as a trustee for the successor to Watauga Academy, Appalachian Training School and Appalachian Normal School, from 1903 to 1927, over 25 consecutive years![39]

Mr. Moore was correct about the "hard pull" ahead, though. Watauga's public schools faced several serious problems, similar to those found elsewhere in North Carolina in 1899. "Attendance was poor because of parental indifference, ignorance, poverty, or lack of transportation."[40] Factor in, also, the economic situation in the mountains and it was most definitely "a hard pull" for the Doughertys.

Since the early 1890s, the area had been scarred by the worst depression since the Civil War. In 1893, the *Watauga Democrat* had reported, "Our business men are much oppressed for the want of money, and a hard struggle is going on between creditor and debtor."[41] Times were still hard at the end of the decade.

"Shocking illiteracy, and general backwardness" is how Daniel J. Whitener characterized public schools in North Carolina during the three decades prior to 1900.[42] Another North Carolina historian, Hugh Lefler, wrote of that period: "The masses of people were apathetic and indifferent toward education. Some were even suspicious of book learning. Some of the wealthier people were opposed to the whole principle of public education and patronized the academies and other private schools."[43]

Attendance in Mountain Schools: Challenges to Education

The Doughertys were constantly preaching the importance of attendance and further education. This became an important aspect of Blan's work as superintendent. Although attendance might not become a serious problem for Watauga Academy's boarding students and nearby town families, out in the county the situation was different. Without regular attendance during their early years, students would not be strong enough academically to consider high school or Watauga Academy.

Eustace and Mary Sloop, both medical doctors, who established Crossnore School in 1913, south of Linville, in Crossnore, faced many obstacles similar to those that faced the Doughertys. Speaking of their rural North Carolina mountain location, Dr. Mary Sloop told her biographer that "many of the pupils of that day quit school about the 4th grade. Few if any compulsory school attendance laws were on the books, and for years after we had such laws there was virtually no enforcement of them."[44] Dr. Sloop lamented that the main "problem was attendance, getting parents to send their children to school and send them regularly.... Uncle Abe [at Crossnore] was keeping his boy, now in his teens, at home to run the gristmill."[45]

A wagon is pulled up the road from Lenoir toward Blowing Rock, c. 1900. Often a team of oxen (seen in this photograph), horses or mules was taken from one wagon and double-teamed to another, allowing four animals to pull a heavy load up a steep section of road where it was "a hard pull." The arduous journey would take two days down and two days up the mountain. Bailey's Camp was the mid-point, where drivers slept under their wagons (courtesy Blowing Rock Historical Society).

Parents placed little value on regular attendance for a reason: their children were needed at home. "Between the ages of six and twenty-one, children moved in and out of school according to family needs, often attending when they were very little, then remaining at home for several years, and finally returning when younger brothers and sisters were old enough to relieve them of field work and household duties."[46] Yet many older teenagers, now "adult" students, feared returning to the classroom and facing the ridicule of being older and on a level with young children.

"Many parents kept their children out to help gather in the crops. If a frost was expected, the whole family had to stay at home to strip or cut cane. Children had to help with molasses and apple butter making and with hog killing."[47] Children were required to help with daily chopping of wood, carrying water to the house, driving cows, getting chickens and turkeys into coops at night. Washday involved extra water and extra wood. "The baby also had to be tended while the mother washed." This often kept two children at home. To make less washing and save clothes, children changed into old clothes when they returned from school.[48] In Watauga County, attendance was often poor because of bad weather, sickness, or indifference.

Historian James LeLoudis records one humorous and pathetic incident that illustrates the common situation in the mountains: "One seventeen-year-old boy presented a note to his teacher explaining a string of absences: Dear Cir—Pleze to eggscuse Henry.... We made sour-krout and he had to tromp it down. Also he had to Help butcher too pigs. Respeckful yuers, His Pap."[49]

At the turn of the century, North Carolina had the worst schools in the South and the nation, according to historian Rob Christensen. "North Carolina spent $0.50 per pupil per capita for education, tying Alabama as the lowest in the South. The national average was $2.84. The average length of the school term in North Carolina was 70.8 days, the lowest in the South. The national average was 144.6 days. The illiteracy rate among white North Carolinians (19.4%) was the second highest in the South and four times the national average of 4.6%."[50]

The Watauga County school records of 1900 showed an average daily attendance of less than half of those enrolled. "This, together with the lack of interest in public education by the parents, explains in a measure why a fourth of the population of Watauga County was, for all practical purposes, illiterate in 1900."[51]

Sacrificial Effort: A Community Project

All of the school board members and trustees knew about the challenges of education in the state, and especially in their county, in the summer and early fall of 1899. First and foremost, a fund-raising campaign was launched. The trustees led the way in contributing sacrificially to support Watauga Academy.[52] "Watauga Academy was a joint effort of a lot of people in the town and county," Etta Dougherty Greene said. "Some of the folks gave materials and money while others donated labor toward the construction of the building. My brothers [Dauph and Blan Dougherty] spent weeks enlisting the support of Watauga's for the school."[53]

Although many people helped, the majority of the load fell to trustees and to the Doughertys. Sacrifices made by Dougherty family members—emotionally, physically, and financially—can be verified with many examples from these early years and decades to follow. "The [Dougherty] family had pooled their cash and assets to raise nearly half the anticipated cost of $2,000 for the new school building," wrote Ruby Lanier, B.B. Dougherty's biographer and a meticulous researcher.[54] It seems that the initial $1,000 on the table came from the Dougherty family, although many in the town would later give to provide what was needed. Obviously, $1,000 was a large amount of money at that time. Perhaps the deaths of several extended family members provided some inheritance money for the Doughertys to give so generously towards the school, but how much is unclear.[55] A *Watauga Democrat* article in 1905 quoted B.B. Dougherty as saying that few people "really knew how much expense, hard work, and nervous anxiety it took to agitate this enterprise, ... [and the] heavy personal and financial load."[56]

Meanwhile, construction work on Watauga Academy continued, as did the campaign to finance it. Local people gave labor, materials, and money. Even a recorded gift of 25 cents showed important support when little cash was available in the area. It was truly a community project.[57]

Planning and erecting the new school on the six acres of donated land south

Lumber is being sawed for the school building, c. 1899, Howard's Knob in the background. The community gave sacrificially with cash, supplies, and labor for the construction of Watauga Academy (Doris Stam Collection, University Archives, Special Collections Research Center, Appalachian State University, Boone, North Carolina).

of the Boone Cemetery would take months. The advertised date of October 1 was overly ambitious. Without a dedicated schoolhouse, options for a building to hold classes were few, other than the courthouse and the Masonic Hall.[58] The few churches in Boone at that time were too small, housing congregations of two dozen or less.[59]

The old Three Forks Baptist Institute (or Boone Academy) stood empty and in serious disrepair, but it would suffice.[60] During the last three days of August 1899, the minutes of the Three Forks Baptist Association record that Three Forks High School was given to the Boone Baptist Church, because "the property is becoming almost worthless as a school building." Immediately the Boone Baptist Church gave the use of it to Watauga Academy while construction continued on the new academy building.[61]

On Horseback: Building Trust and Offering Hope for a Better Future

Traveling over the county by horseback in the late summer and early fall of 1899, Blan surveyed the "84 teachers in 73 schoolhouses, three of which were designated for Negroes."[62] He encouraged the students to continue their education and promoted the new subscription school and secondary classes in Boone.

In the years following 1899, Blan would take the helm and teach in the multi-level one-room schoolhouses (many of them log structures) demonstrating new ideas and teaching tips for rural teachers. Many horseback trips over the pathways and wagon roads of rural Watauga County brought him in close contact with teachers, parents, and pupils. His horse became a well-known figure to all. For most of his life the horse was simply called "Bob," and in old age was referred to as "Old Bob."[63]

Blan Dougherty rode his horse throughout the county, exhorting students to continue their education and not drop out, as so many did.[64] One pupil, Mrs. McKinley Ayers, remembered one of Blan's recruiting visits to her school, during which he told the class, "You should count at $5 each day you come to school. That is how much it will be worth to you." She recalled thinking that was a fantastic amount. She had just hoed corn for 10 hours at $0.05 an hour for her grandfather so that she could buy a ribbon that she wanted badly. Five dollars a day was just unheard of.[65]

The Doughertys were giving hope for a different future, not only economic improvement, but of improvement for the mind, an elevation of morals, and a refinement of culture.[66] They were also on the continual look-out for potential future teachers and leaders who would do the same for other mountain people.

The Doughertys had earned the trust of the county's citizens and families unlike any that could have developed with "outsiders." Daniel was well-known from his role with the *Watauga Democrat* and his involvement in local politics. Dauph was admired for his success at Wake Forest College and his contributions to the *Democrat*. Blan had become acquainted with and respected by hundreds of families while teaching public school on three sides of the county in the 1890s.[67]

The *Democrat*'s July 1899 forecast of the school's "permanent success" due to the efforts of "Professors D.D. and B.B. [Dauph and Blan]" may have been influenced by their father, Daniel, but it appears to be a legitimate reflection of local respect.[68] And succeed it did!

11

Watauga Academy Begins (Fall 1899)

Watauga Academy Begins in a Battered Building

On August 24, 1899, the *Watauga Democrat* announced:

WATAUGA ACADEMY
For Young Women and Young Men
 D.D. Dougherty, A.B.
 B.B. Dougherty, B.S., Ph. B.
 Principals
Fall term opens Tuesday, September 5, 1899. Three courses offered: Common School Course; Academic Course; Two Years' Collegiate Course. Instruction will be given in music, art and business. Special attention will be given to public school teachers. Students will be thoroughly drilled in Debate and Declamation. Board $6 per month. Splendid opportunities for students to board themselves. Tuition from 1 to $3 per month. For more information write or call on the Principals, at Boone, North Carolina.[1]

School began, as promised, on September 5, 1899. The *Watauga Democrat* reported that the school opened "with flattering prospects on Tuesday and the principals express themselves as highly pleased with the outlook."[2] They met in the abandoned Three Forks schoolhouse, "a two-room building, with one room above the other connected by rickety stairs running up the outside wall."[3] No photograph exists of this structure, which stood behind what was to become sites for the Boone First Baptist Church and the former Methodist Church (now the Turchin Center for the Visual Arts).[4]

"About 53 children, none above the third grade, appeared for the opening," according to a later account written by Blan Dougherty.[5] The battered structure was in poor repair and destined for demolition.[6] Recalling those first days, Blan said in his mountain accent, that "ev'ry winda was out on the first floor."[7] Knotholes in the pine wood went straight through the thin walls, exposing the rooms to cold weather and canceling any effects from the pot-bellied stove. Blan himself filled the knotholes with corn cobs.[8]

"I taught the third graders," Blan chuckled with genuine delight as he reminisced about that first day in a 1956 recorded interview with his friend and Boone lawyer, Wade Brown. Lillie "taught the primary work. We had quite a time of it. It was really fun," Blan continued. "Some of the third graders could hardly read."[9]

> # WATAUGA ACADEMY.
> ### FOR YOUNG WOMEN AND YOUNG MEN.
> ### D. D. DOUGHERTY, A. B.,
> ### B. B. DOUGHERTY, B. S., Ph. B., PRINCIPALS.
> ### FALL TERM OPENS TUESDAY, SEPTEMBER 5th, 1899
> Three courses offered: Common School Course; Academic Course; Two year's Collegiate Course. Instructions will be given in Music, Art and business. Special attention will be given to public School teachers. Students thoroughly drilled in debate and Declamation. Board $6 per month. Splendid opportunities for students to board themselves.
> ### TUITION FROM $1. TO $3. PER MONTH.
> For other information write to, or call on the Principals, at Boone N. C.

Announcement of the new school first appeared in the *Watauga Democrat* newspaper on August 8, 1899 (https://newspapers.digitalnc.org/lccn/sn82007642/1899-08-24/ed-1/seq-3).

A bell tower majestically topped the Watauga Academy, built in 1899 on land donated by Daniel Baker Dougherty and John F. Hardin (*The Dew Drop*, Volume XXI, No. 3 (May 1924), University Archives, Special Collections Research Center, Appalachian State University, Boone, North Carolina).

Boone had a population of 155 when Watauga Academy began, according to the U.S. Census of 1900. Boone township had 1,811 residents, while Watauga County was reported to have a population of 13,417.[10]

The trustees and the Doughertys contacted families about subscribing to Watauga Academy. Enrollment was rather flexible, and a few joined or left during each month of the school term. Families within walking distance of the new school signed up their children for the public school term, and most of them also enrolled in the winter subscription term. Among the families were many familiar Boone surnames: Bingham, Blackburn, Blair, Bryan, Coffey, Cottrell, Councill, Culler, Farthing, Greene, Hagaman, Hardin, Henson, Herman, Hodges, Mast, Miller, Moody, Moore, Norris, Penley, Presnell, Reese, Sherril, Shull, Story, Taylor, Thomas, Todd, Trivette, Winkler, as well as others that first year.[11]

Some Students in the First Class at Watauga Academy

When Blan had canvassed the western part of the county in August of 1899 he visited the Beaver Dam (Bethel) community where his cousin Sarah Dougherty Perry lived. This was the same Cousin Sarah who had come to live with the Dougherty family when Dauph and Blan were perhaps 4 and 5, before their mother died, and before their baby sister Etta Mae was given to relatives to raise. Sarah loved to recount that she was the one to teach Blan his letters and early reading.[12] Although only a teenager when she cared for the Dougherty children, Sarah was almost a substitute mother during a formative season of the children's lives and lived with them for a year or longer. In decades to come, Dauph's wife, Lillie Shull Dougherty, would welcome this beloved Cousin Sarah into her home in Boone many times.[13]

Sarah's teenage son, Henry Perry, and his father had been working in a field of rye when Professor Blan came by on horseback. A discussion ensued, and the decision was soon made to send Henry to the first year of Watauga Academy. Family funds for schooling were nonexistent, but Blan assured the Perrys that young Henry could earn his tuition by working on the building site after school and on weekends.[14] Many other new students would tell similar stories of how they came to enroll at Watauga Academy.

When classes in the old, temporary building ended each day, Henry and several other young men assisted with construction of the new Watauga Academy building. A day ledger belonging to D.D. Dougherty shows the tuition credits for this work-study arrangement.[15] Tom Beach, another early student, brought water to the carpenters working on the construction, one of whom was his father, and together they earned Tom's tuition fee.[16]

Some students bartered for tuition and others, like Henry Perry, Tom Beach, and Pink Harrison, worked on the construction.[17] T.H. Hines worked on a well and "the backyard" for tuition credit.[18] Dauph Dougherty's ledger from 1899 to 1903 contains fascinating details of various debts and payments for tuition and books, bartering with produce (corn, potatoes, molasses, buckwheat, beans) and building supplies for the new building, and work for tuition.

The Shull family of the lower Cove Creek area signed up their two daughters, Addie and Minnie, to attend Watauga Academy. Today it would take less than 10 minutes to drive to Cove Creek Store from Boone, but 125 years ago things were different.[19] The girls packed their trunks for the trip to Boone and their anticipated stay of several months, but their trip was delayed for several days by bad weather.[20] When they finally arrived in Boone, the Shull sisters and some other students boarded at the home of a local resident, where they would stay until the end of the term.[21]

In the same edition of the paper announcing the opening of Watauga Academy, an advertisement was printed for the well-established Cove Creek Academy: "Honest instruction that makes for character, by competent teachers/ Board at $5 or $6 per month living expenses. Moral and Religious influence of the community. No thoughtful parent will place his child in school when the influence of the people is not good. Fall Term begins Sept. 14, 1899."[22]

"Thoughtful parents" all over the area did indeed regard the Doughertys as a "good influence" on their children. Cove Creek Academy, ten miles west of Boone, ended with the seventh grade. With the opening of Watauga Academy, people finally had a school where study beyond the seventh grade was possible. High school also opened the door for students to prepare for teacher certification examinations. Teaching in the one-room schoolhouses was one of the only cash-paying jobs available in rural communities. Earning higher marks on the examination test could result in a higher-ranked certificate and higher pay.

In the same newspaper issue that announced the opening of Watauga Academy, it was reported that a Normal School, or teacher training school, was being considered nearby in Blowing Rock. However, the new Normal School did not come to fruition.[23] What Watauga Academy offered for teacher training was much needed in the area.

Lillie Teaches: Working Mother and Bargain for Boone

It was the end of September 1899 before Dauph was able to return to Butler, Tennessee, and move his wife and daughter to Boone and into his father's home on King Street with the family farm beyond. The brothers had been consumed with preparations in August and teaching the first weeks of school in September. The two-day journey by buggy or wagon from Butler with an 18-month-old child could not have been easy.

With Lillie's arrival, the instruction in music and art that had been promised in the *Democrat*'s August 24, 1899, advertisement of the school's curriculum was finally available.[24] Music and art were areas in which the brothers had no training.[25] Common School (public school) classes were divided into three levels and ended with the seventh grade.[26] The Academic and Collegiate Course listed in the advertisement was a college preparatory curriculum.[27] The school's advertisement continued to run in the paper, and new students continued to enroll during the fall, even after classes had begun on September 5.

Soon after her arrival, Lillie Dougherty not only commenced teaching music classes, but also began serving as the regular substitute teacher while Blan, as superintendent, was away for many days at a time to examine or train county teachers.[28]

While Lillie taught at the Academy, others cared for their young daughter. Blan, Dauph, Lillie, and little Clara initially lived in Daniel's home on King Street. Dauph and Blan's sister Etta and her husband already resided in the house to care for Daniel. Etta likely watched Clara along with Etta's own young son, Bonner.[29]

The salary from the Watauga County School Board for teaching at Watauga Academy was only $25 for both D.D. and B.B. Dougherty together.[30] Lillie was apparently not compensated. The 1926 school catalogue, *The Dew Drop*, whose content was written or supervised by Blan Dougherty, described the history of the school, and the respective roles of Dauph, Lillie, and Blan as follows:

> Messrs. Dauphin D. Dougherty and Blanford B. Dougherty began the school, which was called Watauga Academy, in the fall of 1899. Mr. B.B. Dougherty acted as county superintendent and Mr. D.D. Dougherty conducted the school. The town school was taught in connection with the other work. Watauga Academy was conducted in the old school building till the new house was ready. Mr. D.D. Dougherty and Mrs. D.D. Dougherty taught the public school at a salary of $25 for both. The spring term was begun in the new building, and Mr. B.B. Dougherty helped in the work.[31]

It is not clear from this description whether the $25 salary Blan described for Dauph and Lillie was considered compensation for all three, but Blan's account varies from the School Board's original contract with Dauph and Blan to compensate the two of them for $25.[32] It is more likely, if compensation for Lillie was even considered, that she was assumed to benefit from her husband's share of the $25 salary.

Into the New Watauga Academy Building

By November 1899 Watauga Academy's enrollment had reached 100, and the two little rooms in the old school building were filled to capacity. The shorter public school session ended after 10 weeks, "but the subscription school had continued, with most of the students remaining," and new ones joining.[33]

All during the fall Dauph and Blan worked on the new Watauga Academy building whenever possible, and often into the evening when daylight hours and weather permitted. The brothers were noted for not being averse to hard work. "The Dougherty brothers worked with their own hands to clear the land for the building. They would teach all day at the run-down Boone Academy building then hammer, saw, and haul lumber from the sawmill" until dark.[34]

Tuition was from $1 to $3 per month. Any amount higher than this would have been beyond the means of mountain families, the cost of peer mountain academies was similar at that time. In more economically prosperous regions of the state, tuition was much higher. Even the Lutheran-supported Lenoir College in adjacent Caldwell County (now known as Lenoir-Rhyne College) asked over twice as much.[35]

By the end of the Christmas holidays in 1899, two rooms in the new building were sufficiently completed to be used for classes.[36] In early January 1900, the school moved into the new building, although one class remained in the decrepit Boone Academy (Three Forks) building.[37]

It was a momentous day. The weather was very cold, eight degrees below zero, and although the enrollment had grown, only four students showed up for the high school course that day.[38]

A Whole New World

Reminiscing about 1899 and 1900, one mountain farm boy wrote to Professor Blan in 1946:

> I ... have seen you riding in on horseback to see us. I've heard you talking with my father and mother about sending me to Boone, to attend school at Watauga Academy. It was winter, and dark and cold and snowy. Then I have found myself living in a second story room, nearest the home of your brother and his family, and hear again the cheery, bantering voices of the boys and girls as we stamped the snow from our shoes on the front porch of the new building, even then not fully completed; we match wits with one another in the classrooms; *we find a whole new world being opened up to our wondering eyes and minds.* ... [italics added].[39]

After attending Watauga Academy, this young man, W.A. Stanbury, later earned his A.B. and Doctor of Divinity from Trinity College (now Duke University), and became a prominent Methodist pastor in central and western North Carolina.

All the sacrifices the community and Dougherty family had made to establish a new high school in Boone were reaping benefits. Convincing parents to pay for further schooling for their children, and, for many, to send them away from the family farm to boarding school in Boone, had not been easy. Watauga Academy provided opportunities for high school diplomas, teaching certificates, and college entry to students who otherwise would have had no future beyond the family farm. Dr. Stanbury captures the energy and ambition cultivated in the students at Watauga Academy during that first year to open *"a whole new world."*

12

A Whole New World Opens for Students (1900–1902)

As the 19th century ended and the 20th began, Dauph and Lillie Dougherty were determined to expose their students to a wider world beyond the backwoods of Watauga County, where subsistence farming had been unchanged for over 100 years. They had spent their honeymoon in 1897 at the Tennessee Centennial Exposition, held in Nashville to celebrate the 100th anniversary of Tennessee's statehood, which featured exhibits on industry, agriculture, commerce, and transportation, as well as educational and cultural achievements. It celebrated "the social progress of the 'new woman,' the 'new Negro,' and the modern child," and featured the role of Tennessee women, "galvanizing women reformers of the Progressive era."[1]

Agricultural to Industrial

As Watauga Academy opened in 1900, down in the Piedmont section of North Carolina, 217 mills and 101 tobacco factories were in operation. Much of the state had begun a major shift from agriculture to industry. Textile manufacturers "seized upon the labor (and work ethic) of distressed farmers and the tradition of family work (and of large families) to fill the mill villages."[2] Until the 1930s, a "family wage" commonly meant that children and adults all had to tend the factory machinery to earn a livelihood, often basic survival. It was a *hard* life. Although the first child labor laws were passed in 1903, they were not always honored. While industry was rapidly altering a way of life in much of the state, the mountains remained basically unchanged, and practically inaccessible to commerce.[3]

But the need for cash drove many mountain men to seek jobs with logging companies in the mountains, or in the coal fields of West Virginia.[4] At Crossnore School, south of Boone, the Sloops said "many young boys in those days left the home nest early. Frequently they would go off to 'public work,' as it was called. That meant that they got employment at sawmills, or even went into the northwest to do logging, or obtain jobs in the mines."[5]

Dauph, Lillie, and Blan hoped to introduce their students to other options beyond lumbering or mining. They aspired for their students to become teachers, better equipped women and men, or to go on to college and gain skills for other professions.

To house the Fine Arts Building, an exact scale model of the Parthenon of ancient Greece was erected at the center of the exposition grounds for the 1897 Tennessee Centennial, which was attended by Dauph and Lillie Dougherty on their honeymoon (Library of Congress).

Watauga Academy: High Expectations, Humble Surroundings

"Excelsior" was painted on the wall of a classroom in the first years, from a Latin word meaning "higher than." Dauph and Blan Dougherty hoped to motivate their students to excellence. Both brothers, now professors in their own academy, wanted to instill in their students the intellectual rigor and character development they had experienced as students themselves. Ringing through Dauph's mind from his high school years at Globe Academy was Patton's admonishment: "Do Right!"[6]

Enrollment almost doubled the first year, from 53 to 100, creating a great need for student housing. Only a few students lived close enough to walk to classes. Residents of the little village of Boone, which had thrown its support behind the new academy, now opened their doors to the student population and boarded students at break-even rates. Manly Blackburn, who owned a local hotel, offered

Excelsior was painted on a classroom wall in Watauga Academy, exhorting students to loftier goals, excellent work, and ever higher achievement (University Communications Records, University Archives, Special Collections Research Center, Appalachian State University, Boone, North Carolina).

accommodations for students at his hotel for half the customary rate.[7] Only boys took rooms in the hotels. Girls stayed in homes. Among the other families who offered room and board to students were the Hardin, Winkler, Councill and Gragg families.[8]

Serving as the student liaison to homes and hotels, Lillie was also an important emissary to the community and to parents. In her own home she developed the ability to manage a hospitable environment open to ever-changing demands and numbers of people. In October 1899, Dauph and Lillie, with their young daughter, moved into Meadow View—the home/boarding house Dauph had planned to build as part of the establishment of Watauga Academy. Blan moved in, too, and lived in his brother's home his whole life. As a capable woman of 24, Lillie managed the first boarding house on campus in her own home. Soon the number of students living in Meadow View grew to 10.[9] In addition to teaching, Lillie also oversaw childcare for little Clara, cooked, cleaned, and did laundry for the large household of 14.

Jesse Curtis, a student from 1900 to 1904, described what Boone was like in those early years: "The road extending through town was poorly graded and little attention was given to its drainage. There were deep mud holes when it rained and broad dust bowls when it didn't rain. Ravines and small creeks across sidewalks were spanned by boards nailed to a pair of two by fours. Weeds and grass grew everywhere in prolific fashion. A dim kerosene oil lamp atop a post here or there ... more often there ... was the only means of illumination."[10]

Junaluska native the Rev. Ronda Horton, who was born in 1895, described Boone during his early childhood: "Main Street was just a muddy road—the sidewalks were plank. There were just four or five little wooden stores then on Main Street—there were two hotels the old Coffey hotel and the Blair hotel—all the rest of the land around here was just farmland, pastures and corn patches."[11] As sharecroppers, Horton's family grew their own food; some were able to sell part of their produce.[12]

Moses H. Cone and The Dew Drop School Catalogue

The board of trustees was charged with giving and helping raise the money for the new school. In his travels as superintendent, Blan continued to promote Watauga Academy, soliciting student subscriptions and asking every potential donor for money. He approached the founder of Greensboro Cone Mills, Moses Cone, who was in the process of building a summer estate outside Blowing Rock (known now as the Manor House and Parkway Craft Center on the Blue Ridge Parkway). Blan later recalled:

> I remember well when I first met Mr. Cone. It was a cold day, the wind scarce. I knocked at the door of a small cottage—it was before he had done much building. Mr. Cone opened the door and asked me what I wanted. I told him I wanted an interview for 10 minutes. He said come in. I was trying at that time to raise money for Watauga Academy. I told my story [as] briefly and pointedly as I could. When it was finished, he replied that he did not know me, nor had he heard of our enterprise. "Go," said he, "and send me a catalog and printed matter, then you will hear from me." This was done and soon a letter came from his New York office with these words: "Yes, I will contribute to so worthy an enterprise. Here is my check for $50."[13]

The Dougherty brothers, who had seen the value of cheap printed material to advertise their former schools,[14] purchased a press as soon as possible after January 1900. On March 29, 1900, the first edition of the Watauga Academy Catalogue, titled *The Dew Drop*, was printed and mailed, with the assistance of a student who received tuition credit for his work.[15]

The importance of offering financial help or tuition credit for the county and mountain area students cannot be overstated. Evidence of how lives were changed abounds.[16] The Doughertys made what was essentially a work-study program available to many needy students. Higher education made a hopeful future possible.[17]

Winter and Spring Classes 1900

Classes continued during the winter and spring with private subscription students after the public school term ended for that year. Work on the new building progressed as weather permitted. In April 1900 the carpenters had laid the floor in the auditorium.[18] People of the town and county gave labor, materials, and about $1,100 for its construction, but the need was only about half met. More was required.[19]

As the first school year came to an end and the closing celebration approached, Lillie prepared her young students to provide music for the closing ceremonies and rehearsed for her own performances in the program. Dauph and Blan drilled the literary societies on their debate speeches; speakers were arranged and details were planned for the festivities. The Reverend Stanton agreed to give the Baccalaureate sermon. Hon. J.F. Spainhour, who had taught the Doughertys at Three Forks Institute, New River Academy, and Globe Academy, accepted the invitation to give the commencement address.

When the very first Watauga Academy commencement exercises were held on a Friday in May 1900 at the new building, the entire school took part. The *Watauga Democrat* recorded the event. First, the children of the primary department "delighted the audience with songs, recitations."

Moses H. Cone (seated) and brother Caesar Cone, 1870. Moses Cone gave generously to Appalachian for many years and served as a trustee (courtesy Blowing Rock Historical Society).

> Promptly at 11 o'clock our quantum [sic] friend and townsman, the Hon. J.F. Spainhour, of Morganton, delivered the literary address, which was a rare treat to all who heard it, especially to his old students of twenty years ago, many of whom were present. ... The exercises of the entire day were interspersed with most delightful music on different instruments, by the gifted wife of Prof. D.D. Dougherty and the school.[20]

An "immense audience" came to hear the orations, debate, guest speaker, and singing. Those who had sacrificed to make this education possible were pleased with the school and with the Doughertys, who were deemed "gifted educators." The newspaper bragged: "It is needless to say that Watauga is justly proud of her school and that the three gifted educators at the school have decided to cast their lots among us and work for home and native land."[21]

An exhortation followed, with the aim of stirring contributions to meet the unmet costs of the new building:

Friends of Watauga, it is needless of us to urge you to work shoulder to shoulder with these men whose sole aim is to work for you and do you good. Let's all work together in an unbroken phalanx and labor for the cause of education in this our mountain home. We feel all who were present left with a resolution formed in their minds that they would do all that lay in their power for the good of the school.[22]

The future of the new school was not yet solid or secure.

Charles B. Aycock Campaigns for Governor in Boone

Only a few weeks after Watauga Academy's first commencement, the town gathered for an event that swept the crowd up in enthusiasm for the political campaign of Charles B. Aycock, a renowned orator and Democratic nominee for the North Carolina gubernatorial race. Aycock had unanimously been nominated by the Democratic party as their candidate on April 11. The election was to take place on August 2, and inauguration in January 1901.

On May 31, 1900, Aycock arrived in Boone. Historian Rob Christensen explained that "[i]n the 1890s, campaigns were still conducted mainly at political rallies that were part serious debate and part entertainment, and which often lasted for hours," where powerful debaters dominated.[23] "In the golden age of political speech making—an age when public debates were spectacles that sometimes lasted five hours—Aycock was the most celebrated political orator in North Carolina."[24]

The Democratic party embraced and promoted the educational movement in a deliberate plan to draw more votes to the Democratic ticket and soften the provocation of the polarizing white supremacy focus.[25] Aycock won the election. The newly inaugurated governor declared at the very beginning of his term in office that it would be his aim to aid the cause of education.[26]

Mr. Rivers, owner and editor of the decidedly biased *Watauga Democrat* newspaper, glowingly endorsed his party's candidate and was unhesitating in his support. The crowd that gathered to see and hear Aycock was estimated to number 700 to 800 people. The *Democrat* recounted that the Morganton Brass Band, in new uniforms, paraded on:

> our beautiful new school grounds ... [with] [i]nspiring and patriotic music, arousing enthusiasm.... Amid wild cheers and applause the Hon. C.B. Aycock appeared before the people. The peerless man, invincible Democrat, matchless orator and Christian gentleman held his entire audience spellbound for an hour and a half and left everyone sorry that he had stopped.[27]

The crowd was totally swayed by Aycock. Most likely the Doughertys, as staunch Democrats, were, as well, though there is no record of their response to Aycock. Nor is there a record of how the Doughertys felt about the role of the Democratic party with respect to the Wilmington massacre of 1898. In the Wilmington coup and massacre, a group of white supremacists in the Democratic party overthrew a duly elected government and massacred African American and white citizens to seize political power. Aycock and the Democratic party misled the public about the massacre, claiming it had been a race riot led by Blacks, and overlooked the atrocities committed by the party's white supremacist leaders, to the everlasting shame of Democrats. The political climate in Boone was prime soil for both Aycock's racism and his promotion of education.

Even for Republicans in the mountains, who joined together with African Americans for the benefit of Republican party goals, "blacks were regarded as inherently inferior, and this attitude had been formed and accepted long before the Reconstruction period."[28] Boone had its separate section of the village for Blacks, called Junaluska, which sat on the hill above the center of town. Junaluska natives Frazier Horton and Morris Hatton explained that race relations, while far from equal, did not have the same level of general animosity experienced in the Piedmont. "At the same time, whites and blacks had to work together most of the time to survive on this mountain [in Boone, North Carolina]. Slavery didn't catch on as much here because there were no big fields, but, of course, there were slaves...."[29]

Everyone in the crowd was aware of the growing educational awakening across the South. North Carolinians were proud of their part in the larger movement. The education crusade grew, in part, out of the white supremacy campaign of Aycock's road to the governorship. Blacks were intended to be excluded from voting by a state Legislative Amendment in 1899, which imposed a literacy test. This test "was not required for whites because of a grandfather clause. But the clause would expire in 1908, and the Democrats promised to make sure all white boys could read and write by then."[30]

In this era before the visual mass media of television and internet, finding balanced and honest information was difficult. The *Watauga Democrat* and other newspapers were often "mere partisan megaphones rather than independent sources of reliable information."[31] Networks of political supporters including local leaders, lawyers, businessmen, county and precinct chairmen "had considerable influence in both persuading voters and getting them to the polls."[32] Aycock's appearance in Boone was a boost for the prevailing Democratic party views in Watauga County, views that persisted for decades to come.

Summer 1900: Blan Considers a Job Away from Boone

During the summer of 1900, after Aycock's visit, Professor Blan made the rounds of Western North Carolina, and was paid by the state to teach at a summer Normal Institute at Mars Hill College required for regional public school teachers. The county newspaper, *The Madison Enterprise*, wrote that B.B. Dougherty had been impressed with "his sound common sense ability as a teacher. Without pretension, he nevertheless convinces you that he has the true make-up of the able, original instructor."[33] The trustees of Mars Hill College took note and promptly offered Blan a position as co-principal of the school where Dauph's close friend from Globe, Bob (Robert L.) Moore, was president. After conferring with Dauph, who assured Blan that he was needed at Watauga Academy and in Boone, Blan turned it down.[34]

While Dauph stayed in Boone for most of the summer, Blan was called upon to deliver the commencement address at his alma mater, Carson-Newman College, near Knoxville, Tennessee.[35] Blan's good friend and classmate from Carson-Newman,

Virgil Jones, was head of the Masonic Institute school in Mountain City, Tennessee. Both young men were admired by their alma mater.[36]

On August 6, 1900, the public school in Boone opened for the second year at Watauga Academy, with a large attendance. The *Watauga Democrat* ran the same advertisement as before and described the new Academy building: "There were two classrooms on either side as one entered the building and several small rooms just above these. The two back rooms downstairs cared for two classes and the large room over them was an auditorium, first used as a Chapel and later housing the library."[37] In October the order for new desks was placed, and the homemade benches and make-shift furniture would be replaced with proper school furnishings.[38]

Recruiting on Horseback and Adult Students

Out in the rural areas of the county, Blan encouraged young men and women he met to attend Watauga Academy. Capable adults with very limited education also showed interest, but as a rule they were ashamed to go back to school lest they would have to start in the lower grades with children.

Many adult students, as well as teachers with little preparation for teaching, were persuaded to enhance their futures by attending Watauga Academy. The Doughertys were ever on the lookout for adult workers with potential they could recruit to become teachers. Blan traveled to a sawmill in the Blue Ridge section some four or five miles from Boone in pursuit of a bright young man, and there he probed the young man with questions: "Did he intend to spend all his life at a sawmill? Wouldn't he like to go to school again and prepare himself for a more satisfying and more effective life?"[39]

Such questions started that young sawmill worker, Roy M. Brown, thinking. Brown enrolled at Watauga Academy in the fall of 1900, prepared himself for college, and soon entered the University of North Carolina at Chapel Hill. After graduating from the University, he returned to Watauga Academy—by then, Appalachian Training School—and headed the English Department. Later he earned his Ph.D. degree at Chapel Hill and once again returned to Appalachian.[40] The opportunity that an education at Watauga Academy gave the poor mountain farm children and adults endured long after the lumber boom ended and all the saw mills closed.[41]

Many adult students, as well as teachers with little preparation for teaching, were persuaded by the Doughertys to enhance their futures by attending Watauga Academy. In March 1901, it was announced in The *Watauga Democrat* that "more than 100 grown pupils, to say nothing of the scores of smaller ones, answered to their names at roll call."

As in schools across the country, literary societies were an essential part of the institution from its inception. The Watauga Literary Society for young men had been formed in 1899, providing academic encouragement as well as a social gathering on Friday evenings. A Literary Society for young women was established soon after.

Great emphasis was put on debates and public speaking, both significant features at commencement exercises and other special occasions.[42] Professor Blan studied the arguments on both sides of debates and instructed students in the correct forms of

12. A Whole New World Opens for Students 95

Early student body gathered on the front steps of the First Administration Building, c. 1906 (from O. Lester Brown's book, *Blanford Barnard Dougherty: A Man to Match His Mountains* [1963]).

Literary Society room, c. 1906, in Lovill Home dormitory for young women (University Archives, Special Collections Research Center, Appalachian State University, Boone, North Carolina).

delivery.[43] Speeches were limited in length and were required to be written, memorized, and rehearsed before delivery. One student reported that Professor Blan's "optimism and contagious enthusiasm stimulated the participants" in each contest. This was said to be "an antidote for any inferiority complex or timidity of speakers."[44]

The second school year concluded with several days of events, culminating in the commencement exercises with musical performances, speeches, and the awarding of diplomas. Hon. J.F. Spainhour, Dauph and Blan's former teacher, again gave the address for commencement in May 1901. Dauph's close friend the Rev. W.R. Bradshaw, of Wilkesboro, gave a sermon entitled, "How can a young man cleanse his way?" to an appreciative audience of 800.[45] Little Clara Dougherty, age three, recited a short poem before the large audience.[46]

Summer and the Third School Year 1901–1902

Over the summer Dauph drove his wife and daughter in their buggy to see her family in Tennessee. Lillie and young Clara apparently stayed in Butler while Dauph returned to work in Boone during June and tend the family garden. As in the previous year, in the summer of 1901 Blan designed and taught a teacher institute sponsored by the state. Caldwell, Mitchell, and Watauga County public school teachers met at Globe Academy, the central point of the three counties.[47]

School began in late summer. Although enrollment fluctuated during the fall of 1901, depending on farming needs and family income, in January 1902 the *Democrat* reported: "The school at Watauga Academy resumed work Monday of last week, and the boarding pupils have been arriving almost daily ever since. We are told that there are now more than 100 in attendance and that fully ninety per cent of them are grown pupils. The outlook for the school this year is most flattering."[48]

February 1902: Daniel Baker Dougherty Dies

Daniel Dougherty's heart was failing. Although the school was thriving, there was little joy in the family as he lay gravely ill. Daniel died on February 22, 1902, and was buried beside the young wife he had brought to Boone 30 years earlier. He was 68.

R.C. Rivers, who had succeeded Daniel as owner and editor of the newspaper, had once described D.B. Dougherty as "the old war horse," … who "knows when to say a thing and how to say it."[49] Upon his death the *Watauga Democrat* mourned him: "He was a man of rare common sense, broad judgment and even temper. He was perhaps consulted by more people than any man who ever lived in the county. He will be more deeply missed than any man who could have died in the county."[50] Daniel Baker Dougherty was remembered for his influence in the community. Later, a history of the newspaper includes the following biography of Daniel:

> A man with little formal education, Dougherty, known to some as "Squire," had established himself in Boone as a farmer, miner, blacksmith, and grist mill operator. Dougherty served as justice of the peace from 1890 to 1900, a title that granted him the power to regulate elections, appoint judges and county commissioners and to approve or veto the commissioners' actions. He also served as Boone's mayor for two terms and as postmaster, a position in which he is credited with expanding postal service in Watauga County. As editor of the *Democrat*, Dougherty wrote of the plight of the farmer and supported the Farmers' Alliance. Although

when the Alliance's leader Leonidas L. Polk split from the Democratic Party and formed a third party in 1892, Dougherty urged Watauga farmers not to follow suit. Dougherty also pushed for improved roads and the growth of the railroad in western North Carolina, and he advocated for increased support for public schools. Dougherty's sons, Blanford Barnard and Dauphin Disco, would go on to form Watauga Academy, the forerunner of today's Appalachian State University in Boone.[51]

Commencement 1902 and Beyond

Elaborate preparations were being made for the closing exercises at Watauga Academy in April 1902, and the Hon. Locke Craig was invited to deliver the commencement address.[52] Craig, who later became governor of North Carolina, made a remarkable prediction during his address: "Only a few years until you will eat breakfast in Boone, go to Raleigh for a day of business, and be back home for supper."[53] This was an astonishing statement for his audience from rural Watauga County, for whom walking was the main mode of transportation, even in the early 1950s.[54] Until the mid-century, few poor farming families in Watauga County could afford anything beyond the horse that plowed the garden and pulled the wagon.

Fellowship and food concluded the celebration, as the paper had advertised: "The Principals of Watauga Academy request us to say that all the friends and patrons of the school are requested to bring out their baskets, boxes, etc. well filled with good things and all join in having a good old fashioned picnic."[55]

Henry Perry, son of Dauph and Blan's cousin Sarah Dougherty Perry, graduated from Watauga Academy in 1902 with grand aspirations. He and several others from that class were headed to the State University in Chapel Hill. The cost of transportation alone was a challenge for Henry, much less tuition and expenses. The family made deep sacrifices to meet those costs. Henry recalled helping rebuild a log dam at his father's mill to power a saw and cut lumber that Henry then hauled in a wagon across the steep Stone Mountain and down to Butler, Tennessee, where a railroad line had recently been extended.[56] Henry's parents filled all extra space on the wagon with apples and anything else from the farm that might be sold. The wagon and contents—as well as the valuable mules, which brought $190—were sold to pay Henry's tuition and expenses.[57]

After a year at Chapel Hill, Henry transferred to the North Carolina Medical College at Davidson, where he entered in 1903. His first year of medical school was at the Davidson College campus, but his second (and last) year of medical training was in Charlotte. Henry graduated in 1905 and set up a medical practice at the Mast Store in Valle Crucis.[58] In later years the Doughertys would be able to offer scholarships to outstanding high school graduates, one to UNC and one to Trinity College.[59]

A Summer School for Teachers

Watauga Academy offered a new summer school program for teacher training in the summer of 1902. A letter to the editor of the *Watauga Democrat* in April

1902 encouraged all teachers to attend this program. Pointing out the public demand for good teachers and that "many teachers over the state are failing the examinations," the writer saw the summer school and an "Institute" to follow in July as "a much-needed training that every teacher should have." Writing independently, as one deeply interested in the cause of education, he urged, "We hope that all our teachers will attend this school. The principals of Watauga Academy are thoroughly competent to give training, and the teacher who fails to keep step with the rapid progress being made along educational lines will soon be a back number."[60]

Citizens out in the county supported the growing educational movement in the state and the new opportunities being offered by the Doughertys. The June 12 newspaper announced that "the summer school continues to grow, and the professors do the pupils the honor to say that they are the hardest working body, to take them as a whole, they have ever seen."[61] This meager start was the beginning of decades of popular and ever-expanding summer school instruction for teachers in Boone.

After the initial summer school classes at Watauga Academy were completed, a teachers' "Institute," comprising two weeks of Normal training for area teachers, was held in July in the courthouse. Important educational leaders were expected.[62] The *Democrat* cautioned, "Committee men shouldn't employ teachers who have no certificate from the Institute. This is made compulsory by the School Law, and those who fail to attend will not be employed as teachers, unless providentially hindered from attending the same...."[63]

Boone also anticipated a visit from Governor Aycock in September 1902 in connection with his efforts to promote education throughout the state. With annual financial aid from the Southern Education Board, an organization composed of philanthropists and educational statesmen for the promotion of public education in the southern states, he called a statewide conference of educational workers. Rallies were held all over the state and citizens were urged to vote for local taxation, to consolidate school districts, and to provide for more and better schoolhouses, longer terms, and larger salaries for teachers.[64]

Summer 1902: Planning a New Home

The Meadow View boarding house where Lillie, Dauph, and Blan lived afforded little privacy for the young couple. A private home had been their dream as well as their need. Together Lillie and Dauph worked on the plans for the family home, which would overlook the campus from the south, on what became Rivers Street, although there was no "street" at that time. An abundant spring flowed just east of the site chosen by Dauph and Lillie on the family farm.[65] From their front porch they would be able to see their cultivated fields, the old Dougherty Mill on the Boone Creek with the Academy building beyond it, and the south faces of Howard's Knob and Rich Mountain. Their son would later say that he grew up in the county, even though the home was a short distance from the center of Boone.

13

Poorly Trained and Poorly Paid Teachers

Seeking State Aid (Fall 1902)

Aycock Returns to Boone: Anglo-Saxonism

The Dougherty family joined a huge crowd at the Boone Courthouse to hear Governor Aycock speak about public education on September 30, 1902. The *Watauga Democrat* for September 18, 1902, had promoted the event: "It is seldom our people have the opportunity of hearing such a speaker, and they should attend *en masse*."[1] And indeed, the masses showed up. Speeches began outside but were moved inside the courthouse because of rain, leaving many outside when "every inch of room in the building was occupied." For almost two hours Aycock "held his audience in rapt attention."[2] The Dougherty family must have remarked among themselves how their

Watauga Academy (1) with its bell tower is visible in the distant pine grove, in this east-facing photograph of Boone. The 1905 brick courthouse (2) is at left and the Boone Baptist Church (3) with steeple is at center right. Across from the courthouse (4) is the original Boone Methodist Church (courtesy Historic Boone Collection, Digital Watauga Project).

politically active father, Daniel Baker Dougherty, who had died in February earlier that year, would have enjoyed this day.

Meeting Governor Aycock in person was the thrill of a lifetime for many in Boone. Historian Rob Christensen points out that "travel by candidates over poor, muddy roads were [sic] difficult, so most people never met those they were voting for. But when they did meet the candidates, it was often a memorable experience."[3] Seeing the man they had voted into the governor's office return to Boone was memorable indeed. To understand Aycock, one must understand that he was a product of his time and place, who rarely questioned the basic assumptions of most whites. "All his life, Aycock was an advocate of 'Anglo-Saxonism,' a popular intellectual fad of the day that combined white supremacy with the glorification of all things English. It was a Rudyard Kiplingesque age of European colonialism around the world," Christensen explains, "and many believed it was the white man's burden to rule over people of color whether in Africa, Asia, or the United States."[4]

It is difficult to unravel how much of this ideology was woven into the commitment to godly service in the minds of Dauph, Lillie, and Blan. Many histories of that day boasted that the best blood in America flowed in the veins of the isolated Scotch-Irish and German immigrant communities in the back hills of the Appalachians.[5] Cultural norms and pride blinded people to their own racism and belittlement of other races.

Progressive Political Paradox

In 1900, political leaders, ministers, and educators, including northern philanthropists such as John D. Rockefeller, Jr., set in motion a campaign to improve public education in Dixie. "The pivotal figure was Aycock—the voice of white supremacy who became the voice of educational reform; the man who helped engineer the Jim Crow laws but who was regarded by his contemporaries as a leading progressive voice."[6]

Christensen describes North Carolina at the turn of the century "as a progressive paradox"—as a state that was

> shaped by both fundamentalist churches and great universities, by poor yeoman farmers and industrialists, by an urge to move into the national mainstream and a reverence for the traditions, both good and bad of the Old South.... The state frequently oscillated between its progressive impulses and its broad conservative streak, sometimes swinging back and forth in ugly, violent spasms.[7]

Christensen characterizes the history of politics in North Carolina as "nuanced, multilayered, and at times contradictory."[8]

Nowhere is this paradox more apparent than in Charles B. Aycock, "the poster boy for North Carolina schizophrenic politics," but he was not alone in holding what seemed to be diametrically opposed views. "Other progressive voices of that era, such as President Woodrow Wilson and Raleigh newspaper editor Josephus Daniels, mixed progressive reforms with racist tactics or policies—a combination that is difficult to comprehend today, when many people equate liberalism with racial justice."[9]

Dubbed "the education governor," Aycock had promised the crowds who thronged to hear him in all parts of the state during his campaign for governor in 1900: "If you vote for me, I want you to do so with the distinct understanding that I shall devote the four years of my official term to the upbuilding of the public schools of North Carolina. I shall endeavor for every child in the State to get an education."[10] He was committed to the education of Black as well as white children, which may seem surprising to some. When legislation was introduced to decrease financial support of public Black schools in North Carolina, Aycock, "who had no veto power, privately told members of the legislature he would view passage of the bill as a violation of his campaign pledge, and if the measure passed, he would resign as governor."[11]

Aycock explained that "whites had always seen it as their duty to look after the education of blacks, even in the days of slavery. He said the times called for 'statesmanship and not passion or prejudice.'"[12] Christensen sees this as "the first step away from the virulent racism of the white supremacy campaigns."[13]

A statewide drive for better education had been initiated in February 1902, and speakers dispersed throughout the state to promote the cause. The newly founded Southern Board of Education was strongly influenced by Governor Aycock, who appointed Charles McIver to lead the North Carolina arm.

With the 1890 census had come the shocking news that North Carolina was "the most illiterate in the whole Union, with the single exception of only South Carolina."[14] Up to 90 percent of people in Appalachia could not read in 1890.[15] During the summer of 1902, "Aycock organized a group of speakers that held more than 350 rallies in 78 of the state's 97 counties" to promote education.[16] The executive committee "concentrated their efforts on communities that seemed eager to take action for better schools."[17] And, thus, Boone was chosen. The governor would visit Lenoir after leaving Boone.[18]

Dauph Dougherty and his family heard Aycock's remarks in 1902 and began to dream of its implications for Watauga County. Although Blan would be given credit for changes that would come, Hon. J.F. Spainhour, former teacher and family friend of the Doughertys, credited Dauph Dougherty with the push for a state-supported school in Boone. Spainhour wrote, "When Governor Aycock made that magnificent educational campaign throughout the State, declaring that every child should be educated, D.D. Dougherty caught the vision."[19]

Conundrum: Poverty, Poor Pay, and Short Terms

As Watauga County superintendent of public education, Blan knew well the North Carolina educational leaders involved in the Southern Education Board. During Blan's school year at Chapel Hill (1898–1899), he became familiar with James Y. Joyner, Charles D. McIver (president of the State Normal and Industrial College in Greensboro, now UNC-Greensboro), and Edwin A. Alderman (president of UNC 1896–1900), the movers and shakers of the educational revival in North Carolina.

Joyner, who had been promoted by Governor Aycock to state superintendent in early 1902, exhorted the public to raise local taxes for the support of local schools and the increase of teacher salaries.

Superintendent Joyner submitted his first biennial report on the state's public schools in 1902 and did not hesitate to decry the situation before him.

> As long as the annual salary paid the teacher who works with the immortal stuff of mind and soul is less than that paid the rudest workers in wood and iron, less than that paid the man that shoes your horse or plows your corn or paints your house or keeps your jail, the best talent cannot be secured and kept in the teaching profession.[20]

Without changes, he warned, the teaching profession will "continue to be … but a stepping stone to more profitable employments or a means of pensioning inefficient and needy mediocrity."

Blan Dougherty recognized from low scores on teacher certification exams that the one- or two-week teacher training institutes in Watauga County were inadequate.[21] Mountain teachers needed more training to advance beyond the "mediocrity" that Joyner decried. The only way to raise the quality of education for students in the county was to improve the education of teachers.[22] Those who needed teacher training most could afford it least. Even those who contemplated entering the teacher workforce could not afford to spend the money preparing for it.

Robert L. Madison, president of Cullowhee High School (predecessor of Western Carolina University), is seated far right with a summer Teachers' Institute group, c. 1897 (he has a beard and is holding a hat). Madison and Blan Dougherty jointly led a western North Carolina Teachers' Institute at Mars Hill College in the summer of 1902, where Madison told Blan about seeking state support for Normal classes to train teachers (courtesy Western Carolina University Hunter Library).

Watauga County teachers could teach only a limited part of the calendar year because weather, poor roads, and family needs on the farm prevented students from attending, and their average monthly salary was $21.25—"less that what was paid the man who shoes the horse or plows your corn," deplored Joyner.[23] Counties with better teacher salaries and longer school terms attracted the best-trained teachers. In the more remote regions of the mountains, the county superintendents were forced to grant certificates to unsatisfactory applicants.[24]

Robert L. Madison had made this argument before the Legislature when seeking funding for his school, Cullowhee High School, to be able to offer teacher-training classes in the southwestern mountains of North Carolina.[25] Cullowhee, south of Asheville, near Sylva, North Carolina, was granted money for Normal classes beginning in 1893.

Low teacher salaries resulted from low taxes, and low taxes resulted from low income from a live-at-home economy. Watauga Academy "rested upon a precarious and almost starvation financial foundation," Appalachian State Teachers College historian and former dean Daniel J. Whitener noted.[26] Whitener was insistent that the founders had no goal of making money for themselves out of the school. "With the meager fees and the little public-school money, [the Doughertys] were able to keep going, using these to supplement a living earned from their father's farm and a big garden. But the school needed more money to enable it to reach the people—the teachers, for whom it was conceived. The state of North Carolina had the money, and it was to this source the founders now turned."[27]

Letters to State Superintendent Joyner: Mountain Areas Overlooked

In October 1902, Blan Dougherty complained to Joyner of the "dearth of well-prepared teachers" in northwestern North Carolina and suggested that a year-round, academic, "state-supported normal school" might be the answer to the problem.[28] Thus began a six-month fight.

State Superintendent Joyner refused to seriously consider the idea, endorsing only short summer school sessions for teachers.[29] The General Education Board, in Washington, D.C., and Joyner feared that the establishment of smaller teacher training schools, particularly those associated with private academies, would lower standards of professional training, as well as dilute and diminish funding at existing teacher-training schools. Joyner warned Blan not to expect too much, for many sections of the state were clamoring as well. After the November meeting of county superintendents in Winston, which Blan attended, Joyner made clear he would entertain no other options than summer schools for teachers.[30] With this response from Joyner, Blan was jolted into action.

Citizens in Watauga County "were demanding that the superintendent hire well-trained teachers; the people were realizing, he [Blan] said, the difference between 'a teacher and a keeper of the schools.'"[31] When Blan had planned a summer school for Watauga, Caldwell, and Mitchell counties in 1901, he had quickly run into trouble, because the male teachers in the mountains could not afford to be away from home in the busy farming season; only women could attend a summer school. "To reach the teachers in this section of the state, a winter term was needed."[32]

Resisting Blan's pleas to establish teacher-training schools in northwestern North Carolina,[33] Joyner responded in October of 1902: "It is my opinion, one of the poorest things in the world and one of the most deceptive is a half-handed normal school.... Would it not be better to begin with a series of summer schools, running for one to two months in districts of two or three counties each, requiring the teachers attending to pursue regularly organized classes? Let these schools take the places of the institutes."[34] When it became evident that Joyner expected all summer schools for teachers to be held in Chapel Hill, Greensboro and Raleigh, and only at the state-supported colleges, Blan's resolve to push for his area of North Carolina grew.[35]

The Dougherty brothers took note of the fact that the entire state had been taxed to support the University of North Carolina, and very little benefit had fallen to their northwest section,[36] nor had their area felt any benefit from the tax-supported major railroads crisscrossing the state.[37] And somehow these railroad companies had found loopholes to avoid paying taxes that could have helped public education.[38] Wealthier towns could raise extra local money to fund graded public schools, but the mountains were poor. If the governor expected every citizen to pay higher taxes to fund secondary schools and colleges, then every citizen should benefit from those schools.[39]

The state-supported University at Chapel Hill and the college in Raleigh were out of reach to most in the northwest area of the state because of tuition cost and distance. The Normal and Industrial School for White Women had been established in the central section of the state, in Greensboro, in 1891. Normal Schools had been established for African Americans in Greensboro (Agricultural and Mechanical College for the Colored Race, now known as A & T), in the eastern town of Elizabeth City (Normal and Industrial Institute), and in five other cities.[40] When the southwest area below Asheville begged for help, Cullowhee—which already had the advantage of a railroad in Sylva supported by state taxes[41]—was granted support.[42] The Doughertys reasoned that the state required as much of the isolated northwestern mountain people, who had so few opportunities, as it demanded of those in areas of wealth and progress.[43]

A deluge of letters from Blan to Joyner, and from Watauga County citizens to the state superintendent, begged for the unique situation facing the mountain teachers.[44] Other sections of the state had special schools to educate teachers. The "lost provinces" of the North Carolina mountains needed their fair share.[45]

Robert Madison and Blan Dougherty served together as instructors in the summer Institute for teachers in 1902 at Mars Hill College, north of Asheville. When Blan learned about Cullowhee's appropriations from the state, he returned to Boone "fired with ambition for such a program for his own school."[46] "By the end of the summer, Blan was determined to turn Watauga Academy into a teacher-training school with state support."[47] Citing Governor Aycock's praise of recently granted state support at Cullowhee, Blan argued that citizens of the northwest counties should benefit in the same way.[48]

The Need for Good Teachers: Alderman, McIver and Noble

Educating mountain children was not only a matter of getting children into the classroom; they must be kept there by good teachers, longer terms, and better schoolhouses.[49] "A well-trained teacher was 'worth twice as much to the state as an untrained one.'"[50]

While a student at Chapel Hill, Blan had been heavily influenced by Dr. Marcus C.S. Noble, chair of the department of pedagogy (established in 1885)[51] and Edwin A. Alderman, UNC president 1896–1900, who impressed on him the importance of teacher training. As a public school teacher and later county superintendent, Blan had again encountered Alderman and McIver, president of the State Normal and Industrial College in Greensboro, at summer teacher-training institutes held in the mountain counties in the 1890s.

After an Institute get-together held in 1887 north of Boone in Alleghany County, McIver submitted a report to the state superintendent describing the situation facing the mountain teachers and ways to address their needs. In that report he noted:

> [F]rom 80 to 90 percent of the attendant teachers at Sparta had never seen any Normal School before. This indicates that the majority of teachers do not (often they cannot) go a great distance to attend normal schools. Small salaries and short terms render it, in many cases, impossible. Generally, too, these cases need Normal instruction more than any others. Normal Schools, or efficient County Institutes, should be brought within the reach of every teacher in the state.[52]

During his year as a student at Chapel Hill, Blan likely read this particular report, or at least learned of its substance, in his pedagogy classes under Marcus Noble, who had also taught at the county institutes in western North Carolina in the 1890s.[53] Indeed, Dr. Noble wrote a letter of recommendation for Blan in which he said:

> During his senior year Mr. Dougherty was a member of my classes in pedagogy and I was struck with his studiousness, earnestness, and enthusiasm. I believe that he is eminently qualified to conduct most successfully a school of the highest grade. His professional training for special work of teaching qualifies him to give young men and women wishing to teach valuable instruction for work in the classroom. I cheerfully commend Mr. Dougherty to anyone seeking the services of a well prepared teacher.[54]

Having earned the respect and endorsement of Professor Noble, Blan now sought support and recognition from State Superintendent Joyner.

As a mouthpiece for Aycock's educational plans, Joyner had reported to the Legislature in 1900, in grand and flowery language, about the "infinite power of ... universal education" and "equality of opportunity."[55] Clearly, the state of North Carolina had some work to do in the northwestern part of the state. If universal education carried such force, then teachers were the key.

More Letters to State Superintendent Joyner

Blan Dougherty tried appealing in writing again to Joyner for help with teacher training in early January 1903, to no avail. Joyner's reply was to send a copy of his *Biennial Report of the S.P.I., 1901–1902* promoting the same summer school program.[56]

Joyner was in cahoots with McIver, it appeared. Charles McIver, a forceful personality, hoped to secure a special summer school railroad discount rate that would cement his school as the destination for teachers across the state. Such a discounted fare, offered by the newly completed Western North Carolina Railroad in 1884, had contributed to the success of a teacher's chautauqua in Waynesville, and a summer Normal School in Franklin.[57] Two hundred teachers from the middle of the state, Goldsboro and Raleigh, responded to the advertisements for the events in the beautiful mountains.

Attendance had been optional at county institutes; however, teacher attendance became compulsory in 1889. But superintendents in distant counties informed McIver that it would be impossible even with a special fare to go to Greensboro for teacher training.[58]

George Winston, president of the North Carolina College of Agriculture and Mechanical Arts (now N.C. State University), and Francis P. Venable, UNC president from 1900 to 1914, pressured Superintendent Joyner to support their proposals for Normal Departments in the Piedmont before the Legislature. Venable had previously requested funding from the General Education Board in Washington, D.C., which Joyner apparently seconded, but the General Education Board did not agree, and funding was not forthcoming for Venable's plans.[59] But a central piedmont school was still Joyner's focus. Had Joyner really studied the unique needs of the mountain sections? It certainly did not appear so.

Blan Dougherty wrote to Joyner yet again, identifying the many obstacles that prevented mountain teachers from attending distant summer training institutes: (1) Teachers needed to work on their farms during the summer growing season; (2) summer school sessions were too short to bring the mountain or rural teachers to a higher qualification level; (3) Physically getting the rural mountain teachers to the summer schools was a challenge; (4) An influx of hundreds of these teachers would overcrowd the summer school; (5) The mountain teachers could not afford to pay the costs of summer school training; and (6) The hot summer climate of Chapel Hill, Raleigh, or Greensboro, where these state summer schools were to be held, would injure the health of students from mountain climates.[60]

Trying a different tact with Joyner, Blan called Joyner's attention to a magazine article stereotyping mountaineers, and revealing a condescending view held by some of the northern and western denominations in America about "missionary work" in western North Carolina. "Were the churches to do what should be done by the state? Were these 'Westerners' to sit down and let the church build schools and prepare teachers for the public schools?"[61] But Joyner remained unmoved.[62]

Relentless Blan Dougherty continued to pursue for his northwestern constituents what he knew had already been provided for teacher training in the southwestern corner of the state, and for African American teachers in the central and eastern parts of the state. He insisted that the proposed school in the northwestern part of the state could operate for only two or three thousand dollars a year from state money, and that citizens in that area would be willing to contribute part, if not all, of the building costs. He also pointed out that training teachers in the northwest would prepare a great many to seek a higher course of study at the state colleges.[63]

Citizens from Watauga and surrounding counties also wrote to Superintendent Joyner asking for the creation of a teacher training school.[64] R.C. Rivers, editor of The *Watauga Democrat,* added his voice: "You know the world has laughed at our people; you know that this section has long been neglected, and under the existing circumstances something *must be done*" (italics in original).[65] Still Joyner remained unmoved.

While Blan's correspondence with Joyner in 1901, 1902, and January 1903 records his determined efforts, Dauph's role is less well-documented but no less constant. "The Dougherty brothers were always talking school and making plans for increasing the capacity and the efficiency of the Academy," Dauph's son-in-law later recalled about their campaign for teacher training during this period. "Breakfast, dinner, supper all had as part of their menu a large share of such talk. The topics were carried to the classrooms and the hall of the school building. The leaders saw the need for greater financial help and of more teacher-training support. They began to let their ideas be known to the students as well as to others."[66]

In his *"Memories of Watauga Academy and Appalachian,"* former student (1901–1904) Jesse Curtis remembered how Blan "insisted that the teachers in the public schools in this little nest of counties should be better trained, and that the children deserved educational opportunities. He reminded them that these counties were cut off from the rest of the state, with no railroad or adequate highway connections." Blan sought students' input on his proposal to locate a teacher-training center in northwestern North Carolina, illustrating with a map which "he could duplicate from memory and locate each county. He pointed out to his small audience the counties of Alleghany, Ashe, Watauga, Mitchell, and Yancey (Avery County was not yet formed)."[67] Curtis recalled the enthusiasm among the boys over the proposal, and how with elation they pledged their support.[68]

Impromptu Bill Drafted with Lovill

Repeated refusals from State Superintendent Joyner did not deter Blan Dougherty. It was incomprehensible to both Dougherty brothers that the state would do nothing to help. The people's need in their part of the state was too great. In an interview with B.B. Dougherty recorded in 1956, a few months before his death, he recalled details of a pivotal day in the school's history (late 1902) drafting a bill with Capt. Edward F. Lovill, a state legislator from Boone:

> I went up to Capt'n Lovill's one evening, a Sunday evening. We used to go up there often and we would sit and talk. Now, the Captain was progressive in his makeup, and I told him that I'd been dreaming about establishing a permanent teachers' training school here. And we talked and then he said, "By golly, let's just write it out right now."[69]

Captain Edward Francis Lovill, born in 1842, had settled his family in Boone in 1874, studied law, was admitted to the bar in 1875, and "enjoyed a widespread reputation as a lawyer of uncommon ability and integrity."[70] Lovill served in the North Carolina

Will R. Lovill with his typewriter, c. 1905. Captain Lovill's son, Will, was "the only one in Boone who could use a typewriter," according to Blan (courtesy Lovill House, Boone, NC).

General Assembly for many years beginning in 1883,[71] and had taken a big part in establishing the summer teacher training Normal School that operated in Boone in 1885 for three weeks, and in 1888 for one week, indicating his commitment to public education.[72]

Blan Dougherty continued in his informal mountain dialect:

> And he [Capt. Lovill] called Will [Lovill's son] in, and he began to dictate. We'd talked through it and found out what we was trying to do.
> We didn't have any idea it would be anything like this. But we had an idea of getting all the teachers in from Alleghany, Ashe, and Watauga; and Avery, Mitchell and Yancey; Wilkes and Caldwell [counties]. This area was behind—the most illiterate belt in the state. We's right in the middle of it.
> And, we wrote it. And then we rewrote it. And Will produced a typewriter, and he typed it.[73]

Dougherty Brothers: Differing Opinions, Different Personalities

According to Blan's account from the end of his life, Ed Coffey, another lawyer in Boone and Dauph's former roommate at Wake Forest, learned of Blan's meeting with Lovill about founding a teachers' college. The conservative Coffey strongly opposed the idea and told Dauph about the bill draft. Apparently Blan had not told Dauph yet. "He [Ed Coffey] got Dolf onto me. He [Dauph] tried to keep me from going [to the Legislature]. Nobody did ever know that," Blan said.[74]

The brothers presented a united front in promoting a teacher-training school, but perhaps they were not so united on the notion of presenting a bill to the Legislature. Losing control of the school and relinquishing it to the state was a serious concept in Dauph's mind. It also seems that Dauph—pronounced "Dolf" by his brother and sometimes by others—was concerned about Blan being away for weeks, which is what the endeavor would require.

"My brother was a very impulsive man. He would do a thing, ya know, just on the spur of the moment—he might close the thing down. I didn't think he would, but...," Blan's voice trailed off, indicating he had no further comment about his brother.[75] Dauph was described by his son-in-law as possessing "great energy of both mind and body. He was not well satisfied unless he was in study or engaged in work," while Blan, who "differed in his manner of expression," would walk slowly around the campus and the town, "and often, as he sat among others, seemed to be lost in thought."[76] Smaller than Dauph, Blan "was about average in size and was more given to taking the philosophical view of things. He enjoyed talking and often took no notice of the passing of time."[77]

Dauph Dougherty was known for the very strictest morality and behavior, which he felt was his duty as a role-model to students and peers, and as a Christian gentleman.[78] What Blan called "impulsive" may have been Dauph's moral certainty and determination to follow only his own conscience—what Dauph's close friend called "moral courage."[79] By the time Blan took the bill to Raleigh, the brothers might have agreed on the idea. They must have discussed it before Blan left for Raleigh. It was understood that Dauph would stay to operate the school and care for his family, as was their normal practice whenever Blan traveled over the county as superintendent.

Blan revealed to Wade Brown that before the school had secured state support, he had wondered sometimes if his brother would rather that he, Blan, was somewhere else than at Watauga Academy. But the response from Dauph was "No"—he wanted his brother with him. Dauph told his brother to not accept another job; he needed him to remain by his side in Boone.[80] Each brother had leadership capacity. A tribe cannot have two chiefs, but somehow the brothers worked side by side, shared a home, and shared a bank account. Dauph had probably left Butler in 1899 with the dream of heading his own school. Blan may have had similar aspirations.

Blan's First Trip to the Legislature

After the repeated refusals from the state superintendent for financial help, Blan resolved to approach the Legislature with the bill he and Lovill had developed to propose a new teacher-training program in Boone. Although the Baptists were expanding their support of academies in Appalachia at this time,[81] and perhaps church-backed funding could have been sought, Blan preferred his chances with the Legislature. As he recalled in the 1956 recorded interview, "I had thought to myself that I'd get along with the Legislature better than I could with the Baptist State Convention. You know, I just thought that out myself, and I didn't have any connection to either place at the time! [Blan chuckled quietly.] But a man's always a thinkin'."[82]

To the Legislature he went. Several people witnessed Blan setting off down the mountain on horseback on a cold, blustery Sunday afternoon with the bill in his pocket. Jesse Curtis, who was to teach his classes during his absence,[83] described Blan's departure: "[A]s he rode his horse slowly down the muddy road, veering to the right or left to avoid mud holes, one hand was observed going up quickly to rescue his hat from the force of a strong gust of wind. His overcoat collar was turned up snugly about his neck as a further protection from the cold wind."[84]

Curtis said Blan rode a horse to Blowing Rock and spent Sunday night, then went on to Lenoir the next morning. Etta, his sister, said he took the family horse to Blowing Rock and down the mountain where he would catch the train the following day. *Time Magazine* later published a feature on Dr. B.B. Dougherty in 1949, romanticizing the momentous day by reporting he walked to Lenoir, which Blan had certainly done at times. Whatever the mode of transportation, it was a long journey. The train from Lenoir to Raleigh alone required several transfers, several days, and many stops. He would be away in Raleigh pushing the bill for three weeks.[85]

14

The Fight to Establish State Support

Appalachian Training School (Winter 1903)

In Raleigh: Opposed and Ignored

Before leaving Boone for Raleigh, Blan's arguments had been carefully prepared, and a copy of the bill was given to the newspapers. Even if Dauph had some reservations about seeking state aid for their proposed teacher-training school, he stood with his brother as Blan took on the struggle to persuade legislators. The rest of the family remained in Boone where Dauph continued to operate the Academy and eagerly awaited news from Blan in Raleigh.

When Blan arrived in Raleigh with the proposed bill to establish a state-supported teacher-training school in northwestern North Carolina, to his surprise, he found tremendous opposition.[1] Despite that opposition, he persisted in trying to recruit a sponsor for the bill. He later recalled: "We couldn't find anybody that would introduce it. Honorable William Newland, a young lawyer from Lenoir, was in the legislature. He came to me and said, 'Blan, I'll introduce the bill. I cannot promise you that it will pass; but I'll give them the best I have in my shop.'"[2]

After the bill was introduced on the House floor (January 27, 1903) it went to the House Education Committee.[3] Over two weeks went by without a Committee hearing on the bill. On the 17th day Blan confronted the chairman of the Education Committee, who was from Granville County in the central section of the state.

As a result of that encounter, Blan and Capt. Lovill were given a hearing that afternoon with the House Education Committee. However, at the appointed time of three o'clock, the chairman appeared briefly, passed the hearing to another legislator on the committee, and promptly left. Other members of the committee made it clear, *without* politeness, that they would *not* approve the bill no matter how long Blan Dougherty spoke.[4] But speak he did, and persuasively. So did Lovill. When those in the hearing showed disrespect and their attention lagged, according to his dictated account of the events, Blan rapped his fist on the table and said, "Wake up! Wake up! I am about to say something you need to hear."[5]

When Blan and Lovill finally got their hearing, they met opposition from the powerful Dr. Charles D. McIver, president of the Normal and Industrial School for Women in Greensboro (which became UNC-G). Although Dr. McIver was a member of neither the committee nor the Legislature, both Blan and Lovill were provoked by his attempts to dominate and control the scene in the committee meeting and in the Legislature.[6] Unafraid to oppose the influential man, Blan challenged him face to face. Blan felt that McIver had an inflated view of himself and was a man who relished an audience for his orations.[7]

During the committee hearing, Blan reminded Dr. McIver that he (McIver) "had taken an offering at Blowing Rock a summer or two before, after making a speech there in favor of a teacher-training institution for the northwestern part of the state. The collection amounted to some $3,000 dollars."[8] According to Blan, Dr. McIver replied: "O yes, I did make the speech and take the collection, as has been indicated, but I had in mind a school to be run under the auspices of the Women's Normal and Industrial College [in Greensboro]."[9]

McIver's statement revealed not only that he had misrepresented the purpose of the $3,000 he had collected, ostensibly for a northwestern teacher institute, but that the real source of his opposition to an Appalachian Training School was competition with his plans in Greensboro.[10]

Blan Dougherty's "Maiden Speech"

After three weeks of waiting, Blan spoke before the House Committee on Education on Friday, February 13.[11] The *Raleigh Morning Post* printed the entire speech on Sunday, and the *Watauga Democrat* gave a summary and the highlights the following week. In the speech Blan argued that the northwestern counties were the last section of the state to be settled and the slowest to be developed. These counties also represented the largest section in North Carolina without railroad facilities, without graded schools, with the fewest high schools, and with fewer well-trained teachers.[12] For this part of the state to catch up, he proposed that another Cullowhee be created.[13]

Blan asserted that the teacher training school would prove profitable to the state and went on to provide details of a financial argument that made the creation of a new school seem well within the ability of the state to establish.[14] He concluded eloquently: "We don't ask help because we have merited it, but because we need it. ... [We ask the] great state of North Carolina with all her cotton mills, her tobacco factories, her fine railroad system, her tremendous wealth and the prestige of the University for more than a century to concede a little appropriation, a mere pittance out of the State's treasury to that section of the State which nature has left at a disadvantage."[15]

The "lengthy but persuasive" speech by B.B. Dougherty before the Education Committee included:

> As long as this American republic lasts, North Carolina will be a state.
> As long as North Carolina is a state, there will be a public school system.
> As long as there is a public school system, there must be teachers.
> As long as we need teachers, they must be trained.
> As long as teachers are trained, there must be institutions in which to train them. We submit, gentlemen, that the best place to train a teacher is in an institution that dedicates its all to this task.[16]

A well-trained teacher was worth twice as much to the state as an untrained one, Blan argued.[17]

The *Raleigh Morning Post* printed an editorial on February 15 endorsing the proposal from Boone. "We must remember that the 'Educational Fever' is as violently abroad in that part of our good old State as any other, and equal facilities should be furnished thereof for prosecuting the crusade against ignorance. Pass 'The Newland Bill!'"[18]

In a private meeting with Governor Aycock sometime during his three week stay, Blan had pointed out that the "educational governor" could ill afford to oppose a bill that promised so much for the teacher. "He reminded the Governor that he had boasted the building of a new schoolhouse every time the sun set since being elected, that certainly there was no need for a schoolhouse without a teacher, and that there could be no effective teacher without a place to train him [or her]."[19] "The state has made greater demands upon us than ever before. We take it for granted that the state will allow us to make a little demand upon her."[20] Aycock changed his position and promised his support.[21]

The Newland Bill: More Opposition

The House heard the bill and discussion began on the floor. After "quite a warm fight" the bill was passed "by a majority, amid hard clapping all over the floor."[22] William C. Newland made a "magnificent appeal" for the school and won the accolades of both the *Morning Post* and the Raleigh *News and Observer* on March 5, 1903. The *Morning Post* remarked that Newland's speech was "one of the finest efforts made in the House at the present session."[23] Even Superintendent Joyner was persuaded to reverse his stand on the Bill.

However, an editorial on March 5 by the influential Josephus Daniels, editor of the widely read Raleigh *News and Observer,* criticized those representatives who voted for the bill for being swayed by Newland's oratory skills without evaluating his message. Daniels pointed out that Cullowhee High School had secured $5,000, but was requesting another $2,000; he feared the bleeding of state funds. Ridiculing the mountain dialect, he wrote: "Where will this thing stop? ... The state should 'stop right thar'; it should support, enlarge, equip its three great educational institutions without multiplying the number...."[24] The eastern part of the state had come to the Legislature in 1901 with ample money to start a normal school in their section, but had "wisely," in Daniels' view, been turned down.[25]

Fearing that Mr. Daniels' editorial would kill the bill, Blan requested that Watauga Academy students and friends write letters to the newspaper asking it to withdraw its opposition.[26] When Blan returned to Boone in early March, where Dauph was consumed with the day-to-day operations of running the academy, teaching, and caring for his pregnant wife and four-year-old daughter, the brothers conferred daily in person. An account written by Blan more than 40 years later gave this report of what transpired:

> Here [in the House] Hon. R.A. Doughton, of Alleghany County, with his powerful influence, joined Mr. Newland and his arguments for the bill. It was passed by a good majority.
> However, in the Senate the measure was turned down by the Committee on Education, but

Senators Clyde R. Hoey, of Cleveland County, R.B. White, of Franklin County, and E.J. Justice, of McDowell County, all young men who distinguished themselves later as orators and statesmen, signed a minority report and carried the bill to the Senate floor, where, on the last day, each made a speech in behalf of the bill that marked the beginning of a larger career for himself.[27]

Although he had declined to introduce the bill, Hon. R.A. Doughton "brought the prestige of his unexcelled reputation for wise statesmanship to the support of the bill—a support that never wavered throughout the years in loyalty—in a powerful speech."[28]

The speeches of Hoey, White, and Justice carried the Newland bill to the final vote and victory. The bill required a two-thirds majority to pass because it called for the appropriation of money and had not been previously considered by the Senate. To this hurdle was added an unfavorable committee report. In the final vote, Senate presiding officer Clyde R. Hoey of Cleveland County broke the tie, and the bill passed by one vote.[29]

Blan was in Boone when the Newland Bill finally passed on March 9, 1903,[30] establishing the Appalachian Training School for western North Carolina, which later became Appalachian State University. Hoey would later become governor of North Carolina and a U.S. senator. Hoey, Newland, Justice, White, and Lovill, each of whom played a significant role in the passing of the bill, would later be memorialized by naming campus dormitories after them.

It is hard to appreciate today the obstacles the Doughertys faced in expanding their initial school to secure state funding. Blan's courage, boldness, persistence, and zeal were crucial in achieving such results for the mountain people. Lanier expressed it this way:

> It is surprising to find the Newland Bill passing after facing such opposition. Dougherty, whose face was unfamiliar in Raleigh, was the prime mover in its passage, for he helped write the bill, carried it to rally, found an influential sponsor, and made a persuasive speech before the education committee as well as one in the governor's office. Dougherty, alone, could not have brought about the bill's passage; he had realized that the power of the press, public opinion, the governor, and certain legislators were the key, and he had persuaded them to use their influence in getting the bill passed.[31]

For the next 40 years, Blan continued to use his friendships with governors, newspaper editors, and politicians to promote the Appalachian school and to persuade them to do the same.

Board of Trustees of Appalachian Training School: Where to Locate the New School

The Newland Bill provided the school with an annual sum of $2000 to pay teachers and maintain the school. Tuition would be free for all who pledged to teach in the state's public schools for at least two years. The sum of $1500 was appropriated for new buildings, on the condition that private contributions would match public money dollar for dollar. It was enough, barely.

For weeks after the bill passed, the Doughertys engaged many in conversation about the anticipated school, hoping to raise the matching funds and to secure the school's location in Boone. The *Watauga Democrat*, hoping to sway public opinion in support of Boone, reported: "Mr. Moses H. Cone came up from Greensboro last week to his home in Blowing Rock. He was in the village Monday [April–, 1903]; took in our school plant at this place, and expressed himself as being highly pleased with it."[32]

A Board of Trustees for the new school was appointed by the General Assembly to represent the northwestern counties (except for Avery County, which was not formed until 1911). The inaugural board comprised W.C. Fields and A.S. Carson of Alleghany County, J.D. Thomas and T.C. Bowie of Ashe County, Adolphus Taylor and W.P. Horton of Wilkes County, F.P. Moore and J.M. Bernhardt of Caldwell County, Moses H. Cone and E.F. Lovill of Watauga County, J.R. Pritchard and T.A. Love of Mitchell County, and J.B. Ray and E.F. Watson of Yancey County.[33] They first met on May 15, 1903, in Blowing Rock to "organize by electing a president, secretary, and treasurer," and to "open books of subscription for the purpose of erecting buildings suitable and necessary for the establishment of the school."[34]

D.D. Dougherty was elected principal of Appalachian Training School, and B.B. Dougherty was elected superintendent. Blan continued as superintendent of the county public schools, which included the new Appalachian Training School.

A public meeting to discuss potential locations was announced, to be held in Blowing Rock. Blan again approached Moses Cone, now a member of the Board of Trustees for Appalachian Training School, about funding the establishment of the school in Boone. Cone pledged to donate $500 to locate the school in Boone, provided the citizens of Boone matched his gift, and that the county raised $1,000.[35]

The May 21 meeting of the Trustees in Blowing Rock was an important public event—so important that the usual toll for the road to Blowing Rock was waived. "[T]he toll gate was thrown open; the day was perfect; and a very large crowd was present."[36] The meeting was attended by all of the trustees—except for Ashe County's—and by county superintendents from five of the seven assigned counties. Board of Trustees officers were elected: E.F. Lovill, president; W.C. Coffey, treasurer; B.B. Dougherty, secretary and financial agent.[37]

Several locales, foreseeing economic benefit to their communities, competed to be the home of the new school: Blowing Rock, Shulls Mill, Valle Crucis, Montezuma (between Linville and Newland, North Carolina), and, of course, Boone. Decades later, Blan confessed that he had favored Ashe County, where property was much cheaper and taxes were lower, but no one representing Ashe County attended the May 21 meeting to advocate for their community.[38]

According to the *Watauga Democrat*, E.S. Coffey, Dauph's college roommate and Boone lawyer who had supposedly (according to Blan) balked at Blan and Lovill's idea to draft a bill for a state-supported school, now praised "the superior advantages [of Boone] when compared with other sections and tendering on the part of Watauga and Boone, $1,500 and the free use of our handsome and commodious school property, until the Training School building could be completed."[39] Finally, the representatives present voted 10 to 3 to locate the school in Boone, and "[r]ound after round of applause" followed.[40]

Finding the Required Matching Funds

The amount of local money required to match funds for the new school was daunting for the poor mountain counties, yet they gave. Names of donors were printed in the newspaper.[41] The largest amount listed was $100 from W.C. Coffey (equivalent to approximately $3,672 in 2024); 75 others pledged amounts between $75 and $1, with $75 coming from each Dougherty brother and Manly Blackburn.[42] Blan Dougherty and W.C. Coffey were tasked with soliciting subscriptions for the Training School. They sought paying students as well as further donations.[43]

The Executive Committee of the Appalachian Training School sent the General Assembly a formal request for personal contributions from them and their constituents, noting that the appropriation from the state was only $1,500 towards the erection of the building, leaving the substantial balance to be raised by public donation.[44] A modern brick building, "amply sufficient for the needs of the school for generations to come," was estimated to cost "not less than $5,000"—a formidable sum that the mountain counties could not supply. Each teacher in the seven counties was also asked to raise $10 for the building.[45] The following month, another 31 women and men from Boone pledged a total of $63, in amounts from $1 to $7, to be paid January 1, 1904.[46] Though each dollar given or pledged was a genuine sacrifice, more was needed.

Almost 1,000 people gathered under the pines near the Watauga Academy building to enjoy the music and hear the patriotic speeches on Independence Day, 1903. A huge bonfire was built on the campus to celebrate locating the new state teachers' school in the community.[47] North Carolina Congressman Romulus Z. Linney delivered the address on the occasion, and promised to give $500 to the Training School fund if the trustees would inscribe over the door of the school: "Education, the handmaid of loyalty and liberty; a vote governs better than a crown."[48] E.F. Lovill, chairman of the Trustees, "wasted no time in assuring Mr. Linney that the inscription would be on the new building."[49] In 1956 Blan recalled, "It was big money then even if it may appear now as insignificant in contrast with larger amounts received later."[50]

Romulus Zachary Linney, a congressman from Taylorsville, North Carolina, offered $500 to Appalachian Training School if the trustees would place a motto over the door: "Education, the handmaid of loyalty and liberty; a vote governs better than a crown" (public domain).

"Tater Hill": Romulus Z. Linney's Generous Gift

Hon. Romulus Z. Linney was a popular lawyer and politician from Taylorsville, south of Wilkesboro, North Carolina. Known as the "Bull of the Brushy Mountains," he would dominate the legislative or court room proceedings with his stories and antics.[51] In 1902 R.Z. Linney purchased a large tract of land north of Boone on Rich Mountain that he called "Tater Hill," where he built two rock houses. "He was influential in getting a wagon road built along the top of the Rich Mountain range from the gap above Boone to a gap just north of Silverstone."[52] Col. R.Z. Linney became interested in Watauga County in the 1880s, wrote historian John Preston Arthur. Linney served four times as a state senator, three times as a Republican congressman, beating Rufus A. Doughton, a Democrat, and defeating William White, a prohibitionist.[53]

Linney gave a barbecue on the Tater Hill where he had built a summer home. A vast crowd gathered to enjoy the feast, celebrate Boone as the location for the Training School, and to delight in the mountain summer. Adam Dougherty, paternal uncle to Dauph, Blan and Etta, read his poem "Tater Hill," written in Linney's honor, as the highlight of the afternoon's entertainment. A colorful person, Adam Dougherty, bachelor brother of Daniel Baker Dougherty, was a frequent visitor to Boone and had probably developed a friendship with Linney during court week in 1903, or during the celebrations for the establishment of Appalachian Training School.[54]

In one stanza of "The Tater Hill," Adam Dougherty describes another nearby and well-known mountain:

> The old "Grand-father" makes his home,
> And thousands come to make their bow
> And gaze on his imperious brow,
> Which well adorns a splendid face
> So human-like in style and grace.
> His hair reached back upon his head
> Is mountain shrubbery green and red.
> His face is twenty feet across,
> His long white beard is made of moss;
> His Roman nose is fifteen feet,
> And suffers not from cold or heat,
> But shelters with commanding style
> Two massive lips that never smile.[55]

"Ode to Elk Knob" and "The Land of the Sky" were Adam's most enduring and celebrated poems, all three of his poems reprinted by popular request in a 1917 edition of *The Dew Drop*. "Will you come to Watauga, the 'Land in the Sky,' where a banquet of glory is spread for the eye, where scenes of enchantment enravish the soul, and reasons to rapture surrender control. ... Ye seekers of pleasure, oppressed by the heat, come to this region, tis a pleasant retreat; ye ones that are feeble, why linger and die? Come up to this beautiful 'Land in the Sky.'"[56]

The Search for Funding Continues: Opening of School Delayed

Money pledged for the new school trickled in during the summer of 1903, though not as quickly as the Trustees or the Doughertys had hoped. A contract for the new school building had been given to a Wilkesboro company, but the building costs had risen. Blan Dougherty alerted State Superintendent Joyner of the increase. Joyner gave permission for the Trustees to seek funds from state offices and faculty at state institutions, but he, personally, could offer none.[57] A letter went out from the trustees, for the second time, this time to state officers as well as the faculty of the state supported secondary institutions, requesting their personal contributions.[58]

Although the new Appalachian Training School was to open in September 1903, its opening was delayed because the matching funds that were required had not been paid in full. Even though a majority in the Baptist Association opposed using public funds for higher education because they feared it would permit "skepticism and higher criticism" without "the safeguards of religious instruction," the pastor of the Boone Baptist church declared his support for the state-funded teachers' school in Boone in late August.[59]

On September 10 the *Watauga Democrat* reported that less than $1300 had been paid into the treasury of the new school.[60] Moses Cone withheld his promised $500 until the additional $1,500 in donations from the county and other citizens, on which his gift was conditioned, had been collected. The state auditor likewise waited for local matching funds before transferring the promised $1,500 of state money.

The *Democrat* printed an "earnest appeal" from Blan Dougherty that those who had pledged to donate would send the funds they had promised so that building materials could be purchased and delivered. His appeal concluded:

> We certainly can raise this money; We ought to do it; We must do it. The load is heavy on a few of us. We are working with hands and hearts and pocketbooks. Can't you help a little just now? We have 200 cords of wood to haul, and a very good road to it. Men and teams could help wonderfully by hauling a part of this wood. We are making a tremendous effort to start the school by October 1st. Let those who expect to attend take note of this, Very sincerely, B.B. Dougherty[61]

In the same issue, the newspaper urged subscribers, almost all of whom were of very modest means, to read the appeal for the Training School. "Think about it. There is but one way to get the building up, and that is by private subscription. Then ought not every good citizen to help? It is a duty you owe to your children, your country, and your state. You can make nothing else out of it."[62]

October 5, 1903: Appalachian Training School Begins

At last, the final funds arrived and were sent to Raleigh. After four years as Watauga Academy, the school opened with a new name on October 5, 1903, for a fifth year of operation. For the next two years, students of the new Appalachian Training School crowded into the old Watauga Academy, where they awaited completion of their new building.[63]

15

Appalachian Training School Begins (1903–1906)

A New School, a New Home, and a New Baby: The Dougherty House

As the students of Appalachian Training School anticipated the completion of their new building, Dauph and Lillie Dougherty anticipated moving out of their cramped boarding house full of students.

Dauph and Lillie had begun designing a home just for their own family in early 1902, before any plans for seeking state support for the school were seriously entertained. When they had moved into Meadow View, late 1899, and boarded 10 students in the crowded house, Clara had been a toddler. The couple needed privacy away from the hubbub of students and classes and were now confident that Watauga Academy would survive for the long term as a high school. If their optimism was misplaced, the family farm and property would sustain them. Construction began during the summer of 1902. Soon Lillie was pregnant, with the baby due in the spring.

By January 1, 1903, Dauph, Lillie, and Clara had moved to the new residence, and another family moved into their former home and took over the boarding house.[1] The next week the local newspaper reported that Dauph was also erecting a five-bedroom cottage near the existing boarding house to provide additional student housing until a new boarding house, and eventually a dormitory, could be built.[2]

The new residence for Dauph and his family was built with lumber from the Doughertys' land. It was regarded by many town residents as one of the finest homes in Boone,[3] originally with 10 rooms (five up and five down) and four fireplaces, until two additional rooms and a bathroom were added around 1915 to 1918.[4] The house was wired for electricity in 1915, and is believed to be the first home in the region to have indoor plumbing when that was added in 1918.[5] Two central rooms on the second floor served as offices for the Dougherty brothers.[6]

Dauph Dougherty said he had intended to build a finer home for his wife. By the time he died in 1929 the school was the only state college without a president's home. After Dauph's death, bachelor Blan continued to live with his brother's family. Several times during Blan's many decades as president of Appalachian, legislators approached him about allowing the state to build a president's house. Blan declined the offer, feeling no need for a grand home.[7]

The Dougherty house was completed in 1903. In 1987–88 efforts were made by local citizens to preserve the house, which was moved to the school farm property on State Road. Tourists can now visit the house as the Appalachian Heritage Museum, located on Blowing Rock Road (Elizabeth Brown Scoggins Collection, University Archives, Special Collections Research Center, Appalachian State University, Boone, North Carolina).

Dozens of students had been taught during the four years of Watauga Academy's existence, but it was a meager beginning, with only 15 high school graduates in total. No one could foresee the hundreds of thousands that would be taught in the future decades.

The commencement for 1903 was held the third week of April, to the relief of the very pregnant Lillie Dougherty. To Lillie's delight, her younger sister Vinnie (Victoria), who was visiting, played the pedal pump organ at graduation.[8] Although commencement was not favored by good weather—a recent snowstorm and freeze had killed the fruit crops—orations, declamations, songs, dialogues, music, and speeches by lawyers and county-men were "highly entertaining and instructive."[9] The summer term was to open in May 1903.[10]

Lillie gave birth to a second daughter, Annie Lewis Dougherty, on May 17, 1903, in the new home. A notice in the paper read: "Professor D.D. Dougherty is often heard to remark involuntarily, 'It's another girl.'"[11] In July, Lillie's older sister from Butler, Tennessee, Mollie Shull Smith, arrived with her daughter to visit.[12]

Dauph was in charge of the day-to-day operations, teaching at least four classes daily, managing faculty and students, performing administrative duties, caring for the building, overseeing the boarding of students—all with a new baby.[13] Planting

Lillie Shull Dougherty with her two daughters, Clara and baby Annie, c. 1903 (Doris Stam Collection, University Archives, Special Collections Research Center, Appalachian State University, Boone, North Carolina).

and tending the garden, which supplied the majority of the family food for the coming year, and milking the cow, all fell to Dauph.[14]

Blan was away—often for weeks—to Raleigh for the Legislative sessions in the winter, and for fundraising trips sporadically throughout the year. Or he was out in the county on horseback as superintendent, especially in the later summer and early fall, staying in family homes in each community. He continued to live with Dauph and Lillie, freely coming and going from the home. He often missed family mealtimes and helped himself to leftovers when he arrived home late from his travels, seemingly unaware of any inconvenience to others.[15]

Appalachian Training School: Enrollment, Tuition, and Board

Enrollment at the new school in 1903 involved simply this: "'Just see Mr. D.D. Dougherty and sign your name." By October 5, 1903, 273 students had signed up, and enrollment continued to grow.[16]

The bill establishing the Appalachian Training School stipulated that tuition would be free for those who pledged to teach in the public schools of North Carolina for two years, and some 190 students—about 70 percent of enrollees—took that pledge.[17] For the regular students, no tuition was charged for the fall public school term. Those who continued during the four-month winter/spring term and the two-month summer term paid $1 per month for lower grades and $2.50 per month for high school classes. Preachers' children received a 50 percent discount. An additional fee of 50 cents per term, or $1 for summer term, was charged. Total income from these charges was minimal, but state money made operations possible.

The room and boarding accommodations, costing from $7.50 to $8 per month, or 25 cents a day, were provided by townspeople. For those who desired to do their own cooking and housekeeping, rooms could be rented for 75 cents per month.[18] Boarding rates stayed basically the same until 1918.[19] Expenses at Lees-McRae School in Banner Elk were similar, where income from student fees was "pitifully small, even for that day," recalled the founder's daughter, but "that was all that the local people could afford."[20]

Some students bartered for school costs. One young man of 26 or 27, whom Blan met at a country school while traveling as superintendent and who showed potential as a teacher, bartered shingles and lumber from his sawmill for school costs and enrolled in 1903.

Except for a few hotels in the village of Boone, options for meals were few outside private homes. Some teachers as well as students boarded at the Greene Inn, run

The Greene Inn, on King Street next to the Appalachian Theater, offered boarding to students, faculty, and tourists for at least three decades. It was operated by Etta Dougherty (and her husband Richard Greene), sister to Dauph and Blan, from the remodeled home of their father, Daniel Baker Dougherty (University Archives, Special Collections Research Center, Appalachian State University, Boone, North Carolina).

by Etta Dougherty Greene and her husband, in the former home of Daniel Baker Dougherty, where the Greenes had cared for Daniel until he died in 1902. After Daniel's death, they renamed the Dougherty homeplace the Greene Inn, where they housed and fed between 15 and 18 students and faculty for many decades. Meals were sometimes offered to non-boarders as well.[21]

While arrangements were being made for a new structure to accommodate the influx of enrollees, "students thronged the halls and crowded the classrooms of the Watauga Academy Building. And although Appalachian Training School was launched on a mere shoestring appropriation, it was destined to develop and grow."[22]

1904: Construction Begins, and Money Runs Out

Great expectations accompanied the building committee's purchase of a four-and-one-half-acre plot of land, for the outlay of $212.50.[23] In May 1904, after commencement, ground was broken for the new Appalachian Training School building on a site just east of Watauga Academy. Initially it was referred to as Main, but later as the (first) Administration Building. But building costs had surged. Ever watchful and frugal, Blan Dougherty counted bricks and timed the brick masons working on the new building.[24] He was known to sit with one ankle crossed on his knee and write figures on the sole of his shoe with a pencil, calculating the various tasks at hand, always trying to find the most economical way.[25]

Brick masons working on the First Administration Building, c. 1904 (Doris Stam Collection, University Archives, Special Collections Research Center, Appalachian State University, Boone, North Carolina).

As anticipated, the money ran out. Another campaign for donations to complete the building had been launched, but the new effort fell short of the need, and citizens who had given liberally before could not soon do so again. So the trustees waited for the next session of the legislature to request enough money to finish the building.[26]

Students could barely function in the over-crowded conditions in the old Watauga Academy building.[27] In addition to several major wealthy donors, 500 people had contributed to the new school, and donations totaled $4,000. Considering the village of Boone had a population of perhaps 200, the number of donors and the amount they gave is impressive. Yet these donations, with the state's initial $1,500 appropriation, did not meet the estimated $8,000 construction cost. Construction on the new structure ceased until more funds could be found.

To meet the pressing need for money, the executive committee of the trustees printed a fund-raising "Circular of Information" in December 1904, in which they reported that the school had taught 301 students from 10 counties, of whom 190 were teachers, in the 1903–1904 school year.[28] The trustees used the circular to issue a plea to the state and private donors "for help to finish the present building and to erect a suitable dormitory for young women."[29]

Legislature 1905: Those Who Help Themselves

In February 1905, Blan Dougherty, E.F. Lovill, and Tarlton P. Adams, Chairman of the County Board of Education, traveled to Raleigh to appeal in person to the Legislature for the additional funds.[30] Adams, and possibly the others, went at his own expense—no small matter.[31] Seeking state appropriations took persistence, pluck, and sacrifice. Adams and Lovill spent countless hours together over the years in joint efforts for the school. The *Charlotte Observer* later described Blan as an indefatigable lobbyist and "master beggar."[32] He was adamant, courageous, and undeterred, even when laughed at by those in Raleigh who looked down on his unsophisticated ways and backwoods origins.[33]

When the Legislature met in the winter of 1905, Blan Dougherty, as Financial Agent for Appalachian Training School, prepared to speak to the Committee on Education. He contacted some of his former students who were attending college in the Raleigh vicinity and requested that they be present for his report to the committee.[34]

In March 1905, when Blan addressed the committee, he expressed gratitude for the appropriation that had made the school possible and described the progress of the institution, "which was going ahead in spite of severe financial restraints."[35] The *Raleigh Morning Post* reported that the education committee heard of the "school's growth and the 'tremendous effort' the people of the county and surrounding counties were making for the school."[36] They heard of the accomplishments of the school and what its future might be if money were made available. Blan enthusiastically foresaw "a great summer school with leading educators coming to Boone to escape the summer heat, a place where schoolteachers could escape the dusty classrooms and be renewed intellectually and physically."[37]

The General Assembly agreed and appropriated not only $2000 for salaries and maintenance, but "an additional special amount of $4000 to be used for building purposes, provided the sum could be matched by private donations."[38] This would be enough money not only to complete the administration (Main) building and hire more faculty, but to build a dormitory, they hoped. Competition from other state-supported institutions seeking appropriations was fierce. Unlike Appalachian, which was required to match its appropriation in its first few years, institutions in other parts of the state were not generally required to match state funds.[39] Appalachian generally received the least compared to other state schools and would stay at or near the bottom until mid-century.[40]

The *Raleigh Post* was impressed with Blan Dougherty's report to the Legislative committee and "praised the efforts of the mountain people": "They have caught the educational spirit and are working effectively and with noble purpose. They deserve and will continue to receive public approval and support. The legislature's response to the appeal of these people was largely due to what the people themselves have done. It was in the principle of helping those who help themselves."[41] To meet the required matching $4,000, the Watauga Academy building was donated (sold) to the state for $3000. With those proceeds, the school needed only to raise $1000 to receive the state's appropriation.[42] Although friends of the school gave, again, yet more aid was needed. Blan traveled as far north as New York, Washington, and Philadelphia seeking donations for the school,[43] but received disappointingly few contributions . The General Education Board in New York, a private organization that supported higher education and medical schools in the United States and helped rural white and black schools in the South had already been overdrawn, Blan was informed, and the John D. Rockefeller Foundation for Higher Education had been designated to be used exclusively by colleges in the South, not high schools.[44] It would be the local people again—"those who help themselves"—who, bit by bit, matched the appropriation.[45]

Lovill Home: The First Dormitory and Travel to Boone

The campus was busy in the summer of 1905 with carpenters working on the new dormitory for women and plasterers finishing Main, the Administration Building. "The school was 'alive with students' representing Alleghany, Ashe, Wilkes, Iredell, Forsyth, Caldwell, Burke, McDowell, and Watauga counties."[46]

The 1905 *Dew Drop Catalogue* announced that a girls' dormitory, "capable of accommodating 100 girls, two in a room, is under construction." Each room would have one double bed for two students.[47] Each boarder was required to do a limited amount of work in the dining room, keep her own room, and furnish her own bedding, towels, table napkins, spoon, and glass.[48] It was named Lovill Home for Capt. Edward F. Lovill, who, with Blan, had drafted the initial bill to found the training school and continued to make major contributions to the school until his death in 1925.[49]

The Dew Drop Catalogue was printed four times a year by students on a small press at the school under the supervision of Professor Dauph. "It told the world about the growing school and its activities. One day when a request was made for extra copies,

Prof. Dauph replied that the *Dew Drops* had all vanished before the rising sun."[50]

Directions were provided in the 1904–1905 *Dew Drop* for students coming to Boone from different areas of the state, particularly for summer school, and described the various train depots from which students would need to hire a hack.[51] Getting up the mountain between Boone and Lenoir was such a challenge that at Lenoir College "the school week was altered in January 1902 to allow professors more time to return to campus from Sunday preaching assignments. In the preceding year, one of the clergy trustees, W.A. Deaton, resigned because of the 24 hours required to travel from his Boone parish to the Lenoir campus."[52]

The *Dew Drop* of 1905–1906 described the Appalachian Training School campus "on seven acres of land, covered for the most part with young white Pines. Little has been done to beautify the grounds. The property joins the town boundary and lies between the Boone and Blowing Rock Turnpike, and a new street is to be opened on the northern side of the land."[53]

Edward F. Lovill (1842–1925) served Watauga County in the North Carolina Senate in 1883 and in the State House in 1885, again elected to the House in 1893 and to the Senate for the terms in 1907–1908, and 1919–1920. Lovill was among the minority of North Carolina legislators who supported women's suffrage (courtesy Joel Olsen and Lovill House in Boone, NC).

The full-time faculty increased from six to eight for the summer of 1905.[54] Summer school sessions would become increasingly popular and would sometimes account for most enrollees in a given year. Tuition for summer terms helped defray expenses, but the lack of special appropriations to operate summer terms was a persistent frustration for Blan Dougherty in later years.

1905–1906: Moving into Main Building, Curriculum and College Scholarships

In the fall of 1905 the high school junior and senior classes moved into the new Main building. Others remained in the Watauga Academy building. With 132 post-primary students, enrollment for the regular terms was the largest in the history of the school. By February 1906 attendance reached 200, and some rooms in the Lovill Home girls' dormitory had been completed and were occupied.[55] But money was still a problem. It would take another $1000 to furnish the new dormitory completely, $300 to paint it, and at least $500 to beautify the grounds.[56]

It had been 18 years since Dauph Dougherty signed loan papers with Bostwick & Co. for tuition at Wake Forest College. The final loan letter, dated February 19, 1906, came from his former classmate G.W. Paschal, associate professor Latin and Greek, curator of library, and collector for the college. Dated February 19, 1906, it read: "My dear Dougherty, Yours with enclosed $104.00 received. I am enclosing with your notes duly canceled. I heartily congratulate you on getting them paid. I knew you well enough to know that there was a sufficient reason for their not having been paid heretofore. With best wishes, Truly your friend, G.W. Paschal."[57]

A third child, a boy, was born to Dauph and Lillie on August 5, 1906. The baby was named Daniel Disco—Daniel to honor Dauph's father, and Disco after Dauph's middle name.

A scholarship to the University (Chapel Hill) and one to Trinity College (which became Duke University) was offered each year to some worthy student at A.T.S. beginning in 1907.[58] The 1910 *Dew Drop* added that it was "through the kindness of the authorities" that a tuition scholarship was given, but neither "the authorities" nor the source of the funds was identified.[59]

First Administration Building, completed in 1905 *The Dew Drop*, Volume XXI, No. 3 [May 1924], University Archives, Special Collections Research Center, Appalachian State University, Boone, North Carolina).

Many curriculum records at Appalachian were lost in two separate fires,[60] but the curriculum was parallel to that at Cullowhee Normal and Industrial School, where records did survive. Both had teacher training classes ("Normal school" work), regular high school classes, and a primary school. Instruction at Cullowhee included "...spelling and defining, arithmetic, grammar, composition, English literature, elementary algebra, United States history, North Carolina history, civil government, political and physical geography, physiology and hygiene, physics and elementary Latin. The professional work consisted of theory and practice of teaching, principles of education, history of education, psychology applied to teaching, lectures, and professional reading."[61]

Neither Appalachian Training School nor Cullowhee could compare with larger, well-established colleges. Cullowhee's President Madison explained to legislators how the curriculum and purpose of the mountain teacher training schools differed from those at Greensboro or Chapel Hill : "Our specific work," Madison said, "is to prepare teachers for the rural and village elementary schools.... It is just as necessary that normal instruction of teachers be provided for as that the term of rural public schools should be lengthened [from four to six months]. 'As is the teacher, so goes the school.'"[62] Madison emphasized what may not have been obvious to those making state budgetary decisions: "It should have been manifest that no teachers prepared at Greensboro or Chapel Hill, after expending hundreds of dollars a year for such preparation, would go into the rural districts and teach schools of three or four months duration at $20 or $24 a month."[63]

Another Watauga Academy: In Tennessee

Holly Spring College in Butler, Tennessee, was sold in 1906 and a new name was sought. Dauph and Lillie were aware of all the changes with the school where they had taught, and which had been run by her brother-in-law, Professor James H. Smith. Although the school was in another county and another state, it was on the Watauga River. The Doughertys offered the former name of their school in Boone—now Appalachian Teachers State College—to the new proprietors in Tennessee, the Watauga Association of Baptists.[64]

The name of Holly Spring College was changed to Watauga Academy on September 6, 1906. Now there would be two schools in the regional history books with the name Watauga Academy, causing some confusion.

Music for Boone: Lillie Shull Dougherty

Music had been an important part of the curriculum at Watauga Academy, where Lillie Dougherty taught music and other subjects, and she continued to provide and promote music education at Appalachian Training School. Jesse Curtis, who attended from the spring of 1901 until graduating in 1904, including the summer terms for those three years, recalled Lillie's influence and the importance of group singing in the activities of the students.[65] "In society halls and school assemblies,

This large square Mathushek piano, being played by Michael and Martin Stam in the Dougherty house on Rivers Street, c. 1982, was purchased by Dauph and Lillie about 1903 for their new home. Several strong students would carry the heavy instrument down the front steps, over the creek, and up to Watauga Academy for special events (Doris Stam Collection, University Archives, Special Collections Research Center, Appalachian State University, Boone, North Carolina).

vigorous voices, attuned to the *North Carolina Hills* or other patriotic songs, would 'let music swell the breeze and ring from all the trees,'" under Lillie's direction.[66] She particularly enjoyed teaching choral groups.[67] Music education and performance at the school, and at the Baptist church, benefited.

For many years the school had no funds to purchase a piano. But about 1903, the Doughertys purchased a massive square 1895 Mathushek concert piano, which they kept in their home until it was needed for an event at the school. Then boys would carry it down from Lillie's home, across the little valley, up the steps and stairways and place it on the stage in the auditorium; then return it, back over the creek and up the Dougherty front steps.[68]

There were few amusements for Appalachian students:

There were no picture shows, public dances, or other forms of modern amusement in town, nor did the circus include Boone on its schedule. But whenever Hon. R.Z. Linney ("the bull of the Brushies"), [alluding to the Brushy Mountain area] of Taylorsville, and Hon. W.H. Bower of Lenoir came to town to try lawsuits in Superior Court, all the elements of entertainment and intellectual combat were present. "Rom" Linney and "Hort" Bower were ex-congressman and were considered the peers of the best lawyers in the state; and when Linney and Bower appeared on opposite sides of a case "the fur would fly."[69]

The boys enjoyed the fun and would request to be excused early to go "courting"; … "when the small auditorium of the old courthouse would be packed to the aisles."[70]

The courthouse was essentially the social center when court was in session. People traveled from all over the county to hear the lawyers "plead their cases and the judge charge the jury."[71] Covered wagons provided a place to sleep and camp during the week, and swapping and trading activities enlivened the time. That was the extent of entertainment in 1906.

Ashe, Alleghany, and Watauga counties were hemmed in and separated from the rest of the state by the mountains of the Eastern Continental Divide. Since access to the mountain areas from the east was difficult, these three counties were more closely tied economically to Tennessee to the west and Virginia to the north. Commerce and society with the rest of North Carolina were generally unavailable until roads were built from the east in the 1920s.[72] Differences that emerged in the legislature between the wealthier eastern sections and the remote western sections of the state with respect to teacher training would threaten the continued existence of Appalachian Training School.

16

Joys and Sorrows, Threats, and Farms (1907–1911)

North Carolina Legislature 1907: East Carolina Teachers Training School

The stability of Appalachian Training School faced challenges in 1907. Throughout the next 15 years, uncertainty about state support was a constant weight for Dauph, particularly, to shoulder.

Faculty for Summer School, c. 1906, are posed in front of Watauga Academy's front porch. Emma Horton Moore, librarian for decades at Appalachian, is seated far left. Prof. James M. Downum is seated far right, with B.B. Dougherty standing behind him. (Elizabeth Brown Scoggins Collection, University Archives, Special Collections Research Center, Appalachian State University, Boone, North Carolina.)

In this 1907 winter panorama, taken facing northwest with Howard's Knob in the background, the positioning of campus buildings is visible: Watauga Academy (1), the brick First Administration Building (2), and the wood-framed Lovill Home (3) far right (courtesy Historic Boone Collection, Watauga Digital Project).

The Legislature of 1907 was considering a bill that would provide state funds for high school instruction across the state—a massive undertaking. Up to this time local communities were responsible for high school education, most of which was provided by private academies. Also vying for legislators' attention was the call from eastern North Carolina for a teacher training center. Competing voices from all the state-supported schools and institutions were clamoring for appropriations, as at every legislative session.

Convincing politicians that Appalachian Training School needed more than the pittance allotted to it was never easy for the Doughertys. Dauph helped prepare the supporting facts and figures, but Blan was better suited to making appeals to the Legislature in Raleigh. Dauph remained in Boone, teaching and managing the school and maintaining a busy home with three children, plus the family farm.

The eastern section of the state had an extensive plan for their teacher training school. They also had some of the most powerful leaders in the state to make certain the bill for their school passed, particularly Greenville resident Thomas Jordan Jarvis. Having served as governor from 1879 to 1885 and as U.S. senator from 1894 to 1895, Jarvis had hoped to establish teacher training schools in the east. However, his efforts had been hindered by State Superintendent Joyner and McIver, president of Greensboro's Normal and Industrial School—the same two who had hindered the Doughertys' efforts to establish the school in Boone.

Discussions about Greenville dominated the 1907 Legislature. Again, McIver and friends of the State Normal and Industrial School for White Women at Greensboro, "seeing the eastern training school as a possible competitor for students and state funds, were against its establishment."[1]

In contrast to the tiny, remote mountain community of Boone, Greenville, with a population of over 4,000, was a prosperous town located on the railroad lines that traversed the state. When cotton was still king, Greenville had expanded in the 1870s with stately homes and flourishing new businesses. The railroad had reached the area in 1890, spurring more growth, and Greenville (60 percent white, 40 percent African American) became the largest tobacco market in the state. Tobacco money flooding into the city built beautiful mansions, expanded boundaries, and brought new industries for Greenville.²

The opposition of McIver and other Greensboro advocates did not succeed in 1907.³ State Superintendent Joyner finally lent his support for the new school, and a bill establishing a teacher training school in eastern North Carolina was passed.⁴ Even though the General Assembly required petitioners for the new school to pledge at least $25,000 for buildings, Pitt County and Greenville residents approved two $50,000 bond referenda to meet that requirement.⁵

When Eastern Carolina Teacher Training School was established in 1907, it was part of the same general plan of high school instruction and teacher training for the state as Appalachian, but with higher expectations for its graduates. E.C.T.T.S. oriented "the course of study to the preparation for entrance into the freshman class of the University of North Carolina. It carried with it a special appropriation of $50,000 for high school instruction."⁶ Greenville, which was not as large as some other eastern towns, like Wilmington, rejoiced to have raised the money and to be the chosen site for the school.⁷

Former Governor Jarvis, as head of the executive committee for the Greenville school, saw to it that the new school's architecture reflected some characteristics of mission-style architecture, with red tile roofs, a gilded dome, copper gutters, and sandstone block quoins. Compared to the elusive funds for the modest buildings at Appalachian Teachers School, constructed from humble local timber, bartered shingles, and bricks calculated on the sole of Blan Dougherty's shoe, the scale of funds and construction at the Greenville school was incomprehensible to mountain farming families.⁸ Superintendent Joyner, who had been instrumental in mustering support for the bill that created East Carolina Teachers Training School, claimed he intended "to bring in the Appalachian and Cullowhee schools as a part of the uniform correlated plan for high school instruction and teacher training, with the State Normal and Industrial College [McIver's school in Greensboro] as the head and center of the whole."⁹

In the face of these other demands for state funds, Appalachian asked the 1907 Legislature for a larger appropriation: $10,000 to complete the girls' dormitory, build a boys' dormitory, and to purchase some available land.¹⁰ The Doughertys and the trustees were thrilled and relieved that $5,000 would be appropriated to them annually for two years. In May 1907, the trustees of the school purchased a 200-acre farm nearby for $4,000, where livestock, orchards, and a large vegetable garden could provide food for the school.¹¹

The situation in the mountains could not compare, and certainly not compete, with the eastern and central sections of the state. They were different worlds. Greenville was granted an appropriation nine times that of Appalachian Training School. The isolated mountain areas like Boone were still, as some calculated, 50 years behind the rest of the state.

Newland Hall: The First Boys' Dormitory

A six-acre lot was purchased for the boys' dorm site,¹² and in June 1908 work began on a frame building intended to house 40 male students. A few months later the trustees purchased another residence adjoining the campus for $1200 to house about 10 girls. By November two stories of the boys' dormitory were completed.[13] Two years later the boys' dorm would be named Newland Hall for William C. Newland, the Democrat from Lenoir who had sponsored the bill creating the school in the Legislature, and who later served as lieutenant governor from 1909 to 1913.[14] The town of Newland is named for him as part of a political deal to secure his aid in passage of the bill that established Avery County in 1911.[15]

Superintendent on Horseback: Bob, an Intelligent Horse

Over half of the 337 students who were enrolled at Appalachian in 1907 were from the Watauga public schools, most of which were one-teacher operations where Professor Blan Dougherty, visiting on horseback as superintendent, had seen and encouraged each child to continue their education past seventh grade.[16]

Bob, his horse, was recognized by almost everyone in the county.[17] After Blan retired as county superintendent in 1915, Bob continued to work on the A.T.S. campus, sometimes teamed with another horse, Doll, to pull a wagon around the campus hauling wood, delivering goods, and collecting trash. Bob and Doll worked at Appalachian until Bob's death at age 28. "In the summers he worked in the gardens with a degree of intelligence seldom known."[18] "He did away with every doubt as to whether a horse has intelligence. No one could have watched his movements without knowing that horses think."[19]

Lovill Home Girls' Dorm: Strict Oversight

With the 1907 summer session, Mrs. Emma Horton Moore took over the position of matron of the Lovill Home for Girls.[20] Emma had grown up with the Dougherty boys and attended New River Academy with them, near her family home northeast of Boone. She had been a schoolteacher in another county and had a four-year-old son who accompanied her when the Dougherty brothers hired her as matron for the girls' dormitory. Her husband, who did not go with her to Appalachian, died in 1914.[21] Mrs. Moore worked at the school for most of the next 40 years and became something of a legend as the enforcer of silence in the library, the chaperone of young ladies under her care, and the strict overseer of campus policy on separation of males and females.[22]

Mrs. Moore later recalled her early days at Appalachian: "Students would be brought to school in hacks, wagons, buggies, and on horseback. Most of them were local country girls and from the surrounding counties. … We had from 50–75 girls in the dormitory when I came."[23] Describing conditions in the dormitory, Mrs. Moore later recalled that "each room … was equipped with a pitcher, bowl, and slop jar.… When they wanted water they had to carry it from the pump."[24] There was no indoor water or plumbing.

Mrs. Moore collected the room and board money. In addition to staples purchased

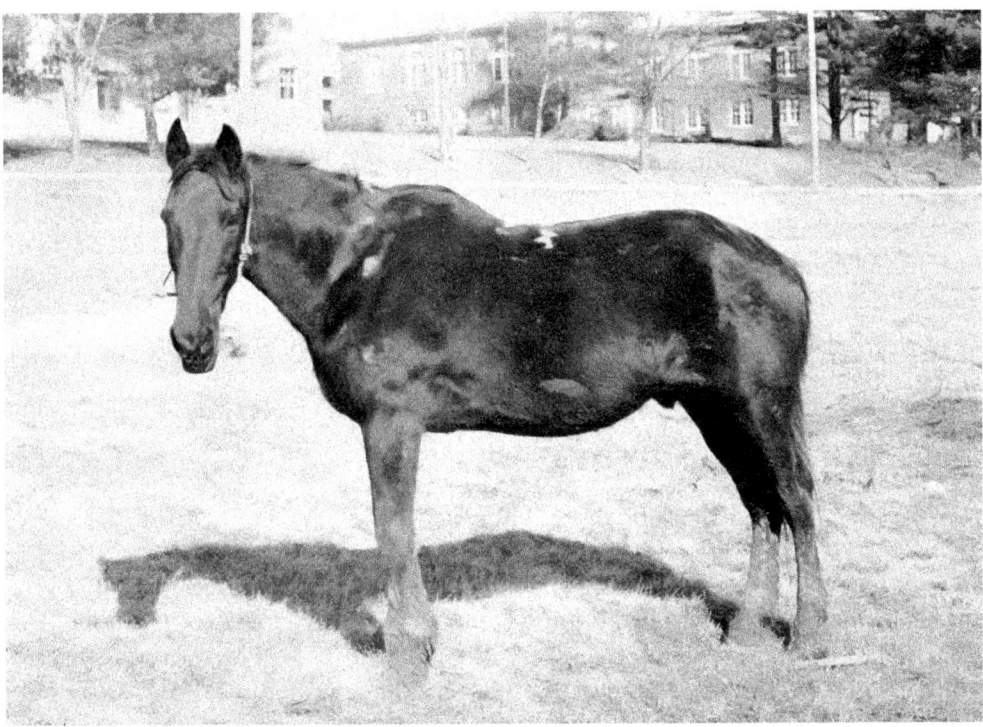

Bob, c.1926, B.B. Dougherty's faithful horse, known all over the county because of Blan's travels as county superintendent. After Blan left the superintendency in 1916, Bob worked on the campus until his death in 1928. A tribute to "Old Bob" was written for the 1929 school yearbook by history professor I.G. Greer (*The Rhododendron*, 1929, University Archives, Special Collections Research Center, Appalachian State University, Boone, North Carolina).

by the Doughertys, Mrs. Moore bought other food staples for the dorm from a school fund. Supplies were hauled up the mountain on wagons. The "country people" delivered hams, which she purchased for the dormitory kitchen.[25] Mrs. Moore also chaperoned the girls' dorm residents for shopping or church: "I had to ring the bell in the hall to get the girls together to go up the street. We all marched in a line. All girls had to stay in line and together at all times no matter where or what store they wanted to enter. When we went to church we did the same. I think we all went to the same church, having reserved seats. All the persons in the church remained seated until we marched out."[26]

For over a decade the same short admonition was printed in *The Dew Drop*: "A Regulation: young women and young men are not expected to board at the same places or to associate together on any occasion. There may be a few times when this regulation is suspended. At these times the suspension is announced at Chapel."[27]

Other schools had similar requirements for female students at that time. At Lenoir College in 1903, girls "were not permitted to answer the phone or doorbell, or to talk or communicate in any way from windows with persons on the outside of the building. Neither could they attend a social function in town unless chaperoned by a member of the faculty."[28] At Cullowhee Normal and Industrial School, "Females were allowed to go down the hill and across the bridge to the small village of Cullowhee only twice a week, on Tuesdays and Fridays, and only in groups with a matron to chaperone them." The school explicitly aimed "to throw around the young ladies the influences of a refined and elegant home, and thus to develop in them the desire and power to create and preside over such homes, and the ability to inspire such desires in the pupils who shall later come under their care."[29]

At East Carolina, Kate R. Beckwith, who oversaw female students as a teacher and administrator beginning in 1909, "worked to instruct the rural daughters of the east in the concept of public service, proper attire, and polite demeanor as drawn from the existing ideal of southern womanhood. Her admonitions included no yelling from dormitory windows, especially if young male visitors were on campus. Each Sunday evening, she made a gathering of the girl's dormitory students, she discussed such topics as art, literature, and architecture and their roles in her students' futures."[30]

Extended Family in the Dougherty Home

Extended family often lived in the Dougherty family home, requiring Lillie to cook and clean for a large family, as well as impromptu guests, for over 40 years. Annie Dougherty Rufty, Dauph and Lillie's second daughter, recalled, "There were not many hotels or eating places in Boone. When families brought children to school they landed at our house. We never knew when we would actually sit down as a family. We did a lot of cooking!"[31]

Dauph and Lillie also hosted many meetings and events in their home for the Baptist Church, where they had been active since their earliest days in Boone. In addition to attending twice-monthly services, Dauph also served as superintendent of Sunday schools from 1899 until at least 1913.[32]

Lillie's brother Edgar Shull, 12 years younger than her, enrolled at Appalachian in 1907 and lived in the Dougherty home. At 20 years old he had not completed high school because Holly Spring College, the school he attended in Butler, Tennessee, had been sold. Living with Dauph and Lillie enabled him to graduate from Appalachian in 1908.[33]

While living in Boone, Edgar became acquainted with Mary Lillington Hardin, the only surviving child of John F. Hardin, who had donated land for the beginning of Watauga Academy and remained a strong supporter of the school. Edgar lingered in Boone to pursue Mary and continued to take classes after graduation.

Appalachian Acquires More Property: The Edmisten Farm

In 1908, Appalachian Trustee T.P. Adams insisted that the school purchase the Edmisten farm, two miles east of Boone. Over opposition from the other trustees, the purchase was completed.[34] This second farm property comprised 60 acres of meadow land and 140 acres of timber land, and proved essential in providing garden vegetables and milk for the school cafeteria, as well as ample wood for fuel.[35]

The Edmisten Farm, purchased in 1907, remains valuable school property and the source for the name of State Farm Road (University Archives Photograph Collection, Appalachian State University, Boone, North Carolina).

Illness and Death in the Family

"Little Disco," the delightful son of Lillie and Dauph, was barely two years old when he was suddenly stricken with membranous croup, or diphtheria, and died on September 11, 1908.[36] Clara was 10 when her little brother died, old enough to recall the details and the sadness.

The threat of death before the development of penicillin and other antibiotics always loomed, and childhood deaths were not uncommon. Lillie's sister Nettie's baby died suddenly in 1903, only two hours after contracting croup. The agony of watching a child suffer and die and the painful void of their absence is surely one of life's deepest sorrows. In their grief, the family comforted one another with their shared Christian faith. Sister Alice wrote: "I hardly know how to begin. I feel so sorry for you and Prof. and the children. We heard today that little Disco had passed away into that better land where there is no sorrow and no tears."[37] Her sister Nettie (Virginia) wrote: "My dear Lillie, I do not want you to grieve after little Disco for he is in the arms of our Dear Redeemer. I do not grieve for our little Virginia for I feel the Lord can take care of her far better than I can."[38]

Lillie's sister Vinnie (Victoria) wrote: "We know at this time our sympathy seems cold and cruel, yet God knows how sad we are for your dear son ... left in the hands of the all-wise Ruler who knows what is best for all of us. And in these dark powers of sorrow and sore trials, we must abide by His decision.... We remain very sad, James and Vinnie."[39]

On the heels of this overwhelming sorrow, Lillie was consumed with the care of two more children, Clara and Edgar, who fell sick with typhoid fever. The sickness was either fatal or would take weeks to run its course, which included fever up to 104.9 degrees, "headache, weakness and fatigue, muscle aches, sweating, dry cough, loss of appetite and weight loss, stomach pain, diarrhea or constipation, rash, and extremely swollen stomach."[40]

When the children passed the crisis and began to improve, Lillie, their caregiver, broke from the strain. The doctor did not know what to do, other than watch and wait.[41] Distraught and exhausted, Lillie was unable to shoulder all the demands on her. Daughter Annie was six years old, and still needed a full-time mother. The college still demanded full-time oversight from her husband, who had his own grief to bear. Lillie's mother traveled to Boone from Butler, Tennessee, to care for Lillie after the death of Disco. Everyone who knew the Doughertys was concerned about Lillie. Even the newspaper commented, to help relieve the anxiety in the community: "Mrs. D.D. Dougherty has been very unwell for some days, but we are glad to know that she is now some better."[42]

1909 Legislative Session

Hoping to secure a larger appropriation for the next two-year funding cycle, Blan Dougherty and Board of Trustees Chairman Capt. E.F. Lovill traveled to Raleigh in 1909, armed with their report on the impressive progress their small mountain school had made. They sought allies to promote their cause, and distributed a pamphlet explaining that the school property was now worth $35,000 to the state, having grown in value from its original cost of $23,410 (of which the state had spent only $15,780, and the people had raised $7,629). With the two farms and five buildings on a 13½-acre campus, the property's value was—over twice what the state had spent on the school.[43]

"Over one hundred students are in our higher grades," the 1909 report said. "The course of study is a full four years above the public-school course," which ended with seventh grade. (High school did not include the twelfth grade until 1942.[44]) "With all this, the state does not spend over $1 per capita for a whole year on our students," boasted Board of Trustees Chairman E.F. Lovill.[45]

The needs of the school were many. The grounds were muddy and unimproved; desks, blackboards, and furnishings for the boys' boarding hall were urgently needed[46]; and the growth of the school required that waterworks and sewage systems be installed. In addition, requesting additional funding for the purchase of a third farm to produce hay and other products for the school, and to establish a test farm that would employ students, Lovill claimed that "no institution in North Carolina has accomplished so much on so little."

"The school has had a healthy and an uplifting influence for public school education throughout this mountain country," B.B. Dougherty wrote at the end of his report. "It reaches all classes of people, rich and poor. That the spending of money on such an institution is wise, no thoughtful, observing person will any longer doubt."[47]

A newspaper reporter from the *Raleigh Times* relished in the stories Blan Dougherty told about the first years of the school and published a favorable article under the heading "A Great Institution: The Appalachian Training School Makes Report."[48] "If the *Times* man were called upon to name the state's most economically managed institution," the article claimed, "the one with the greatest future and the one doing the most good with the least expenditure, he would not hesitate to name the Appalachian Training School. In saying this there is no exaggeration. Only one who knows the mountain section and who knows conditions there can appreciate the work being done."[49]

The 1909 Legislature awarded A.T.S. an annual appropriation of $6,000 for salaries and maintenance and $8,000 for the completion and furnishing of the boys' dormitory, purchase of land, and other necessary improvements.[50] With the increased appropriation, *The Dew Drop Catalogue* for the following school year announced that "bath rooms will be fitted up in the Lovill Home"—the first bathrooms at Appalachian.[51]

As summer was ending, the enrollment at Appalachian Training School increased to 388 students for 1909–1910, with students coming from 21 counties in the state. Lillie was pregnant again. Clara, now age 13, continued with piano and art lessons, helped her then very pregnant mother do the cooking and cleaning, and often watched over her sister Annie, age 9. The baby, David Barnard Dougherty, was born August 20, 1909.[52]

1910 Haley's Comet, a Marriage and Thanksgiving School Open House

The following year, in the summer of 1910, Edgar Shull, Lillie Dougherty's younger brother who had enrolled at Appalachian Teachers School to finish his education, married Mary Lillington Hardin, to the delight of his sister. The Hardin family, who had been so generous in encouraging the Doughertys' work in Boone, were very happy with the match.

Earlier that year, Haley's Comet had appeared at 3:00 a.m. one night in May. With no light pollution—the rural areas in the Appalachian Mountains had no electricity until the 1940s and 1950s—the atmosphere was dark and clear, and the comet with its tail spread across the sky was memorable.[53] Lester Brown, one of those who clearly remembered seeing the comet, accompanied his older sister, Lillie Belle Brown, from their remote Ashe County farm to Boone in 1910, where she took teacher training classes and became a teacher. Their older brother Charles was also enrolled at Appalachian at that time and also became a teacher. There were few ways to earn a living in the mountains, and it was common for mountain families to send several family members to the school to train as teachers.

On Thanksgiving, 1910, the townspeople were invited to an open house at the school. A tour of the campus ended in the auditorium of the Administration Building, where the Doughertys presented the portraits of three men who had been invaluable in the founding of A.T.S.: "William C. Newland, the representative from Caldwell County, who had introduced the 1903 bill establishing the school; E.J. Justice, the senator who had signed the minority report in 1903; and J.R. Gordon, a Guilford County legislator and chairman of the Appropriations Committee for two years who 'had shown great friendship to the school.'"[54]

Because the new brick Science Hall was still under construction, only Newland Hall was on the public tour. The Science Hall, when it was completed the following year, contained a laboratory, lecture room, and four recitation rooms on the first floor, and four recitation rooms on the second floor with an alumni hall.[55] "A portico on monumental columns fronted Science Hall (later used for music, then home economics), making it the first of the classically inspired buildings that would dominate the campus in coming decades."[56] In his county history, J.P. Arthur commented that T.P. Adams, long term Watauga County school board chairman and Dougherty family friend, carried mortar and brick for one month until the roof was on the science building, so that it was not left exposed to the elements all winter.[57]

1911: Appalachian in Jeopardy Again

The beautiful campus and academic quality of East Carolina State Teachers Training School became an object of envy for the leading citizens of Asheville, in the mountainous western part of the state. Many of them had received fine college educations themselves and were now political and business leaders for this growing city. When the railroad connected this mountain town to the major arteries of the state, Asheville grew to become the dominant economic center for western North Carolina. Lacking direct train access put both Cullowhee and Boone at an extreme disadvantage, although Boone was far less accessible than Cullowhee.

Dr. George T Winston, former president of the University of North Carolina, and of the State Agricultural and Mechanical College in Raleigh (later, N.C. State University), upon his retirement to Asheville and Buncombe County, envisioned a teachers' college for the west, far above the high school level work offered at Boone and Cullowhee. He remarked to State Superintendent Joyner that it was only a question of time until a fine school on a par with the Greenville and Greensboro teacher schools would be established in the west: "Let the little schools at Cullowhee and Boone go on as they are: they can never fill the bill for western North Carolina. We need them also and indeed many others like them. They will do good."[58]

Aware of the threat that Asheville posed to Appalachian, Blan Dougherty had been communicating his concern to State Superintendent Joyner, who advised him to "have a 'full report' of his school printed in pamphlet form, containing, if possible, a 'nice cut' of the buildings for distribution to all members of the General Assembly that they might know of the work going on in Boone."[59] Advertising Appalachian, as had been demonstrated by the effectiveness of the 1909 pamphlet, was of great importance in influencing legislators. A school such as Dr. Winston envisioned in Asheville would draw state appropriations away from Boone and Cullowhee.

The Asheville group used their political weight in Raleigh. In his inaugural address in early January 1911, Governor William W. Kitchin noted that neither Boone nor Cullowhee was accessible by train. "Without detracting from the importance and usefulness of these schools," Kitchin said, "I recommended the establishment at some suitable place of another school to be known as the Western Carolina Teachers Training School."[60] The "suitable place" Kitchin had in mind was Asheville.

Soon after this speech, the committee from the west, chaired by future governor Locke Craig of Buncombe County, held meetings in Raleigh with legislative representatives to promote the proposal for a school like East Carolina Training School in the Asheville area.[61] Pressure for the new western school continued to grow, and the bill to establish it passed the Senate by a vote of 37 to 4. Only one senator spoke in opposition, arguing that the state should take better care of its existing schools before establishing new ones. The bill was sent to the House and from there to the Joint Appropriations Committee.[62]

Both B.B. Dougherty and Robert Madison, president of Cullowhee, were in Raleigh working against Dr. Winston's Asheville measure.[63] A vote of 15 to 11 in the Joint Appropriations Committee killed the Winston bill. "In 1911 [Dr.] Winston was called away from Raleigh as his bill appeared for a vote before the Appropriations Committee." He telegraphed Frank Ray, representative for Macon County: "We are looking to you and God for the western training school." When the bill was narrowly defeated, Ray wired back: "Me and God on other side. Your bill has failed."[64]

Improving Curriculum, Fall Fair and Family Sadness

After surviving the scare with the Asheville contingent, the Appalachian Training School announced in the *1911 Dew Drop Catalogue*: "a year of college work will be added." Considering that the school had begun as a "substandard high school," adding college level courses was a significant improvement, but the emphasis on teacher training remained.[65] "In the establishment of the Appalachian Training School for teachers the state has purchased more intellect for the money invested than by any other investment it has made," local lawyer Frank Linney boasted in a 1911 speech. He remarked that 200 teachers had already been sent out to the rural schools, where they had influenced thousands of young lives.[66] Without question, mountain communities were improved through education.[67]

Well-known Boone lawyer Stacy Eggers, Jr. (1924–2018), recalled that his family had moved from rural Watauga County to Boone so the children could get an education. Getting one was not easy, but people were eager for their children to "do better." Egger's mother was one of 10 graduates of Appalachian Training School in 1911.[68] Many generations of Eggers lawyers continued to practice in Boone because of the education afforded them at Appalachian.

A Fall Fair was held on the school campus in 1911, with "a parade, military maneuvers on the groomed grounds," and a speech in the auditorium by State Superintendent Joyner. Afterwards, dinner was announced, and "the doors of the old Watauga Academy building were thrown open and people thronged in to see the wonderful exhibits of farm products … a magnificent array of fruits and vegetables." Dauph Dougherty submitted produce samples from his garden and won first and second prizes in four categories: carrots, collards, Swiss chard, and kohlrabi. The Ladies Department judges included Mrs. D.D. Dougherty and two others. Annie Dougherty entered some Indian artifacts from her father's collection.[69]

Soon after the celebration the family learned that Edgar Shull's wife of just over a year, Mary Lillington Hardin, had died of tuberculosis after unsuccessful treatment in several sanitoria. Mary was the only child of Mr. and Mrs. J.F. Hardin, who were devastated at the loss. Lillie's mother, who had come for the funeral of her son's wife, accompanied the grief-stricken Edgar back to Tennessee.[70] Soon after, Lillie's mother begged her to go to Nettie, Lillie's sister, who was struggling with illness, probably cancer. Such were the demands of extended family on Lillie for most of her life.

Caldwell County Campus Considered

Worries about the future of Appalachian Training School continually weighed on the Doughertys. As Dauph carried out the day-to-day operations, Blan focused on sustaining state financial support. Superintendent Joyner had come in October to discuss opposition from the Asheville contingent. If "remoteness" was the major obstacle to a secure future, Blan reasoned, then they should relocate the school near a train. Joyner was shown a 55-acre tract in Caldwell County, with a two-month option to purchase it for $3,000. But Joyner was hesitant to endorse the transaction.[71]

When Joyner returned to Raleigh, he reported that he was "pleased and

Male faculty for 1906 at Appalachian Training School near the Administration Building: from left, Dauphin Disco Dougherty, Augustus Masters (seated), D.W. Read, W.J. White (seated), Charles M. Dickson (bowtie), and Blanford Barnard Dougherty. In 1905 the faculty included three females, Maude Harris, Julia Hardin, and Margaret B. Rhea, who taught with William Francum, B.B. and D.D. Dougherty (Doris Stam Collection, University Archives, Special Collections Research Center, Appalachian State University, Boone, North Carolina).

Appalachian Training School summer school faculty seated on the stage, B.B. Dougherty at far left, c. 1906 (Elizabeth Brown Scoggins Collection, University Archives, Special Collections Research Center, Appalachian State University, Boone, North Carolina).

encouraged" with the work of Appalachian Training School. He found it "filled to capacity" with a "fine body of capable, enthusiastic young men and women."[72] He was pleasantly surprised "that such 'excellent buildings' had been built for so little money. The state was 'certainly getting more than value received for every dollar' that it had appropriated for the school."[73] Joyner remarked on how the school had "greatly improved the teaching forces of Watauga and many of the surrounding counties." "Appalachian Training School was not 'seeking or aspiring to be a college,' but was 'devoting itself wholly to its useful mission' of providing high school instruction 'for the mountain boys and girls.'"[74]

In December Blan was assured by some wealthy businessmen that a railroad would soon be connecting Wilkesboro, Lenoir and Boone. Trusting this assurance, Blan told Joyner the "good news," and let the Caldwell County option lapse. But no railroad came to Boone. "Boone used to be the most inaccessible place in the world," Blan later said in his retirement speech, in 1955. Blan Dougherty worked continually with local leaders for decades to bring a train to Boone and safeguard the school's longevity.[75]

Boone remained isolated and remote, with an uncertain future. The Asheville contingent would continue their attempts to establish a state-supported teacher training college, like Greenville's East Carolina, in Asheville. The next governor would resume this campaign in 1915 for a school in Asheville to replace those in Cullowhee and Boone.

17

More Children, Extended Family, and an Elopement (1912–1915)

Respect and Trust

Although the future of the teacher training school in Boone seemed uncertain because of Locke Craig and the Asheville contingent, its leadership by Dauph and Blan Dougherty was trusted, respected, and untarnished.

By contrast, although Cullowhee was also under pressure from Craig and the Asheville contingent, more serious was the damage to the school's reputation caused by widespread rumors about President Robert Lee Madison's conduct, rumors seemingly reflected in the sharp decline of female student enrollment.[1] Also, the school's curriculum had remained virtually unchanged since Madison's arrival in 1889, and his skills as an administrator did not grow with the school's increasing complexity.[2] Another possible source for concern was Madison's undying allegiance to the Southern cause and his personal desire to be a military commander. He required military uniforms for students from the 1890s until 1906.[3] Male students had drill practice with rifles. In 1912 he was replaced by Alonzo C. Reynolds, superintendent of Buncombe County schools.[4]

Mars Hill College had faced a similar situation before 1900 when Charles Patrick Stapp, a brilliant 1893 graduate of Wake Forest, became president at age 21. Stapp, who was described as pleasure-loving, with little interest in religion, and unsuited "in temperament or interest for the sober responsibilities placed upon him at Mars Hill," was replaced after only one year.[5]

Later a scandal with President Sams of Carson-Newman College brought disgrace to the college with his resignation in 1924.[6] And East Carolina's President Leon Meadows was jailed in 1944 for three years for mishandling school funds.[7]

Trustworthiness and honesty was never questionable at Appalachian with the Doughertys.

Clara Dougherty and a New Student

In the summer of 1912, the summer training program was flourishing, as indicated by an overabundance of applicants for summer school positions. Dauph worked in the school office after the spring term ended, while Blan traveled to give commencement addresses at Oak Hill, Taylorsville, and Spring Hope. Dauph and Lillie enjoyed enough free time to take their family on picnics in Blowing Rock by horse and wagon.[8]

Dauph and Lillie's first-born, Clara, was a 14-year-old high school student at Appalachian in the fall of 1912. The last student to arrive to Latin class the first day of school was a skinny, freckle-faced, 17-year-old student named Lester Brown, an unsophisticated farm boy newly arrived from Creston, in the backwoods of Ashe County. Surveying the crowded room of total strangers, the boy was immediately enchanted by Clara, a pretty brunette with round, rosy cheeks, dark eyes, and friendly countenance, seated in the back of the room. Clara also took special notice of him, and later revealed that she envisioned him as her future husband. It was love at first sight. He had no idea that the girl was the daughter of the Doughertys.

Lester Brown was one of the 50 or more boys housed in Newland Hall dormitory. His older sister, Lillie Belle, had enticed him to attend high school at Appalachian Training School by giving him a horse, which he could sell for school expenses.[9] Lester admitted that the boys in the dorm sometimes violated the rules by "slipping out from the second floor room at night via the fire escape" and would ramble in the nearby fields for a while.[10]

On a Sunday in October, an older student, Bill Garvey, told Lester he had a secret date with his girlfriend, Lillie Campbell. Lillie's cousin Clara was invited "to keep down suspicion. ... [it being] strictly against the rules to date, on or off campus without permission." He asked Lester to go along to look after the cousin.[11] The foursome met off-campus and walked to Winkler's Creek, "a famous trysting place" not far away.[12]

The next day Lester and Clara shared glances in the halls and the classrooms and passed notes. Soon they were meeting secretly—sometimes in the music room of the Academy, where she often practiced, or in the art room, where she spent much spare time painting.[13] Clara was a child of many talents, which her parents were eager for her to develop to their fullest. Lessons in drawing and piano had begun when Clara was age eight. In her teen years Clara gave many piano recitals and completed numerous oil paintings.[14]

During the 1912–1913 school year, Clara's parents were consumed with work and family matters and were not always aware of Clara's activities. Lillie was pregnant again, caring for three-year-old Barnard and nine-year-old Annie, and hosting official campus visitors. Clara was assumed to be busy with high school when not at home helping with the cooking, washing, and cleaning. When Lillie and Dauph discovered that Clara was "courtin' on the sly," the reins tightened at home and closer supervision followed.[15]

The autumn of 1912 was a difficult time for the Doughertys' extended family. Lillie's younger sister and dear friend Nettie (Virginia), whom Lillie had visited in late November 1911 to help with her children during her illness, was terminally sick. Though her condition had worsened, Nettie wanted to leave the hospital where she was undergoing treatment and go home to her family. In October of 1912, Nettie died, leaving four small children.[16] Her husband of 13 years was Dauph's close friend the Rev. A.C. Sherwood, and Lillie and Dauph helped to raise their children after Nettie's death. One daughter, Martha Sherwood, often lived in the Dougherty home in Boone. In addition to the loss of Lillie's sister, Richard Greene, the husband of Dauph and Blan's sister, Etta, was badly injured in an automobile accident, in which Blan was also injured to a lesser degree.[17]

Early November brought the county fair, a welcome diversion from the sadness of October. The prize for the best biscuits and the best calico quilt went to Mrs. D.D. Dougherty.[18] But in late November Lillie's mother died, adding to the family's grief.[19]

Pauper Counties

By December 1912, the perennial issue of taxes for education had escalated into an ugly battle for resources between wealthier counties and the poorer ones. In March *The Evening Chronicle* (*Charlotte Observer*) had run an editorial claiming that the poorer counties were essentially robbing the wealthier ones of money that municipalities needed for fire and police protection and for infrastructure improvements. Editorials in Greensboro and Wilmington called poorer areas of the state "delinquent" and accused them of "insufficient management" if they needed state assistance to operate their public schools. It was suggested that the richer counties annex these poorer counties, "convert them into good public assets," and eliminate the "State scandal."[20]

These words were offensive to the Doughertys and others from less wealthy areas of the state. Every county received help, but the local tax base of isolated counties like Watauga did not generate sufficient funding. This imbalance in the tax base led to "the charge that the 'pauper counties' were trying to live off their more provident neighboring counties."[21]

Wealth was growing in the larger cities of the state because of the textile and tobacco industries. Many citizens of Winston-Salem were "opposed to paying over so much money to educate children in other sections of the State."[22] The *Charlotte Daily Observer* editorial declared an unjust burden was already imposed upon the cities, and charged promoters of higher taxes for education with "a dwarfed sense of justice."[23]

Blan Dougherty responded immediately and vigorously to these attacks with an editorial refuting the wealthier counties' arguments and pointing out that while every citizen in the state had paid for the railroads, only certain areas had access and advantage from them. "They have enjoyed the opportunities for the building of factories, the starting of many enterprises, the coming of outside wealth. They have not only had the advantages of this railroad, but they have also prospered from local taxes on this railroad property, for the most part owned by the state itself; and still, the pauper counties have not murmured."[24]

When analyzed properly, Blan argued, the "pauper counties" paid a higher educational tax than citizens living in richer counties. He urged that all the tax money designated for education be put into the state treasury and appropriated in such a way as to "give every child an equal chance," not kept within each county. "North Carolina is a unit. County lines should not interfere with the education of our children. No state can be great when even a part of her children are neglected."[25]

A gross inequality existed, to the disadvantage of the less wealthy counties. Blan hoped to see the day when public schools of the state were maintained from not only property taxes, but from income taxes. Blan Dougherty would continue to champion the cause of parity in public education for decades.[26]

Biennial Report for 1911–1913

The Appalachian trustees carefully prepared their report to the governor and the General Assembly to be delivered in January 1913, with the intention of thwarting any new challenges from Locke Craig and the Asheville contingent. Noting that the physical plant at Appalachian was valued at $100,000 and calling "attention to the fact that the State has spent only about one-half this amount, the people and economy [frugality] having done the rest," it was hoped that the doubling in value would impress the legislators. "Next year will bring to us splendid railroad facilities," the report stated optimistically claimed, "giving us a fine outlet to every section of the State."[27] The latter assertion was meant to assure the legislators that Boone would be more accessible soon, negating the claim from the Asheville contingent, which included Governor William Kitchin and Senator Julius C. Martin, that travel to Boone was difficult.[28]

E.F. Lovill, chairman of Appalachian's Board of Trustees, acknowledged "the difficult task the General Assembly has now in providing funds for the pressing needs of all our institutions. ... We have improvements on hand, but the work has been stopped for the lack of funds."[29] The number of applicants exceeded the school's capacity. Expenses were kept very low so "that the School may be in reach of all our people, however poor." Lovill argued that "this is the most economically managed institution, public or private, in North Carolina."[30]

The report stated that the aim of the Appalachian Training School was "to be of the greatest service to the State." To effectuate that mission and reach the "great mass of young people, wishing to teach in our State, the plant must be greatly enlarged, and the expenses must be kept at the lowest possible point." There was a pressing

Lovill Home, painted white, with the brick Administration Building, looking south, c. 1910. Faculty and student boarding houses are visible on each side (University Communications Records, University Archives, Special Collections Research Center, Appalachian State University, Boone, North Carolina).

Appalachian Training School graduates holding lovely bouquets on graduation day, c. 1910 (University Archives, Special Collections Research Center, Appalachian State University, Boone, North Carolina).

need for men's and women's dormitories with kitchens and dining rooms, a domestic science building, a laundry, and a central heat and light plant, which alone was estimated to cost $15,000. In 1914, attendance was expected to exceed 400, compared to 344 students from 24 counties in the 1912–1913 school year. The school had sent about 200 teachers each year to public schools in every section of the state.[31]

State Superintendent Joyner responded with a commendation for Appalachian's "marvelous" work and "remarkably economical administration."[32]

After a visit to Boone in September 1913, the editor of the *Charlotte Observer* wrote a lengthy article praising Appalachian Training School, suggesting the state had never made a better investment and received a better return for its money, and praising the 1913 Legislature for appropriating funds for a new building. The editorial pledged that the *Charlotte Observer* would endorse future requests from A.T.S. to the Legislature by A.T.S.[33]

1913: Another Baby Boy and Asheville's Failed Legislative Attempt

To the great joy of the family, another son, Edwin Shull Dougherty, was born to Lillie and Dauph on March 30, 1913. This would be their last child, and a great friend

Lillie Shull Dougherty in the front yard with her daughters, c. 1910, Annie (front) and Clara (beside); the boy is unidentified. Howard's Knob and the future campus are in the background (Doris Stam Collection, University Archives, Special Collections Research Center, Appalachian State University, Boone, North Carolina).

for David Barnard who was then three years old. Having lost their first son, the joy over yet another boy was great.

While Blan was in Raleigh petitioning the legislature for much-needed funds, Dauph had shouldered all the responsibilities of managing the school and teaching a full load. All were relieved that nothing had transpired in the Legislature to endanger the school that year. High hopes for a railroad from the Yadkin Valley up the mountainous terrain to Boone were disappointed when grading proved very difficult and the expense exceedingly large. Citing the perennial inaccessibility of Boone and Cullowhee, Locke Craig and the Asheville contingent tried again to persuade the 1915 legislature to close the teacher training schools in Cullowhee and Appalachian, but their attempts failed.[34]

As the school year drew to an end, while Dauph and Lillie were busy with the new baby and preparations for commencement, they "relaxed their supervision

The Dougherty children, c. 1914. Clara is holding Edwin in her lap, with Barnard in front and Annie to the left (Doris Stam Collection, University Archives, Special Collections Research Center, Appalachian State University, Boone, North Carolina).

and opened the way" for Clara and Lester "to roam about somewhat at large."[35] The young couple treasured their time together on long walks away from her parents' awareness. At the 1913 spring recital, displaying the musical talent inherited from Lillie, and years of practicing, Clara performed on the piano. Lester listened.

Summer School Thrives, New Faculty, and Games

Enrollment for the 1913–1914 school year numbered 256 students, beginning with the seventh grade. The summer term had enrolled 197, totaling 453, including one student from China. Lester Brown and Clara Dougherty were among the second-year high school class members.

Several new teachers were hired in 1913 who brought a higher level of academic credentials, and who would faithfully serve the school for decades: Roy M. Brown, English (A.B. University of North Carolina); James M. Downham, Latin (A.B. Trinity College); Isaac G. Greer, history (student in University of North Carolina); Carrie M. Michael, instrumental music (Cincinnati College of Music); J.A. White, mathematics (A.B. Wake Forest College).

An excellent "ball ground" was provided for the young men, with these caveats: "No games are allowed during the regular school hours. The baseball team cannot leave the neighborhood to play match games without permission from the faculty." "The young women will in the near future have grounds for croquet, tennis, and other games," *The Dew Drop Catalogue* promised.[36]

Students were "urged to be in the open air as much as possible." Professor Dauph

Dougherty identified the indigenous wildflowers and other plants with labels and encouraged interesting walks near the school.[37] However, "Young women do not leave the school grounds for walks without a teacher."[38] One regulation remained each year: "Young women and young men are not expected to board at the same places or to associate together on any occasion."

Lester Brown at the Blair Hotel: John Preston Arthur

When Lester Brown returned to Appalachian in the fall of 1913, he found work in the Blair Hotel, doing chores for his board and lodging. There he met a lonely but distinguished-looking man, John Preston Arthur, around 60 years of age. Mr. Arthur was "portly, bald headed and attractively dressed." Their rooms were adjacent; they shared meals at the same table and became well acquainted. Arthur, a bachelor and native of Asheville, had recently finished his *History of Western North Carolina*, a project that had taken 10 years, and was working on *A History of Watauga County*. Estranged from his family in Asheville, Arthur had made Boone his permanent home. Although he was a lawyer, he had trouble getting work and was soon broke. Arthur was willing to do any odd jobs, and Lester later helped arrange with the Doughertys a few weeks of work for Arthur cataloging library books at the Training School.[39]

Lester and Clara resumed meeting secretly, against the "unrelenting rules" of her parents to prevent Clara from dating. Grieving over "being fenced in," Clara grew more unhappy. Her aunt Etta, who felt that Dauph was too hard on his daughter, allowed Lester and Clara to meet in her home, the Greene Inn.[40]

In October of 1913, Dauph hired a new handyman whose grandfather had run the mill on Boone Creek for Daniel Baker Dougherty prior to 1900.[41] Ed Culler was a colorful personality, full of stories peppered with expletives. Dauph persuaded Culler to leave his job on a farm at $0.60 per day to work at the school for $0.75 per day, plus a place to live and firewood. Culler started by milking cows twice a day for the dining halls, feeding the pigs, cutting and stacking wood for the dining hall fireplaces and the dorms.[42] When Culler began his 45 years of employment at Appalachian, he also delivered milk, filled oil lamps, and drove a mule team to Wilkesboro or Lenoir—a two, or sometimes, three-day trip—for supplies, collecting 100-pound bags of flour and other necessities.[43] During his first years, on Mondays, when no classes were held, he carried water from the creek and built a fire for the girls to do their washing in big iron wash tubs. Clothes were dried outside or inside, and ironed with heavy flatirons heated on woodstoves.[44,45]

Strict in the Dougherty Home and on the Campus

Rebecca Greene was a student from out in the county who lived and worked in the Dougherty home for her tuition and board around the years 1913–1917. She told her life story to her nephew, who transcribed her words, some of which follows.

I stayed with the Doughertys and went through the 7th and 8th grades. I did housework, cook, wash dishes, make beds, clean the house…. We cooked three meals a day. We cooked on a woodstove, the old thing wouldn't half heat….

I went to school from 8 to 12 noon, went home and helped Mrs. Dougherty. About 11:30, I had my last morning class and went home and helped her for lunch. She'd have it on. Everybody went home for dinner. It's just across the meadow there [sic]. Wouldn't no buildings hardly, just across the meadow, you could walk it in five minutes….

Ol' Mrs. Dougherty would work your butt off. Her name was Lillie. She was the prettiest woman ever been in Boone. She wanted you to work all the time. But she was good and kind to me.[46]

Campus discipline was also strict. The daily schedule for teachers and students, as described in the 1914 *Dew Drop Catalogue*, was rigid:

    1. Each teacher must be in his room 10 minutes before time for the bell and see that his room is in order.

    2. The students are allowed three minutes to change rooms. Three bells will ring:

        a. For boys to change rooms,

        b. One and one-half minutes later for girls to change rooms,

        c. One and one-half minutes later *for all to be in rooms.*[47]

A group of musicians holding guitars outside the Watauga Academy building, c. 1910. Prof. I.G. Greer stands centered amid the group (University Communications Records, University Archives, Special Collections Research Center, Appalachian State University, Boone, North Carolina).

17. More Children, Extended Family, and an Elopement

Graduates line up in front of Science Hall in 1916, girls and boys separated, as was the common practice. Watauga Academy is to the left (University Communications Records, University Archives, Special Collections Research Center, Appalachian State University, Boone, North Carolina).

Lester Brown, a poor mountain farm boy from Creston, walked all day from his home, up and over Elk Knob, to get to Appalachian Training School. While there he "batched it" with a few others for at least one semester, "shaking it," as in this photograph of students at another North Carolina mountain school, c. 1914 (courtesy Western Carolina University Hunter Library).

The Doughertys were particularly strict with respect to the segregation of boys and girls, as was culturally expected at the time. But many students, especially the older ones, resented the ban on dating and in protest carried out the school's first student strike.[48]

A rumor was spread that three teachers would lead a hike to Howard's Knob on April Fool's Day. Believing that teachers were heading the hike, Clara and Lester and the large majority of students quickly left campus for the rumored hike when the class change bell rang. But clever students had played a joke and fooled their peers.

"All who went on strike were expelled from the school then given the opportunity to go before the faculty, one by one, and apologize for breaking the rules. Afterwards, about all of them were readmitted to classes."[49] Girl offenders living in dormitories were confined to campus, each for as long as her active part seemed to require. Clara and her classmate and cousin Lillie Campbell, who lived in the Dougherty home, were confined to the house. Clara felt her punishment was more severe because, as the principal's daughter, she was expected to be an exemplary student.[50]

No closing exercises were held at the end of the spring term, possibly as a result of the student strike. At the close of the first summer school session for that year, the Commencement Day graduating exercises took place on July 11, 1914.[51]

Shocking Elopement

Lester and Clara became secretly engaged in the spring of 1914. After they parted for the summer, Clara's brooding about their separation led her unsuspecting parents to send her to visit relatives in Butler, Tennessee, where Lester and Clara secretly met and eloped.

When Clara returned to gather her baggage from her aunt's house and sneak out to join her new husband, she was discovered. Clara's Aunt Alice Campbell phoned Lillie to tell her of the elopement.[52] When Lillie heard the news, "her scream was heard all over the campus."[53] Without a clear plan for the future, the newlyweds moved in with Lester's family. Clara had some adjustments to make in the six-member Brown home, living in an isolated community.[54]

Dauph forbade the couple to return to Boone. The elopement was distressing to Dauph and Lillie and had ended their dreams for Clara. Neither Lester nor Clara had finished high school. Lillie and Dauph worried about Clara, whom they did not see for several months. They sent his sister, Etta Greene, and her husband Richard to check on the newlyweds at the Brown homeplace. Clara was homesick. Etta and Blan, according to Lester's later account, had been pleading with Dauph to allow the young couple to return and finish their high school studies.[55] Dauph relented.

"After a cold horseback journey of eight hours Clara's parents welcomed them in the front room of the house where a big log fire blazed out its light and warmth. Annie and Clara's two young brothers were all thrilled over what was happening. Lester was taken in as a member of the household and included as one of the family."[56] The couple lived with the Doughertys, and the two were readmitted to school. Lester had no income or employment but helped with odd jobs for the family.[57]

One night, soon after the newlyweds returned, they were awakened at midnight by reports of a fire on campus. Dauph, Blan and Lester raced across campus where McNeil Cottage, where several female students lived, was ablaze. Within half an hour it was a heap of burning timbers and household goods. Rosalie Lackey, teacher and matron, was able to save all the students and most of their belongings. This was the first big fire on campus.[58] The destruction of the cottage hastened efforts to build a new dormitory for girls.[59]

Fall 1914: Preparatory Department

In the fall of 1914 Professor Dauph Dougherty needed an assistant for his science classes and chose his wife's niece, Lillie Campbell, who had just graduated and was still living in the Dougherty home. An enrollment of 286 that fall, and the great differences in student abilities, created a challenging situation for the professors and the need for assistants.

Many students who enrolled at A.T.S. came from areas of the mountains where public schools were inadequate to prepare them for high school. Hard-working and ambitious, these disadvantaged teenagers and their families were willing to sacrifice and save a little money for education—a true hardship. "A lot of them were borrowing money. At that time I know that many of them got hungry.... They were highly motivated and knew what they wanted to do," future Appalachian president Herb Wey commented about the students attending the school during that time. "The fact that they had not achieved to a certain level did not mean that they were lacking the native intelligence and ability to do the work," Wey insisted.[60]

The Dew Drop for 1914 announced a two year preparatory department for those who were unprepared for the first year of high school. The first preparatory year consisted of a review of public school studies and supplementary work; the second year covered the usual eighth grade work.[61]

Andrew Jackson Greene was hired to teach these remedial classes. Born and raised in Watauga County north of Boone, Jack Greene brought a wealth of experience from teaching in the rural county schools since 1906.[62] After graduating from Appalachian Training School, he had attended Wake Forest College.[63] Jack Greene was "considered a very capable, thorough, and conscientious teacher of the preparatory department."[64]

1915: Locke Craig

The Asheville contingent re-emerged in 1915, again championed by Locke Craig, now governor of North Carolina, and again threatened the survival of the schools at Boone and Cullowhee. "Cullowhee President Reynolds joined the Doughertys in combating Gov. Craig's latest drive to either move or close the two institutions."[65]

The city of Asheville, North Carolina, and the busy Pack Square, between 1910 and 1920 (courtesy North Carolina State Archives).

In his gubernatorial address to the General Assembly of 1915, Governor Craig and Asheville[66] businessmen pressured the General Assembly to adopt Craig's plan, to combine the Cullowhee and Boone schools into a new one in Asheville, Governor Craig's hometown.[67] Governor Craig praised East Carolina "as a splendid and well-equipped school" and complained that "for a number of terms the Legislature has not considered a school for the western section similar to that established at Greenville."[68] He claimed that many teachers in the western part of the state "lacked training from convenient schools of proper character and facilities," and therefore "have not been able to equip themselves sufficiently for their work."

Craig was likely influenced by Dr. George T. Winston, former president of the University of North Carolina (Chapel Hill) and of North Carolina State College (Raleigh), with whom he shared a deep friendship. When Winston retired from State College and moved to Asheville, his friendship with Craig grew even closer. They may have shared a belief that neither Boone nor Cullowhee would ever grow into a first-class college and that North Carolina should have a genuine senior college located at a more accessible site in the western part of the state. The Asheville Chamber of Commerce may also have exerted some influence over Craig.[69] The *Watauga Democrat* expressed some surprise at the governor's political infidelity to Appalachian:

> [O]ur mind reverts to the time when he (the Governor) as a candidate for gubernatorial honors, and his speech, in Boone, spoke in the highest terms of the school, lamenting the fact

that this good county of ours was cut off from railroad communications, and promising better prospects for both when he was elected governor. The county stood solidly behind him; he was elected, and now in his message, absolutely overlooks the fact that such a school is in existence. Can it be that the ghost of a western training school for Buncombe, the governor's home county, has again bobbed up? Maybe so.[70]

But the legislators were not convinced by Governor Craig in 1915. They favored expanding the existing two western schools, which could accommodate the anticipated students who would be training for teaching careers at costs far below those of establishing a brand-new school. A legislative committee who had visited Appalachian in February gave a glowing report on the school, commending the management for their use of state money, helping to persuade the voting in favor of Boone and Cullowhee.[71]

Sanitation on Campus

Seeking approval of distributions, even for things like toilets, required the most dogged determination before the legislators. In county schools the sanitary facilities were very poor, and sometimes nonexistent. Toilets were built over streams where possible. Luckily many buildings were close to the woods and streams, and other shrubs were used to provide some measure of privacy. Boys would often go up the road and the girls down the road.[72] Unclean water was the root cause of many illnesses, especially typhoid. In addition to human and animal waste, farmers would often throw the carcasses of cows and other large animals in the streams.[73]

The Legislature of 1915 approved the funds for Appalachian Training School "to put in an electric plant, ... to make plans for a steam plant, sewerage," to raise the salaries of the Dougherty brothers, and add new faculty members.[74]

Remodeling Dougherty Home

Dauph Dougherty used his salary increase in 1915 to add electricity to his home, as well as a bedroom on the main floor and a tiny bedroom above it on the second floor. A bathroom was added, but possibly not until a year or so afterward.[75] Rebecca Greene, a student boarder and helper in the home, recalled:

> They had water in the house, but they had a wonderful spring right down under the bank there. And we'd go down there and get good spring water to drink. And they had on the porch, kitchen porch, a little room built off for the bathroom. They had a bathtub and wood heater there and before you could get your bath you had to go in there and build a fire and warm up that room and take your bath. Hot water was from the hot water tank in behind the stove, heated from the stove, the cook stove. That was why it wouldn't heat hardly, too much on it. The coils went into the pipe of the stove or something. ... They didn't have no heat in the house, just wood heaters [fireplaces with wood stoves]....
>
> You know what, everybody had a slop jar, they called it. Go under their bed with a lid on it. Every morning you'd carry that down and pour it out there in the bathroom, down the commode and flush it down ... they had a sewer somewhere, I don't know where it went to.

The southwest side of Dougherty house, c. 1987, where the 1915 rear bedroom addition is clearly visible ("The Dougherty House: Appalachian State University Buildings Survey Project," by Diane Cook Barefoot, January 1987, University Archives, Special Collections Research Center, Appalachian State University, Boone, North Carolina).

> They had running water in the house. The water was piped in somehow from up on those mountains.[76]

Library Linked to Accreditation

The Legislative Committee on Education for North Carolina visited Appalachian Training School in 1915 and gave another glowing report. Several items in the report specifically praised the work of Dauph and Lillie Dougherty. The first was the mention of a good library and reading room, consisting of about 5,000 volumes, noting that "considerable interest is being taken in the library and its usefulness is rapidly growing."[77]

Having an adequate library had been a particular objective of Dauph, who knew that certification by the Southern Association of Colleges and Secondary Schools (SACSS) depended partly upon the requirement of an adequate library and the funding for it.[78] From the earliest years he "directed plays to raise funds for the purchase of books and to pay newspaper and magazine subscriptions."[79] Although accreditation from SACSS was a long way off, it was nonetheless an aspiration for the Doughertys. The Southern Association of Colleges and Secondary Schools had voted in

October of 1914 to admit certain junior colleges, and Mars Hill was making preparations to become a junior college in 1916.[80]

Professor Dauph Dougherty was a voracious reader and lifelong scholar, who started the school library from his own collection by 1904, and encouraged donations of books and periodicals from friends of the school.[81] Mars Hill College did not begin a library until 1919, and Western North Carolina College not until 1923.[82]

The Legislative Committee praised the chemical laboratory at Appalachian, which was the direct domain of Dauph as the science professor. The art and domestic science departments was also of great interest to the committee, both areas being the fruit of a joint initiative from Lillie and Dauph.[83]

Farm to Table at Appalachian

The 1915 Legislative Committee noted that the state's investment of $128,000 has been spent at Boone for buildings, farmland and maintenance of the school. "We would estimate the entire plant, consisting of buildings, electric light plant, cattle farm implements and farm lands to be worth at least $150,000."[84] "Reporting about the two school farms, it was noted that the school owns a fine herd of Holstein cattle, four nice mules, wagons and other necessary farm implements. The apples,

The *Lusitania*, pictured here, was a British passenger ship, first launched in 1906. Built for the transatlantic passenger trade, it was luxurious and noted for its speed. The *Lusitania* was sunk by a German torpedo, a precursor to World War I, resulting in great loss of life and shock to the world (public domain).

LUSITANIA SUNK BY A SUBMARINE, PROBABLY 1,260 DEAD; TWICE TORPEDOED OFF IRISH COAST; SINKS IN 15 MINUTES; CAPT. TURNER SAVED, FROHMAN AND VANDERBILT MISSING; WASHINGTON BELIEVES THAT A GRAVE CRISIS IS AT HAND

Headlines from the *New York Times*, May 1915, announcing the sinking of the *Lusitania*.

vegetables and other farm products are utilized at the dormitories. All the wood for fuel and building purposes comes from the woodlands belonging to the school."85

In an effort to keep the cost of board low, at $6.50 per month for women and $7.50 for men, a work program was introduced whereby boys worked on the school grounds and girls in the dining room for 12 hours per month.86 The school farm supplemented the food in the dining rooms with vegetables, meat, and milk. Pointing to the economy with which the school was run, the committee noted: "The farm, orchards and gardens will always enable this institution to give board at a very low rate."87

Potential War on the Horizon

On May 7, 1915, a German U-boat torpedoed the British-owned luxury steamship *Lusitania*, killing 1,195 people, including 128 Americans. "The disaster immediately strained relations between Germany and the neutral United States, fueled anti–German sentiment and set off a chain of events that eventually led to the United States entering World War I."88

Widely discussed in the newspapers, this event was shocking to Americans and solidified the public's opinions towards Germany.89 Thoughts of war and how it might affect their lives emerged in people's minds, even those people in the far-off mountains of North Carolina.

18

While Appalachian Training School Grows (1915–1916)

Blan Resigns as County Superintendent

Appalachian was growing and needed Blan's full-time attention. The school's trustees had offered to increase Blan's salary when he could arrange to give up the office of county superintendent. In July 1915, Smith Hagaman was elected to take his place, and the Watauga County Board of Education declared their appreciation for Blan's 16 years of "untiring devotion and unswerving fidelity to the cause of education in his beloved native county."[1]

Through his contacts as county superintendent with students, teachers, and families all over Watauga County, Blan influenced many to continue their education past seventh grade, and encouraged hundreds to attend Appalachian Training School.

New River Light and Power

Before fall classes of 1915 began, wheels were set in motion to bring electricity to the campus. A large brick dormitory for women was under construction and *The Dew Drop Catalogue* enticed new students with the promise, "All modern conveniences, water, steam heat, and electric lights are being installed."[2]

The school in Banner Elk begun by the Rev. Edgar Tufts, now known as Lees-McRae College, also faced the exciting prospect of electricity to provide heat and lighting. There, the school term ran from April to Christmas but was suspended during the coldest winter months because the frame buildings could not be adequately heated. The installation of electric lights to replace smoky oil lamps was a notable improvement there as well.[3]

Searching for a potential site to generate electricity for the school, Blan Dougherty visited a 100-foot waterfall on Howard's Creek with Ben Ward, a student at Appalachian who was a genius with numbers and mechanics.[4] Ben's father operated a dam on the Watauga River, and Ben had been around waterpower all his life. As Blan calculated the kilowatts that might be generated with the power of the water, Ward commented, "Prof. Dougherty, you've taught me a lot of things. Now I'm gonna teach you. You're forgetting that you must store that water in a reservoir."[5]

The 1899 Watauga Academy building amid the campus pine trees, from the 1916 *Dew Drop Catalogue* of Appalachian Training School. The wood frame building was used until a fire destroyed it in 1949 (University Archives, Special Collections Research Center, Appalachian State University, Boone, North Carolina).

Finding a site from which to generate electricity was now an urgent priority for 1914–1915. David Shearer, a young electrical engineer from Knoxville, Tennessee, was employed to oversee the construction of a dam, installation of machinery, and planning for a steam plant and sewerage. The site chosen for the plant was on the South Fork of the New River, at the lower end of the state-owned Edmiston Farm.[6]

The New River Light and Power Company plant "housed a 75 KW rope driven generator powered by a 10-foot dam built of heavy timbers."[7] Their remains can still be seen today on the Greenway Trail in Boone, North Carolina. The system consisted of "15 miles of line run on poles made from local chestnut trees. There were three employees responsible for maintaining service to the school and six Boone residences."[8]

Boone Is All Ablaze with Beautiful Lights

The building of the transmission lines and the wiring of school buildings, and later of town residences, were met with enthusiasm. Replacing oil lamps in the

Opposite: Lester Brown's 1916 report card from Appalachian Training School, when he was a newlywed, having eloped with Clara Dougherty in August of 1915 (Elizabeth Brown Scoggins Collection, University Archives, Special Collections Research Center, Appalachian State University, Boone, North Carolina).

Appalachian Training School
Boone, N. C.
ADVANCED DEPARTMENT

Report of _____ Lester Brown _____

_____ 4th Year, for C term, 1915-1916.

	Absent	Excused	Grade
Absent from Chapel	8	4	4
Absent from Class	6	6	
Deportment			98
Industry			98
Initiative			a
Attention			a
Attitude			a
Improvement			B
Society Work			
Housekeeping			
Library			B

A denotes high; B, medium; C, low.

	Absent.	Excused	Grade
Mathematics,			
English	2	2	2
History			
Latin	2	2	1
German,			
French			2
Science	2	2	2
Domestic Science			
Instrumental Music			
Vocal Music			
Book Keeping			
Type Writing			
Drawing			
Painting			
Writing			
Spelling			2
Short Hand			
Methods			
Current Events			

A figure 1, 2, 3, or 4 indicates passing grades; a figure 5 indicates a new examination; and a figure 6 indicates that the work must be taken again.

EXPLANATIONS

INDUSTRY means working power applied continuously and actively in the mastery of assignments.

INITIATIVE means the ability to plan and to execute.

ATTENTION means withholding thought from diverting subjects and fixing it upon the problem in hand.

ATTITUDE means the disposition of the pupil toward the work of the school.

IMPROVEMENT means the amount of progress and accomplishment

school and town with electric lights, although subject to flickering and a bit erratic, was a momentous improvement.⁹

Professor A.J. Greene wrote on August 18, 1915: "There is a new experience for the boys. The electric plants are in operation, and they have electric lights for the first time. The little town of Boone is all ablaze with beautiful lights. This is a new thing for the people in this section. ... The school buildings and the town of Boone are brilliantly lighted. The electric plant is in, and it adds much to the school." The next day he recorded, "School opens today with the largest attendance in the history of the institution."¹⁰

Former Appalachian State University Archivist Ruth Currie recalled:

> The hardship of those first few years required the pioneering spirit that came to characterize the school. In the rather primitive separate boarding facilities for male and female students, and those for faculty as well, there was no running water or indoor plumbing. In 1915, electricity and steam brought welcome changes. Occupants, however, found the new Lovill Home and Newland Hall dormitories cold even with the much-touted steam heat, since the Doughertys taught by example a frugality with the school's meager resources. Electricity must be reserved for evening; no need to compete with sunlight through the daytime hours.¹¹

A female high school student at Appalachian recalled when a new girls dormitory was constructed: "The students were excited about the modern conveniences

Wooden scaffolding on the south fork of the New River headwaters showing construction of the first New River Light and Power hydro-electric dam. Electricity arrived at the Appalachian campus, and six homes in Boone, in August of 1915 (Doris Stam Collection, University Archives, Special Collections Research Center, Appalachian State University, Boone, North Carolina).

New River Light and Power Company original dam with the rock power house, 1924 *Dew Drop Catalogue* of Appalachian Training School. Several other power plants were built through the years. These plants have been a source of revenue for the college (University Archives, Special Collections Research Center, Appalachian State University, Boone, North Carolina).

they would now have, such as electric lights and steam heat, compared to the oil lamps and coal heat they had used in their old dorm."[12] When winter came, however, the new building didn't meet their expectations.

> We were excited about getting those steam heaters, but about halfway through the winter we just weren't getting any heat. We found out Blanford Dougherty was turning it down because the school couldn't afford the bill. Then we kept thinking about those old stoves and how warm they were. ... I had to practice the piano with my gloves on.[13]

The large building was not "energy efficient," using large quantities of coal and electricity. Originally a 200-horsepower generator was installed at the hydro-electric power plant that put out 100 kilowatts, and later a 600-horsepower generator that put out 500 kilowatts. "Dr. [B.B.] Dougherty would come down to the plant and ask me how many kilowatts we'd put out that morning and how much coal we'd used," remembered employee Ed Culler. "He'd figure on the heel of his shoe and in nothin' flat tell me if we'd made money or not."[14] He was well-known for ciphering on the sole of his shoe.[15]

Teachers and students were continually exhorted to turn the lights off. Ed Culler told of Blan Dougherty coming into the little restroom where Ed shaved every morning:

> "Now Ed, what size light bulb is that?" he asked.
> "A 75 watt," I told him.
> "Ed, you don't need that big bulb in here."
> I told him I needed it to shave by.
> "Well, Ed, you put a 25 watt in there and when you go to shave you put the 75 in and take it out when you're finished," he told me.
> "And that's the truth as I'm living today."[16]

Ed Culler, at left, with workers on the Appalachian State Teachers' College campus outside the New River Light and Power headquarters. Culler was the right-hand worker for the Doughertys at Appalachian from 1913 until his retirement in 1957 (University Archives, Special Collections Research Center, Appalachian State University, Boone, North Carolina).

The 1916 and 1917 *Dew Drop Catalogues* required students to furnish their own light bulbs or pay a fee of 15 cents per month.[17]

A Vacation and a Grandchild Born

There was little leisure for the head of the school. Lillie longed to be with her extended family in Butler, and usually Dauph drove her in the buggy once a year. One year the family had set out in the buggy, Annie recalled, and were a few miles from Boone when Dauph slowed to a stop and, to the great disappointment of Lillie, said, "Lillie, I just can't leave the school."[18]

However, in July 1915, after the first term of summer school ended, Dauph and Lillie took Annie, Barnard, and toddler Edwin to the Baptist Conference Center near Black Mountain. The newspaper trumpeted their return: "Prof. D.D. Dougherty and family, who have spent several weeks at Ridge Crest, are at home again and the outing has doubtless been of very great benefit to them all, especially to the Professor, who has hardly known what the word rest means for several years."[19]

Lester and Clara remained at the house, where a bathroom and another bedroom on the main floor were added in the family's absence.[20] Lester worked 60 hours a week that summer at 10 cents per hour, draying with the wagon and mule or horse team, occasionally making trips as far as 10 miles out.[21]

Clara and Lester's first child—Dauph and Lillie's first grandchild—Emma

Lillie was in her early 40s with her own young boys, when she became a grandmother. Mama and Papa Dougherty were the agreed upon names for the young grandparents. Clara holds her first child, the first grandchild for Lillie and Dauph, flanked by Edwin, in front of Lillie, and Barnard, to the right. Annie stands behind Clara and a cousin is behind Barnard in this photograph from 1916 (Doris Stam Collection, University Archives, Special Collections Research Center, Appalachian State University, Boone, North Carolina).

Lester Brown, son-in-law to Dauph and Lillie Dougherty, stands (top row, far right, closest to the window) with his A.T.S. graduating class of 1916 (Elizabeth Brown Scoggins Collection, University Archives, Special Collections Research Center, Appalachian State University, Boone, North Carolina).

Virginia Brown—was born on August 27, 1915. When they eloped, Clara had been only 16, and Lester 19. Lillie was only 40 years old when she became a grandmother, and had her own two-year-old child. Lillie refused to be called "Grandmaw," but agreed to "Mama and Papa Dougherty."[22] Clara, Lester, and baby Virginia stayed in the Dougherty home until an apartment in Meadow View, the very house where Clara had lived as a toddler and young girl, was ready.

Satie Hunt and Ed Broyhill

Clara and Lester were not the only couple who formed a romantic liaison despite the school's efforts to segregate male and female students. When 15-year-old Satie Hunt arrived on horseback to start high school at Appalachian in 1915, there were no paved roads, and it took Satie and her father two days to cross the mountains from Grandin, North Carolina, near Lenoir, to Boone.[23] Satie recalled for a 1988 interviewer: "Everybody had work. We all had duties. … The dormitory rooms were simple and had to be kept in perfect order, … Everything was white—curtains, bed covers and coverlets—and the rooms had to be swept. Everything was so plain— we weren't allowed to put things up on our walls like students do today."[24]

Before moving to North Carolina, Satie had been educated in Pennsylvania, where she had studied Latin grammar and verse, English, mathematics, piano, and voice. Having learned to read music almost before learning to read English, she was exceptionally talented in this area.

She recalled the Dougherty brothers' strictness about campus rules: "We were sheltered, but you couldn't really blame them for that…. Boys and girls were required to sit on opposite sides of the classroom and were not allowed to talk or pass notes. They were separated outside of class as well; the girls' dorm and boys' dorm were on opposite sides of the campus."[25]

Male students were allowed more freedom to roam.[26] Satie recalled that boys and girls did manage to mingle when changing classes. Once a year the school held a field day when male and female students were allowed to fraternize. "On field day they gave us each a rake and we got to rake leaves. We didn't mind, though, because we got to do it together."[27]

Ed Broyhill, a classmate of Satie Hunt, had left his father's farm in 1913, at the age of 21, to attend Appalachian Training School. Ed had met Satie's father, Hartley Hunt, while Ed was working as a barber in Boone, and he encouraged Hunt to send Satie to Appalachian, where they met in 1914.[28] Ed showed his interest in Satie by offering to sharpen her pencils. Broyhill's biographer wrote:

> Tuition at the school was provided by the State of North Carolina, but the students were required to pay $7.00 a month for room and board. The determined young man traveled 35 miles to the school, mostly on foot, arriving with the grand sum of $5 in his pocket. He was receiving no financial help from his father so, in order to pay for the tuition, he opened his own barber shop in downtown Boone and charged 15 cents for a haircut and 10 cents for a shave. His career as a barber lasted only a few months, but this would not discourage him. He then set up shop on the lower floor of his dormitory and began pressing clothes for students and faculty. This enterprise was not extremely lucrative and at times he was forced to borrow from his older brother, Tom. Ed worked during the summers at various jobs, saving every penny so that he could return to school in the fall.

Ed never received his high school diploma. In 1917, during his fifth and final year at the school, he was drafted. He was never sent overseas, however, because he was diagnosed as tubercular. "While he was recuperating at Walter Reed hospital, he learned his skill which he would later say gained him entrance into the business world—he learned to type. In 1918, Ed was discharged from the army."[29]

In 1918, Satie left Appalachian to attend the North Carolina College for Women, now the University of North Carolina at Greensboro. Before Ed returned home from the army, he stopped in Greensboro to ask Satie to marry him. Seven years after they had met, Ed and Satie were married. Ed entered the furniture-making business in Lenoir with his father and brother and helped build the largest furniture manufacturer in the country (1927–1980).[30] They raised four children, all of whom possessed, according to the family biographer, the Broyhill drive and ambition, and sense of obligation toward the community.[31] The Broyhills have been generous benefactors of Appalachian for decades.

Rowdy Students

Fifty new students had enrolled just before the new year in 1916, and discipline problems arose.[32] Money had been stolen from Professor Greene's room in Newland

Hall that winter, and some young men were disciplined for bad behavior.[33] Professor Greene complained: "Some boys are boisterous and rude.... There are many boys who take a special delight in teasing and annoying other boys. No elevation of character can come from such practice. Often, I get disappointed in my work with students. They are indolent and do not care whether they do their work or not. It is sad to see so much valuable time wasted. There are but few students who work unless they are held strictly responsible for it."[34]

Prolonged bad weather did not improve the mood on campus. In January there had been three weeks of rain and fog. "The mud on main street is about one foot deep and looks like that it is ready to flow." Even the mail had trouble getting to Boone because of the mud on the roads leading up the mountain from Lenoir.[35] However, spirits seemed to improve when an evening social was held in the Auditorium at the end of the month. "The young people have a good time. I never have heard so much noise. It continues for 2 hours or longer," Greene commented.[36]

Local citizens complained about public disturbances on the campus, particularly the discharging of pistols. On one such occasion, Professor Blan Dougherty sent a reply to the newspaper, admitting that there had been some shooting, but "less than in years past." He asked eloquently for the citizens' understanding and patience:

> We can imagine how pleasant it is to think how a large student body like this should be controlled, and how a young man, untutored but promising, should be transformed at once into a polished, refined gentleman, but it takes patience, time, tact, and oftentimes we are doubtful as to the best course to pursue. It would not be difficult for a man on the ground to suggest to a friend how to walk a rope high in the air, but it would be a thousand times more difficult for the man to walk the rope himself.[37]

No commencement exercises were held in 1916 until July. Commenting that Professor D.D. Dougherty had high standards and would not simply pass a student who had not done the proper work. Lester Brown, who graduated in July of 1916, noted that he had seen diplomas which his father-in-law, Dauph, had refused to sign.[38]

Summer Terms and State Textbook Commission

Long and tedious faculty meetings were held in the fall of 1915 to discuss improvements for the school. The next spring faculty met with trustees and they jointly developed a list of 14 possible improvements: (1) more athletics; (2) an Appalachian press; (3) manual training and agriculture departments; (4) a "continuous" school; (5) a better preparatory department; (6) more teacher training; (7) rules for the superintendent, principal, and teachers; (8) a canning factory; (9) a systematic plan for development of the school; (10) better equipment in art; (11) uniforms for the girls; (12) departments with heads and tutors; (13) milk and better gardens; (14) more religious training.[39]

Dauph did not normally teach during the summer sessions, which were run by Blan, but in the summer of 1916 Blan was in Raleigh meeting with the State Textbook Commission, to which he had been appointed by Governor Locke Craig.[40]

Forty textbook companies submitted bids, and the summer was spent reviewing the options. Again, Blan was the public representative of the school in state-level meetings, while Dauph remained in Boone and oversaw the summer school in Blan's absence. Blan was gaining a state-wide reputation.

Cultural Life: Revivals and Faculty Club Meetings

Boone's Baptist Church sponsored a series of revival services each spring. In 1916, the Rev. Rufus Bradshaw, by this time well established as a preacher in Hickory, drew unusually large crowds to the meetings. "A preacher of force and ability preaches.... The church is packed to suffocating. ... The people come from many miles to hear Mr. Bradshaw. You rarely see so many people at preaching. ...[Bradshaw] made a very eloquent plea for us to lead better lives. ... At night I attend church at the Courthouse ... the people are in great expectation...."[41]

As Principal, Dauph encouraged other faculty to read, and suggested materials for discussion. Professor Dauph Dougherty was a life-long learner and reader, particularly periodicals and professional publications. According to his son-in-law, Dauph's days were so full that he did most of his reading in bed at night.[42]

A teachers' club was organized, which met on Saturday nights, sometimes in the Doughertys' home. The programs were varied, but generally there was discussion of a literary nature, singing, recitations, and talks, and a two-course meal prepared by Lillie Dougherty. Professor Greene delighted in one evening at the Dougherty home: "In fact, the time is so pleasant it is almost midnight before we are aware. I have never enjoyed an occasion better."[43]

John Preston Arthur's Book and the 1916 Flood

At a spring faculty meeting Dauph Dougherty gave each teacher a copy of John Preston Arthur's *History of Western North Carolina*.[44] A group of citizens, including the Doughertys, had commissioned Arthur, then living in Boone, to write a history of the area. Arthur was impoverished, but a man of sophistication and ability who needed work. *A History of Watauga County, North Carolina, with Sketches of Prominent Families* was the result of this commission.[45]

After the book was finished, Arthur became desperate for income, even seeking manual labor. The livery stable turned him down after seeing his age, his fine clothes, and hands that had never done manual work. Digging potatoes and picking up apples for 50 cents a day was his last income, which was a short-lived employment. Finally, reduced to utter poverty, Mr. Arthur grew despondent, took to his bed, and died within a week. The hotel owner and Lester Brown were with him when he died.[46]

The school attended the burial of Mr. John Preston Arthur in December of 1916, with Training School students as pallbearers. Professor Greene noted the sad occasion: "A crowd of little girls, who were his friends, followed the casket as chief mourners. He had not a relation here to see him put away."[47]

> FACULTY CLUB
>
> The Best Thing in the Current Magazines.
>
> (Meet with Mr. Downum by Invitation)
>
> 8 to 10 P. M.
>
> 1. Mrs. Beatty---Geographic Magazine
> 2. Miss Bridge---Cooking Magazine
> 3. Mr. Brown---The Bookman
> 4. Prof. B. B. Dougherty---The Independent
> 5. Prof. D. D. Dougherty---Atlantic Monthly
> 6. Mr. Downum---Review of Reviews
> 7. Mr. Greene---Outlook
> 8. Mr. Greer---Ladies' Home Journal
> 9. Miss Kincaid---Everybody's
> 10. Miss Matney---Century
> 11. Miss Parsons---Physical Culture
> 12. Miss Reid---Literary Digest
> 13. Miss Stanbury---Musical Messenger
> 14. Mr. Stedman---World's Work
> 15. Miss Stephenson---Illustrated World

A.T.S. Faculty Club reading assignments, c. 1920 (Doris Stam Collection, University Archives, Special Collections Research Center, Appalachian State University, Boone, North Carolina).

Commencement 1916: Celebrations for the Doughertys

Lester Brown graduated from Appalachian with a high school diploma in the class of 1916. Clara gave a "post-graduate recital of instrumental music" in April and a graduate piano recital on July 15 with her cousin Lillie Belle Campbell, as part of the commencement events, but Clara is not named as one of the graduates.⁴⁸ Annie Dougherty was listed with the eighth-graders among the 319 students that school year. Another 237 students, mostly teachers seeking further training, were at Appalachian for only the summer term.⁴⁹

Lillie Shull Dougherty's younger brother, Edgar Shull, had been a widower for several years by this time. While visiting his sister in Boone he had met Miss Rosalee Lackey, the art teacher, and they were married in 1916.

The second term of summer school ended in mid-summer of 1916. Professor Greene mailed his suitcase and started the long walk home to Mabel, near the Tennessee state line north of Boone. The walk took a full day, and left him footsore despite stops along the way to soak his feet in the creek.⁵⁰ Today the journey takes 15 minutes by car.

On July 7, 1916, heavy rains began and lasted 10 days. On one day in Hickory, 13.9 inches of rain were recorded; 10 inches fell in one mountain county in less than 24 hours; and 22.22 inches were recorded in one day by the National Weather Bureau near Grandfather Mountain.⁵¹ All that water came rushing down the mountains, bursting out from underground streams with booming sounds, and causing excessive flooding in Asheville and Charlotte.⁵²

John Preston Arthur contributed significantly to the history of North Carolina with his two books: *Western North Carolina: A History from 1730–1913*, printed in 1914, and *A History of Watauga County North Carolina: With Sketches of Prominent Families*, completed in 1915 at the request of local Boone citizens, including the Doughertys (University Archives, Special Collections Research Center, Appalachian State University, Boone, North Carolina).

The torrential rains and high winds that pounded Watauga County for days during July 1916 were the most severe ever known in the county and caused extreme loss of crops and property. The hydroelectric plant machinery of the New River Light and Power facility was destroyed when water cut around the ends of the dam, even though the dam itself withstood the water pressure from flooding. Power was out for two weeks.⁵³ Thirty-one miles of railroad track from North Wilkesboro to Darby, laid with hopes of extending the final 18 miles from Darby to Boone, were ruined by the rains and abandoned.⁵⁴

Globe Academy, the Doughertys' high school alma mater, and the entire community of Globe were washed away when the Johns River violently overflowed its banks. Globe never recovered and is remembered by very few in the state today.⁵⁵

A flood in 1916 caused major damage in the mountains, completely washing away the Globe community and damaging roads and railroad tracks, as seen in this image from the area near the North Carolina-Tennessee state line west of Boone, 1916 (courtesy Butler Museum, Butler, Tennessee).

Ed Broyhill (in uniform) met his future wife, Satie Hunt (pictured here with her parents), at Appalachian Training School in 1915. Ed was drafted for World War I and never completed high school (courtesy Broyhill descendant Anne Stevens).

World War I draftees with a marching band approaching the train depot in Ashe County. Draftees from Watauga County traveled to a train depot in either Ashe or Caldwell counties, North Carolina. Boone had no train until late 1918 (courtesy Ashe County Historical Society).

Draftees Leave for Camp Jackson

In 1917 "Miss Chessie" Neal observed an ominous sight in nearby Jefferson which left a lasting impression on her:

> When our railroad was at last finished [1915], we went to see the first train arrive…. There were very few motorcars then. Most of the people rode horseback, and buggies, and walked. I drove my trusty little white mare Kitty latched to the phaeton and took my three young children as I wanted them to see what was making history … the next time I took them to the train was when the first draftees left for camp and World War One. That was a sad occasion. Some of the relatives of the draftees were there weeping.[56]

Ed Broyhill, a student at Appalachian Training School, was one of the draftees. He never finished high school. Many young men left the classroom during the pre-war and war years, and many did not return. Those who did return looked forward to peaceful years before them.

19

Changes Come with World War, the Flu Pandemic, and Tweetsie Railroad (1917–1919)

War on the Horizon

War in Europe had been raging since 1914, and the possibility of the United States' participation loomed as the year 1917 began. On April 7, President Woodrow Wilson and the U.S. declared war on Germany and entered World War I. Although many new students had joined the school in January, the war and the Spanish Influenza epidemic would take a toll on enrollment and attendance at A.T.S. for the next two years.[1]

"These are such perilous times that people are thinking about something else besides school," wrote a teacher at Appalachian later that spring. "Many boys are expecting to be called into the army, others are working at home in order to make a great supply of food. We are in this war...."[2]

Before the declaration of war, Dauph and Blan had prepared the biennial report for the 1917 Legislature. Reporting the largest enrollment in the school's history, 556 students in 1916, this and other facts about the school facilities and use of state funds made a positive impression.[3] As was his practice, Blan stayed at the Raleigh Hotel during the legislative session, mixing and mingling with the legislators. Appalachian was appropriated $40,000 for support and maintenance and $50,000 for permanent improvements for the biennium.[4] There would be funds to build a new dormitory for boys, as well as much-needed other improvements.

World War I soldier from Butler, Tennessee, name unknown (courtesy Butler Museum, Butler, Tennessee).

When the summer term opened on May 30, the focus quickly turned to fears about the war. A program on June 4 in the school auditorium "for the encouragement of the boys who must register for military service tomorrow" featured an opening prayer, the school choir singing "Onward Christian Soldiers" and "Columbia the Gem of the Ocean."[5] Four messages were given: "Our Christian Duty," "Our Patriotic Duty," "Women's Duty in the War," and "Why we are Fighting."[6]

A Victrola, but No Dancing

Dauph's purchase of a wind-up Victrola record player and classical music records for the college brought a welcome distraction from the ever-present concerns about the war. Hearing an orchestra for the first time, even from a machine, was magical.[7] Between sessions at the school, Dauph took the Victrola home for the family to enjoy.[8] As staunch Baptists opposed to dancing, there were no dance tunes for the record player; dancing was strictly forbidden on campus until the mid-forties. However, some managed to sneak over to the Critcher Hotel (originally the Coffey Hotel) where dancing was available any afternoon.[9]

Organized outings and walks also provided relief from the heaviness of war news. W.W. Stedman joined the faculty in 1917 to teach Mathematics, but his outstanding contribution to A.T.S. was the many sports activities and hikes he sponsored.

That summer Dauph and Professor Stedman attended summer school in Raleigh

The Critcher Hotel, on the corner of Depot and King streets, was quite busy until after World War I. During the Depression, there were few guests and little money was available for upkeep. When the Daniel Boone Hotel opened on May 16, 1925, it took much of the business away from the Critcher Hotel, which soon failed and was torn down in 1935 (University Archives, Special Collections Research Center, Appalachian State University, Boone, North Carolina).

Prof. Stedman with the A.T.S. student outing club on a hiking trip. Stedman was involved with several athletic teams (University Archives, Special Collections Research Center, Appalachian State University, Boone, North Carolina).

at the A & E College (NC State University),[10] where they were introduced to better ways Appalachian's farms could support the school.[11] Lillie had her hands full at home. Annie was already 15, studying art, and contemplating becoming a teacher. Barnard, age eight, and Edwin, age five, were active young boys.

Dauph sent loving letters to his wife and children while he was in Raleigh. To Lillie he wrote about visiting A & E College's farms; to Annie he wrote about the girls he saw studying to be teachers, and encouraged her to help her mother and behave well; to Barnard he described the cotton and tobacco plants he had seen and how cigarettes were made; and to Edwin he wrote of seeing little schoolboys learning to play games, sing songs, and read; about seeing young calves being fed milk from a bucket; and urged him to be good to the other children.[12]

His grandchildren—Virginia, age two, and Pauline, who had been born in April—were often at the Dougherty family home. The Sherwood cousins, children of Lillie's deceased sister Nettie, also stayed with the Doughertys for extended periods. In early August, Lillie's sister Vinnie (Victoria) died in a Philadelphia hospital, leaving her husband and one young son. Grieving the loss of yet another younger sister, Lillie did what she could to care for her motherless nieces and nephews.[13]

New Buildings and Landscape Improvements

The fall term of the school opened in September, noticeably affected by the war. Professor Greene wrote in his diary: "There are hardly so many boys. Many of our students have been called into the army."[14] The entire school attended a patriotic rally held at the courthouse "in honor of the boys who are soon to go into the training camps," with marching bands and patriotic songs sung by students of the school. William C. Newland, the original sponsor of the bill that founded the school, gave a speech, followed by a community dinner. An address by Romulus Z. Linney, and music by the Blowing Rock Band, with Fife and Drum, drew the evening to a close. Despite the rousing music, the mood was described as sober.[15]

Even in the context of a world war, Blan tried to spread optimism about the school, where students and teachers could "rejoice in the amount and in the excellency of their work. ...where each one ... may realize that he is the equal not the superior of his fellows." He spoke of a vision for "an institution where health is preserved, economy taught, honor developed, and morality and religion encouraged; an institution dedicated to mountain homes, to the rebuilding of mountain schools."[16]

The previous fall, public traffic had been excluded from the campus because of damage to drives and the nuisance of public visitors.[17] In September 1917, a landscape architect from Knoxville was hired to make suggestions for how the campus grounds could be improved. "New Hall" for boys, a dormitory, was under construction.[18] It would be named Justice Hall. The generalized term "New Hall" was also the original name of the first brick women's dorm (1915), which was later designated as "White Hall," and finally "Lovill Hall."[19]

June Davenport, an African American from Lenoir, oversaw the molding and burning of the thousands of bricks used in this new dorm, later named Justice Hall. The first bricks were laid by trustees, teachers, and friends of the school on October 1, each having written their initials on the back of a brick.[20]

A boys' gym was completed in 1917 and in November, with the first basketball match against another school, the gym officially opened. Although it was called the "Arts and Crafts Building," its main function was as a gymnasium. The second story of the wooden 40-foot by 60-foot building housed four rooms used for manual training for men, what would later be known as "shop" in high school curricula. Later school catalogues indicate that women also used the gymnasium, but at different times than the men.[21]

War Savings Stamps and an Ideal for Appalachian

The Doughertys, the whole school, and the town participated in the war effort. As the appointed Watauga County Food Commissioner, Dauph headed the collection of food for the war effort.[22] The school became a center for the War Savings Stamps Campaign, with Blan Dougherty as campaign chairman for the county.[23] Chapel exercises were held to honor the boys in the war training camps.[24] Everyone had a friend or family member involved in the war.

In late March 1918 the courthouse was again packed to capacity for a patriotic meeting of Watauga County citizens, at which Dauph Dougherty gave a slide-show lecture about the history of the flag and "patriotic songs ... were sung with a great deal of life and enthusiasm."[25] In May townspeople gave a play in the school auditorium for the benefit of the Red Cross.[26] In June the school lined up on the campus and marched to the courthouse where they met with the townspeople for the purpose of selling War Savings Stamps, accompanied by patriotic speeches and songs.[27] Dauph and Lillie each bought $1,000 in War Savings Stamps to benefit the school loan fund, which was a very large and sacrificial amount.[28] During the summer term, the Doughertys and the Training School hosted a Fourth of July event, at which the town's residents were invited to campus for dinner, patriotic skits by students, and a social mingling of the school and town.[29]

As the fall 1918 term began, the effects of the war were still felt in the noticeably smaller number of male students, as well as economic strain.[30] "The high cost of living and the new changes in the law make it very hard for any school to exist. There are only a few boys. In the past we usually had a large number of boys, but the war is keeping them away."[31] Its effects cut even deeper when four Appalachian professors registered for military service.[32]

A Spoof on Bachelor B.B. Dougherty and Other Programs

In July the town gathered for what must surely have been an evening full of laughter, and a total diversion from the war. Professor Greene recorded the event, no doubt smiling as he noted: "At eight o'clock this evening the school and a few town people meet in the auditorium for a General Social and a very short program which proved to be the supposed 'Life of B.B. Dougherty.' Mr. James Farthing played the part of the bachelor and several girls took the parts of the bachelor's girl, Miss Anna Mae Shipley being the bride. Miss Robertson sang as the different girls came in. Very pleasant evening but the Supt looked a little cross."[33]

French Independence Day, July 14, was celebrated in Boone with an address given to a nearly full auditorium by "Maj. Du Pont, a native Frenchman, who has been at the front, was wounded and is now helping train Americans." All were hoping and praying for an end of the war.[34] The war figured again in the summer graduation events, where the speaker exhorted the audience to enlist "in the war against indifference, ignorance, filth & disease, graft & corruption, and sin."[35]

Spanish Flu Pandemic

Dr. Henry Baker Perry, a Watauga Academy graduate with degrees from the University of North Carolina and North Carolina Medical College, established his medical practice in Valle Crucis in 1905 from the Taylor-Mast Store, which had added a room to its building for his sleeping quarters. When not engaged in treating patients, Dr. Perry worked at the store and took his meals across the road at the Taylor house, which was full of boarders in summer. If there was an illness or emergency in the community, a family member came to the store to "fetch" the doctor. Dr. Perry rode his horse all over the remote hollers and mountains to provide medical care.[36]

During the winter of 1916–17, Dr. Perry traveled weekly by horseback between Boone and Valle Crucis to examine young men for the draft.[37] As soldiers returned from the war to their home countries they brought the Spanish Flu, creating the first world pandemic. Mrs. Perry later wrote about her husband, whom she called H.B., working through the epidemic:

> H.B. was spared and ministered to hundreds through the hills and mountains, many of whom recovered, and many who did not.
>
> The epidemic in 1918–1919 was a time that required skill and physical strength. I remember a man coming to the house and saying, "Please Doctor, come! Everybody in our holler has them flu's."
>
> H.B.'s one precaution against catching the flu was to smoke a cigar while he was ministering to the patient. This worked, until the third year I believe, he was called to see a patient, and not suspecting flu, failed to light his cigar. This time he caught it and so did the family.
>
> The "Flu Flyer," also called a Skeeter, which was a stripped down Ford chassis with a seat and an 18 gallon gas tank, was used to visit patients. This contraption could usually manage to get through the mud, the creeks or climb the mountains, but help was needed when it slipped off the road, which happened at least once, and a rail was used to help get it back on the road.
>
> [An older boy] was carried along to help push or right the car on the road, and to crank the thing, for this was a feat that called for strength. This could also cause a broken arm when the coughing machine backfired.

After consulting with his father-in-law, Dauph Dougherty, Lester Brown accepted a six-month stint teaching in the public schools outside Raleigh in January of 1918. When that proved disappointing, Lester and Clara returned to Boone, and Clara joined the summer school faculty to teach music for a small income. Lester, who did not qualify for the war draft, continued to do odd jobs on the campus until he got a position as a railway postal clerk in Washington, D.C.[38] After a few weeks of loading heavy mail bags and lodging on a cot among hundreds at the Union Station YMCA, he caught the Spanish Flu.

Lester alerted the family to his illness, took the train to Lenoir, and rode up the mountain with the mail carrier in his car. For three weeks Lester had barely enough strength to lift his arm. Soon Clara, who was with him in their little campus cottage, became ill, suffered a miscarriage, and almost died. Lester remembered "how they watched through the little window, longing to see even a dog pass by. It was three weeks before they saw anybody except Papa Dougherty [who left food at the door] and the family doctor. After what seemed ages, they were strong enough to have the children brought home and to care for them."[39]

From September to November of 1918 the flu epidemic killed more than 13,000 North Carolinians, including Edward Kidder Graham, president of the University of North Carolina.[40] Almost one in four people in the state was sick with the flu. Nearly one-third of the world's population was infected.[41] When Appalachian students became ill, the school was quarantined.[42] In Lenoir health officials were forced to quarantine the whole city and county. No schools, movies, church services, Sunday schools, fairs, or public gatherings were permitted for a period of 14 days, later extended to 21 days.[43] A Butler, Tennessee, resident traveling to Baltimore, Maryland, in 1918 on business, told of "seeing train cars filled with coffins, and of how the coffins of the flu victims were stacked like lumber on every station platform."[44]

Tweetsie passes Appalachian Training School, c. 1920, with Howard's Knob in the distance. Tweetsie was a narrow-gauge train, part of the East Tennessee & Western North Carolina Railway (ET&WNC) which extended to Boone from Shulls Mill, a lumber boom-town seven miles to the south on the Watauga River. Its tracks were three feet wide rather than a standard four feet, eight inches. "Her locomotives and cars were smaller than standard cousins. She looked for all the world like a burro," wrote E.T. Campbell, "when sized against the standard horses. But, no Sissy, this train. With locomotives starting at near 50 tons, she was tough, and ideally suited to the limited right of way, to the narrow tunnels and cliff hugging mountainsides she ran through and around, up 4% grades and around 32% curves" (*Tweetsie Tales* 2) (University Communications Records, University Archives, Special Collections Research Center, Appalachian State University, Boone, North Carolina).

End of World War I: Boone Celebrates

September ended with North Carolina troops in the Army's 30th division taking part in a decisive breakthrough of German lines in France.[45] Hope was high for an end to fighting, but the following week's newspaper warned, "The War Is Not Over." Allies were fixing terms for a peace treaty which might take a few weeks to finalize. Then, the Germans might turn down the treaty and continue the war. The newspaper issue included letters from Wataugans on the front lines in France.[46]

To the relief of everyone, an Armistice between Germany and the allies was signed on November 11, 1918, ending World War I. The campus celebrated with a parade and Chapel service.[47]

Tweetsie: The Train Finally Arrives

The Town had another big reason to celebrate—the arrival of the railroad to Boone, familiarly called Tweetsie. After more than two decades of anticipation and failed attempts from the east and center of the state, the train tracks finally reached

19. Changes Come with World War

Looking west toward the train depot in Boone, North Carolina, c. 1940, before the flood that caused severe damage in the mountains. "In addition to lumber, Tweetsie hauled pulp wood for processing into paper, certain woods and bark for tanning leather and fabric. Oak, chestnut, white pine, ash, balsam, maple, poplar and hemlock went out. Rhododendrons and laurel found a market. Wreaths and garlands made from evergreens found favor for use as holiday decorations.... Brick and cement and crushed stone came in, livestock and cabbages and potatoes went out. And Friday, said Clyde Simerly, was 'chicken day.' 'We'd have eight to ten carloads of coops full of chickens going out,' he said. 'In came fertilizer, salt and sugar and flour, even whiskey'" (E.T. Campbell, *Tweetsie Tales*, 54) (courtesy Reba Smith Moretz).

Boone from Shulls Mill in the west as an extension of the East Tennessee and Western North Carolina Railway. Construction of the link from Tennessee through Linville, North Carolina, was completed late in 1918, signaling an end to arduous travel by wagon over often impassable roads. As the mayor of Banner Elk put it on the celebratory opening day, "Before the arrival of the railroad the only way a person could get to Boone was to be born there."[48]

When the Linville River Railway reached Boone, progress came with it in the form of construction supplies for the "Watch Boone Grow" campaign, which local businessmen had developed and had begun to promote.[49] One resident recalled: "I remember when they first began to put gravel on the streets at the close of World War One, because I helped haul and lay that gravel. ... The gravel came from the cranberry ore mines in Avery County. They shipped it here on the Tweetsie railroad."[50]

From 1830, the railroad had been "regarded as the substitute for the improvement of public roads." North Carolina saw the railroad as "a promise of release from its ancient bondage in mud." It was not until the automobile became a competitor to the train that the people began to "clamor for good roads as a pressing necessity."[51] The Watauga County roads were still so poorly graded in 1918, so muddy in wet weather, so full of ruts and holes in dry weather, that the train brought new life and finally enabled Boone's commerce and economy to grow. Farmers began shipping their produce, and freight was brought in regularly. "She hauled coal and fertilizer and crushed stone and bricks and bolts of cloth in, and herbs, cabbages, potatoes, timber and lumber out."[52]

Tweetsie had a trestle by the college's power plant and "they dropped coal down the trestle to concrete and they'd wheelbarrow it and stoke it into boilers at the plant," recalled Shuford C. Edmisten.[53] The plant was able to accumulate enough coal to last the whole winter.[54]

Passenger service between Shulls Mill and Boone began on January 2, 1919, and the first real passenger train arrived on May 9, 1919. Highways were soon to compete with the railroad transporting passengers and freight, but business was booming over the tracks in 1919.[55] The potential for development included the anticipated tourist industry. The school joined hands with the town officials to promote the growth of Boone.[56]

In about 1917 Dauph and Blan together had bought a new Ford automobile. A student boarder and helper living in the Dougherty home recalled:

> It was an old fashioned car. You had to crank it. If I'm not mistaken, it had curtains instead of windows. ... Everybody was thrilled to death when we went for a ride in that car. You had to learn yourself them days to drive it. They showed him a little bit about it, you'd even run them into a bank to stop. There was no traffic like now to get [you] killed.[57]

After some months Blan began taking driving lessons but never mastered driving. To the relief of his friends and family, Blan would ask someone else to drive him places, or he rode the bus, which became his choice of transportation for many years.[58] Boone had a Ford dealership by 1920, but one of the owners, who lived in Valle Crucis, rode a horse from Valle Crucis to Boone in bad weather and bad road conditions to sell cars.[59]

Soldiers Return Home

Chapel topics at the school in January and February often focused on the issues in the world: peace, the Russian Revolution, prohibition, women's suffrage, and issues facing returning soldiers. To save coal, heating was used sparingly.[60]

As servicemen returned and resumed their studies, enrollment began to rebound.[61] For each soldier who died in the war, a tree was to be planted on campus.[62] Watauga County celebrated the end of the war and the return of its soldiers on July 4, 1919, with a school holiday, parade, speeches, and picnic. The crowd was estimated to number 5,000 to 7,000 people.[63] The Tweetsie Railroad's new passenger service added to the excitement.

Change came to North Carolina after World War I, when 15,000 men and women in uniform returned home to the state from distant places bringing new ideas. "Military service gave many of these people new skills and broadened their perspectives, and numbers of them lost old prejudices. Their return contributed significantly to the blunting of class lines in the state...."[64]

As the November 1918 Armistice ended the warfare, it also presented new problems for the state Teachers Assembly. Soldiers did not want to return to low-income jobs like teaching. The war had disrupted the nation's teaching corps. The president of East Carolina "estimated that 180,000 teachers over the nation had left school

A large crowd on the A.T.S. campus celebrating the return of soldiers and the end of war, July 4, 1919. Background: Watauga Academy building front porch (courtesy H.L. and Gladys Coffey Collection, Digital Watauga Project).

rooms for more profitable employment."[65] This problem would affect the structure and organization of Appalachian Training School in major ways.

In 1919 North Carolina was the second most industrialized state in the South, with an output of a billion dollars per year. The state's top industrial goods were textiles, tobacco products, and furniture. The 19th amendment of the U.S. Constitution, giving women the right to vote, was ratified in August 1919, despite opposition from North Carolina legislators.[66] Times were changing.

Temperance on the Campus: In Loco Parentis

The 18th amendment to the U.S. Constitution passed Congress in January 1919, enacting a national prohibition of alcoholic beverages.[67] Dauph had long been a passionate proponent of temperance and was surrounded by friends and mentors of the same persuasion. In high school, Bob Moore and Dauph had debated the issue, both arguing for prohibition.[68] Dauph's college friend, Rufus Bradshaw, who became a well-known preacher and was described as "[p]ure in life and chaste in demeanor, he is yet the stern and uncompromising enemy of evil in every form, especially of the liquor evil."[69] Professor J.F. Spainhour and Robert L. Patton, who had taught Dauph and Blan when they were younger, were also determined lifelong temperance men.

Testifying to the Dougherty brothers' avoidance of cultural ills, Spainhour declared: "It has been said that neither of them ever took a chew of tobacco, ever smoked a pipe, cigar, or cigarette, ever took a drink of whiskey, or ever swore an oath."[70] B.B. Dougherty refused to patronize a store in Wilkesboro that sold beer.[71]

The founders of Crossnore School continually fought moonshiners in Crossnore, south of Boone. "In making our fight for better school facilities and better teaching," Dr. Mary Martin Sloop said, "I pointed out that education and liquor just didn't go along together.... I've fought liquor with every means I could devise.... I should make it clear that it was so much easier to make corn into whiskey and sell it to people who would come up here for it than to attempt to haul the corn itself off to market."[72]

Overseeing the student population *in loco parentis* was a responsibility the Doughertys took very seriously. No drinking was allowed on campus by students, teachers, or workers, as was the rule at all schools of the era. Radford College, a teacher training school in Virginia, was even more strict than Appalachian, according to one student who had attended both schools.[73]

Ed Culler, long-term campus employee, beginning in 1913, related the following story about how Dauph dealt with an employee who admitted to having drunk on the weekend:

> They were strict back in those days. I remember one day when me and this other man were unloading coal off of Tweetsie.....
>
> I saw Professor Dauph comin' down the road toward us. I knew he was mad; He was walking with hands on his hips with his coat flappin' around him.....
>
> He came up to the man that was helping me and said, "I heard you got drunk this weekend." "Sure did," the man said. "Well, here's your paycheck. Now just go on. I can't have that kind of going on with these students around."
>
> "You want me to finish doing this?" the man asked. "No, you just get going. Ed can finish this. If you ever think you can quit that kind of thing, you come back and see me, and I don't care how many men I got workin' I'll find you a job," Professor Dauph said.[74]

Flu Again, Memorial Trees for Fallen Soldiers, More Joys and Sorrows

Another health scare erupted the second week of February 1920, when several cases of influenza were reported in the school. Miss McCarney, a trained nurse from the Health Department, was instructing students in caring for the sick, but had come down with the flu herself.[75] Because of the illness on campus, the town authorities quarantined the school. Mid–March brought heavy snow, more sickness, and postponement of Superior Court. Classes were interrupted by outbreaks of influenza, recorded Professor Greene, "...many being sick with it and most not sick being required to wait on the sick. A truly heroic spirit is being shown by many of the students, going where they can be of help to the sick even at the risk of contracting the disease. There are some noted examples of these, some going to wait on poor families where they do not hope for any remuneration other than to be of help to the needy—a noble spirit indeed."[76]

Dauph had gathered the names of those from Watauga County who had died in camps and in France during the war, and prepared to honor them by planting memorial trees at marked sites on the campus. Plans for a special ceremony had to be abandoned because of the amount of illness.[77]

Diphtheria struck and took the life of Dauph and Lillie's grandchild Pauline, age three, in August 1920. Clara and Lester Brown were distraught to lose their second-born child, and feared losing Virginia, their first-born, as well. Dauph and Lillie's youngest son, Edwin, age seven, and Virginia, now five years old, contracted the disease at the same time as Pauline. Being older helped them to survive. Remembrances of their three-year-old, Disco, dying from diphtheria (membranous croup) in 1909, filled the minds of Dauph and Lillie. It was hard to see another child, a beloved grandchild this time, die.

Clara was seven months pregnant when Pauline died. A third girl was born on October 13, 1920, named for Clara's mother.[78] Baby Lillie Alene Brown moved with the grieving family into Justice Hall men's dormitory, basically next door to the Dougherty home, where Clara and Lester Brown lived and worked for four years. Dauph and Lillie loved having the little girls in and out of their house.

Dauph suggested that Lester be trained to supervise the manual training department of Appalachian, which had a temporary head at that time. During the summer of 1919, Lester attended Eastern Kentucky State Normal in Richmond, Kentucky. During the summer of 1920 Dauph arranged for him to attend Bradley Polytechnic Institute in Peoria, Illinois. Dauph wanted to help Lester and Clara gain the financial ability to care for their growing family. With the skills he acquired, adding to what he had learned growing up on a farm, Lester was able to join the faculty at Appalachian.

In addition to teaching, Lester had oversight of the students in this male dormitory, while Clara worked as matron of Justice Hall. The fact that neither Lester nor Clara had any college education remained a disappointment to Dauph and Lillie, yet their loving support and respect for their daughter and her husband never wavered. Life had taken several unexpected turns for Dauph and Lillie. Yet even more unforeseen challenges and changes lay ahead for the school and the family.

20

The State Mandates a Major Reorganization: No Longer a Regional High School (1920–1924)

The State Mandates a Major Reorganization

In 1917 Governor Thomas W. Bickett ordered a thorough investigation of the entire North Carolina public school system. However, World War I intervened, and it was not until 1920 that the North Carolina Educational Commission completed its study, which revealed a crisis in education and a major shortage of teachers.[1] As a result, the Commission initiated changes that would alter Appalachian Training School in major ways.[2]

"The state government discovered physical deficiencies [in schoolhouse structures] and an appalling illiteracy in its young men." More high schools were needed to remedy statewide illiteracy. The General Assembly of 1919 and the special session of 1920 addressed the urgent need for well-qualified teachers by passing legislation that set teacher certification standards and standardized the scale of teachers' salaries, which depended on the level of each teacher's academic achievement in higher education.[3] Although salaries were increased and better-prepared teachers were guaranteed higher salaries, 403 public schools were closed during the 1919–1920 school year for lack of teachers.[4]

As had been clear to the Doughertys when they founded Watauga Academy and Appalachian, the need to train teachers was paramount. "About 2,000 new white elementary teachers and 350 Negro teachers were needed in North Carolina annually," the Educational Commission's report stated. A major cause for the teacher shortage was lack of adequate training facilities, especially for elementary teachers.[5] Accordingly, the Commission recommended that existing state-supported teacher training schools be enlarged, strengthened, and reorganized to concentrate on teacher training.

For the teacher training schools in Cullowhee and Boone, the report meant major changes. No more were they to function as regional high schools with incidental teacher training programs. They were to move toward omitting high school instruction entirely and focus on training elementary teachers for the public schools. The University in Chapel Hill and North Carolina College for Women in Greensboro would provide stronger courses for training high school teachers, as well as

The Second Administration Building, completed in 1925, had an auditorium seating capacity of more than 1,000. Restrooms, a new phenomenon at the time, were provided "for the female teachers" inside the building. Exterior doors were clearly marked with separate women's and men's entrances. This building allowed for the school's expansion to a two-year junior college (Appalachian State Normal School) in 1925, and a dedicated four-year college (Appalachian State Teachers College) in 1929. A fire, possibly arson, destroyed the building and contents, with a loss of valuable documents on December 29, 1966 (*The Dew Drop*, Volume XXI, No. 3 [May 1924], University Archives, Special Collections Research Center, Appalachian State University, Boone, North Carolina).

specialized courses, such as music and physical education. East Carolina Teachers Training School in Greenville was to be elevated to a four-year college qualified to train high school teachers.[6]

The Commission judged that neither Boone nor Cullowhee functioned at the level of a standard high school, and that any students who graduated from a standard four-year high school should attend Chapel Hill, Greensboro, or Greenville for college. Only students who had graduated from non-standard high schools should be admitted to the new normal classes to be offered at Boone and Cullowhee because, in the Commission's assessment, "only three counties in the western part of the state, Cherokee, Buncombe, and Haywood, have standard high schools."[7] Both Appalachian and Cullowhee were "well located to serve their respective sections, ... and if properly developed and equipped should graduate at least 100 elementary teachers a year."[8]

State Superintendent Brooks Receives Faculty Complaints

Soon after the North Carolina Educational Commission report was made public, State Superintendent of Public Instruction Eugene C. Brooks visited Boone not only to help the county teachers, but also to "look after the interests of the Training School with a view to re-organizing and raising the standard of the school."[9]

Brooks praised the fiscal management of Appalachian Training School, which, he said, had "gotten more for the money spent, than any school in the country." It was Brooks' opinion that "this institution must become a standard State Normal College open to the people who want higher education, as well as to the teachers." He also recommended that "[t]he departments of Science, Pedagogy, Manual Training, Domestic Science, Agriculture, and Business should be enlarged so that the school might rank with the best institutions of the country."[10]

During Dr. Brooks' visit to ATS he asked that faculty submit suggestions about the school to him. One respected, long-term professor wrote confidentially to Superintendent Brooks, commenting on a number of issues he saw as detrimental to the school. First, he noted that Blan, as superintendent, and Dauph, as Principal, disagreed on most policy issues regarding the school, and that Dauph was "by far the more capable man so far as school room work and management are concerned." Second, he faulted Blan for refusing to institute "a definite policy as to entrance, management, discipline, graduation, curriculum, and other things." Third, he complained that Blan did not hold faculty meetings or solicit input from the faculty, refused to delegate any responsibility, and insisted on handling all details himself without the faculty's knowledge, with the result that many matters were neglected because the duties were too much for a single person. Fourth, he complained that the superintendent allowed insufficient heat in the girls' dorm for their comfort.

The professor also noted that faculty salaries seemed to be set at Blan's sole discretion; that even the trustees did not know the faculty's salaries; that they were not paid regularly, and not at all until "each teacher hunts up the Superintendent each and every time and asks for it." He reported that Blan tried to bargain with the teachers individually to reduce their pay, so that even some of the best teachers were "not getting more than that set by the state for the highest public school salaries."[11] Finally, he reported that the grounds and buildings were neglected, and the farms were too expensive because of the way they were managed.

Brooks' response, if any, is not documented; however, Superintendent Dougherty was in Raleigh in late November of 1920 to discuss the school's needs with the Budget Commission, and the Appalachian trustees met in Boone with State Superintendent Brooks at the end of the month.

1921: Big Changes and Transitions at Appalachian

In January of 1921 the General Assembly made Appalachian Training School a normal school, equated with a junior college, but its name remained the same. Cullowhee Normal and Industrial School was already designated a normal school.[12] The letterhead on Dauph's stationery—*Appalachian Training School: A State Normal, Boone, N.C.*—clarified the status of the school in 1922, but the school's name remained unchanged for several more years, even though it had been reorganized by the state to focus on a "normal department" to train teachers in the "norms" of education.[13]

The State Board of Education was also authorized to organize normal schools in Elizabeth City, Fayetteville, Winston Salem (Slater State Normal School), and Pembroke (Cherokee Indian State Normal School) like the normal schools at Appalachian and Cullowhee, or to change the organization to suit conditions.[14] The Commission feared that local interests might "easily divert small teacher training institutions from the purposes for which they were intended."[15] With the reorganization, these schools were placed under the control of the State Board of Education, which then appointed a seven-member board of trustees for each school.[16]

D.D. Dougherty Leaves the Classroom; B.B. Dougherty Becomes President

In February 1921, the General Assembly approved $50,000 to enable ATS to make the transition to a normal school.[17] In May, Appalachian's Board of Trustees met in Boone with Blan and Dauph Dougherty, Superintendent Brooks, and the state's director of teacher training and voted to elect Blan as president and Dauph as treasurer and general manager.[18] Most of the existing faculty members of the faculty were retained, a number of new teachers were added, and two years of normal work above high school level were provided.[19] Dauph assumed the administrative duties that Blan had failed to address, but unfortunately, this meant he had to stop teaching, at which he excelled.

The General Assembly approved an appropriation of $200,000 for the biennium for permanent enlargement and improvements at Appalachian, and the same amount for Cullowhee. Salaries for Appalachian's president and teachers were significantly increased.[20] Members of the state Department of Public Instruction and the Building Commission surveyed the existing plant at Appalachian, and planned improvements, including a new heating and water system. The old Watauga Academy building received a new roof and a thorough overhaul.[21]

By 1921, the campus contained 40 acres, plus two farms of 200 acres each. The biennial report sent to the legislature listed a horse barn, dairy barn, herd of 28 Holstein cattle, two teams of heavy farm mules, and farm equipment on the Coffey Farm adjacent to campus, in the location of the current football stadium. By conservative estimate, its worth was $500,000, the state having contributed only $72,500.[22] In early April, the state supervisor of teacher training took a detailed inventory of the school's equipment to determine its capabilities and needs to function as a normal school under the state's new plans and approved of the school's equipment and efficiency.[23] The state's appropriations, particularly those later in 1923, represented a substantial investment in the newly reorganized normal school in Boone.[24]

The school had 18 teachers in 1921, with salaries totaling $20,000, compared to the five teachers it had employed in 1903, whose salaries totaled $2,000.[25] The 1921 *Dew Drop Catalogue* claimed that 193 students had graduated to date from Appalachian with high school diplomas. The population of Boone was 500 according to *The Dew Drop*, unchanged since 1917. Its people were described as rural, quiet, and industrious.[26] The catalogue boasted, "The town is lighted by electricity. Improvements are being made on the sidewalks and streets," but actually getting to Boone from the eastern or Piedmont sections of the state was still difficult. Students were

The Watauga Academy building received a new roof and a thorough overhaul in 1921 as part of the state's plans to expand Appalachian into a college-level teacher training school (University Communications Records, University Archives, Special Collections Research Center, Appalachian State University, Boone, North Carolina).

advised to take the train to Lenoir, which required several transfers, and from Lenoir to arrange for automobile transport to Boone.

All of the school's buildings and science laboratories, except for the cottages, had running water and toilets by the summer of 1921, replacing the outhouses that had been the subject of public complaint and a source of disgrace for the school.[27] In November a new water system was installed on campus.[28]

During this time of transition and construction, Dauph, Blan, and Etta Dougherty Greene, who still retained title to some of the property used by the school, sold several pieces of property, including six acres with buildings, to the state for $8,000.[29]

A Normal Department, a Yearbook and the Flu Again

By January 1922 the Normal Department was officially opened with James E. Hillman as Dean. Dean Hillman had undergraduate and master's degrees from

Organized athletic teams and matches with other schools began around 1920. The men's baseball team took the competition seriously. The 1921 *Dew Drop* included this comment: "A very good diamond for baseball is provided for men. Women have a tennis court, a croquet ground and an outside basketball ground. In the Arts and Craft building there is a good gymnasium for the joint use—at different times—of men and women. No games allowed during school hours. No games allowed without consent of the faculty. A teacher is expected to be on the grounds at all times" (University Communications Records, University Archives, Special Collections Research Center, Appalachian State University, Boone, North Carolina).

The 1922 women's basketball team, *The Rhododendron* yearbook. Note that the women are wearing bloomer uniforms. Prof. Greene noted in his diary relating school events: "The faculty meets to discuss the athletic situation. Much talk but no conclusions. There are too many views" ("Greene Diaries," February 16, 1921). "Faculty meets. Everyone seems to be the head of the institution. We have to sacrifice self to uphold the good of all" ("Greene Diaries," January 20, 1921) (*The Rhododendron*, 1922, University Archives, Special Collections Research Center, Appalachian State University, Boone, North Carolina).

Peabody (now the Peabody College of Education and Human Development at Vanderbilt University in Tennessee), and Mary Jarrell, also a graduate of Peabody, was employed as teacher of primary methods.[30]

By the end of January, the senior class had decided for the first time to raise funds, write, prepare, and publish a yearbook, *The Rhododendron*, with two professors as manager and editor in chief. It was dedicated to Manly Blackburn, local hotel and store owner, local leader, a generous supporter and trustee of the school for over 20 years, who had died that spring at the age 63.[31]

Student morale was high, boosted by school basketball games, until the flu hit the campus again in February 1922, and the county health officer quarantined the school for scarlet fever and the flu.[32] Dauph Dougherty's family and Blan Dougherty were ill with the flu.[33] Daughter Annie, the first of Dauph and Lillie's children to go away to college, was a student at Carson-Newman College in Jefferson City, Tennessee, when she heard about the quarantine at Appalachian. The severity of the Spanish Flu epidemic of 1918–1919, and the near death of Clara and Lester, was fresh in everyone's minds. Dauph reassured her that, although there were several cases of flu in the dormitories, they were not serious. He also encouraged her not to care too much for grades. "Grades are often made without much knowledge," he wrote.[34]

20. *The State Mandates a Major Reorganization*   195

The Watauga Literary Society, for men, from the 1922 *Rhododendron* yearbook (University Archives, Special Collections Research Center, Appalachian State University, Boone, North Carolina).

The Calliopean Literary Society, for women, from the 1922 *Rhododendron* yearbook (University Archives, Special Collections Research Center, Appalachian State University, Boone, North Carolina).

The Manual Training class, from the 1922 *Rhododendron* yearbook (University Archives, Special Collections Research Center, Appalachian State University, Boone, North Carolina).

Bobbed Hair for Female Students

By the time Annie Dougherty had graduated from high school, she was allowed to join the bobbed hair craze sweeping the nation.[35] The *Rhododendron* yearbook displays the same change in hair fashions at Appalachian in the 1920s that were sported at similar institutions—"from sedate bun to jaunty bob to carefully coifed 'permanent wave' styles."[36]

Even though female students were beginning to feel emboldened by bobbed hair, many other rules and regulations regarding girls remained strict. Zetta Barker, from Ashe County near the Virginia–North Carolina border, attended a summer session for teachers at Appalachian in the mid-1920s and wrote home to ask her father's permission to have her hair "bobbed." "No. Absolutely NOT," was his answer.[37]

She graduated from Virginia–Carolina High School in 1924, where the commencement speaker was Professor Blan Dougherty. His remarks—"Whatever you plan to be, be the best"—motivated her to continue her education and get a teacher certification. She recalled, "We were from farm families and accustomed to work—hard work—and we knew our parents had made it possible for us to attend high school and wanted us to make the best of our efforts. …[They] instilled ambition and determination in us. Despite the fact that our parents could not afford to send some of us to college, many of us found a way to get started and then work our way through a bachelor's degree."[38]

To qualify for a teacher's certificate at that time, students had to have completed high school, be 18 years of age or older, and be known to be sedate, modestly dressed, and respected in their community.[39] The bar for qualification was being raised beyond the conditions that had been common in remote, rural areas, where teachers in one-room schools were not required to have graduated from high school.[40] At age 18, Zetta completed the training program and was certified to teach elementary school reading and writing.[41] After teaching for one year, she could afford summer sessions at Appalachian Teachers College. Many poor mountain students had to travel far for their teacher training and interrupt their education to earn enough money to continue. One such student at ATS recalled,

Annie Dougherty, second child of Dauph and Lillie Dougherty, with bobbed hair, 1921 *Dew Drop* (*The Dew Drop* [1921], University Archives, Special Collections Research Center, Appalachian State University, Boone, North Carolina).

> When I would run out of money, Dr. B.B. Dougherty would issue me a Teacher's Certificate. I am sure the recording angel overlooked the fact that I was too young to have such certificate. When my school was out where I taught for $20 and $30 per month, I would re-enter Appalachian. I did this until a year of college was added. Dr. Dougherty said I was the first student to register for college work. Taking this work enabled me to finish at Wake Forest in three years.[42]

During the first summer term of 1923 there were 341 students and teachers, and for the second summer term, 155. "These, with the high school students, made an enrollment of 770 from 64 counties. During the 1923–1924 school year a total of 1,097 students from 71 counties were enrolled. The school was no longer an institution only for mountain boys and girls."[43]

D.D. Dougherty's 1923 Editorial, Entertaining, and Another Granddaughter

Dauph Dougherty continued to advocate for improved conditions in mountain schools. In January 1923, he wrote a letter to the editor of the *News and Observer* entitled, "Educational Needs of Children in Rural Sections,"[44] in which he identified two weaknesses in the North Carolina educational system that needed to be addressed by legislators: better schoolhouses and longer terms. First, he was particularly distressed that appropriations neglected the poor children in the state and pleaded for legislators to prioritize the needs of poorer, rural children over those of the colleges and universities. The higher institutions should wait until the poor children have school buildings, he argued.

Second, the length of the school term and the curriculum needed adjustment. In the mountains, as in other rural schools of North Carolina, the school term was only six months, yet the year's curriculum was designed for eight months. Since students were often unable to complete the material in the abbreviated term, they lagged behind their grade level. The disadvantage was compounded because each year teachers in rural schools had to spend time on the material from the end of the previous year, and then attempt to cover the new material for the new grade year. As a principal, Dauph had studied the difficult task set before the rural teachers and urged that the course of study be designed for six-month terms, until the term could be extended to eight months in rural areas. Streamlining the curriculum with less padding, fewer books, and less supplemental work would allow students to complete the grade curriculum within six months, and would also be a great relief to teachers.[45]

The Friday Afternoon Club was a social highlight for the ladies of Boone and drew public attention with a newspaper feature about the entertainment, decorations, and menu provided by Lillie Dougherty and her daughter, Clara Dougherty Brown.[46] In addition to entertaining, Lillie had her two boys to supervise; Edwin was notorious for getting into mischief and sustained a serious head injury in the summer of 1923, from which he ultimately recovered.[47]

Clara and Lester lived in Justice Hall, where Clara served as matron, overseeing the kitchen and dining room. Lester, who headed the Manual Training Department at the school, also supervised the boys living in Justice Hall. Lester and Clara's daughters, Virginia and Lillie Alene, were now six and two, respectively, when another girl, Elizabeth ("Lib"), was born.

1924: Second Administration Building and a New Power Plant

Construction of several major building projects continued in 1924 with state funds, the most substantial of which was the second Administration Building. The new, multi-purpose Administration Building would house all teaching activities and replace the old, overcrowded structures of Watauga Academy and Science Hall. The modern brick and concrete building contained an auditorium comfortably seating more than 1,000 people and furnished with stage equipment.[48] The school boasted of restrooms for female teachers near the auditorium, as well as reading rooms, writing rooms, and bathrooms equipped with showers—a novelty in Boone. The main entrance faced south, so the sun could help melt the winter ice. Separate entrances for male and female students were designated on opposite sides of the building.[49]

The main offices of the school were located on the main floor, where, *The Dew Drop* crowed, "records and other valuable papers will be stored in fireproof vaults. ... The entire building will be heated by steam.... Their stairways will be enclosed in fireproof towers, making them absolutely safe in case of fire."[50]

Despite the fireproof vaults, when tested by a real fire in December 1966, the building and all the documents were destroyed, except a few boxes quickly tossed

Lester and Clara Dougherty Brown worked at Appalachian for several years. Clara helped with music, and together they oversaw the Justice Hall men's dormitory. Lester taught Manual Training before leaving for seminary training in Atlanta (Doris Stam Collection, University Archives, Special Collections Research Center, Appalachian State University, Boone, North Carolina).

out the window.[51] The fire was spread by heavy winds and engulfed the three-story building within a matter of minutes, destroying college records, publications, pictures, and furnishings, as well as the valuable libraries of several administrators and department heads. Only the outer shell remained of the brick structure that had served as the Administration Building for almost a half century.[52]

Funds for a new power plant had been requested from the legislature, who did not consider it urgent until another fire in March 1923, caused by a short circuit from an overworked generator, left the campus in the dark. The campus was forced to revert to oil lamps, and the need for a new plant advanced up the list for special legislative appropriations. Electrical service was disrupted for almost four months, while construction began on a new plant and dam with constant water flow to provide consistent electric current to the campus and community. In 1924, a steam plant and generator were added for additional power, and in 1925 electric home cooking ranges were introduced in Watauga County.[53]

Chapel and Church Requirements

Christian religion continued to be intertwined with school life, as at similar institutions of the period. "Always the school had a religious atmosphere. ... Church attendance was required. Daily chapel periods were given a distinctive religious flavor, opening with Scripture reading and prayer."[54]

Similarly, at Cullowhee, all boarding students were required to attend Sunday school and church services, as well as daily chapel. Card-playing during study hours and on Sundays was prohibited.[55] Cullowhee "stressed the importance of Christian values and serious intent in all aspects of college life. The catalog listed the denomination of each teacher. In addition to requirements for church and Chapel attendance, the president went to considerable lengths to provide Bible study courses on campus."[56]

At East Carolina, "Speakers used Christian themes at their required weekly assemblies to encourage students to aspire."[57] In the late 1920s "Christian themes continued as a part of the college's programs."[58]

Dr. Mary Sloop of Crossnore School explicitly based her views on education on her Christian faith: "I firmly believe that Christian education is the cure for all the ills of this sick world." The school's effort to cultivate conscience and its motto, "Noblesse Oblige," she associated with "conduct in line with all of the Ten Commandments, upon which are based the teachings of Christ."[59]

Dauph Attends Peabody and Sends Lester to Seminary

To equip the school to develop its curriculum and business practices into those of a two-year junior college and normal school, Dauph attended the 1924 Winter quarter at Peabody College for Teachers in Nashville, Tennessee.[60] Beginning in 1924, the Normal Department was put under the direction of a new head, Chapell Wilson, who replaced Professor Hillman when the latter took a new post in state government. Wilson had taught in the summer session of 1922 and joined the faculty in 1923 to teach education and psychology, giving up his pursuit of a doctorate in history at Blan Dougherty's urging for him to stay. As head of the Normal Department, Wilson developed two demonstration schools, Appalachian Elementary and, a few years later, Appalachian High School.[61]

Lester Brown, Clara Dougherty Brown's husband, felt a strong calling to enter the Methodist ministry and to leave Boone and his position teaching Manual Training behind. Blan urged Lester to stay in his position with the prospect of a salary increase, and persuaded him to wait a year. At the end of the year, Blan renewed his pleas that Lester change his mind about entering the ministry, but Lester's conviction remained, and Blan reluctantly gave in.[62]

Dauph advised Lester to get at least one year of training before entering the ministry. and made arrangements for him to attend Candler School of Theology at Emory in Atlanta. Clara remained in Boone as matron of Justice Hall during Lester's year of seminary, with Dauph and Lillie's help to care for the three children.[63]

Dauph's Health Begins to Fail

When Lester was able to visit from Atlanta in late fall of 1924, he found his father-in-law suffering from shortness of breath, which required him to sleep sitting in a chair. Lester and Blan took Dauph to a doctor in Lenoir, who concluded that Dauph had a heart ailment and ordered him to bed. Carefully following the doctor's recommendation, for about a year Dauph directed his work as business manager of the college from his bedroom. Later he was able to return to his regular office and work for several years. The stresses of planning for all the changes at the school, taking on the responsibilities of business manager and treasurer, overseeing the new buildings, curriculum changes, and additional students, took a toll on Dauph's health.

Lillie prevailed upon her sister's granddaughter, Ruth Barker, to take a temporary leave from her job with the Red Cross in Tennessee to work as Dauph's secretary and assistant. Ruth stayed in the Dougherty home with Lillie and Dauph. Within two weeks of arriving, Ruth wrote to her cousin, Annie, who was away at college, that Dauph had improved enough to sit up and give directions.

Ruth later reminisced about Dauph and her duties as his secretary when she first arrived in November 1924. Dauph "paid the bills, ordered the equipment, paid the teacher salaries, and did anything else that had to be done."[64] Despite being upset by a disagreement with Dauph about a new bookkeeping system, Ruth remembered, "He wasn't angry—I never really saw him angry. ... He was a kind man and a gentle man; he was mighty easy to work for."[65]

After a season of cutting back and working from home, Dauph was able to return to work. Just in time, too, for the school was transitioning and changing, yet again.

21

From a Normal School to a Four-Year College (1925–1929)

Appalachian State Normal School and the Death of D.D. Dougherty

Appalachian Training School became Appalachian State Normal School (ASNS) in 1925, with a new charter and a new name given by the legislature.[1] Finally, Appalachian's name reflected its status as a Normal School.[2] Appalachian now offered two years of college-level training and became essentially a junior college, as planned in the 1921 reorganization of state-supported institutions to provide more trained teachers for the public schools.

Although the official Normal Department at Appalachian had been in place from January 1922, the school's name had remained the same, and the majority of its students were high school students for several more years. The school year 1925–1926

Campus snapshot panorama, c. 1926 (Doris Stam Collection, University Archives, Special Collections Research Center, Appalachian State University, Boone, North Carolina).

21. From a Normal School to a Four-Year College

Campus snapshot panorama, c. 1925 (Doris Stam Collection, University Archives, Special Collections Research Center, Appalachian State University, Boone, North Carolina).

saw 245 in the Normal Department, 266 in the High School Department, and 1,025 new students during the summer terms.[3] Phasing out the high school came gradually. The eighth and ninth grades were discontinued after 1926 and were taken over by the county.[4] The total elimination of high school classes came in the spring of 1928.[5]

Graduation from the Normal Department required 96 quarter hours of work, with the prerequisite of a high school degree. "Students who had state certificates were allowed to take the normal work to raise the certificate from the elementary to the primary and grammar grade. Correspondence courses, taught by regular professors, were offered to those without normal school training who desired to prepare themselves for more efficient teaching."[6] Chapell Wilson initiated changes with the new certification exams in mind, which were set by James Hillman as the new director of certification for the state.

Cullowhee Normal and Industrial School (CNIS) was renamed Cullowhee State Normal School (CSNS) in 1925. Neither Cullowhee nor Appalachian could offer a four-year program comparable to that at East Carolina in Greenville for another decade.

East Carolina had been elevated to a four-year college in 1920 to help answer an anticipated demand for teachers with bachelor's degrees. Greenville benefited from transportation connections with the centers of economic and political power in the state. Appalachian and Cullowhee in the western mountains lacked those connections that served the central and eastern parts of the state.

Amid the changing concepts about education in the 1920s, normal training was scorned by some academics at liberal arts colleges. Appalachian was far removed from the ivory towers of academia, as was Cullowhee. Yet the Doughertys embraced their charter: "the central purpose of the Appalachian State Normal School shall be to prepare teachers for the public schools of North Carolina." Likewise, the president of Cullowhee fought the contempt and open scorn from some traditional liberal arts adherents, affirming its focus on teacher training with the motto: "This one thing we do."[7]

Emphasizing the development of character over the priority of curriculum, Blan Dougherty addressed the summer school session in 1927, and "set forth 14 points outlining such training as the Normal [school] should, in his opinion, give the large body of teachers enrolled here [at ASNS]." These functions of a Normal are:

> To know that children are citizens in the making.
> To give the science of teaching.
> To give the art of teaching.
> To develop a judgment as to dress, where and with whom to be.
> To develop a judgment as to what to say, where and to whom to say it.
> To recognize the obligation of the school to the taxpayer.
> To encourage economy and habits of thrift and industry.
> To impress the importance of health habits.
> To inspire one with a willingness to work.
> To train for tactfulness and adaptability.
> To emphasize the importance of teamwork and full cooperation with local, county, and state authorities.
> To emphasize the idea that character and service are the high ideals of life.
> To lead teachers to see that it is what they are, not what they teach, that counts most.[8]

Permanent Endowment Fund

The law that changed the school's official name to Appalachian State Normal School also authorized by the trustees to establish "a permanent endowment fund to be loaned to needy and worthy students." The endowment was to be funded by gifts and donations, as well as by selling excess current from Appalachian's power plant to the people in the community.[9] Blan Dougherty would make the fund a priority, and late in his life was proud to say, "I have raised more money for the Endowment Fund than the state has ever paid me."[10]

The Doughertys had always sought to make education available to any student who truly desired it, regardless of financial status. Countless students benefited from the quiet ways the Doughertys devised to allow needy students to attend high school during the first 30 years of Appalachian's existence, and in later years, college. Blan Dougherty stated his plain and simple goal: "I want to make it so that every boy and girl in this whole region, no matter how poor, can have the opportunity to get a good education, not just the real smart ones but everyone."[11]

Gordon Winkler, who was mayor of Boone for 24 years (1943-1961 and 1969-1975),[12] was making bricks for the Methodist Church building in 1922 after attending high school at Appalachian Training School when Blan Dougherty walked by and asked if he was going to college. Gordon replied that his family had no money to send him. Blan made arrangements for Gordon to receive a scholarship. Many years later Gordon donated the cost equivalent of that scholarship to Appalachian in gratitude for his education. "The college wanted to put his name on the former hospital building, but Gordon said no, and the building was named Founders' Hall at Gordon's insistence."[13]

Another example from the early 1950s was Ned Trivette, whose family, like most Watauga County farming families, had no means to send him to college. His mother, who had earned a teaching certificate at Appalachian Training School, encouraged him to see President Blan Dougherty, who found a way for Ned to attend. Later, as Vice Chancellor of Business Affairs from 1964 to 1990, Trivette oversaw the explosive expansion at Appalachian after the school became part of the North Carolina University system. He remained forever grateful for his education and resulting career, and thereafter "spoke with reverence" about the Doughertys.[14]

Dr. Perry Comes to Boone in 1925

Boone was a town of about 1,100 permanent residents plus about 400 college students in 1925. Tweetsie (the railroad), the telephone, and electricity had modernized the town. The train was able to deliver building materials such as steel to the area that trucks had been unable to bring. The town was in the middle of a building boom. "New brick store rooms and numerous fine bungalows" were being built. "The streets are full of people every minute of the day and they appear to be busy buying goods and attending to other things."[15]

With 21 faculty members, the 1925 school year began in September and ran nine months, followed by two summer sessions of six weeks each. The summer sessions were more popular than the full year. "There were 395 students in their regular school year and 649 in the summer school. In those days, teaching was clearly a pursuit for women: the 1924 summer session drew 600 women and only 49 men."[16]

Dr. Jones, who had been the town's doctor for at least ten years, died in January 1925, and a new trained doctor was needed to treat townspeople and Normal School students. Dr. Henry Perry, who had begun practicing in Boone more frequently in 1924 from his home and practice in Valle Crucis, often staying for several days or weeks while his wife and children remained at home in Valle Crucis.[17]

The only doctor in the county with surgical training, Dr. Perry, was asked to take over Dr. Jones' practice. In 1925 the town's first hospital (now the Daniel Boone Restaurant) had recently been built by R.K. Bingham of Emeryville, Tennessee. Dr. Perry lived in the hospital for a period as the surgeon, until Bingham's family moved in, and Dr. Perry found quarters nearby on the Appalachian campus.[18] Electricity was erratic in 1925, making surgery a challenge at times for Dr. Perry.[19]

When the Perry family permanently moved from Valle Crucis in 1926 with their two children, Johnnie (my father), age six, and Gertrude, age 11, they moved into Lovill Home, the original wooden dormitory built on the school campus in 1906. The thin-walled building, constructed mainly for summer school students, was cold

Dr. R.K. Bingham built his home in Boone in 1922 to create the first hospital in the town. Dr. Henry Perry, who opened the first hospital in the county in his home in Valle Crucis, came from Valle Crucis to perform the surgeries for Bingham. In 1959 the Whitaker family opened the Dan'l Boone Inn as a family style restaurant in the former Bingham residence and hospital. This eating establishment remains a favorite landmark and food destination in Boone today (courtesy Bobby Brendell Postcard Collection, Digital Watauga Project).

in the winter. Dr. Perry worked at the Bingham house hospital but also ran a clinic for students at Lovill Home for five years before building an office downtown and a family home on Cherry Drive in 1929.[20] His wife, Doris Taylor Perry, cooked and cleaned for the clinic patients and sometimes served as a nursing assistant. Teachers and students boarded at the Perrys' Cherry Drive home from 1929 to 1945.

Dr. Perry took care of the Dougherty family until his retirement in 1954. His son, Johnnie Perry became a doctor, and married D.D. and Lillie Dougherty's granddaughter, Lillie Brown, and practiced medicine in Boone with his father for five years.

Academic Freedom, Better Roads, and an Honorary Doctorate for B.B. Dougherty

Following the clash of traditional and modern views in America with the conviction of John Thomas Scopes in July 1925 for teaching evolution in Ohio, religious fundamentalists from Tennessee turned to North Carolina to fan the flames of the textbook-banning movement. An anti-evolution bill had been defeated in the 1925 North Carolina General Assembly by a vote of 67 to 46, but its advocates warned of a renewed attempt to come in 1927.[21]

William Lewis Poteat, former president of Wake Forest College, was a moderating

Future teachers at Appalachian State Teachers' College benefited from the public Boone Demonstration School, which was erected at the north end of campus behind the Boone Baptist Church. Johnnie Perry (in overalls), son of Dr. Henry Perry, stands next to the teacher, 1931 (Doris Stam Collection, University Archives, Special Collections Research Center, Appalachian State University, Boone, North Carolina).

voice when many North Carolinians "were passively fundamentalist and disturbed by the secularism around them." Poteat, a prominent Baptist and biologist, and Dauph Dougherty's former professor at Wake Forest, was "willing to grant freedom of thought and teaching to those who held different views." The militant minority of book-banners, by their extremism, "lost the support of large numbers of moderate people who might have joined them."[22]

Dauph Dougherty held Dr. Poteat in highest esteem. Poteat's tolerance influenced Dauph; both men were serious Baptists and serious science educators. East Carolina president Wright invited Dr. Poteat to East Carolina during the Scopes controversy. "As a major player in defending academic enquiry, he [Poteat] spoke to the students concerning the pursuit of truth and understanding."[23]

At the 1926 graduation ceremonies of Elon College, B.B. Dougherty was awarded an honorary doctor of letters because of his "signal service in the field of educational statesmanship." When an announcement about the honor was made at Appalachian during chapel, it was met with a standing ovation and cheering. Blan "simply rose and bowed, but said not a word."[24]

The Watauga Democrat acknowledged Blan's new title when it reported on the address given by "Dr. B.B. Dougherty" to the Good Roads Association in 1926, in his folksy, storytelling style. Dr. Dougherty, as he was now called, "knew whom to

> We are inviting a few friends who worked so faithfully in the early nineties to establish this school to a Thanksgiving dinner in the Central Dining Room. Come to the Auditorium at 11:30.
> Your friends,
> *D.D. Dougherty*
> *B.B. Dougherty*

Signatures of D.D. and B.B. Dougherty on this personal invitation to a dinner in Appalachian's Central Dining Hall, c. 1925, to honor those who helped support the founding of the school in 1899 (Doris Stam Collection, University Archives, Special Collections Research Center, Appalachian State University, Boone, North Carolina).

contact to get the most done" for roads in the western counties, and displayed a passionate pride in the future growth and development of northwest North Carolina.[25] But it was a long wait for roads in the mountains, where roads were much harder and more costly to build than in the Piedmont and coastal regions.[26]

The first hard surface road in Watauga County did not appear until 1929.[27] Blan continued to press for roads in the county until the 1950s.[28]

Dr. Dougherty, as he was now called, was appointed to the State Equalization Board in March of 1927, where he helped to write North Carolina public school law.[29] It was an investment of intense mental energy and time, during which Blan honed his political skills, recognizing that the road to advancement in public school policy required succeeding with politicians.[30] He trumpeted an equal chance for every child, coupled with an equal chance for every taxpayer. "He declared it was not right for North Carolina to 'allow' an eighty-five-cent tax upon property in Watauga County to run a six-months' school, and at the same time 'allow' a levy of twenty-seven cents in the 'great county of Forsyth,'" which benefited from the R.J. Reynolds Tobacco Company.[31]

Cultural Changes

Culture was changing rapidly after World War I, evincing a shift towards respect for women and their expanding abilities and roles. At East Carolina, President Wright "observed that World War I had 'smashed all of civilization's traditions and liberated youth from the hand of the past.' Technology fueled this transformation. Radios, automobiles, and motion pictures nurtured new clothing styles, slang,

Appalachian Orchestra, 1926 *Rhododendron* yearbook. At her classmates' request, Lola Rebecca Thompson gathered her fellow students for the formation of the school orchestra. Lola Thompson is seated on the first row, in white dress, playing guitar. Lola earned a teaching degree in May of 1928, and graduated from Appalachian State Teachers College in August 1932 (Mary Moretz, interview with Doris Perry Stam, 7 June 2021) (University Archives, Special Collections Research Center, Appalachian State University, Boone, North Carolina).

and demeanor. ... Women's hairstyles progressed from jaunty bob to carefully coifed 'permanent wave' style."[32]

Convenience was the reason for the popularity of bobbed hair, according to one contemporary journalist, who said the hairstyle accompanied the rise of "the low-priced generally available automobile. Riding in automobiles, as everyone knows, is destructive of any coiffure ... just find a means of fixing the hair attractively, yet in a style which would withstand the breezes." One mountaineer in Avery County opposed the bobbing of hair and suggested his state representative submit a bill to the General Assembly that would "exterminate bobbed haired flappers" from teaching in the public schools![33]

Appalachian student Lola Thompson and her sisters, also Appalachian students, embraced not only the new hairstyles, but more importantly, they embraced the educational opportunities that freed them from their impoverished farming background. A major gift to the School of Education at Appalachian from their descendants celebrated the lives of these women.[34] A plaque currently hanging in the Reich College of Education building reads:

> All seven of the Thompson sisters attended Appalachian Training School and two of them completed teaching degrees at Appalachian. ... Betty and Lola were lifelong educators.... The

deep religious beliefs and high ethical standards of this closely knit family were expressed in altruistic acts of generosity and benevolence. This endowment to Appalachian State University is another expression of the Thompson sisters' belief that paying it forward is both a spiritual and civic responsibility.[35]

Maxie Greene Edmisten, the daughter of professor and diarist A.J. Greene, attended Appalachian State Normal School from 1927 to 1931, and also sought new opportunities amidst continued restraints. "The school was very strict then, but nonetheless," Maxie said, "I always enjoyed school. I enjoyed most of my classes, enjoyed studying and even enjoyed taking exams…," yet she still found time for minor rebellions against school rules, such as a midnight picnic in her dorm room after the 11:00 p.m. "lights out" curfew. "We ate by flashlight and it tasted good because we were sneaking," she recalled. She graduated cum laude and was a member of the Phila-Retian Society, earned a B.S. degree in elementary education, and later served as Dean of Women at Appalachian for 14 years, beginning in 1957.[36]

LeVerne Fox lived on the campus where his father worked on facilities. As a teenager, LeVerne found it "difficult to think of something to do for fun because the regulations were so strict." The options were limited: pitching horse-shoes (a "big event"), hunting chestnuts on the hill, and boiling molasses at the old State Farm in the fall.[37]

Students were not allowed to talk or call out of their dormitory windows, Fox remembered. "There was a story I heard, and I am not really sure if it is true," Fox related. "Boys used to go by the girls' dormitories in the evenings and sheets would be hanging from an upper level window of the girls' dormitory. After a few boys got up to the room, the boys would proceed to pull the rest of the boys up to the window. It was said that Dr. B.B. Dougherty heard about this, so one evening he decided to try this little trick. He tugged on the sheet, and as he was being pulled up towards the window, the young men 'caught sight of his bald head' and instantly let go of the sheets. There were no records of Dr. Dougherty being injured from this fall, if this story is true."[38]

As a young man, Fox had been full of enthusiasm for girls and for moonshine, unconcerned about rules and regulations. "Girls were not allowed out of their dorms after dark," he recalled, but he arranged to "have a young lady meet me in her dormitory laundry room," where they could make their way through underground maintenance tunnels to the other side of campus and then "proceed to a wooded area."[39] This was definitely against the school rules!

Blan frequently discovered delinquent students and foiled their plans.

High School Classes End: Appalachian State Teachers College

The huge growth in enrollment caused overcrowding. Classes were too large—several numbering more than 100 students—for the number of teachers, who felt the heavy workload.[40] To relieve the pressure of too many students, the Normal School had to "confine its efforts to normal work,"[41] and at last the high school department was removed in 1928.

Summer school enrollment was also growing. Blan Dougherty was dissatisfied

Men's basketball, from the 1925 *Rhododendron* yearbook (University Archives, Special Collections Research Center, Appalachian State University, Boone, North Carolina).

with the appropriations for Appalachian's summer school, which was the largest summer school that the state operated except for the University. Blan reported to the Joint Committee on Appropriations that by previous records, at least 1,000 students from almost every county in the state would attend the summer school in 1929 and again in 1930, but the recommended appropriation was barely half of what was needed for the summer school teacher salaries.[42]

Appalachian State Normal School had become a member of the American Association of Teachers' Colleges and Normal Schools in April of 1926.[43] Aspiring to become a four-year school, the Doughertys looked to East Carolina as a model for what Appalachian could become. In March of 1928 Blan spoke with the faculty about the possibility.[44] Dauph and Blan continued to pursue their goal of becoming a four-year college.

On February 28, 1929, the legislature changed the name of the school to Appalachian State Teachers College.[45] Improvements were needed to become an accredited school. Preparing for accreditation was an enormous process, and drastic internal reorganization was required, much of which did not take place until the mid–1930s.[46]

First, the school sought recognition from the State Department of Education for the degrees it offered. The demand for elementary grade teachers was so urgent that there was no difficulty getting recognition for grammar and primary grade teaching degree programs. However, a higher-level certification was required to teach high school.

Co-ed tennis team, from the 1925 *Rhododendron* yearbook (University Archives, Special Collections Research Center, Appalachian State University, Boone, North Carolina).

An urgent shortage of high school teachers in physical education, mathematics, and science created an opportunity for Appalachian to be accredited in 1929 in these subjects, but in these subjects only. In 1933, after some reluctance by the state, the college was recognized in the fields of history and English, with full recognition following for French in 1934, home economics in 1937, library science in 1940, public school music and business education in 1946, all standard four-year college courses.[47]

State Superintendent Arch T. Allen did not expect the state accreditation for Appalachian in 1929. Allen had communicated this hesitation to Cullowhee's President Hunter. But Hunter was "convinced that if Appalachian State Normal School is made into a teachers' college with degree-granting privileges that Cullowhee should certainly be given the same status." On March 18 the western school name was changed to Cullowhee State Normal School, on a par with Appalachian.[48]

Consistently insufficient appropriations had left Appalachian with the choice of either raising fees or reducing enrollment to meet Southern Association of Colleges and Secondary School (SACSS) standards of per-capita expenditure for instruction. However, a drop in enrollment due to World War II allowed Appalachian to meet the required per-capita expenditure standard. This and the prior years of reorganization enabled Appalachian to be accredited by SACSS as a four-year institution in December of 1942.[49] Western Carolina was accredited by SACSS in 1946.[50]

The Hancock Bill of School Tax Equalization

Throughout the years the Doughertys continued their efforts for those students from the rural mountains who had little opportunity for education. Dauph had written his editorial to the Charlotte paper in 1923 pleading the needs of children in rural sections. Both Blan and Dauph preached that education was a state function, and that all the wealth of the state should be put behind all the children of the state.

Blan had waged an active campaign for the "pauper counties," beginning in 1912, "working hard to spread what he later called the 'Gospel of Equalization.'"[51] He gave public speeches, wrote letters, and campaigned for lower taxes and more money for public schools. Over the years he served on many state-level boards and committees that affected public education. His years of public service began in 1916 with his appointment to the state Textbook Committee, and in 1937 Blan became chairman of the state's Committee on (Teacher's) Salaries.[52]

Governor Angus McLean had begun the year 1925 with great enthusiasm for expanding education and increasing the equalization fund that could help the poorer sections of the state. However, "an unexpected deficit of nine million dollars in current revenues" was discovered before the legislative session ended, and appropriations were sacrificed—a set-back for public schools in rural areas.[53]

By 1927 the inequalities between rural and urban schools were at the forefront of Superintendent Allen's report to the Legislature, largely due to Blan Dougherty's efforts.[54] When the State Board of Equalization was established that year, Blan, as one of its leaders, undertook a thorough and complex study of land values, district maps, and tax values, which proved controversial. School budgets, transportation, and other associated costs were also considered. Blan did the lion's share of writing the legislation, the Hancock Education Bill, which passed in early March of 1929.[55] *Time Magazine* later lauded Blan Dougherty and his efforts, which finally resulted in total state funding for public schools in 1933.[56]

Blan Dougherty was appointed a member of the State Board of Education in 1929, on which he served, except for two years, until his death in 1957. He wanted to make a worthy contribution to the state's public school system, and believed that writing the Hancock Bill was his greatest contribution to the state, more important even than his five decades at Appalachian.[57]

Dauphin Disco Dougherty Dies

In the spring of 1929, Dauph Dougherty was seriously ill. Unable to leave his brother to attend an important state meeting of superintendents, Blan Dougherty explained his absence to State Superintendent Allen[58]:

> Since last January I have suffered as no man ever did.... My brother remains very unwell. He is unconscious almost all of the time. His wife has also been very ill; his daughter is just from the hospital in Greensboro where she underwent a serious operation; our sister has also been for days and weeks lingering between life and death. We had a time with 150 cases of "flu" in the school. I am now up many times every night, try to sleep a little, but it is very little.[59]

A few days later Blan again wrote Allen to tell him he would be unable to attend the next meeting as well because his brother was still seriously ill and he could not leave him "under any circumstances."[60] A few days later Dauph was hospitalized in Statesville.[61]

After some recovery time back in Boone, Dauph improved and was able to return to the classroom. Then, he unexpectedly died on June 10.[62]

Because students were already arriving on campus, the faculty decided that summer school registration would be held as planned. "At 8:30 Wednesday morning Dougherty's body lay in state in the auditorium of the Administration Building and at 10:00 o'clock his funeral was held in the First Baptist Church in Boone. His minister, P.A. Hicks, presided over the service. Several visiting ministers also participated.... Dougherty was buried in the Boone cemetery, which overlooked the newly chartered Appalachian State Teachers College."[63]

The *Winston-Salem Journal* carried the following article:

> Educator Passes. Death Claims Dr. Dougherty. Prominent Educator of Boone Succumbs to a Long Siege Sickness. Funeral on Wed. Connected with Appalachian Teachers College.
>
> D.D. Dougherty, Treasurer and Co-founder of the Appalachian State Teachers College, died at his home here at 6:00 o'clock tonight after an illness of nearly three months. In spite of the extended nature of his illness, his death came unexpectedly, as it was believed he had passed the danger point. Only two weeks ago his brother posted a notice on the bulletin board of the college that his brother ... was out of danger. Late today, however, he had a sudden relapse and at 6:00 o'clock he was dead.
>
> Mr. Dougherty became ill during the spring term at the college and had to be taken to a hospital at Statesville for treatment for kidney trouble, complicated by a heart condition. After he was brought home, he gradually regained his strength until he was believed to be out of danger. His sudden death, therefore, came as a distinct shock to his friends and relatives.

The Dougherty family in their yard after the funeral of D.D. Dougherty in June 1929. From left: Edwin, Barnard, Annie, Clara, and Lillie (Doris Stam Collection, University Archives, Special Collections Research Center, Appalachian State University, Boone, North Carolina).

... The Dougherty brothers once drove ox teams and plowed and cultivated on the very land on which the college now stands. Both worked their way through college and came back.... Dauph Dougherty was the scholar ... Mr. Dougherty's death came just when he had seen his dream of more than a quarter of a century realized when the state legislature made this school a four-year college.[64]

22

Lillie Shull Dougherty's Last Years (1930–1945)

Lillie Shull Dougherty: Business Manager and Treasurer

During Dauph's extended illness, Lillie Shull Dougherty had shouldered Dauph's responsibilities as business manager and treasurer with the assistance of her niece, Dauph's secretary, Ruth Barker.[1] After his death, Lillie carried on that work in the same spirit of self-denial and dedication, and shared the long hours, dreams, disappointments, and triumphs of Dauph and Blan Dougherty.

The transition to a four-year college was well underway as Lillie took on more duties, despite her great loss. She still had two sons and Blan to look after, and a home to maintain, as well as many hostess duties. Keeping busy was a balm for the grief.[2] Lillie worked with Blan in conducting the business of the college—ordering all food and supplies, paying bills and payroll, and managing the daily cash—assisted by her son, Barnard, who had attended Berea College and would finish his degree at ASTC. Working on the campus and finally earning a salary as business manager and treasurer—her first paychecks from the school—was rewarding, and she enjoyed the regular interactions with staff, teachers, and students.

A shared commitment and vision for Appalachian created a camaraderie and sense of family that carried the faculty and staff through the challenges of the Depression years. Living on campus since the school's inception had given Lillie a knowledge of

Lillie Shull Dougherty became business manager for Appalachian State Teachers' College upon the death of her husband. She remained in this position until her retirement in 1938 (photograph in the 1930 *Rhododendron* yearbook, University Archives, Special Collections Research Center, Appalachian State University, Boone, North Carolina).

Dauph and Lillie Dougherty in their yard adjacent to campus, c. 1927 (Doris Stam Collection, University Archives, Special Collections Research Center, Appalachian State University, Boone, North Carolina).

school operations and a unique familiarity with its people. Lillie cared for them in tangible ways as her dear friends. Many of those who worked at the college struggled, as she did, to make ends meet, especially during the Depression years. Ed Culler, faithful campus employee of many years, loved Lillie, according to granddaughter, "because she paid him on time" and was concerned for his family.[3]

Dr. Herb Wey, Chancellor of Appalachian from 1969 to 1979, said of the faculty and staff during the 1920s and '30s that there were many people with "outstanding" abilities and credentials. "They worked for practically nothing. ... [President Dougherty] would give them groceries. They had a state farm. The school was pretty much the kind where if you would come and join them you would manage to get enough to eat and a place to live and a little salary, and a lot of people just had that missionary spirit." These people stayed because they believed in what Appalachian was doing to offer education to mountain youngsters.[4] "Back then everybody knew everybody."[5] Lillie nurtured that Appalachian family and sustained the sense of belonging and fellowship.

Dr. Wiley Smith came to Appalachian in 1936 with a doctorate in psychology, one of only a handful with PhDs, having been a faculty member at the University of South Carolina. Because of the Great Depression his position had been eliminated there, and, after farming for a few years, Smith had taken a temporary job at Asheville Normal College. B.B. Dougherty met Dr. Smith and offered him a job at Appalachian. Even though the salary was less money, the offer of a job with food and a home secured Smith for the next fifty years.[6]

Frugality: Returning Money to the State

As business manager, Lillie helped keep expenses as low as possible. The reports to Raleigh and the requests for funding, which Lillie helped Blan prepare, reflected the Doughertys' frugality.[7] Managing public funds with prudence and economy was a sacred duty to them, and Blan *returned* any money unspent, or any extra income, to the state.

Boone native Carl Day was keeping the books for the cafeteria in the 1930s when Dr. Dougherty insisted on having the books from every department turned in on the very next day after classes ended for the school year. "I finished the books and got ready to go see Dr. Dougherty," Carl recalled. "Well, that year the cafeteria had made a little over $6,000 profit. Dr. Dougherty said, 'I'll write a check this afternoon and pay the state back.' That was Dr. Dougherty!"[8]

When Blan thought an architect's estimate for a campus building was too high, he visited cement and brick factories, consulted railroad officials, and secured reduced prices on all materials and freight, reducing the $175,000 estimated cost to $80,000.[9] In the 1930s, he delayed the construction of a building for which the state had already allotted money, saying, "I'm waiting on the price of nails to come down."[10]

This extreme economy was lauded by some, but was not always effective to secure future funding—thrift did not beget generosity. And some were critical of this frugality, believing the savings resulted in poorly constructed buildings.[11] Lillie stood by Blan's decision, economizing and supporting the school in every way that she could.[12]

Lillie and Blan shared a commitment to honest handling of money that was sometimes lacking at other institutions. The reputation of the Home Mission Board of the Southern Baptist Convention was clouded in 1928–1929 when its treasurer was accused of embezzling $900,000 from the Board.[13] Western Carolina Teachers College lost $23,000 in the failure of the Tuckaseigee Bank on April 25, 1930, and was forced to cut back its building program.[14] In the 1940s, Eastern Carolina's President Leon Renfroe Meadows was charged with mishandling student funds, "which resulted in his resignation, arrest, trial, and conviction; the school, which had enjoyed an impeccable reputation, was left scarred by scandal."[15] Largely through Blan Dougherty's influence, the banks in Watauga County did not fail in 1930 and did not go into receivership in 1933.[16] Appalachian and the Doughertys remained solvent and trustworthy.[17]

The Great Depression: Hard Years at Appalachian

As Lillie collected fees from students during enrollment, many did not have the required amount, but allowances and provisions were often made. No eager student was turned away.[18] One such student in the 1930s, who admitted to Lillie that he did not have enough cash to enroll, recounted later that she softly said, "It's all right. We'll make a way. Now, you go on down to the school farm. I'll make arrangements, and you can work your way through school."[19] He was allowed to enroll and began work that very day. Through all their years with the school, Dauph and Blan had quietly and privately made arrangements for students who lacked means.[20]

In 1929 Appalachian's appropriation was far below the 10 other state schools. Although six percent of all North Carolina students enrolled in teacher training at Appalachian, only three percent of the appropriation to state supported schools was designated for Boone.[21] Yet, the next appropriation reflected only a nominal increase for Appalachian.[22] The *Charlotte Observer* would later describe this pattern with state appropriations as a sensational disparity.[23]

With the national financial collapse, Appalachian's requests for an increase in the maintenance and summer school appropriations in 1929 had been denied, leaving the Doughertys to press on with a shoe-string budget.[24] Despite cutting costs wherever possible, financial problems persisted. Salaries were cut 10 percent by the Legislature in 1931, and the State Budget Bureau informed all institutions in late December 1931 that appropriations would be cut by at least 30 percent for 1932, and it was rumored that state allocations might be even more severely limited in 1933.[25] All schools received cuts.

Student unrest at the school during the 1930s reflected a nationally changing culture,[26] which was also felt at other schools having to deal with changes in students' standards of conduct.[27] Lillie was a source of encouragement for Blan as president of Appalachian during these challenging days, providing a stable home environment as she had done since her first days of marriage to his brother.

Her Brother-in-law's Keeper

After her husband died, Lillie continued to care for Blan, enabling him to function in his expansive role as president and ensuring his personal appearance was appropriate. "If she noticed that he was a bit untidy as he was leaving the house, Blan would usually say, 'Oh, I'm just going to my office and won't see hardly anybody.' But she knew better and saw to it that he was dressed suitably for meeting any and all he might see during the day."[28]

To her brother-in-law, time meant little; his big silver-cased watch often went unwound and he missed family meals.[29] "Unless he brought a guest home, he might take a cup and go to the [cooking] pots to get his food," or, in later years, help himself to food in the refrigerator, leaving his dishes anywhere in the house when he had finished eating.[30] Having a simple appetite, a sensitive stomach, and picky eating habits, he ate mainly vegetables and fruits. Sometimes without notice, he would bring a friend or two for a meal, not appearing to realize that he created an embarrassing situation and one that required more work for his sister-in-law, who often had to change her plans altogether.[31]

When sickness came upon the family, Lillie tended not only to her children, but also to her brother-in-law, whose constitution was not strong. After Dauph's death, Blan moved to the apartment above the garage springhouse, only a few yards from the main home, but Lillie continued to do his cooking, laundry, and house cleaning. Lillie and Dauph's son Barnard took on more and more responsibility as assistant business manager. Eventually, Blan and Barnard were able to manage without Lillie in the office and she was able to retire. She was 63 years old and high blood pressure was beginning to afflict her.[32]

Expansive Roles for Lillie and the Wives of Other College Leaders

Heads of similar educational institutions in the mountains of North Carolina and their wives followed a similar pattern of service to Lillie Dougherty, the wives constantly assisting their husbands during their lifetimes or taking on their duties after they died.

Bessie Tufts, wife of the Rev. Edgar Tufts, gave her abilities to Lees-McRae College in Banner Elk. Her piano and organ music, like Lillie's, added greatly to occasions at the school the Tufts founded in 1900.[33] When Edgar died prematurely in 1923 from exposure to winter's cold and ensuing pneumonia, Bessie continued to serve the school, church and community alongside their son, who was appointed to lead the school.[34] Another presidential couple, Ella Richards Madison and President Robert Madison, served at Cullowhee (now Western Carolina University).[35] The Eldridges, husband and wife team leading Glade Valley School in Sparta, North Carolina, devoted themselves sacrificially to humble life-long work and leadership at their school.[36] Edna Moore took on management duties, as "lady principal and treasurer," at Mars Hill College, a title which later was changed to "bursar," when her husband, President Robert Moore, became overwhelmed with his work and she took on more of his responsibilities. Edna continued at her position after her husband's retirement until her death in 1950 for an amazing total of 51 years at that college.[37]

Lillie's official paid position at Appalachian ended with her retirement in 1938, but her vital, unpaid position as College Hostess continued.[38]

Hospitality was instinctive to Lillie, part of her expansive role as Dauph's wife and as homemaker for both Dauph and Blan. Being constantly on duty to entertain guests strengthened relationships with the college and the community. "Until her health began to fail in the late thirties, Lillie was Appalachian's hostess. Men in high educational circles, including state superintendents of public instruction, were entertained in the Dougherty home—not in a 'university mansion.' Not infrequently the commencement speaker was among guests, for in those days it was not the custom to send visitors to a hotel. Many others came on school business and remained for a meal or two if not for the night."[39]

Lillie also hosted meetings in her home of the Faculty Club and the Faculty Dames, a local ladies' social club that Lillie formed and fostered for the faculty spouses and female faculty, similar to those at peer schools like Lenoir-Rhyne where the president's wife began Lenoir Dames in 1914.[40] The Faculty Dames met for teas,

22. Lillie Shull Dougherty's Last Years

BARNARD DOUGHERTY, B. S. —— *Business Manager*

Appalachian is glad to have you here and we hope you will be happy in your new environment.

The physical plant of this college has been specifically designed so as to give each student every comfort and opportunity that can be afforded.

While you are here seeking knowledge, may you use these facilities in such a way as to receive all the benefits the college desires you have.

BARNARD DOUGHERTY,
Business Manager

Barnard Dougherty assisted his mother, then took over as business manager in 1938 and became vice president and comptroller for Appalachian State College. "Uncle Blan" gave strict oversight to his nephew. Barnard worked at Appalachian until his death in 1965 (Elizabeth Brown Scoggins Collection, University Archives, Special Collections Research Center, Appalachian State University, Boone, North Carolina).

failed is an elective one he may drop it by paying a change fee. No failure may be made up by taking the course at another institution.

The teacher may set a time for the removal of "Incompletes" and "Conditions", provided the work is done within three residence quarters.

Dating

The dating program at Appalachian is under the supervision of the Student Council, and it is open to all students of the college. The following rules pertain to its functioning for those who are eligible:

1. Senior girls may date as often as they wish.
2. Junior girls may date three nights per week.
3. Sophomore girls may date twice per week.
4. Freshmen girls may date once each week.
5. This applies to the girls rooming in the dormitories.
6. All dating is carried on in the dormitory living rooms. Students do not date on nights when there is a program sponsored elsewhere on the campus. Dates begin at 8:00 and end at 10:00. Student hostesses and the matrons are in charge of the dating rooms during dating hours.

Rules for students stayed the same in 1938 as they had been for decades (Elizabeth Brown Scoggins Collection, University Archives, Special Collections Research Center, Appalachian State University, Boone, North Carolina).

Lillie (at left) started the Faculty Dames Club, which she enjoyed hosting (Doris Stam Collection, University Archives, Special Collections Research Center, Appalachian State University, Boone, North Carolina).

special events, and holiday gatherings.[41] For Christmas each year Lillie gave each Faculty Dames member a gift.

Another group, the Friday Afternoon Club, was an important and regular part of Lillie's and the local community's life.[42] Her daughters joined her to host this club periodically. Later her granddaughters, and, after her death, her great-grandchildren would sometimes attend these club meetings when they were visiting Boone. The friendship and fellowship of these women was a great support to Lillie through the years, especially as a widow. The club later changed to Saturday meetings but retained the name, often needing the humorous explanatory comment, "the Friday Afternoon Club which meets on Saturdays."

Ever a hardworking woman, Lillie kept the home going and the food flowing. She was skilled at making plans and carrying them out. All six granddaughters have consistently expressed how beautiful "Mama Dougherty" was, how kind she was, *and* how *hard* they had to work when they visited her.[43]

Eldest granddaughter Virginia remembered the all-day job of laundering and preparing the starched collar shirts that her Uncle Blan wore. Always a luncheon, dinner or tea was in the making, or company expected, requiring extra cooking or cleaning or other special preparations. Helping to make delicate cucumber or nasturtium flower sandwiches, along with cakes and pies for ladies' gatherings, and setting the dining room table with starched linens and fine china, were special memories for the granddaughters.[44] In addition to assistance from her daughters and grand-daughters, Lillie often hired helpers such as John Adams and Zula Lewis, a very small woman from Ashe County who was beloved by all the grandchildren.[45]

Lillie hosted many other college events throughout the years. Today colleges and universities have development and alumni divisions, food and hospitality services, catering and venues, conference and guest services; back then they had the "College Hostess."

The unofficial position of "College Hostess" persisted at least into the 1980s and beyond as part of the assumed and unofficial job description of institutional leaders and spouses. A *New York Times* article described what was required of those who headed large schools during the 1980s: "Many presidential couples live in official university mansions, the campus equivalent of the White House. They [or their spouses alone] are administrators, hostesses, menu planners and decorators. They also attend dozens of events outside the home, ranging from faculty teas and freshmen orientation to football games and alumni reunions."[46]

A commitment to Christian service ordered Lillie's actions, motivated her moments, and dominated her decisions. Her duty, as she saw it, was done as a grateful and loving response to Christ, whether it be in the home, at the school, or in the community. She served as president of the Woman's Missionary Union (WMU) at Boone Baptist Church some 25 years. "Time and again she was re-elected to the office over her protests, but the society was unwilling to let her go because of her able leadership and her superb personality."[47] Church workers and pastors visiting in Boone always found a welcome at the Dougherty home and a sympathetic interest in their labors. Some of these people were top leaders in the Baptist State Convention or preachers for revivals or other important meetings.[48]

What is today termed "people skills" came naturally with Lillie's genuine interest in others. She was at ease with all manner of people, as noted at her funeral by her pastor who said: "I have had people who could neither read nor write along with the leading college professors to tell me that she was a most thoughtful woman. She was concerned about the welfare of all, and she showed it in her daily life and work."[49]

Lillie's Last Years

It was a great joy for Lillie to see her daughter, Annie, marry Roy Rufty in 1937, and then to see her son, Barnard, marry Grace Stacy Boyd in 1941. Helping host these celebrations were highlights during her later years.

When her grandchildren visited, Lillie sometimes "played the piano and guitar, or sang old songs, many about the virtues of being a good girl," granddaughter Lib recalled.[50] Ellen, born in 1927, clearly remembers observing Lillie with her guitar singing "The Church in the Wildwood" and other songs. "The North Carolina Hills" was a family favorite and was also sung frequently at the college.[51]

In 1939, after an illness, Lillie wrote to her daughter Clara: "I am feeling stronger. My blood pressure was higher when the doctor examined me. He gave me some medicine. I shall go back this week to see him again. ... We are ticking some quilts. When you come up bring your quilt I made of papa's clothes ... and we will tack [sew] it for you...."[52] The family felt someone should be in the house with elderly Lillie. Her sons were still living at home, but were out each evening. Lib (Elizabeth)

Brown, Clara's daughter, stayed with Lillie at night and helped care for her in 1939–1941 while she attended college for two years before transferring to Greensboro College to finish her degree.

When she felt good and the weather cooperated, Lillie worked in her garden or on the campus grounds, cutting flowers from the yard to carry to sick friends, or making floral sprays for funerals, and planting flowers around the campus.[53] Lib was walking across campus one day with a fellow student, "and there was Mama Dougherty working in the flower beds on the campus, down on her knees!" Lib did not acknowledge seeing Mama Dougherty. She did not want her friend to know "the lady working in the flowers" was her grandmother—"she was dressed in her work clothes, for heaven sakes!" Lib exclaimed.[54]

In her final years, Lillie often stayed with her daughters, Clara and Annie, in the Piedmont of North Carolina during the harsh mountain winters. In late May of 1942 Edwin wrote to his oldest sister: "Barnard, Grace and I went to Annie's Sunday afternoon and brought mom back. She stood the trip well, seemed to enjoy the scenery and had a good time. She has been hitting it hard since though. She and John have been setting out flowers and we have had the painters here.... I think we can get her to spend most of this summer here.... I may go to some branch of the Armed Services almost any day."[55] Edwin soon thereafter entered the Air Force.

A long and newsy letter from Lillie to a dear family friend in May of 1944, nine months before her death, mentioned many faculty, staff, friends and family members, and expressed delight in the beauty of the natural world around her:

> I do hope you shall be feeling much better when this letter reaches you. I'm so glad you have been going to a good doctor. I believe you will be helped, for you're giving yourself a chance. While you worked with all that bunch of girls [in Dauph-Blan Residence Hall] it was almost impossible for you to improve.... The commencement went off well. Mrs. [Emma] Moore said she thought the breakfast was the nicest one they have had. I went over for the first time. I ate at the table with Dr. and Mrs. Hunter [from Western Carolina College] and Dr. Dougherty. The girls in the May Day exercises looked beautiful. Their dresses and flowers were so pretty. I sat in the window between the dining room and kitchen in the cafeteria. I could see well. It was rather cool, and I have had rheumatism in my shoulder and breast, so I did not risk it out there. I did not go to the commencement, neither the play.... Everything is looking so pretty now. The grass is so pretty and green, the leaves are coming out, several flowers in bloom. You should see the dogwood and mountain magnolia in the yard. They are so full of bloom....[56]

Lillie left this earthly life on January 22, 1945. The newspaper announcement read: Lillie Shull Dougherty "died in Watauga hospital this morning. She had been seriously ill for three weeks and for several years prior to that time had been in bad health.... She took a keen interest in the college almost to the end."

Upon receiving news from Clara of her mother's death, the former Boone pastor, the Rev. F. M Huggins, wrote back: "I always regarded Mrs. Dougherty as one of the best and most refined and cultured women that it has ever been my privilege to know. I knew her as a devout Christian and a loyal member of the church. Your mother and your father were two of my best friends while I was in Boone. It is good to reflect upon the noble lives that they lived."[57]

The Watauga Democrat reported: "Four children survive: Mrs. O.L. Brown of Mount Holly, Barnard Dougherty of Boone, Mrs. Roy Rufty of Statesville, and Edwin

S. Dougherty of the USAAF, now stationed at Columbus Army Air Field, Columbus, Miss. She is also survived by seven grandchildren, four great-grandchildren, a brother, E.L. Shull of Elizabethton, Tenn., and two sisters, Mrs. L.W. Campbell of Elizabethton and Mrs. James H. Smith of Johnson City, Tenn. … [B]urial will be in the family plot of the town cemetery."[58]

Blan was despondent after Lillie's death, according to Clara and Lester Brown.[59] "Perhaps no other woman could have meant so much to Dr. Dougherty's career as his sister-in-law, Lillie Shull Dougherty," Lester Brown wrote. "Perhaps he did not know how great his reliance on her was until after she had gone from the stage of life. When he found only himself left of the three who started and who fostered the growth of Appalachian, his physical strength, already somewhat depleted, weakened even further and the will to carry on was at low ebb."[60]

It took time to restore Blan's determination to press on without either Dauph or Lillie, but he would thrive as president of Appalachian for another 10 years. In 1949, four years after Lillie's death, Watauga County celebrated its Centennial with a week of events including pageants and parades, climaxing in a day-long tribute to honor Blan (Dr. B.B. Dougherty) on Education Day, held on Appalachian's campus and highlighted by Frank Porter Graham's speech.[61] After Lillie's death, Barnard and Grace Dougherty, then Annie and Roy Rufty, cared for Blan in the Dougherty home where he had lived since it was built in 1903.[62] Grace and her three children spent

In the center of this April 1939 photograph can be seen the Daniel Boone Hotel (1) with the Appalachian Theatre (2) across the street. The Greene Inn (3), which was the original Daniel Baker Dougherty house, is next to the theater. The WPA Boone Post Office (4) lot is cleared for construction next to the Linney home (5). In the foreground is the train depot building (6). Bobby Snead donated this print to the Town of Boone Cultural Resources Department about 2011. He gave permission for its use in this book. The image is originally from the Cy Crumley Scrapbook.

two winters in Florida assisting Blan after he retired in 1955. Blan died in the spring of 1957, having outlived Lillie by 12 years, and his brother by 28 years.

Steadfastness of Purpose to Serve

Behind two remarkable men, Dauph and Blan Dougherty, was a remarkable woman, Lillie Shull Dougherty. Her strengthening influence and relentless service contributed heavily to Appalachian's success. The brothers were "temperamentally opposites," yet each depended heavily on Lillie.[63] "Having been denied the care and solicitation of their mother," who died when the boys were young, they appreciated and benefited from Lillie's counsel, which offered good "insight and judgment" when differences of opinion arose between the brothers.[64] In every challenging situation the brothers faced, Lillie Shull Dougherty's skill, understanding, and faithful labor sustained them.

The life of Lillie Shull Dougherty can never be measured solely by her visible achievements or official jobs as teacher or business manager, her informal role as hostess, or her domestic role as homemaker. Although it is hard to quantify her accomplishments, it is now acknowledged that Appalachian had three founders. She was a founding teacher and contributor not only in the first years, but from 1899 until after her retirement in 1938—more than 40 years of devotion. Her contributions as peacemaker, counselor, caretaker, and stabilizing force in the Dougherty home were essential and pervasive. What is clearly evident is her steadfastness of purpose to serve the school and the integrity of her character in doing it.

23

Dauphin Disco Dougherty
The Dougherty Family Legacy and the Brothers Compared

Humble, Behind the Scenes

Dauphin Disco Dougherty has been an enigma, a quiet, earnest, dedicated educator and administrator, overshadowed by his brother Blan's more public, political personality and long tenure as president of Appalachian. But Dauph seemed to prefer working behind the scenes. In the estimation of others, Dauph worked for an audience of One, his Lord God, without regard for what others thought of him.

"He was absolutely indifferent as to whether others agreed with his thinking and planning," his former teacher, Spainhour, wrote in 1929. "He never went out of his way, by word or act, to gain the applause of any human being. If the thing was right, he endorsed it; if it was wrong, he rejected it."[1] The *Watauga Democrat*'s announcement of Dauph Dougherty's death described him thus: "He did not aspire to public preferment but served his county for a number of years as a member of the Board of Education, going out of office during the past winter only because of ill health. He did not, however, allow the cares of his daily life to interfere with his manifold duties to his community. He was an organizer, Sunday school worker and teacher, Sunday school superintendent and a well-loved Christian gentleman, and in his going Watauga County and the state at-large have sustained a loss which seems irreparable."[2] His professional colleague, A.J. Greene said of him, "He is so modest that only a few know and appreciate his true worth."[3]

A Study in Contrasts: the Dougherty Brothers

Hon. J.F. Spainhour gave remarks at D.D. Dougherty's memorial service in October of 1929, which were printed in the 1929 *Rhododendron* yearbook. Spainhour, who had taught both Dougherty brothers as young teenagers and remained closely associated with them and the school, wrote:

> The Dougherty brothers have been, in many respects, a remarkable pair. I doubt if their like could be found in this state again. They were different in almost every detail of life, but they were both honest, both truthful, both sober, both modest, both ambitious, both bright, both studious, and later, both fine scholars and great educators. Notwithstanding their differences in taste and sentiment, they worked together in perfect harmony. It was the planning of

B.B. Dougherty on the day of his retirement from the office of president of Appalachian State Teachers' College, 1955, at the age of 85. He died in May of 1957 (University Archives, Special Collections Research Center, Appalachian State University, Boone, North Carolina).

a common task and both working at the same thing, but each with his own initiative, in his own peculiar way, made his contribution to the Institution. Neither ever complained of the other. When things turned out bad, it was dropped—never to be referred to again.

... While these brothers were very different, their differences were means of strength, rather than weakness. Although so different, and oftentimes they did not agree, they had absolute faith in, and were deferential always to each other. They kept but one bank account, and each drew on it as he pleased without consulting the other, and so far as their most intimate friends ever knew there was never an unpleasant word between them about their private matters.[4]

Blan noted the differences in a letter to Santford Martin, editor of the *Winston-Salem Journal*, about his brother LeRoy Martin, who had educational leadership on the State Board of Equalization with Blan: "My brother and I were more unlike than you and LeRoy. Yet we worked together, lived in the same house, and had the same bank account. He spent more money to promote the church and I spent more money to advance the college."[5]

Dauph's Christian Faith and Home Church

Though both brothers were religious men, their faith manifested itself in different ways. Dauph was deeply involved in the life of the church. "D.D. was always going to church, but I never knew Dr. [B.B.] Dougherty to go to church. Pretty often he said that he felt he could worship God best by being out in these mountains, and he took walks out in the mountains quite often. Sometimes he would be gone for hours. I think they both thought they were doing God's will by being here at Appalachian."[6]

"He [Dauph] had a plain, simple personality that was charged with an indescribable force," wrote a former student of D.D. Dougherty, the Rev. Elbert H. Hicks. "He never seemed to design its use, for it operated spontaneously.... At the base of his personality was a character unsurpassed for sterling work." Hicks concluded his letter: "Deep down beneath the moral structure we call his character was a very profound Christian experience almost too sacred for discussion."[7]

Blan's mentor in Globe, F.P. Moore, exhorted him to move his church membership to Boone Baptist Church, but Blan never did.[8] He never went to church unless he was invited to give a speech, "but this didn't mean he wasn't religious."[9] Often he spent Sunday morning at the office and presumably joined the family for Sunday dinner.

By contrast, Dauph was committed to the church. "Prof. [Dauph] Dougherty was an exceedingly busy man, but he made a large place in his life for his religious activities," his former student, Superintendent of Watauga County Public Schools Smith Hagaman wrote. A few days before his death, from his bed Dauph asked his wife to write and send a check to Hagaman, "to be used in alleviating some case of distress of which he [Dauph] had heard so many on first Mondays in the office of the County Welfare Superintendent."[10] Hagaman said Dauph Dougherty was:

> A Sunday school teacher of a rare ability and power, a member of the executive board of the Three Forks Baptist Association, he gave much time and thought to the development of the churches of the county. Each Christmas he mailed a check to the preachers of the county. Realizing that he might not live to the next Christmas, he mailed his usual check to the preachers two months ago [in April]. The last time I saw him in life was when he, with his wife and brother, signed a deed conveying to Boone Baptist church the valuable lot on which the new church [Sunday School] building is to be erected.[11]

The church sanctuary stood on property which had been given to the Three Forks Baptist Institute in 1873 by Daniel Baker Dougherty, who also gave land to Boone Episcopal Church in 1882. More land was given by D.D., Lillie and Blan in 1911, 1914, and 1929, and yet another property was given later by Blan, for a building to be named in honor of Daniel Baker and Ellen Bartlett Dougherty.[12]

Dauph (D.D.) Dougherty had given an address at the evening service dedicating the 1923 brick Boone Baptist Church. His wife, Lillie, was president of the Woman's Missionary Union (WMU) during these years. "What of the Future" was the title of his message, given the year before his health began to fail.[13] The *Watauga Democrat* said of Dauph after his death, he was a "well-loved Christian gentleman, and in his going Watauga County and the state at-large have sustained a loss which seems irreparable."[14]

Developing School Departments and Sharing Enthusiasm for the Natural World

In the early years D.D. Dougherty led the Science Department, "which listed: Advanced Physiology, Geography, Zoology, Astronomy, Elementary Physics, and Botany."[15] He also taught all the mathematics classes, algebra and geometry.[16] The library was established by 1904 from his personal collection, added to by community donations.[17]

"Prof. Dauph was always interested in Art, Music, Home Economics, Industrial Arts, Agriculture and Printing. He organized and developed these and other departments in the earlier years of Appalachian," his daughter Annie wrote.[18] Lillie shared these interests in artistic things and "the practical side of life," and, together with her husband, influenced the founding and strengthening of these departments of the college.[19]

Described as one who thoroughly enjoyed the art of instruction, Professor Dauph "was jubilant when a student grasped some difficult truth he was presenting. At such times he would bang a ponderous fist on the table in front of him and exclaim, 'That's it! That's it!' He was quick to recognize effort and ability and to encourage them," but had little patience with those who had made little effort and came poorly prepared for class.[20]

Dauph displayed a contagious enthusiasm for the natural world throughout his life, inspired by his grandfather Elijah, who had made a scientific study of the wild grasses in his area of Tennessee, and by his Wake Forest College professor, Dr. W.L. Poteat. "The professor was a lover of the outdoors and all within its vast domain. ... If in his excursions he discovered a flower or tuft of grass he was not acquainted with, he would bring specimens home and from his books learn all he could about them."[21]

Observant and curious about plants, particularly mountain wildflowers, Dauph was on the lookout for new specimens whenever he was in the woods and pastures.[22] In the location of the current football stadium, he created nature paths with identification markers for native plants. Dauph would place a native plant or wildflower on a table at the library entrance, with genus and species in Latin.[23] Aware of the damage and loss of soil due to the clear-cutting practices of the lumber industries, in 1923 he wrote letters to leaders and an editorial exhorting "Forestry Preservation"[24]

Lillie and Dauph enjoyed gardening, and setting out flowers and native flowering shrubs around their home and on the campus.[25] "Prof. Dauph, an intense lover of order and beauty, wanted the Appalachian campus to have harmonious connection with its setting, and devised a master plan with this in mind.[26] Dauph would plan picnics, hikes, and other field trips for the Appalachian student body to enjoy the beauty in the mountains. His last outing was with the faculty at Blowing Rock where he took his colleagues to witness a majestic sunset."[27]

A Good Friend

Satie Hunt (Mrs. Ed Broyhill), a generous benefactor of Appalachian for many years who knew both the Doughertys from her days as a student beginning in 1915 and as an active alumna for her entire life, regarded Blan as much more conservative than Dauph, which she attributed to Blan being unmarried and Dauph having a family.[28]

"These two men were different as night and day," remarked LeVerne Fox, who lived on the school campus beginning in 1924 and was close friends with Dauph's two sons. "Blan was more tight on things; more rational about things; D.D. would talk easy to ya.'"[29] Dauph's death "hit us all very hard…. It was like losing one of the family."[30]

The *Watauga Democrat*, whose publisher and editor, R.C. Rivers, had known the Dougherty brothers all his life, noted that the brothers "complemented one another.

The D.D. Dougherty family in 1905: from left, Dauph, Clara, Lillie, and Annie (Doris Stam Collection, University Archives, Special Collections Research Center, Appalachian State University, Boone, North Carolina).

Blanford had the vision and the ability to make other men join with him and help work dreams into facts. Dauphin possessed the warm spirit and the great heart which built lifelong loyalties among the mountain families in the 'lost provinces.'"[31]

Lester Brown noted that Dauph Dougherty dealt with all classes of people and was highly respected by them. "He believed in the common man and cared little for titles. Once when he was presiding at the Three Forks Baptist Association the question came up as to whether a certain man's name should have the word 'Reverend' before it. He settled the matter by saying, 'Put *mister* before it, there is no better title than that.'"[32]

Dauph once told Lester Brown: "The wants of my brother and me are few and simple." According to Brown, "Both men had learned a priceless lesson in early adult life: that they could enjoy living and working with little display of dress and with no pretentious spending. As honest, willing servants in a great cause they found abiding satisfaction."[33]

At a fundraising meeting at the Baptist Church, the minister had requested contributions for a building project, stating that donors would be acknowledged by name. When Dauph objected because many did not have the means to donate even a dollar, one member thought Dauph was trying to get out of giving a large gift. But when the meeting was over, Dauph, without drawing any attention, left a generous check.[34]

Dauph was known for his integrity, gaining the full confidence and respect of farmers who sold produce to the college for many years.[35] Over the many decades that Ed Culler worked on the campus, he became well acquainted with the brothers, and he sometimes referred to them as "Dr. Dauph and Prof. Blan."[36] "I don't guess they have anybody over there now any solid-er than the two Doughertys. All those years I worked under them they were just straight, honest people."[37]

Two Leaders with Two Different Sets of Skills

A *History of North Carolina* recognized the work of both Dougherty brothers, although the article entry was entitled "Blanford B. Dougherty."[38] In 1919, when the *History of North Carolina* was published, Appalachian had not yet been reorganized and Blan was not yet president. Dauph was the principal and Blan the superintendent until 1921.[39]

Blan was becoming known all over North Carolina through newspaper articles about his work on the State Textbook Committee (beginning in 1916) and with the Legislature on behalf of Appalachian. Blan attended every session of the legislature, beginning in 1903, until his retirement and knew every governor from that time until his death.[40] Blan was a member of the North Carolina State Board of Education for many years (1929–1957). He was already the public face of the school by the time this article was written in 1919.

But this biographical entry on B.B. Dougherty defined Dauph as "the main man" on the Appalachian campus, for his everyday, relentless, behind-the-scenes work: "by a straightforward and direct manner of life, by his tireless work in every capacity, by his thoughtfulness and carefulness in every detail of schoolwork, by his loyalty and devotion to every interest of this school, as well as every one with whom he comes in contact, he is generally thought of as the main spring if not the right arm of Appalachian training school."[41]

"As long as he lived and was able to be around, Professor Dauph was decidedly the most powerful figure on Appalachian's campus," according to Lester Brown.[42] Yet in her enthusiasm for her former professor, Ruby Lanier, in her doctoral thesis and important book, *Mountain Educator: Blanford Barnard Dougherty*, overlooks the contributions of D.D. Dougherty, and makes little mention of him.

Dauph had a commanding stature of six feet, with a brisk, energetic walk—no doubt gained by walking being the main way of getting places for most of his life. For some 20 years Dauph

B.B. Dougherty in 1955, on the cover photograph of *Our State* magazine in July 1955. He was so well-known and recognized around the state that his name is not mentioned on the cover of the magazine issue (courtesy *Our State* magazine).

taught full-time and did much of the secretarial work himself since there was no money available to pay a full-time secretary. "All this was enough to have kept two men busy."[43]

Dauph was able to carry his heavy load because he was a capable administrator who "had his systematic way of doing things. He knew what to do and how best to do it. Then, he was a man of decision who was widely respected for his opinions and actions."[44] Dauph changed from teaching as his main occupation to become the school's business manager and treasurer in 1921 and was working quietly behind the scenes by the time Blan Dougherty rose to statewide prominence.[45]

"What I remember most about my father is that he was constantly planning for the college and community," Dauph and Lillie's son Barnard recalled.[46] There was much to be done aside from teaching, Lester Brown wrote: "the buying of food supplies, the administration of two school farms, arranging for the heating of the school buildings, including dormitories, the making up of the payroll, keeping the books, and so on."[47]

D.D. Dougherty was remembered for unselfishly serving the state, "quietly and without ostentatiousness." After interviewing B.B. Dougherty in 1934, a journalist wrote that his older brother, D.D. Dougherty, "was a constructive thinker, a great planner of practical things. His keen intellect and powerful initiative brought into the life of the institution new ideas and principles. His constant ideals of modern and progressive education played no small part" in the rapid growth of Appalachian.[48]

At Dauph's funeral the Rev. Rufus Bradshaw paid tribute to the life and character of his dear friend, organizing his words about Dauph as "the student, the scholar, the builder, the Christian gentleman."[49]

Scholar

Dauph read a great deal, according to his son-in-law. "All along the way he had been hopelessly committed to the life of a scholar."[50] A former student wrote of Professor Dauph: "He was the first and in many respects the best teacher I ever had. ... He had an appreciation of genuine values and an intellectual integrity that is rarely equaled in the world of teachers."[51] Appalachian librarian Mrs. Emma Moore commented that Professor Dauph "was a scholar of the deepest type. His life's work centered about the cause of education."[52] His secretary for five years prior to his death, Mrs. Ruth Barker Redmond, described him as "a wonderful person to work with. He was well read and, indeed, a true scholar."[53]

Dr. A.P. Vandusen of Syracuse University, who also taught in the summer school at Appalachian during Dauph's lifetime, remembered Dauph as "the best-informed man, the most thorough in several fields, that I have ever known. His great knowledge made you wonder at the breadth and depth of his thinking."[54]

Will R. Lovill, son of Capt. E.F. Lovill (chairman of the Trustees for most of the years from 1903 until his death in January 1925), "paid eloquent tribute to the career of the deceased cofounder—a man of great vision, one of fixed purpose, a deep thinker, a scholar, builder—[and to] his educational genius and his Christian influence."[55] The first issue

A family snapshot of the Dougherty brothers, Blan (left) and Dauph, one of the few of them together, standing in front of the Second Administration Building, c. 1927 (Elizabeth Brown Scoggins Collection, University Archives, Special Collections Research Center, Appalachian State University, Boone, North Carolina).

of the Appalachian Alumnus publication was dedicated to Dauphin Disco Dougherty—"Scholar, Thinker, Christian."[56]

Blan Dougherty had many leadership qualities and abilities, yet he was not known for scholarship, as was his brother.[57] Blan's areas of expertise included politics, business and banking, and persuading voters, elected officials, and legislators to influence development for Appalachian and for Boone.

The brothers shared the same ambition, and each "richly supplemented the other."[58] They had "perfect confidence in each other."[59] Both held strongly to "the idea of every child having a chance to get an education," particularly with the Hancock School Equalization Bill.[60] As the younger brother, Blan lacked the educational opportunities given to the first-born son. As youngsters, Dauph was 19 months older, but three years ahead in schooling, according to Blan. As young men, Dauph obligingly gave Blan "exercises" to advance his education, yet Dauph continued to remain ahead of his brother academically.

J.F. Spainhour described the Dougherty brothers, his former pupils, in his eulogy at the memorial service for D.D. Dougherty in 1929:

> ...They both led their classes in every school or college they ever attended. The only thing about which they agreed perfectly was that they were going through College in spite of hindrances....
>
> ... The plans to enlarge from year to year were largely the product of the brain of D.D. Dougherty. The execution of these plans was accomplished mainly by B.B. Dougherty....
>
> B.B. Dougherty, as I have said, is bright, capable, honest. He studies people; he keeps his ear to the ground; he knows what the people are thinking; he goes to work; he captures the folks and carries out the plans originated by his brother—and in this he is an artist. He does his work so quietly, so successfully that the public is unaware when or how it is done.[61]

In 1929 the *Charlotte Observer* mistakenly designated D.D. Dougherty as "Dr. Dougherty," revealing an assumption that the scholarly brother who had led Appalachian for so many years was the PhD holder.[62]

Gracious and Friendly

The Dougherty brothers differed in how they related to people. Although not an elected official, Blan was a public servant and was appointed to several state boards and committees, which took a great deal of his time and thought.[63] He gave hundreds of speeches, to both small and large groups, promoting the Appalachian, good roads, tax equalization for North Carolina public schools, and many educational causes.[64]

But he could exasperate others by his silence, or by asking questions of others, but keeping his thoughts and experiences to himself "in a superb manner," and closing up "like a clam."[65] After his death in 1957, the State Board of Education members wrote a resolution of respect and tribute, characterizing B.B. Dougherty as "The Silent Man," noting B.B. Dougherty's "characteristic pose was that of an attentive listener; but when he did speak, it was with devastating clarity."[66] Often doodling on the sole of his shoe, Blan was always thinking and figuring.[67]

Contrastingly, Dauph's son-in-law Lester Brown described Dauph as gracious and friendly, and one who enjoyed children.[68] He was a warm and loving father, his daughter Annie affirmed. Blan didn't talk much to the children when they visited during the years after Dauph's death, according to Dauph's granddaughter Elizabeth "Lib" Brown. Lib, who stayed with Lillie at night while attending Appalachian for college in the late 1930s and early '40s, felt that Blan was focused on Raleigh and "politicking."[69] Blan, who lived above the garage at this time, came to the main house to eat meals, often at odd hours, sometimes kept his hat on while he ate, she said, and always seemed to be caught up in his own thoughts.[70]

Stewards for the State of North Carolina

The Doughertys personally practiced the simple way of life that they promoted, "with little display of dress and with no pretentious spending."[71]

While Dauph Dougherty supported substantial buildings and adequate equipment for Appalachian,

> [Dauph] did not believe in lavish spending for the sake of showiness. In all this he wanted it kept in mind that most of Appalachian's students came from modest homes, and that many were from poor families. He would not make the gap between home and school too great but would build all around with the idea of making the transition of students [to school] as natural as possible.... He was not enthusiastic about any college becoming a big institution lest the striving for mere bigness outweigh the standard of quality. He could hardly envision more than 1000 students at a time at Appalachian, if the college were to keep the quality of its work high.[72]

Stewardship and frugality defined all the Doughertys. "As was later said of his dollar stretching brother, Prof. Dauph could also make a dollar do the work of a dollar and a half. He knew well as anybody the value of money, which was hard to get during his boyhood and youth and on through college days. During those days he learned how to spend wise money wisely, whether it was his own or whether it belonged to the citizens of the state. In either case, it was a sacred trust."[73]

High Ideals and Thorough

"There is no man in this county that thinks more—and thinks [more] deeply—than he," Professor Greene wrote about Dauph. "He is so modest that only a few know and appreciate his true worth. Some think that he is cold and easy to become angry; but he is often hurt. His ideals are so high that he appears to be too exacting."[74]

Dr. Graydon Eggers began working at the college in 1922 and knew Dauph professionally for seven years. "He was a brusque man—very thorough," Eggers told a *Watauga Democrat* reporter.

> For instance, I recall one of the last times he and I saw each other. It was just a few days before his death.... At the time, a football team was being organized and I was presenting the budget to him for consideration. He wanted to know not only the amount of the proposed budget but, among other things, how long the uniforms and equipment would last and what the game would contribute to the betterment of the institution.[75] ... [I]f you want to get a good insight into his character, look at his portrait which is hanging in the auditorium of the Administration Building. Notice, in particular, his penetrating eyes.[76]

A professional portrait of D.D. Dougherty was presented to the college at his memorial service by his former students. This portrait hung in the Second Administration Building but was burned in the fire of 1966, as was a professional portrait of B.B. Dougherty. Clara Dougherty Brown, an amateur artist, painted a replica of her father which currently hangs in the B.B. Dougherty Administration Building entrance.[77]

Blan was also known for his penetrating gaze, which could unnerve his subjects. "You could never forget those dark, keen eyes," Lester Brown wrote, "that seemed to be looking through you as if the owner were reading your innermost thoughts. Sometimes his glasses were a hindrance and he would then incline his head forward and look over them."[78]

"No one can think or speak of one without thinking of the other. While D.D. Dougherty was married and had a family and a home, all their property was owned jointly and the home of the one was the home of the other and their hospitality was unbounded."[79]

Perhaps the divergent pathways of marriage and bachelorhood magnified and further developed the differences in the brothers' personalities. At Dauph's funeral in 1929, the Rev. W. "Rufus" Bradshaw a minister from Morganton and perhaps one of the closest friends of Mr. Dougherty, commented that "the brothers were temperamentally opposite, yet cared deeply for one another."[80]

Community Minded in a Quiet Way

Professor Downum, Latin professor and registrar at Appalachian, wrote "A Tribute to a Friend" in honor of his close friend and colleague, D.D. Dougherty:

> He seemed always ready and planning for the comfort, pleasure and the benefit of others. A special program for the student body was often his objective. For long years, until the last few when he has been sick, it seemed to be his one purpose to be helpful to others. Even for the past few months during the fall and winter terms he kept up the fine work. At one time he took some students in a school bus to Blowing Rock, and at another time he took the faculty over to the rock to see a sunset, and at that time the sunset was so beautiful that it almost seemed that it was made for the occasion. …all these things were done in such an unassuming and quiet way that often many did not know who laid the plans.[81]

"He was one of the most generous men I ever knew," wrote Smith Hagaman. "Without show, he was always displaying charity wherever he could relieve suffering or want."[82]

Ruth Barker Redmond, Dauph's secretary, pointed out: "He was a man who was very much interested in his fellow workers—teachers, auxiliary workers, and so forth. Each Christmas he would give them a book or some other present. And he was periodically helping out county ministers by mailing checks to them." Remembering his professor, a former student described him as "one of the greatest friends to the struggling youth of the hill country and recall[ed] touching incidents of the manner in which he had always extended a helping hand or dropped a word of cheer."

At Dauph's memorial service, college classmate Rev. Bradshaw remarked that D.D. Dougherty "had as much moral courage as any man I have ever known ... contributing liberally of his time to church and other Christian activities. A man could have no better friend than he whom we revere this evening."[83]

To Better the Conditions of Those Around Us

When Dauph died, Professor A.J. Greene of the English Department wrote: "No member of the faculty has done more hard work than he. The best man in Boone has passed.... Many of us have lost our best friend."[84] Spainhour ended his remarks at the June 1929 funeral for Dauph with these words: "In his death the college, as well as his brother, has lost its right arm. No man can be found who can fill the place of this great and good man who has so modestly and so efficiently done his work...."[85]

Dauph Dougherty was noted to be "a pioneer in mountain education work."[86] Dauph's peer, Professor J. Downum, called Dauph "a distinguished educator and friend of mankind."[87] The 1931 *Rhododendron* yearbook was dedicated to D.D. Dougherty with these words, describing him as "a leader in civic righteousness, student, educator and co-founder of Appalachian State University, who spared no time, labor or sacrifice to make it a cradle of character, a fountain of knowledge, and a builder of ideals for the teachers of the State."[88]

The legacy of Dauph Dougherty's life can be found on the plaque dedicating the library which bears his name: "This Building Is Dedicated to the Memory of Dauphin Disco Dougherty, Scholar-Thinker-Christian, Co-founder and Business Manager of the Appalachian State Teachers College, Professor of Mathematics and Science 1903–1929, Organizer of the First Library in this Institution, whose vision and devoted labors have flowered into these Ampler Opportunities for Aspiring Youth."[89]

Appalachian thrives today in large part because of one man's aspiration to "better the conditions of those around us," as was his resolve as a 21-year-old.[90] He enlisted the help of his wife and brother to improve "the lost provinces"

Portrait of Dauphin Disco Dougherty, c. 1921 (Doris Stam Collection, University Archives, Special Collections Research Center, Appalachian State University, Boone, North Carolina).

of northwest North Carolina, through the future teachers, future professionals and citizens they taught, enriching hundreds of thousands of lives.

These three Doughertys—Lillie, Dauph, and Blan—lived lives of sacrifice and fixed purpose: to "better the condition" of others. Their persistence towards their goal brought forth a rigorous four-year-college that would flourish into a major regional university. They fought hard for what they gained, and the benefits for generations past, present, and future abound. Their devotion to the cause of education and the good it manifested is incalculable. May they inspire us all to continue in the path of giving for the good of others.

In this south-facing aerial view of Appalachian's campus from June 1950, the Boone City Cemetery (1) is in the center. King Street (2) is visible in the lower left corner to the middle right edge, moving east to west. The ASU football stadium is currently located on the T.S. Coffey farm (3) in the upper right of this image (University Communications Records, University Archives, Special Collections Research Center, Appalachian State University, Boone, North Carolina). *Opposite top right:* In this north-facing aerial view of Appalachian State Teachers College campus, c. 1950, the Second Administration Building is on the left center. The razed area is the former site of Watauga Academy and Science Hall, both of which burned in a 1949 fire (courtesy Palmer Blair Collection, Digital Watauga Project). *Opposite bottom right:* The steel framework of Doughton Residence Hall (1)under construction (c. 1962) on Blowing Rock Road. I.G. Hall (2) is centered in the lower edge of the photograph, on the former site of the Watauga Academy building (courtesy Palmer Blair Collection, Digital Watauga Project).

The Appalachian State University campus in 2023. Clockwise: D.D. Dougherty Memorial Library on the left, Belk Library & Information Commons with cupola, First Baptist Church of Boone with steeple, the Reich College of Education Building, Miles Annas Student Services Building, and Plemmons Student Union, Howard's Knob in the background (photograph by Marie Freeman, Appalachian State University).

Chapter Notes

Chapter 1

1. D.D. Dougherty, written 31 Dec. 1890, among family documents, UA 47: Doris Stam Collection, University Archives, Special Collections Research Center, Appalachian State University, Boone, NC.
2. D.D. Dougherty, 31 Dec. 1890, Stam Collection.
3. D.D. Dougherty, 31 Dec. 1890, Stam Collection.
4. D.D. Dougherty, 31 Dec. 1890, Stam Collection.
5. W.R. Cullom, "Wayside Heroism: The Dougherty Brothers," *Charity & Children* (Thomasville, NC: Baptist State Convention of North Carolina, 1 Feb. 1945), Stam Collection. *Charity & Children* is the Baptist Children's Homes of North Carolina's long-running news publication established in 1887.
6. Rev. William Bradshaw, "Tribute Paid Benefactor of Teachers College at Boone," special to the *Charlotte Observer*, 26 Oct. 1929.
7. James Monroe Downum, "An Appreciation for a Friend (to Prof. D.D. Dougherty)," 25 Nov. 1934.
8. Emma Horton Moore, "A Worthy Tribute to D.D. Dougherty" (Boone, NC: unpublished manuscript, June 1929), UA 30.024, Emma Horton Moore Scrapbook, University Archives, Special Collections Research Center, Appalachian State University, Boone, NC.
9. Bradshaw, "Tribute Paid Benefactor."
10. O. Lester Brown, *B.B. Dougherty: A Man to Match His Mountains* (Charlotte: privately published, 1963), 103.
11. Susan C. Cubbage and Jan E. Moore, "Changes in an Era: 1924–1940: Recollections of LeVerne Smith Fox," a paper presented to Dr. Ruby Lanier, History, Section 101, 7 Dec. 1982, Appalachian State University, Boone, NC, 7–8.
12. Prof. V.C. Howell, "In Memoriam of Dauphin Disco Dougherty," *The Rhododendron 1929*, vol. 7 (Boone, NC: Published by Faculty and Students of Appalachian State Teachers College, 1929), 11, University Archives, Special Collections Research Center, Appalachian State University, Boone, NC.

Chapter 2

1. Rebecca Dougherty Hyatt, *The Dougherty Family in America: 1744–1965* (Ann Arbor: Edwards Brothers, 1965), v.
2. Lester J. Cappon, "Iron-Making—A Forgotten Industry of North Carolina," *The North Carolina Historical Review* 9, no. 4 (Raleigh, NC: North Carolina Historical Commission, Oct. 1932), 331–348, https://archive.org/details/sim_north-carolina-historical-review_1932-10_9_4_0/page/331/mode/1up. "It [the legislative act offering land grants] promised tax exemption for a decade for works set up within three years of the grant if production even amounted to 5000 weight of iron. The August 1807 term of the county court issued the first approval of a land grant to Daniel Daugherty [spelled with an "au"] for the use of iron works built on Big Helton. He later sold to Meredith Ballou."
3. Cappon, 331–348. Bernard Goss, chairman, Ruth Weaver Shepherd, and Ashe County Heritage Book Committee, eds., *The Heritage of Ashe County, North Carolina Vol. 1, 1799–1984* (Winston-Salem, NC: Hunter Publishing Company and Ashe County Historical Society, 1984), 15–16; Ashe County Court, Minute Book (MS.), 10 Aug., 9 Nov. 1807; Arthur Lloyd Fletcher, *Ashe County: A History; A New Edition*, Contributions to Southern Appalachian Studies 14 (Jefferson, NC: McFarland, 2006), 41, 86.
4. Hyatt, 1–2.
5. Brown, *B.B. Dougherty*, 4.
6. http://www.johnsoncountytn.gov/dry-run-tennessee.
7. Morley, 240.
8. Fletcher, *Ashe County*, 231.
9. R. Carlyle Buley, *The Old Northwest: Pioneer Period, 1815–1840* (Bloomington: Indiana University Press, 1951), 227; David McCullough, *The Pioneers* (New York: Simon & Schuster, 2019), 71.
10. Fletcher, *Ashe County*, 41, 88, 167, 222–223, 259. (Fletcher even mistakenly misspells the last name of Dr. B.B. Dougherty with an "a" instead of the "o." Pronunciation of the family name varies across America. D.D. and B.B. Dougherty's extended family pronounce the family name like DAR-I-TY, so it is understandable that it is misspelled!)
11. A concrete pond was created on the property at some point in time, which was filled with the very cold spring water and allowed a trout pond with watercress in shallow areas, both of which

12. Hyatt, 4; Fletcher, *Ashe County*, 89; Wilson, *1860 Census*. David Worth, at Creston, was a tanner by trade and became one of the county's leading citizens. Fletcher writes on page 91: "Not everybody in Ashe County was completely loyal to the South. The institution of slavery was never popular in Ashe County and when the war between the states came there was little enthusiasm for slavery. As a matter of fact, the census of 1860 showed only 391 slaves in Ashe and 142 free Negros. Probably not more than a dozen families owned slaves, and there was no interest in perpetuating slaveholding. However, because the citizens of Ashe were strong for states' rights, they threw their support to the South and went along with the rest of the state when it finally seceded from the union."

13. Hyatt, 4. A woodworking shop and lathe furthered Elijah Dougherty's capabilities. His niece, Rebecca Dougherty Hyatt, reported that "a hundred small spinning wheels were made here for the trade." Metal fittings for these items were created. "This shop contained a heavy trip hammer run by waterpower used in reducing the heavier iron bars to proper size for use in wagon tires, horseshoes, etc."

14. Herman Tester, *Butler: Old, New and Carderview, A Story of Butler, Johnson County, Tennessee 1768–2006* (Johnson City, TN: privately published, 2007), 101–127. Frequent flooding is why the T.V.A. chose this area for a lake after the devastating 1940 flood. Tester records that 15 inches of rain fell in a few hours in August of 1940, which caused major devastation.

15. Hyatt, 1–122.

16. Hyatt, 26–27.

17. Basil Duke Barr, *Jefferson, North Carolina: My Boyhood Town at the Turn of the Century* (Jefferson, NC: privately published, 1975), 34–35.

18. Several of Elijah's brothers also built brick homes in the area around Dry Run; at least one of them is also still in use.

19. Tester, *Butler*, 68–70. President Smith oversaw the making of 200,000 bricks for Holly Spring College in 1865–1866, which took more than a year to make, even with a team of workers and sometimes 24-hour shifts.

20. Annie Dougherty Rufty, Virginia Brown Brown and Lib Brown Scoggins, interview by Dr. Ruth Currie, Boone, NC, 21 and 31 Oct. 1995. Videotape recorded. UA 45: Elizabeth Brown Scoggins Collection, Special Collections Research Center, Appalachian State University, Boone, NC.

21. Hyatt, 4. Joseph Buckner Killebrew (1831–1906) was an American planter and geologist.

22. Tester, *Butler*, 49.

23. Goss and Shepherd, *Heritage of Ashe County Vol. 1, 1799–1984*, 173–174; Ruth Weaver Shepherd, Project Director, and the Ashe County Historical Society, eds., *The Heritage of Ashe County, North Carolina Vol. 2, 1799–1984* (West Jefferson, NC: Hunter Publishing Company and Ashe County Historical Society, 1994), 83. Eve Dougherty's relatives included Benjamin Council (married to her aunt Elizabeth Mast), Dudley Farthing (married to her aunt Nancy Mast), and uncle Ruben Mast. Her grandmother, Eve Bowers Mast (wife of Joseph Mast), had a sister, Sarah Bowers, who was married to the wealthiest land and slave owner in the county, Jordan Council, Jr. Eve Bowers was married to Joseph Mast.

24. Sanna Ross Gaffney, ed., and the Heritage of Watauga County Book Committee, *The Heritage of Watauga County, North Carolina, Volume 1* (Winston-Salem, NC: Heritage of Watauga County Book Committee in cooperation with the History Division of Hunter Publishing Co., 1984), 2. Before Watauga County was established, "the nearest county seat from the center of the area was Lenoir, but even that was 26 miles away. Some found it easier to ride the 25 miles to Taylorsville, Tennessee (renamed Mountain City) to obtain a marriage license. Burnsville, county seat of Yancey, was over 50 miles away," to the south.

25. Gaffney, ed., 2–4; Michael Hardy, *A Short History of Watauga County* (Boone, NC: Parkway, 2005), 34.

26. Hyatt, 71–80. Casper Cable, maternal grandfather to Eve Dougherty, inherited many slaves by marrying Elizabeth Baker.

27. The military records for the sons of Elijah and Eve Dougherty are available in government records.

28. Hyatt, 4–5.

29. *North Carolina Troops 1861–1865 Vol. 2* (Raleigh, NC: NC Department of Archives and History, 1968 and 1989), various pages. Eddie Dougherty, interview by Doris Perry Stam, Aug. 2022, Stam Collection.

30. https://civilwartalk.com/threads/the-price-of-a-good-horse.17718/; https://www.quora.com/How-much-did-a-horse-cost-in-1850.

31. https://www.nps.gov/common/uploads/teachers/lessonplans/1870CatalogueofGoods.pdf.

32. Tester, *Butler*, 48.

33. https://warfarehistorynetwork.com/2019/02/02/civil-war-cavalry-units-worth-the-cost/; http://www.civilwar.com/overview/315-weapons/148532-cavalry-62478.html; https://en.wikipedia.org/wiki/Cavalry.

34. https://en.wikipedia.org/wiki/Cavalry_in_the_American_Civil_War.

35. Hyatt, 81.

36. Hyatt, 81.

37. Hyatt, 81–82.

38. Hyatt, 82.

39. Tester, *Butler*, 16; Eddie Dougherty, interview by Doris Perry Stam, Aug. 2022, Stam Collection; Herman Tester, phone conversations, 2021–2022, with Doris Perry Stam, Stam Collection.

40. Morley, 202–203; Tester, *Butler*, 48–49.

41. Tester, *Butler*, 48–49, 54, 57; Herman Tester, interview by Doris Perry Stam, 25 July 2017,

recorded, Stam Collection; Herman Tester, emails with Doris Perry Stam, 2017–2019, Stam Collection.

Benjamin Councill, Jr., and Daniel Baker Dougherty were second cousins (through Eve Mast Dougherty), which may have been another reason for Councill's willingness to sell property to Dougherty. Benjamin, who owned the muster field for the county, had been unwilling to sell the muster field as a site for a courthouse in 1849. His brother, Jordan Councill, Jr., offered 25 acres of land, as did Ransom Hayes.

42. Hardy, *Short History of Watauga County*, 88.
43. Watauga County, North Carolina, *Index, Registry of Deeds*, Book L, 530.

Chapter 3

1. Basil Duke Barr, *Jefferson, North Carolina: My Boyhood Town at the Turn of the Century* (Jefferson, NC: privately published, 1975), 7; Arthur Lloyd Fletcher, *Ashe County: A History; A New Edition*, Contributions to Southern Appalachian Studies 14 (Jefferson, NC: McFarland, 2006), 76, 88, 93, 123.
2. Barr, 5; Alene Hardin, "Private Papers," unpublished manuscripts, Stam Collection; Mrs. C.D. Neal, *Miss Chessie's Memories: Interesting People, Places and Stories in Ashe County History Recounted* (Ronda, NC: Elizabeth Parks Neal, 1982), 3; Barr, 5.
3. Barr, 5; Alene Hardin, "Private Papers"; C.D. Neal, *Miss Chessie*, 3.
4. Barr, 5; https://www.townofboone.net/163/Historical-Population-Information. Basil Barr wrote: "While we had nothing in this part of the world like the class system of Europe, there were what you might call strata of society in Jefferson. Some people, of course, had more money than others, and some families tended to think of themselves as the elite.... Help was plentiful in those days, and almost all the well to do families had servants."
5. Barr, 15–16; Brown, *B.B. Dougherty*, 7. Granddaughter Alene Hardin added some details about the Bartlett house: "If Asa Gray's headquarters were 50 feet from the town, it must have been at the back of Grandpa's home, the lands of Edwin Bartlett running back up the hill, with the chestnut orchards, a spring, and a small farm." A letter dated 27 March 1897, from Daniel Baker Dougherty to his son, Dauph, mentions the tinner tools of E.C. Bartlett inherited by Dauph. Dauph is advised by his father that the tools will not bring much money if being sold. With his home Edwin "had a shop on the premises. I cannot remember back to the time Mr. Bartlett actually lived there," wrote Mr. Barr, "but at his death, a sale was held, and my father bought some tinner tools. I still have two of the tinner's anvils."
6. Barr, 28; Brown, *B.B. Dougherty*, 7; C.D. Neal, *Miss Chessie*, 3.
7. Brown, *B.B. Dougherty*, 7.
8. Zetta Barker Hamby, *Memoirs of Grassy Creek: Growing Up in the Mountains on the Virginia-North Carolina Line*, Contributions to Southern Appalachian Studies 1 (Jefferson, NC: McFarland, 1998), 118–119.
9. John Preston Arthur, *A History of Watauga County with Sketches of Prominent Families* (Johnson City, TN: The Overmountain Press, 1992; originally privately printed, 1915), 129; Fletcher, *Ashe County*, 76, 93, 123, 130, 131.
10. Alene Hardin, "Private Papers."
11. Brown, *B.B. Dougherty*, 7–8; C.D. Neal, *Miss Chessie*, 36.
12. Brown, 7–11.
13. Brown, 11.
14. Daniel Baker Dougherty might have taken part in an event about which Chessie Neal wrote (page 16 in *Miss Chessie*): "From all I have heard from people who remembered, the land where on [sic] the Jefferson school is now situated, was loaned by Major Neal for tournament and gala occasions where numerous riders competed in taking rings off a hook while riding at breakneck speed. This began a few years after the civil war. The rider who could take off the most rings was entitled to crown some girl present the queen of beauty of the tournament."
15. J.P. Arthur, *A History of Watauga County*, 151 and 182; Ben Horton, "Glimpses of Yesteryears in Watauga County" (Boone, NC: privately published, Dec. 1975); Watauga County, North Carolina, *Registry of Deeds, Index* 133, or 317; *Book M*, 248. The historian John Preston Arthur, whose book *A History of Watauga County* was written at the request of Dauph and Blan Dougherty and some other citizens of Boone, lists the date of a transaction between D.B. Dougherty and Jordan (and Sarah) Councill as 1865. He gives the deed page and number. However, the actual Registry of Deeds gives the date for this particular transaction as 1888. The Doughertys probably gave Arthur information to correct the deed book. With court records destroyed in 1865 and again in 1872, only those with proof and duplicate copies could have conveyances prior to those fires recorded in the deed books.

Jordan Councill, Jr., was apparently worried that the U.S. government would confiscate his lands (for siding with the South) and offered to sell his lands to D.B. Dougherty at half their value. Arthur continues on page 182: "Accordingly, on the first day of August 1865, Jordan Councill gave D.B. Dougherty his bond for title to all his land and property in and around Boone when Dougherty should pay him $3,000.00 cash (Deed Book M, 248)." But I, Doris Perry Stam, believe that Arthur is mistaken, or there was a typographical error, for the date in Deed Book M, page 248, is the year 1888. The Watauga County deed books mention a sale from Jordan and Sarah Councill to D.B. Dougherty of 300 acres in 1875 and from Jordan Councill to D.B. Dougherty of 600 acres in 1888.

Arthur goes on to say: "Councill moved away but returned and recovered all the property Dougherty had not sold, the proceeds of that which had been sold having been applied to the bond." Others have quoted Arthur, and confusion may have developed, even among Dougherty family members, myself included.

16. Jordan Councill, Jr.'s wife was Sarah, sister of Daniel Baker Dougherty's great-grandmother, Elizabeth Cable Mast.

17. J.P. Arthur, *History of Watauga County*, 182; Ben Horton, "Glimpses of Yesteryears in Watauga County" (Boone, NC: privately published, Dec. 1975); Bud Altmayer, *A Family History of Watauga County* (Boone, NC: Minor's Printing Co., 1994), 97, 148–149.

18. Altmayer, 119–122; J.P. Arthur, *History of Watauga County*, 157. Rachel Rivers-Coffey, interview by Bud Altmayer.

19. Mrs. Barnard Dougherty file. Some discrepancy exists about his birth location, but the birth certificate lists Boone, not Ashe County. Alene Hardin claims she verified B.B. being born in Boone by talking with the Councills and the Bryans. "Facts" are not always correct in Alene's writings. Dr. B.B. Dougherty claimed he was born in Jefferson in a speech promoting "good roads."

20. Watauga County, North Carolina, *Registry of Deeds, Index Book F*, 301. *Watauga County, North Carolina, Old Deed Books, Book D*, 638. Deed conveying land from Jordan and Sarah Councill (Jr.) to Daniel B. Dougherty: "State of North Carolina, Watauga County, Court of Probate, March 14, 1870.... The written deed is duly registered in Book D 638, this 21st March 1870. Joseph Harrison, C. Register" (300–302). See also Deed book M, page 248.

21. Brown, *B.B. Dougherty*, 13–14.

22. J.P. Arthur, *History of Watauga County*, 151–155; https://chroniclingamerica.loc.gov/lccn/sn82007642/; https://www.ncpedia.org/justicespeace. The relocated and remodeled Councill's store, which became the Dougherty home, stood near the current restored movie theater, on the site of a surface parking lot to the west of the theater.

23. Brown, *B.B. Dougherty*, 13. Dr. William Bower Councill is sometimes confused with his son, Judge William Ballard Councill (1858–1940).

24. Alene Hardin, "Private Papers."

25. Ellen's beloved older sister had died in 1865 at the age of 25. Two brothers had died as two-year-olds, and two other sisters at ages 24 and 45.

26. Brown, *B.B. Dougherty*, 14.

27. Brown, *B.B. Dougherty*, 14.

28. Brown, *B.B. Dougherty*, 14.

Chapter 4

1. Lillie Shull Dougherty's tombstone and family Bible list 1874 as her birth year, but it has sometimes been incorrectly listed as 1875. In *Mountain Educators* Doris Perry Stam used the wrong birth year.

2. Lillie Shull Dougherty's tombstone and family Bible list 1874 as her birth year, but it has sometimes been incorrectly listed as 1875. In *Mountain Educators* Doris Perry Stam used the wrong birth year.

3. James H. Smith, "Obituary of David Shull," Stam Collection.

4. Smith, "Obituary of David Shull," Stam Collection.

5. Gaffey, *Watauga County, 1984*, 166.

6. James L. LeLoudis, *Schooling in the New South: Pedagogy, Self and Society in North Carolina, 1880–1890* (Chapel Hill: University of North Carolina Press, 1996), 13.

7. Smith, "Obituary of David Shull," Stam Collection.

8. Dan Crowe, *Old Butler and Watauga Academy* (Butler, TN: privately published, 1983), 7–11; Michael Depew and Lanette Depew, with the Butler Museum, *Images of America: Old Butler* (Charleston, SC: Arcadia, 2005) 6–7; Tester, *Butler*, 57, 60–61, 66–70.

9. Crowe, 32–51; Harry E. Fontaine, *I Remember "Old" Butler* (Butler, TN: privately published, 1984), 3; Tester, *Butler*, 110–127; Herman Grindstaff, "Aenon Seminary, Another Pioneer Institution," *The Elizabethton Daily Star*, Saturday, 23 May 1942; Tester, *Butler*, 122. The exceptionally fertile river valley around Butler was also prone to major flooding. See note 14, Chapter 2, and map, Cranberry 1895.

10. Brown, *B.B. Dougherty*, 117.

11. Hyatt, 77; George Jenkins, "The History of Watauga Academy of Butler, Tennessee," Masters Thesis, Appalachian State Teachers College (Boone, NC: unpublished manuscript, presented to the Faculty of the Department of Education, 23 Aug. 1950), 24–25, UA 30.026, Ruby Lanier Papers, W.L. Eury Appalachian Collection, Special Collections Research Center, Appalachian State University, Boone, NC; Morley, 32, 39, 40; Tester, *Butler*, 24; Brown, *B.B. Dougherty*, 117. Dougherty relatives lived in the Bethel area of western Watauga County, south of the Stone Mountain ridge that separated North Carolina from Tennessee, with a steep road over Stair Gap or Locust Gap connecting the families and farming areas.

12. Smith, "Obituary of David Shull," Stam Collection.

13. James H. Smith and D.D. Dougherty, *1895–96 Annual Catalogue of Holly Spring College, Butler, Tennessee* (Elizabethton, TN: News Job Office, 1895), 2. Photocopy in possession of the family,

14. Morley, 19, 24, 108; Tester, *Butler*, 8.

15. *The History of Johnson County 1986*, 41; Tester, *Butler*, 72. Aenon is another spelling for the same school. Both spellings have been used in publications. Enon, which means "spring" or "fountain" in Hebrew, is where John the Baptist met Jesus. This was an apt term because of the large spring at this spot near a giant holly tree. Tester

wrote about this spring (page 72 in *Butler*): "Indians had been here in the distant past as their axes, grinding stones and arrowheads were found around this spring. A huge cage cave with ceremonial burial remnants, skeletons, tools and weapons was discovered close by, but was closed off out of respect."

16. The Tennessee Baptist publication *Baptist Reflector* (Nashville, TN) printed a news article about Holly Spring College written by D.D. Dougherty in the 2 Dec. 1897 edition (accessed through newspapers.com on 27 Oct. 2021).

17. Morley, 42.

18. Morley, 41. Pioneers who came across the mountains from North Carolina or down the valley of Virginia and Pennsylvania colonies brought with them a desire for education for their children. But "ill will" developed over the Federal Government Compact of 1806 and the designation of public lands for schools, political wrangling and squabbling over so-called vacant land that was in fact settled, some with permanent homes. These landowners resented the take-over of their property. Taxpayers in Tennessee objected strongly to supporting public schools and felt that people should educate their own children at their own expense. This negative bias toward public education seems to have placed a stigma on "free schools," or Common School, often referred to as schools for the poor. Those with means sent their children to private schools. State funding for public schools was exceedingly low, and the quality of teaching equally low prior to 1873. The U.S. Census of 1870 revealed a significantly dropping literacy rate in Tennessee, prompting interest in education and school legislation in 1875, though not without enraged opposition from opponents of public education who persuaded legislators. The bill passed only because of a pocket veto by Governor Porter, a friend of education.

19. Morley, 13.

20. *Biographical Directory of the Tennessee Assembly 1861–1901* 2 (Nashville, TN: The Tennessee State Library and Archives and the Tennessee Historical Commission, 1979), 596.

21. Tester, *Butler*, 62.

22. Crowe, 7–14; Morley, 42; Tester, *Butler*, 64.

23. Guitars are frequently seen in photographs from this time and were often part of the school's orchestra at Appalachian, as well as accompaniment for solo or group singing. Not complicated to make, this instrument was affordable for purchase, or could be hand-made in the Appalachian Mountains.

24. According to tncourts.gov, Tennessee's 95 counties are divided into 31 judicial districts. Hamilton Smith, father of James Hamilton Smith, appears (based on an article from the Jonesborough *Herald and Tribune* from 28 May 1885) to have presided over the First Judicial District of Chancery Courts, which encompassed Washington, Unicoi, Carter, and Johnson counties. This response is from the Tennessee State Library and Archives, from 21 Oct. 2021.

25. Jenkins, 24; Tester, *Butler*, 65–66. Milligan University archivist Katherine N. Banks reported: "Milligan was founded as Buffalo Male and Female Institute in 1866 and promoted to collegiate level in 1882. Milligan is not associated with the Tennessee Baptists, but it is associated with the independent Christian Churches/Churches of Christ" (email on 18 Feb. 2022).

26. Crowe, 11.

27. Crowe, 11.

28. Smith, *Catalogue*, 8, 14.

29. Jenkins, 21.

30. Tester, *Butler*, 68.

31. Crowe, 10, 14.

32. Elizabeth "Lib" Brown Scoggins, with the help of Annie Dougherty Rufty and Virginia Brown, *A Brief Biography of Lillie Shull Dougherty* (Boone, NC: unpublished paper, 1989), in possession of the author, 1–3.

33. Report card for Lillie Belle Shull, 1889, Box 3, Folder 1, Stam Collection.

Chapter 5

1. Tom Corbitt, and others, *Development of Public Education in Watauga County North Carolina* (Boone, NC: Bicentennial Committee and Appalachian State University News Bureau, 1976), 10, Appalachian State University Archives.

2. Addie Mae Edmisten Love, interview by Doris Perry Stam (Bethel, NC, Western Watauga County, Summer 2007), Stam Collection.

3. Lanier, 10, quoting the *Watauga Democrat* on 23 Apr. 1936 and 4 Feb. 1937.

4. "Mrs. Sarah Perry ... Her Pupil," *Watauga Democrat*, 16 June 1955; Addie Mae Edmisten Love, interview by Doris Perry Stam, recorded (Bethel, NC), 2001, Stam Collection.

5. Boone Creek was called Kraut Creek for decades after the kraut factory in western Boone, established in the 1920s, emitted juice from their vats into the creek, causing a noticeable smell from the fermented cabbage to linger over the town through which the creek flowed until the factory closed in the 1980s.

6. Brown, *B.B. Dougherty*, 19. The wood-framed slates used by Dauph and Blan for their early schoolwork, before paper and pencil were widely used, have been handed down through the family. These slates were given to Appalachian State University. ASU, Stam Collection.

7. Brown, *B.B. Dougherty*, 19.

8. https://www.ncpedia.org/education-public.

9. Brown, *B.B. Dougherty*, 13.

10. Lanier, 10. See also Hight C. Moore, *Patton: Southern Highlander: A Biography of Rev. Robert Logan Patton* (Morganton, NC: privately published, 1964), 13.

11. Lanier, 10. Burning wood was the only source of heat for homes at that time.

12. Brown, *B.B. Dougherty*, 15.

13. Daniel J. Whitener, "Semi-Centennial

History of Appalachian State Teachers College," *History of Watauga County: A Souvenir of Watauga Centennial, Boone, NC* (Boone, NC: privately published, 1949), 44 and 74.

14. D.J. Whitener, "Semi-Centennial History of Appalachian State Teachers College," *History of Watauga County: A Souvenir of Watauga Centennial*, 74.

15. Corbitt, 2; McLeod, 14ff; Daniel J. Whitener, *History of Watauga County*, 64.

16. Corbitt, 2.
17. Eggers, 5–6.
18. Eggers, 5–6.
19. Eggers, 5–6.
20. Ballard, 148.
21. Corbitt, 9. He left Oak Hill in the spring of 1883, having finally earned enough money to attend Wake Forest College, from which he graduated in 1885.
22. Eggers, 5–6.
23. Ballard, 137.
24. The location of the James Elrod home is indicated as northeast from the current bridge over the river on Hwy 421 east of Boone.
25. Brown, *B.B. Dougherty*, 20.
26. Lanier, 10–12.
27. Brown, *B.B. Dougherty*, 19–21.
28. W.M. Moore, "Globe Academy Towers with Majestic Greatness in Garden of Fond and Inspiring Memories," *Lenoir News-Topic* (Lenoir, NC), Sept. 1941.
29. R.L. Patton, Jr., "Sidelight of a Great Life," in H.C. Moore, *Patton*, 63.
30. Van Noppen and Van Noppen, 152–153.
31. W.M. Moore, "Globe Academy … Inspiring Memories."
32. H.C. Moore, *Patton*, 17.
33. McLeod, 161.
34. McLeod, 161.
35. McLeod, 161.
36. R.L. Patton, autobiography, "My Struggle for an Education," *Carter's Weekly* (North Wilkesboro, NC), 26 July 1919, and *North Carolina Education*, Feb. 1920. In possession of the author. The contents are also included, in part, in Hight Moore's biography *Patton: Southern Highlander*.
37. Van Noppen and Van Noppen, 152–153.
38. H.C. Moore, *Patton*, 25. "Hight C. Moore, clergyman, writer, and editorial executive, was born in Globe, Caldwell County," Ncpedia.org.
39. Robert Patton, IV, interview by Doris Perry Stam, 24 Jan. 2022, phone conversation and email correspondence, Stam Collection.
40. H.C. Moore, *Patton*, 28.
41. H.C. Moore, *Patton*, 28.
42. H.C. Moore, *Patton*, 28.
43. R.L. Patton, Jr., "Sidelights of a Great Life," 50–59.
44. H.C. Moore, "Globe Academy, flood 1916."
45. R.L. Patton, Jr., "Sidelights of a Great Life," by the youngest son of Prof. Patton, in H.C. Moore, *Patton*, 58–68.
46. McLeod, 161.

47. H.C. Moore, *Patton*, 31–32.
48. Hight C. Moore, "Globe Academy: Memories by Hight C. Moore," *Biblical Recorder, Journal of the Baptist State Convention of North Carolina* (Raleigh, NC: Baptist State Convention of North Carolina, 11 Oct. 1952). Appalachian professor D.J. Whitener mistakenly says B.B. attended Marshall High School, a school which did not exist. Whitener must have somehow associated Prof. Marshall as the namesake of a school.
49. B.B. Dougherty to D.D. Dougherty, 19 Feb. 1899, Stam Collection.
50. Hyatt, 14. When Dauph graduated from Wake Forest College he had the highest math scores of anyone in the history of the school to that date of more than fifty years, according to Rebecca Dougherty Hyatt in *The Dougherty Family in America 1744–1965*.
51. These thoughts were modeled on the work of David McCullough in his book *The Pioneers*.
52. H.O. Huffman, "I Shall Not See His Like Again," in H.C. Moore, *Patton*, 61.
53. McLeod, 161; George A. Plimpton to Mrs. R.L. Patton, 9 Jan. 1920, in H.C. Moore, *Patton*, 83. Patton's classmate from Phillips Exeter Academy, George A. Plimpton, served on the board of the textbook company publisher Ginn & Company (and later donated 16,000 rare books, showing the development of education, to Columbia University). Plimpton recalled R.L., as Patton's friends called him, arriving at Exeter without any money, but with robust health, splendid character, and the determination to get an education. "We were two years at Exeter and four years at Amherst together. The Lord never made a better man. He saw clearly, he had great courage, and expressed himself with much frankness…. President Bruce Payne of George Peabody College told me once that Mr. Patton was the greatest teacher he had ever had, and that he owed more to him than to any other living man. I have no doubt that this testimony could be repeated by many."

Chapter 6

1. Bob Moore to D.D. Dougherty, 31 May 1888, Stam Collection.
2. Bob Moore to D.D. Dougherty, 31 May 1888, Stam Collection.
3. Bob Moore to D.D. Dougherty, 31 May, 4 July 1888, Stam Collection.
4. Bob Moore to D.D. Dougherty, 4 July 1888, Stam Collection.
5. See Daniel Baker Dougherty to D.D. Dougherty, 21 Sept. 1888.
6. Bob Moore to D.D. Dougherty, 10 Aug. 1888, Stam Collection.
7. Bob Moore to D.D. Dougherty, 17 Aug. 1888, Stam Collection.
8. Bob Moore to D.D. Dougherty, 4 July 1888, Stam Collection.
9. Bob Moore to D.D. Dougherty, 17 Aug. 1888, Stam Collection.

10. Paschal, *History of Wake Forest College*, 251-254. Family financial papers include a record of the final payment in 1906 for Dauph's Wake Forest College loan, 18 years after his entrance, and 14 years after his graduation in 1892.

11. Letter from Daniel Baker Dougherty to D.D. Dougherty, 21 Sept. 1888, Stam Collection. Ike was Isaac Dougherty, one of Daniel's brothers.

12. Brown, *B.B. Dougherty*, 28.

13. A. Jackson Greene, "Greene Diaries," unpublished manuscripts, 27 Aug. 1907, AC 105, Andrew Jackson Greene Collection. W.L. Eury Appalachian Collection, Special Collections Research Center, Appalachian State University, Boone, NC. https://omeka.library.appstate.edu/items/browse?collection=39.

14. Daniel Baker Dougherty to D.D. Dougherty, 9 Sept. 1888; B.B. Dougherty to D.D. Dougherty, 10 Dec. 1888, Stam Collection.

15. Arthur, 155. Mr. Arthur, writing in 1915, avows that D.B. Dougherty built a small house for a post office east of the Critcher Hotel "soon after the Civil War. It was enlarged and improved and used as by D. Jones Cottrell as a store room about 1906 and since."

16. B.B. Dougherty to D.D. Dougherty, 10 Dec. 1888, Stam Collection; Brown, *B.B. Dougherty*, 19-20.

17. Daniel Baker Dougherty to D.D. Dougherty, 15 Dec. 1888, Stam Collection.

18. Arthur, 151-155; Gaffney, ed., 163-164; https://chroniclingamerica.loc.gov/lccn/sn82007642/; https://www.ncpedia.org/justices-peace.

19. https://chroniclingamerica.loc.gov/lccn/sn82007642/.

20. Gaffney, ed., 163-164; https://chroniclingamerica.loc.gov/lccn/sn82007642/.

21. Lanier, 8-9.

22. Daniel Baker Dougherty to D.D. Dougherty, 21 Sept. 1888; *Watauga Democrat*, 1893, Stam Collection; Lester Brown's notes from interviewing B.B. included mention that the Coffey family had been quite involved in founding and supporting the newspaper in Boone.

23. Daniel Baker Dougherty to D.D. Dougherty, 21 Sept., 23 Nov., 10 Dec. 1888, Stam Collection; Daniel Baker Dougherty to D.D. Dougherty, prior to Nov. 1891, Stam Collection. The first page of this letter is lost, so a specific date is unknown.

24. B.B. Dougherty to D.D. Dougherty, 23 Nov. 1888, Stam Collection.

25. B.B. Dougherty to D.D. Dougherty, 10 Dec. 1888, Stam Collection.

26. B.B. Dougherty to D.D. Dougherty, 1 Dec. 1888, Stam Collection.

27. B.B. Dougherty was awarded Honorary Doctor of Letters from Elon College in 1926 and Honorary Doctor of Education from Wake Forest College in 1936.

28. Paschal, *History of Wake Forest College*, 144.

29. Paschal, *History of Wake Forest College*, 438.

30. Paschal, *History of Wake Forest College*, 343, 457.

31. NCpedia, "William Louis Poteat"; Wake Forest University Archives, https://zsr.wfu.edu/special/research/guides/wfu-presidents-papers. Dr. Poteat played a prominent role in the development of both Wake Forest and Meredith colleges and was elected president of Wake Forest College in 1905, serving until 1927.

32. https://zsr.wfu.edu/special/collections/archives/wfu-timeline.

33. Paschal, *History of Wake Forest College*, 379.

34. Paschal, *History of Wake Forest College*, 381-382.

35. Paschal, *History of Wake Forest College*, 380-381.

36. Paschal, *History of Wake Forest College*, 368.

37. Paschal, *History of Wake Forest College*, 368.

38. Paschal, *History of Wake Forest College*, 368.

39. Brown, *B.B. Dougherty*, 103; McLeod, 162-163; Evelyn Underwood, "Robert Lee Moore," NCpedia, https://www.ncpedia.org.

40. Brown, *B.B. Dougherty*, 103. Paschal, *History of Wake Forest College*, 342-334.

41. Brown, *B.B. Dougherty*, 103; W.R. Cullom, "Wayside Heroism: The Dougherty Brothers," *Charity & Children* (periodical of Baptist Children's Homes of North Carolina, 1 Feb. 1945).

42. Brown, *B.B. Dougherty*, 103.

43. W.R. Cullom, "Wayside Heroism: The Dougherty Brothers," *Charity & Children* (periodical of Baptist Children's Homes of North Carolina, 1 Feb. 1945).

44. L.R. Mills, written from Wake Forest College for D.D. Dougherty, June 1891, Stam Collection.

45. Daniel Baker Dougherty to D.D. Dougherty, 10 Nov. 1891, Stam Collection.

46. Ruby Lanier, *Blanford Barnard Dougherty: Mountain Educator* (Durham: Duke University Press, 1974), 10-11; *Watauga Democrat*, 29 May 1890; 9 Apr. 1950; 7 July 1958. The chronology of Blan's education and early teaching is difficult to discern and has been misrepresented in some writing about him. Daniel J. Whitener incorrectly wrote that Blan attended Marshall High School, which never existed, confusing Prof. Marshall from Globe Academy with a school name.

47. Brown, *B.B. Dougherty*, 24.

48. Lanier, 11-12.

49. Lanier, 10-12.

50. B.B. Dougherty to D.D. Dougherty, 31 Oct. 1891, Stam Collection.

51. B.B. Dougherty to D.D. Dougherty, 31 Oct. 1888, Stam Collection.

52. B.B. Dougherty to D.D. Dougherty, 31 Oct. 1891, Stam Collection.

53. Brown, *B.B. Dougherty*, 27.

54. D.D. Dougherty to B.B. Dougherty, 30 Oct. 1891, Stam Collection.

55. B.B. Dougherty to D.D. Dougherty, 31 Oct., undated Dec. 1891; 7 Jan. 1892.

56. Brown, *B.B. Dougherty*, 28. Ruby Lanier

records a further anecdote about Blan arriving at Wake Forest in her book, 12–13.

57. Brown, *B.B. Dougherty*, 28–29; *Charlotte News and Observer*, 9 Apr. 1950.

58. Paschal, *History of Wake Forest College*, 376.

59. *The Biblical Recorder*, 15 June 1892; Elizabeth Brown Scoggins Collection, University Archives, Special Collections Research Center, Appalachian State University, Boone, NC. The envelope in the Scoggins Collection which had contained Dauph's Polar Lights thesis is empty, and it appears that the actual thesis is lost. Wake Forest College archives did not have a copy.

60. Brown, *B.B. Dougherty*, 32; Lanier, 13.

61. Lanier, 13.

Chapter 7

1. T.H. Briggs, Treasurer of Wake Forest College, to Mr. D.D. Dougherty, 13 June 1892, Stam Collection.

2. Crowe, 12; *The Wataugan*, Butler, TN. 1948 Yearbook of Watauga Academy (known as Holly Spring College until 1906). This was the last year of the school before the town was inundated in the T.V.A. project.

3. Crowe, 14.

4. Smith, *Holly Spring College Annual Catalogue 1895–1896*, 3. A photocopy is in possession of the family.

5. Jenkins, 38.

6. D.D. Dougherty to Lillie Shull, 11 Oct. 1894, Stam Collection. Dauph wrote that he had loved her for two years, referring to his first acquaintance with her in 1892.

7. Crowe, 10; Tester, *Butler*, 67.

8. Jenkins, 22.

9. Jenkins, 22.

10. Jenkins, 22; Mrs. A.H. Shoun, interview by George Jenkins, 8 June 1950, Neva, TN.

11. Jenkins, 23.

12. *The Tennessee Tomahawk*, 17 May 1893.

13. *The Tennessee Tomahawk*, 17 May 1893.

14. See Lanier, 12. Blan, who had taught at Shulls Mill, Silvertone, and Blowing Rock—school districts on three sides of Watauga County—was paid a remarkable $40 per month at Hamilton Institute, double the regular rate at most mountain schools.

Chapter 8

1. Tester, 67.

2. D.D. Dougherty to Lillie Shull, 8 Dec. 1894, Stam Collection.

3. Carter County, Tennessee, Board of Education Minutes, Record of Certificates Issued 1890, 1891, 1893, 1894. Alice Shull Campbell to Lillie Shull, 8 Dec. 1894, Stam Collection. The Carter County, Tennessee, Board of Education minutes and records list Lillie B. Shull of Butler as receiving a teaching license in 1890, when she was only 16, and again for the years 1891, 1893, and 1894.

4. Jenkins, 21–23.

5. Henry Drummond, "I Corinthians 13," in *The Greatest Thing in the World* (Grand Rapids: Fleming H. Revell Company, 2011, reprint of original, 1874). https://www.christianity.com/church/church-history/timeline/1801-1900/death-of-christ-like-henry-drummond-11630651.html and https://en.wikipedia.org/wiki/Inherit_the_Wind_(play).

6. D.D. Dougherty to Lillie Shull, 11 Oct. 1894, Stam Collection.

7. D.D. Dougherty to Lillie Shull, 11 Oct. 1894, Stam Collection.

8. D.D. Dougherty to Lillie Shull, 11 Oct. 1894, Stam Collection.

9. D.D. Dougherty to Lillie Shull, 11 Oct. 1894, Stam Collection.

10. D.D. Dougherty to Lillie Shull, 11 Oct. 1894, Stam Collection.

11. It is hard to say for sure, but Miss Emma could be Emma Horton from school days at New River Academy east of Boone where Dauph and Blan boarded a few months for the session of school two different years. Emma lived near the school, attended with the brothers, and later worked with them for decades. Emma may be the mysterious Miss "M" that Bob Moore teased Dauph about in a letter to him in 1888 when they were all just out of high school at Globe Academy. Emma married a Mr. Moore, but what happened to him is unknown. The Doughertys offered her a job as matron of the newly built Lovill Home for Girls in 1906. She moved in with her son, and stayed at Appalachian for 35 years, working for most of those years as librarian. Emma Moore's reputation for insistence upon silence in the library, and for strict oversight of the girls' dorms, became notorious.

12. Alice Shull Campbell to Lillie Shull, 8 Dec. 1894; Mr. Jas B. Compile to Lillie Shull, 15 Jan. 1894, UA. 47: Doris Stam Collection, University Archives, Special Collections Research Center, Appalachian State University, Boone, NC. The handwriting makes it difficult to discern the spelling of Mr. Compile's last name.

13. William Lewis to his children, 8 Aug. 1867, ASU, Stam Collection.

14. D.W. Cress to Lillie Shull, 13 Sept. 1896, Stam Collection.

15. D.D. Dougherty to Lillie Shull, 8 Dec. 1894, Stam Collection.

16. D.D. Dougherty to Lillie Shull, 8 Dec. 1894, Stam Collection.

17. D.D. Dougherty to Lillie Shull, 9 Dec. 1894, Stam Collection.

18. D.D. Dougherty to Lillie Shull, 9 Feb. 1895, Stam Collection.

19. D.D. Dougherty to Lillie Shull, Spring 1895, Stam Collection.

20. James H. Smith and D.D. Dougherty, *1895–1896 Annual Catalogue of Holly Spring College*, Stam Collection.

21. James H. Smith and D.D. Dougherty, *1895-1896 Annual Catalogue of Holly Spring College*, Stam Collection.
22. *Watauga Democrat*, 17 June 1897, 3. A record of Lillie Shull's college graduation has not been located. She might have been hired with only two years of college classes.
23. Lillie Shull to D.D. Dougherty, 26 Nov. 1895, Stam Collection.
24. D.J. Whitener, *History of Watauga County*, 74.
25. Brown, *B.B. Dougherty*, 36.
26. Mr. A.C. Larrimore interview by Doris Perry Stam, 6 June, 10 and 21 July 2022, Stam Collection.
27. Lanier, 18. This information comes from interviews with Mr. and Mrs. Clara Dougherty and Lester Brown; Annie Dougherty Rufty; Mrs. Annie Ray Stemson; Mrs. Frances Blalock; and Mrs. Grace Dougherty, all of whom knew Clara Powell, and all of whom were interviewed by Ruby Lanier in the year 1970.
28. Lanier, 18.
29. Brown, *B.B. Dougherty*, 200.
30. Lanier, 18.
31. D.D. Dougherty to Lillie Shull, 14 June 1896, Stam Collection.
32. D.D. Dougherty to Lillie Shull, 14 June 1896, Stam Collection.
33. D.D. Dougherty to Lillie Shull, 14 June 1896, Stam Collection.
34. D.W. Cress to Lillie Shull, 13 Sept. 1896, Stam Collection.
35. Daniel Baker Dougherty to D.D. Dougherty, 22 Mar. 1897, Stam Collection.
36. B.B. Dougherty to D.D. Dougherty, 27 Apr. 1897, Stam Collection.
37. B.B. Dougherty to D.D. Dougherty, 27 Apr. 1897, Stam Collection.
38. Family letters, 11 Oct., 8 and 9 Dec. 1894; 9 Feb., 26 Nov. 1895; 14 and 17 June, 13 Sept. 1896, Stam Collection. Lillie Shull Dougherty's wedding band was inherited by her granddaughter and namesake, Lillie Perry. Doris Perry Stam, whose husband died at age 58 after 36 years of marriage, currently wears this ring.
39. Annie Dougherty Rufty, recorded interview by Doris Perry Stam, 13 Aug. 2000, Stam Collection.
40. *Watauga Democrat*, 17 June 1897, 3.

Chapter 9

1. Daniel Baker Dougherty to D.D. Dougherty, 22 Mar. 1897; B.B. Dougherty to D.D. Dougherty, 21 Apr. 1899, Stam Collection.
2. Daniel Baker Dougherty to D.D. Dougherty, 22 Mar. 1897, Stam Collection.
3. B.B. Dougherty to D.D. Dougherty, 27 Apr. 1897, Stam Collection.
4. Brown, *B.B. Dougherty*, 89.
5. Brown, *B.B. Dougherty*, 200-201; Lanier, 18-20. This information comes from interviews with Mr. and Mrs. Clara Dougherty and Lester Brown; Annie Dougherty Rufty; Mrs. Annie Ray Stemson; Mrs. Frances Blalock; and Mrs. Grace Dougherty, all of whom knew Clara Powell, and all of whom were interviewed by Ruby Lanier in the year 1970. Neither Blan nor Clara ever married, but they continued to write and see each other until the end of their lives.
6. Heidi Coryell Williams, "Hell and High Water," *Our State Magazine* 80, no. 10, Mar. 2013, https://www.ourstate.com/flood-of-1916/.
7. Brown, *B.B. Dougherty*, 17.
8. Lanier, 18.
9. https://www.nps.gov/people/clara-barton.htm.
10. B.B. Dougherty to D.D. Dougherty, during the school year 1898-1899, mentioned financial need, even urgency of need, many times.
11. There was only one UNC at that time, in Chapel Hill.
12. Letters preserved from early 1899 between Daniel Dougherty and his sons Dauph and Blan indicate that there were other letters mentioning the idea of moving back to Boone in 1899, Stam Collection.
13. Jenkins, 32-33. This information came from a former student who was interviewed in 1950 by Mr. Jenkins.
14. Brown, *B.B. Dougherty*, 101.
15. *Watauga Democrat*, 29 Aug. 1888, and other issues from this time period.
16. "Henry W. Blair," Wikipedia, The Free Encyclopedia, last modified 15 July 2023, https://en.wikipedia.org/wiki/Henry_W._Blair; "The Blair Education Bill: A Lost Opportunity in American Public Education," *Studies in American Political Development* 35, no. 1 (Apr. 2021).
17. Brown, *B.B. Dougherty*, 102-103.
18. Peabody Fund | Encyclopedia.com. George Peabody helped establish a major teacher training center in Nashville, Peabody College for Teachers, which became part of Vanderbilt University.
19. Hugh Talmadge Lefler, *History of North Carolina 2* (New York: Lewis Historical Publishing Company, Inc., 1956), 648.
20. William S. Powell, *North Carolina through Four Centuries* (Chapel Hill: University of North Carolina Press, 1989), 419-420.
21. There is no record of any Peabody Fund monies in Watauga County. As superintendent of Watauga County Schools, Blan Dougherty would later request help from the fund in 1902, but not receive any help for the county schools. The fund was ended in 1914.
22. Willard B. Gatewood, Jr., "North Carolina and Federal Aid to Education: Public Reaction to the Blair Bill 1881-1890," *North Carolina Historical Review* 40, no. 4 (Raleigh, NC: North Carolina Historical Commission, Oct. 1963), 465-488. https://archive.org/details/northcarolinahis1963nort/page/464/mode/2up?q=gatewood.
23. William S. Powell, *North Carolina: A History*

(Chapel Hill: University of North Carolina Press, 1977), 184; D.J. Whitener, "Education for the People: An Introduction to the History of Universal Education in North Carolina, 1900–1933," *North Carolina Historical Review* (Raleigh, NC: North Carolina Department of Archives and History, Dec. 1968), 188. Whitener wrote: "Suffice it to say that the law regarding state taxes for education was amended so that these taxes were not only collected but also spent within the respective county. This practice disadvantaged the poorer counties. The poverty of the people, and a narrow interpretation of the constitution of the state Supreme Court, stifled local taxes." B.B. Dougherty was a state leader in the decades-long fight for the tax equalization Hancock Bill, which finally passed in 1929.

24. James S. Ferguson, "An Era of Educational Change," *North Carolina Historical Review* (Raleigh, NC: North Carolina Department of Archives and History, Spring 1969), 134. See also Lanier, 8–9, for more on Daniel Baker Dougherty and the Farmers' Alliance.

25. "About Watauga Democrat," https://chroniclingamerica.loc.gov/lccn/sn82007642/, provided by University of North Carolina at Chapel Hill Library, Chapel Hill, NC.

26. Ferguson, 134.
27. Ferguson, 134.
28. Ferguson, 134.
29. Ferguson, 135.
30. Powell, *North Carolina*, 178–179.
31. https://www.ncpedia.org/normal-school.
32. Lefler, *History of North Carolina 2*, 650–651.
33. https://www.ncpedia.org/anchor/leonidas-polk-and-farmers; https://www.ncsu.edu/spirit-and-traditions/.
34. Ferguson, 135.
35. Ferguson, 135–136.
36. https://www.ncat.edu/about/history-and-traditions/index.php.
37. Ferguson, 137–138.
38. *Biennial Report of the Superintendent of Public Instruction of North Carolina, for the Scholastic Years 1898–'99 and 1899–1900* (Raleigh, NC: Edwards & Broughton and E.M. Uzzell, State Printers, Presses of Edward & Broughton, 1900), 34, 49–50; https://docsouth.unc.edu/nc/ncinstruction1898/ncinstruction1898.html; Rob Christensen, *The Paradox of Tar Heel Politics: The Personalities, Elections, and Events That Shaped Modern North Carolina* (Chapel Hill: University of North Carolina Press, 2008), 11.
39. *Biennial Report 1898–'99 and 1899–1900*, 49.
40. *Biennial Report 1898–'99 and 1899–1900*, 49–50.
41. Bob Etheridge, *The History of Education in North Carolina* (Raleigh, NC: North Carolina Department of Public Instruction, 1993), 4, https://files.eric.ed.gov/fulltext/ED369713.pdf.
42. Lefler, *History of North Carolina 2*, 655.
43. Ferguson, 135.
44. McLeod, 147; Paschal, 60–62.
45. Deweese, 37.

46. Terry Ruscin, *A History of Transportation in Western North Carolina: Trails, Roads, Rails and Air* (Charleston, SC: The History Press, 2016), 12.
47. DeWeese, 19.
48. William Ernest Bird, *The History of Western Carolina College: The Progress of an Idea* (Chapel Hill: University of North Carolina Press, 1963), 14–16; DeWeese, 14; McLeod, 6–14, 71–73.
49. DeWeese, 20.
50. McLeod, 196.
51. Corbitt, 5–8; McLeod, 201 and 208; https://en.wikipedia.org/wiki/Appalachian_stereotypes.
52. Jacqueline B. Painter and Appalachian Consortium Press, *The Season of Dorland-Bell: History of an Appalachian Mission School* (Asheville, NC: Biltmore Press, 1996), Foreword. See also the 1967 historical fiction novel *Christy*, by Catherine Marshall.
53. Jacqueline B. Painter and Appalachian Consortium Press, *The Season of Dorland-Bell: History of an Appalachian Mission School* (Asheville, NC: Biltmore Press, 1996), Foreword.
54. Margaret Tufts Neal, *And Set Aglow a Sacred Flame: History of Edgar Tufts Memorial Association 1895–1942* (Banner Elk, NC: Pudding Stone Press, Lees-McRae College, 1983), 16.
55. https://www.ncpedia.org/lenoir-rhyne-college. The institution's name was changed to Lenoir-Rhyne College in 1923 in recognition of textile manufacturer, banker, and philanthropist Daniel Efird Rhyne, who made a generous donation to the college in 1922. See also Pfeiffer College, a Methodist-related school which began near Lenoir.
56. *Davenport Female College Catalogue, 1891–1892* (Lenoir, Caldwell County, NC: Davenport College, 1891–1892). Clara Powell is listed as the principal of the Model School, and it is my opinion that this is the same person B.B. Dougherty asked to marry him. As at Holly Spring College, geometry (using Wentworth's text) is a college- level class, taught in the junior year at Davenport. Tuition costs seem comparably high.
57. McLeod, 78–79.
58. McLeod, 204.
59. Deweese, 58.
60. Paschal, 47–49, 58–61. *The Biblical Recorder*, a North Carolina Baptist newspaper, published the names of these academies and details about them during the nineteenth century. In 1905 the North Carolina legislature began a system of state-wide public high schools. Prior to that time the number of state-supported public high schools was limited to the major commercial cities of the state, and numbered less than 20, according to Paschal. Baptist academies were overlooked by Raper, Battle, Mebane and Smith in their histories of academies in North Carolina, according to Paschal, who cites evidence in the *Biblical Recorder* for the many North Carolina Baptist academies of the nineteenth century.
61. Paschal, 58–60.
62. DeWeese, 36; McLeod, 202–203; Paschal, 58.

63. D.D. Dougherty, New Year's Eve diary entry, 31 Dec. 1892/1 Jan. 1893, Stam Collection.
64. Hardy, *Short History of Watauga County*, 104.
65. https://www.encyclopedia.com/history/united-states-and-canada/us-history/panic-1893.
66. Lanier, 27. Blan Dougherty was offered a co-principalship with Bob Moore at Mars Hill in 1900, but declined, probably sensing his options were more attractive elsewhere.
67. https://www.thettomahawk.com/accent/watauga-academy-memories-still-alive-in-butler/, Mountain City, TN, accessed 28 Sept. 2021. President Smith sold the college in 1902 to the Southern Baptist Board of Home Missions, Division of Mountain Schools. The name of Holly Spring College was changed to Watauga Academy at a board meeting of the school on 6 Sept. 1906; Crowe, 16–17.
68. 2018 Local School Finance Study (Public School Forum on North Carolina), https://files.eric.ed.gov/fulltext/ED585762.pdf. In 1901, the General Assembly appropriated $100,000 for public schools, marking the first time there was a direct appropriation of tax revenue for public schools. Today, the constitution mandates that the state provide a "general and uniform system of free public schools" and that the state legislature may assign counties "such responsibility for the financial support of the free public schools as it may deem appropriate." N.C. Const. art. IX, § 2 (see note, "Sources of Local School Finance Law: The North Carolina State Constitution"). See also https://www.ncpedia.org/public-education-part-4-expansion.
69. B.B. Dougherty to D.D. Dougherty, 19 Feb. 1899.
70. Daniel Baker Dougherty to D.D. Dougherty, 20 Mar. 1899, Stam Collection. See also Lanier, 21.
71. Daniel Baker Dougherty to D.D. Dougherty, 10 Apr. 1899, Stam Collection.
72. Brown, *B.B. Dougherty*, 42.
73. B.B. Dougherty to D.D. Dougherty, 21 Apr. 1899.

Chapter 10

1. *Watauga Democrat*, 5 Jan. 1899.
2. Lanier, 23. Lanier does not give a date for the newspaper, only the month of January. *Watauga Democrat* digitalNC issue for 2 Jan. 1899 is missing 3 and 4 which probably had this announcement. Lanier may have seen a copy on microfiche.
3. *Watauga Democrat*, Jan. 1899, cited in Lanier, 23.
4. *Watauga Democrat*, 12 Jan. 1899.
5. Paul. W. Bingham, "The Growth and Development of Education in Watauga County" (Master's Thesis, Appalachian State Teachers College, Aug. 1950), 71; Hyatt, 54. The other members in 1873 were J.T. Coffey, chairman of the Watauga County Board of Education, J.M. Brown, Thomas Bingham, J.W. Farthing, and E.F. Lovill.
6. Brown, *B.B. Dougherty*, 21, 42–46; Corbitt, 29–30; Eggers, 4; Lanier, 24–25; *Watauga Democrat*, 11 July, 3 Oct. 1895, 19 May 1898. Brown indicates that Blan attended Cove Creek at least one short term.

See also Kemp P. Battle, "Sketches of Some of the Old or Extinct Schools in the Counties of North Carolina," *Biennial Report of the Superintendent of Public Instruction of North Carolina, for the Scholastic Years 1896–'97 and 1897–'98* (Raleigh, NC: Superintendent Public Instruction), 716–17. Brown indicates that Blan attended Cove Creek at least one short term.

7. Gaffney, ed., 204. Lillie Shull was Etta Mae Dougherty's classmate. Dauph Dougherty began teaching at Holly Spring College in 1892.
8. Lanier, 24.
9. Lanier, 9.
10. Lanier, 9.
11. Brown, *B.B. Dougherty*, 43; Lanier, 24–25, 36; Powell, *North Carolina through Four Centuries*, 418–19; Van Noppen and Van Noppen, 131.
12. J. Alexander Mull, "Joseph F. Spainhour," *Burke County Heritage, North Carolina* (Morganton, NC: Burke County Historical Society, 1981), 402. See also Maud Patton Anthony, "Historical Sketch of First Baptist Church Morganton, North Carolina and Personal Reminiscences" (Morganton, NC: First Baptist Church Morganton, 1956, reprint, 1995).
13. Brown, *B.B. Dougherty*, 46.
14. B.B. Dougherty, interview by Wade Brown, 29 Nov. 1956. UA 33, University Archives Oral History Collection, University Archives, Special Collections Research Center, Appalachian State University, Boone, NC.
15. Alfred T. Adams, "The T.P. Adams Family," in Sanna Ross Gaffney, ed., and the Heritage of Watauga County Book Committee, *The Heritage of Watauga County, North Carolina, Volume 1* (Winston Salem, NC: Heritage of Watauga County Book Committee in cooperation with the History Division of Hunter Publishing Co., 1984), 89.
16. B.B. Dougherty, "Tarlton Pulaski Adams" (a biography written "by a friend," Blan Dougherty noted about his relationship to the older T.P. Adams), Stam Collection.
17. Adams, 89. Alfred Adams, who was a leader in the Northwestern Bank in Boone for more than 40 years, wrote that his father was called "Uncle Doc" by many of his friends.
18. Alfred T. Adams, "The T.P. Adams Family," in Gaffney, ed., 89; John Preston Arthur, *History of Watauga County*, 279; Bingham, 75.
19. Daniel Baker Dougherty to D.D. Dougherty, 20 Mar. 1899, Stam Collection.
20. Lanier, 23; *Watauga Democrat*, 22 June 1899.
21. Bingham, 75–79; Lanier, 25.
22. Brown, *B.B. Dougherty*, 86; *Minute Book "A" of Watauga County Board of Education*, Lanier Papers.
23. "The General Assembly of 1913 enacted the first statewide law compelling school attendance."

https://www.ncpedia.org/public-education-part-4-expansion.

24. B.B. Dougherty to D.D. Dougherty, 21 Apr. 1899, Stam Collection.

25. Brown, *B.B. Dougherty*, 86.

26. *Watauga Democrat*, 13 July 1899.

27. In family letters from 1897, Daniel and Blan both refer to hired cooks, one of which was not to Blan's liking. Stam Collection.

28. Gaffney, ed., 204; Eric W. Plaag, *Images of America: Remembering Boone* (Charleston: Arcadia, 2021), 2.

29. Lanier, 18–19.

30. LeVerne Fox, interview by Doris Perry Stam, 9 Aug. 2007, Stam Collection; Lanier, 18–19; Clara Powell to B.B. Dougherty, 21 Jan. 1944, Mrs. David Barnard Dougherty, University Archives, Special Collections Research Center, Appalachian State University, Boone, NC; Mrs. Zeb "Nurse" Shook, interview with Doris Perry Stam, Aug. 2002, Stam Collection.

31. Lanier, 26.

32. Gaffney, ed., 256. See subscription lists in B.B. Dougherty papers, and *Watauga Democrat* issues late August and early October 1899.

33. B.B. Dougherty, interview by Wade Brown, Nov. 29, 1956, ASU Oral History Collection. In this interview Blan Dougherty mentioned several men who were helpful in the first years of Watauga Academy but the names of Trustees for Watauga Academy have not been found during Stam's research.

34. *Watauga Democrat*, 13 July 1899.

35. http://www.appstate.edu/~scherlnag/docs/what_in_the_world_is_watauga_mountain_times_text.pdf.

36. F.P. Moore to B.B. Dougherty, 19 July 1899, Stam Collection.

37. F.P. Moore to B.B. Dougherty, 19 July 1899, Stam Collection. See also Altmayer, 21; Susan Anhold, "The Blackburn Hotel," University Archives, Special Collections Research Center, Appalachian State University, Boone, NC.

38. *Watauga Democrat*, 20 July 1899.

39. *Dew Drop* (Boone, NC: Appalachian Training School). Each issue lists the school trustees.

40. *Watauga Democrat*, 13 July 1899, in Lanier, 30–31. (Lanier wrote: "Of the white population, 60.8 percent was enrolled in the public schools, and 54.5 percent of the Negro school population was similarly enrolled, but only 33.3 percent of the white and 30.9 percent of the Negro school population were in actual daily attendance during the term. The school term was far short of the constitutional requirement of four months. Teachers were poorly prepared, salaries were low, and a large number of school houses were unfit for use by reason of being uncomfortable and unsafe for the health of the children. All the difficulties arose from a lack of money for operating the schools.... [Watauga County was] able to keep its schools open an average of 11.25 weeks for white pupils and seven weeks for Negro pupils.... The 1899 Legislature ...lengthened [the school term] to 12.33 weeks for white pupils and to eleven weeks for the Negro pupils.")

41. Hardy, *Short History of Watauga County*, 104; *Watauga Democrat*, 29 June 1893.

42. D.J. Whitener, "Education for the People," 187.

43. Lefler, *History of North Carolina 2*, 648. See also Brown, *B.B. Dougherty*, 33–34; R.L. Patton, Jr., "Sidelight of a Great Life," 59.

44. Mary T. Martin Sloop, M.D., with Legette Blythe, *Miracle in the Hills: The Lively Personal Story of a Woman Doctor's Forty-Year Crusade in the Mountains of North Carolina* (New York: McGraw-Hill, 1953), 63–64. https://www.ncpedia.org/crossnore-school.

45. Sloop, 95.

46. James L. LeLoudis, *Schooling in the New South: Pedagogy, Self, and Society in North Carolina, 1880-1920* (Chapel Hill: University of North Carolina Press, 1996), 13.

47. Corbitt, 29.

48. Corbitt, 29.

49. LeLoudis, 13.

50. Christensen, 8, 42.

51. D.J. Whitener, *History of Watauga County*, 66.

52. Unfortunately, the names of these trustees have been lost, likely in the campus fires of 1946 and 1966.

53. Gaffney, ed., 204; Larry Penley, "Mrs. Greene Reminisces, ASTC Beginnings Recalled," *Watauga Democrat*, 30 May 1963.

54. Lanier, 56.

55. E.C. Bartlett, maternal grandfather to Dauph Dougherty and his siblings, died in 1896. Dauph's maternal aunt, Etta Bartlett Lawrence Hall, wealthy and childless, died in 1895, leaving $10,000 to her nieces and nephews, according to a letter from Daniel Baker Dougherty to his son Dauph, 21 Oct. 1891. If true, then Dauph, Blan and Etta each received $2,500, and their cousin Lena received $2,500. It seems likely that the three Dougherty siblings, possibly with their father's help, together put forward $1,000 for the school.

56. *Watauga Democrat*, 25 May 1905, in Lanier 56.

57. Curtis; *Watauga Democrat*, 14 Mar., 2 May 1901; 4 Oct. 1900, in Lanier, 28; *Watauga Democrat*, 15 and 29 Mar. 1900.

58. J.P. Arthur, *History of Watauga County*, 252.

59. Eggers, 12.

60. J.P. Arthur, *History of Watauga County*, 252.

61. Eggers, 11–12. Boone Baptist is also known as First Baptist Church of Boone, NC.

62. *Biennial Report 1898-'99 and 1899-1900*, 52, 155–60, 267, 278–79, 288–89, cited in Lanier, 31; Hugh Talmadge Lefler and Albert Ray Newsome, *The History of a Southern State: North Carolina* (Chapel Hill: University of North Carolina Press, 1954), 498–506.

63. Eddie Dougherty, interview by Doris Perry Stam, July 2022, Stam Collection. Gunpowder was

the name of another horse that Blan rode during his very first years as superintendent.
64. Corbitt, 14.
65. Lanier, 32.
66. See Greene diaries and Lanier, 67–70.
67. Lanier, 10–12.
68. *Watauga Democrat*, 13 July 1899.

Chapter 11

1. *Watauga Democrat*, 24 Aug. 1899. This same ad appeared in the paper until the end of December, including the start date of September 5.
2. *Watauga Democrat*, 5 Sept. 1899. School was held Tuesday through Saturday, with Monday as "wash day." See Wade Brown's autobiography, 116.
3. Lanier, 26.
4. Doris Perry Stam mistakenly identified the old courthouse as the Boone Academy in her book *Mountain Educators*. There may have been some school classes held at the old courthouse, as well as some church meetings and town gatherings. The photograph in question may have been one of those groups. See Digital Watauga.
5. B.B Dougherty, "Appalachian State Teachers College Founders' Day 1945," event program bulletin (Boone, NC: Appalachian State Teachers' College, 8 May 1945), Stam Collection.
6. Eggers, 11–12; Jim Thompson, *Mountain Times*, 19 Aug. 1999.
7. B.B. Dougherty, interview by Wade Brown, Nov. 1956, ASU Oral History Collection.
8. B.B. Dougherty, interview by Wade Brown, Nov. 1956, ASU Oral History Collection.
9. B.B. Dougherty, interview by Wade Brown, Nov. 1956, ASU Oral History Collection.
10. "Population of North Carolina by Counties and Minor Civil Divisions," *United States Bureau of the Census, Twelfth Census of the United States: 1900, in the Census Bulletin no. 39, 22 Jan 1901* (Washington, D.C.: Government Printing Office, 22 Jan. 1901), 12, https://www2.census.gov/library/publications/decennial/1900/bulletins/demographic/39-population-nc.pdf.
11. D.D. Dougherty, "Day Ledger," unpublished manuscript, 1899–1903, Scoggins Collection, University Archives, Special Collections Research Center, Appalachian State University, Boone, NC. See endnotes for a list of students.
12. Interview with Addie Mae Love, Summer 2007; "Mrs. Sarah Perry. Her Pupil," *Watauga Democrat*, 16 June 1955.
13. *The Dew Drop* (Boone, NC: Appalachian Training School for Teachers, 1917), Stam Collection. (Lester Brown does not include Henry Perry in his list of students, nor does Curtis, but he is listed in the 1917 yearbook as having graduated in the second graduating class in 1902! A ledger for the school from 1899 to 1903 in D.D. Dougherty's handwriting includes Henry Perry as a student from 1899 to 1902.)
14. Brown, *B.B. Dougherty*, 171.
15. Dr. Henry Baker Perry, Jr., about his father Dr. Henry Baker Perry, Sr., notes written in 1993 before his death in 2000. Stam Collection.
16. *Watauga Democrat*, 15 Aug. 1963.
17. Ray and Virginia Ward, interview by Doris Perry Stam, Oct. 2018, recorded, Stam Collection.
18. D.D. Dougherty, "Day Ledger."
19. Brown, *B.B. Dougherty*, 53.
20. Brown, *B.B. Dougherty*, 53. After 63 years Mrs. Addie Shull Sutherland was interviewed by Lester Brown, and she remembered the names of half or more of the students in attendance during her first year in the new institution. Some of these men and women were still alive during the late 1950s and early 1960s when Lester Brown interviewed them for his biography of B.B. Dougherty, written at the request of B.B. Dougherty.
21. Brown, *B.B. Dougherty*, 53.
22. Bingham, 43; *Watauga Democrat*, 7 Sept. 1900, 3.
23. *Watauga Democrat*, 7 Sept. 1900, 3.
24. *Watauga Democrat*, 24 Aug. 1899.
25. *Watauga Democrat*, 24 Aug. 1899. Initial school ads mentioned music and art classes but did not specify Lillie Dougherty as the teacher. Only the principals, D.D. and B.B. Dougherty, were listed in the *Watauga Democrat*.
26. Corbitt, 17, 30.
27. Brown, *B.B. Dougherty*, 53; Smith, *Catalogue*, 8–10.
28. Lanier, 56; *Watauga Democrat*, 5 Sept., 5 Oct. 1899; Brown, *B.B. Dougherty*, 86–97.
29. Gaffney, ed., 204. Bonner died at the age of ten years.
30. Bingham, 75–79c, *Third Year 1905–1906, Appalachian Training School* (Boone, NC: n.p., 1906); Lanier, 25; Carrie Smith, "North Carolina First Southern State to Help Train Teachers: Dougherty Brothers Built Great Teacher Training School....," *Alleghany Times* (Sparta, NC), 23 Aug. 1934.
31. *The Dew Drop Catalogue Edition, Twenty-Third Year 1925–1926, Appalachian State Normal School* 24, no. 1 (Boone, NC: n.p., July 1926). Online *The Dew Drop, Catalogue Edition 1925–1928*, 7–132. https://lib.digitalnc.org/record/34742?ln=en#?xywh=-2257%2C0%2C10130%2C4300&cv=6. Copy in possession of the author.
32. Brown, *B.B. Dougherty*, 50; B.B Dougherty, "Founders' Day 1945," Stam Collection.
33. Lanier, 27; *Watauga Democrat*, 23 Nov. 1899; 11 Jan. 1900.
34. Emma H. Moore, "History of Appalachian," in E.H. Moore Scrapbook.
35. Jeff L. Norris and Ellis G. Boatmon, *Fair Star: A Centennial History of Lenoir-Rhyne College* (Virginia Beach, VA: The Donning Co. Publishers, 1990), 21.
36. Brown, *B.B. Dougherty*, 118.
37. Lanier, 27.
38. Lanier, 27; E.H. Moore, in E.H. Moore Scrapbook. Emma Moore reported that the four

students in the high school course were John Sherrill, Clyde Reese, Julius R. Blair and W.L. Trivette.
  39. Brown, *B.B. Dougherty*, 59.

Chapter 12

  1. https://tennesseeencyclopedia.net/entries/tennessee-centennial-exposition/on/.
  2. Allen Tullos, *Habits of Industry: White Culture and the Transformation of the Carolina Piedmont* (Chapel Hill: University of North Carolina Press, 1986), 15, 19.
  3. Tullos, 5.
  4. Tam Bowie, career politician and life-long friend to B.B. Dougherty and Appalachian, left his Ashe County home as a teenager to work in the West Virginia coal mines. https://www.ncpedia.org/biography/bowie-thomas-contee.
  5. Sloop, 68; *Watauga Democrat*, 18 Sept. 1902.
  6. McLeod, 171–172. With no documents preserved from Watauga Academy's first years, it seems reasonable to study the developments of peer institutions, Western Carolina University and East Carolina University in particular, whose backgrounds and development parallel Appalachian State University.
  7. B.B. Dougherty, "A Tribute to Manly Blackburn," UA 45: Elizabeth Brown Scoggins Collection, Special Collections Research Center, Appalachian State University, Boone, NC. Brown, *B.B. Dougherty*, 54; Julia McFarland, "The Critcher Hotel: A Glimpse of Boone's Beginnings," *Watauga County Times ... Past*, no. 16, Mar. 1985, 2–9, University Archives, Special Collections Research Center, Appalachian State University, Boone, NC.
  8. Brown, *B.B. Dougherty*, 54.
  9. Brown, *B.B. Dougherty*, 118.
  10. Curtis, "Memories of Watauga Academy," 7–8.
  11. McFarland, 2–9; Susan E. Keefe with assistance from the Junaluska Heritage Association, *Junaluska: Oral Histories of a Black Appalachian Community*. Contributions to Southern Appalachian Studies 48 (Jefferson, NC: McFarland, 2020), 16, 81, 108–09, 140, 159–168. See also T.J. McGuire, Oral History, "Boone, North Carolina: In Early Days," AC.111, Tape # 95, Box 44, Folder 10, Transcription, University Archives, Special Collections Research Center, Appalachian State University, Boone, NC.
  12. Keefe, 50–51.
  13. Lanier, 28; *Watauga Democrat*, 17 Dec. 1908.
  14. Blan Dougherty to Dauph Dougherty, 10 Dec. 1888, 27 April 1897, Stam Collection.
  15. D.D. Dougherty, "Day Ledger," UA 45: Elizabeth Brown Scoggins Collection, Special Collections Research Center, Appalachian State University, Boone, N.C., USA; Lanier, 28; *Watauga Democrat*, 15 and 29 Mar. 1900.
  16. Jule B. Warren, "New Economic Empire Blossoms from Educational Vision of Doughertys," in *We The People* 3, Aug.–Sept. 1949, Appalachian State Teachers College, 1903–1954 (Boone, NC: Appalachian State Teachers College News Bureau, 1949), UA 02.01. Office of the President. Blanford Barnard Dougherty Records, University Archives, Special Collections Research Center, Appalachian State University, Boone, North Carolina. I, Doris Perry Stam, have heard this testimony from the lips of citizens countless times in my thirty years of talking to people in the county about Appalachian.
  17. D.D. Dougherty, "Day Ledger"; Mary Moretz, interview by Doris Perry Stam (Boone, NC), 7 June 2021; Ned Trivette, interview by Doris Perry Stam, 2014.
  18. Lanier, 28.
  19. Lanier, 18; *Watauga Democrat*, 4 Oct. 1900.
  20. *The Watauga Democrat*, 10 May 1900.
  21. *Watauga Democrat*, 10 May 1900.
  22. *Watauga Democrat*, 10 May 1900.
  23. Christensen, 17; PBS Documentary, *Becoming Frederick Douglass*, aired Saturday, Dec. 3, 2022, on PBS TV.
  24. Christensen, 14.
  25. Christensen, 41–45.
  26. Gordon B. McKinney, "Southern Mountain Republicans and the Negro, 1865–1900," *Journal of Southern History* 41, no. 4 (Nov. 1975), 493–516.
  27. *Watauga Democrat*, 31 May 1900. NC Museum of History Timeline, 10 Nov. 1898.
  28. McKinney, 495.
  29. Keefe, 16, 81, 108–09, 140, 159–168.
  30. Christensen, 34–35, 38, 42.Bl
  31. Christensen, 38.
  32. Christensen, 38.
  33. Lanier, 27, *The Madison Enterprise*, 5 July 1900.
  34. B.B. Dougherty, interview by Wade Brown, 29 Nov. 1956, ASU Oral History Collection.
  35. Lanier, 27.
  36. Lanier, 2–28; *Watauga Democrat*, 14 Mar., 2 May 1901.
  37. *Watauga Democrat*, 7 Nov. 1901; D.J. Whitener, *History of Watauga County*, 76; Brown, *B.B. Dougherty*, 52.
  38. Lanier, 28; *Watauga Democrat*, 4 Oct. 1900.
  39. Brown, *B.B. Dougherty*, 57–58.
  40. Brown, *B.B. Dougherty*, 56.
  41. Shull's Mill, seven miles south of Boone, exploded as a lumber boom town in 1915, but dwindled in the 1920s when the lumber had been essentially clear cut in the area (https://sites.google.com/appstate.edu/nwnc-theaters-1/watauga/shulls-mills-american-theatre?pli=1; private interviews with: Mr. Larrimore; Ned Trivette's son Mark; Robert Snead).
  42. In our current times schools offer a multitude of clubs and after-school programs to enhance education, such as Mock Trial, where debates in the form of pretend criminal cases are prepared and executed. Outstanding students are given the honor of making speeches at end-of-the year school programs. 125 years ago things were simpler, more streamlined.

43. Lanier, 15.
44. Brown, *B.B. Dougherty*, 57.
45. W.M. Francum, "Local News" section, *Watauga Democrat*, 2 May 1901, 3.
46. Brown, *B.B. Dougherty*, 53.
47. Lanier, 36.
48. *Watauga Democrat*, Jan. 1902.
49. R.C. Rivers, Sr., "From Early Files: Sixty Years Ago, November 18, 1900," *Watauga Democrat*, 17 Nov. 1960.
50. *Watauga Democrat*, Feb. 1902.
51. https://www.digitalnc.org/newspapers/watauga-democrat-boone-n-c/. This article says that Daniel Baker Dougherty was associated with the paper until his death in 1902, however, the actual newspaper indicates that by March 1899 Rivers was the sole owner and editor.
52. *Watauga Democrat*, 17 Apr. 1902.
53. Brown, *B.B. Dougherty*, 53. Brown interviewed Mrs. Addie Shull Sutherland in the early 1960s. Lester Brown states that college level classes began in the fall of 1900. Julia Hardin, of Sutherland, joined the faculty, Brown states, though neither of these assertions can be proved because of missing or burned documents from the early days of the school. *Watauga Democrat* (May 10, 1900) spoke of only the three Doughertys in the report of commencement from 1900. Brown may be referring to college-prep classes, for actual college level classes were not taught until 1911, according to D.J. Whitener, *History of Watauga County*, 82–83.
54. Howell Cook, interview by Doris Perry Stam, 14 Aug. 2020, recorded.
55. *Watauga Democrat*, 17 Apr. 1902.
56. Tester, 76.
57. Dr. Henry Baker Perry, Jr., interviewed by Doris Perry Stam, August 1999, December 1999, recorded, Stam Collection.
58. Dr. Henry Baker Perry, Jr., interviewed by Doris Perry Stam, August 1999, December 1999, recorded, Stam Collection.
59. *Dew Drop* 1906–1907; *The Dew Drop, Catalogue Edition, Fifth Year, 1907–1908, Appalachian Training School* 6, no. 1. (Boone, NC: n.p., Aug. 1908); *The Dew Drop, Catalogue Edition, Sixth Year, 1908–1909, Appalachian Training School* 7, no. 1. (Boone, NC: n.p., Aug. 1909).
60. *Watauga Democrat*, 17 Apr. 1902.
61. *Watauga Democrat*, 12 June 1902.
62. *Watauga Democrat*, 17 July 1902. Former governor Thomas J. Jarvis and Dr. Geo T. Winston, president of the A & M College (Agricultural and Mechanical, now State University) at Raleigh were expected to address the Institute.
63. *Watauga Democrat*, 17 July 1902. On March 11, 1889, the North Carolina General Assembly ratified an act to abolish the eight white Normal Schools in the state and launched county institutes across the state to train teachers and other educators. Each teacher had to attend full time for a designated length of time, most often during summers, and then must pass a written examination to obtain their teaching certificates, which were now good for three years. "North Carolina—Acts on Education Topic: 1889 Public Laws: Chapter 200," 171–172, from Carolana.com
64. Lanier, 31–32.
65. Edwin Dougherty, "Diary," unpublished manuscript, 1929, Stam Collection (son of D.D. and Lillie, from 1929 indicates this mindset of living in the country, although it was only a few blocks away, when Edwin writes: "I drove Mama … .into town," Stam Collection); John Thompson, "Daughter of D.D. Dougherty Remembers Old Spring," *Mountain Times*, 22 Apr. 1999; John Thompson, "Parking DeckORT Development Threatens Dougherty Spring," *Mountain Times*, 22 Apr. 1999.

Chapter 13

1. *Watauga Democrat*, 18 Sept. 1902, 3.
2. *Watauga Democrat*, 2 Oct. 1902, 3.
3. Christensen, 38.
4. Christensen, 14; https://www.ncpedia.org/anchor/governor-aycock-negro.
5. DeWeese, 21–23, 37.
6. Christensen, 43.
7. Christensen, 43.
8. Christensen, 2, 4.
9. Christensen, 14–15.
10. https://docsouth.unc.edu/nc/connor/connor.html, 85.
11. Christensen, 44.
12. Christensen, 45.
13. Christensen, 45.
14. "Moderate Education the Means to Wealth and Progress," *The Daily Free Press* (Kinston, NC), 18 April 1902, newspapers.digitalnc.org/lccn/sn91068514/1902-04018/ed-a/seq-1/.
15. Cratis Williams, "The Appalachian Experience: Historical Sketches of Southwest Virginia," 1977, Ruby Lanier Papers, University Archives, Special Collections Research Center, Appalachian State University, Boone, NC.
16. Christensen, 43; Van Noppen and Van Noppen, 132–133.
17. Van Noppen and Van Noppen, 133–134.
18. "Gov. Aycock at Lenoir," *The Morning Post* (Raleigh), 2 Oct. 1902, 1, newspapers.digitalnc.org/lccn/sn92072955/1902-10-02/ed-1/seq-1.
19. Hon. J.F. Spainhour, taken from the message he delivered at the memorial service for D.D. Dougherty, Stam Collection; Scoggins Collection; also found in Hon. J.F. Spainhour, "The Dougherty Brothers," in *The Rhododendron 1929*, vol. 7, 13.
20. Van Noppen and Van Noppen, 135.
21. Lanier, 34.
22. Van Noppen and Van Noppen, 136. In her enthusiasm for B.B. Dougherty, Ruby Lanier does not mention D.D. (Dauph) Dougherty regarding the fight for a state-supported school, and mistakenly calls B.B. Dougherty the principal, when Blan was co-principal with Dauph.
23. Van Noppen and Van Noppen, 135.

24. Lanier, 34.
25. Van Noppen and Van Noppen, 133. Cullowhee Normal and Industrial School had another name change in 1925 and was renamed Cullowhee State Normal School. In 1953 the school became Western Carolina College, and in 1967, it became Western Carolina University.
26. D.J. Whitener, *History of Watauga County*, 77.
27. D.J. Whitener, *History of Watauga County*, 77.
28. Marcus C.S. Noble, *A History of the Public Schools of North Carolina* (Chapel Hill: University of North Carolina Press, 1930), 399–403, 412–413. Thomas Toon to B.B. Dougherty, 20 June 1901, *S.P.I. Letter Book,* Apr. 6, 1900–Mar. 29, 1901, 262; J.Y. Joyner to B.B. Dougherty, 11 July; 3 and 17 Nov. 1902, *S.P.I. Letter Book*; Lanier, 38.
29. Lanier, 38.
30. Lanier, 42.
31. Lanier, 39.
32. Lanier, 42; Noble, *Public Schools of NC*, 420–427. States that the colored normals were very poorly funded, with resulting low quality, "yet unequal to the needs."
33. Lanier, 42.
34. J.Y. Joyner to B.B. Dougherty, 25 Oct. 1902, *Letterbook of the State Superintendent of Public Instruction, September 19, 1902 to Dec 2, 1902*, quoted in Lanier, 38.
35. Lanier, 40–44.
36. D.D. Dougherty, "Educational Needs of Children in Rural Sections," *News & Observer* (Raleigh, NC), 15 Jan. 1923; Stam Collection. https://www.digitalnc.org/newspapers/ did not have this article.
37. Margaret W. Morris, "The Completion of the Western North Carolina Railroad: Politics of Concealment," *North Carolina Historical Review* 52, no. 3 (Raleigh, NC: North Carolina Division of Archives and History, July 1975), 257.
38. Mebane, 33, 49–50.
39. Van Noppen and Van Noppen, 133–134.
40. https://www.ncpedia.org/anchor/colored-state-normal-schools.
41. Morris, 259.
42. Van Noppen and Van Noppen, 176.
43. D.D. Dougherty, "Educational Needs of Children in Rural Sections," *News & Observer* (Raleigh, NC), 15 Jan. 1923; Stam Collection. https://www.digitalnc.org/newspapers/ did not have this article.
44. Ruby Lanier Papers, W.L. Eury Appalachian Collection, Special Collections Research Center, Appalachian State University, Boone, North Carolina.
45. Van Noppen and Van Noppen, 176.
46. "Cullowhee Is Pioneer in Teacher Training; Founder of School Tells of Early Struggles of Institution," *Asheville Citizen Times* (Asheville, NC), 18 Nov. 1934. See also Curtis W. Wood and H. Tyler Blethen, *A Mountain Heritage: The Illustrated History of Western Carolina University* (Charlotte, N.C.: Delmar Co., Western Carolina University, 1989), 23–29.
47. Van Noppen and Van Noppen, 179.
48. Wood and Blethen, 35–36.
49. Lanier, 33; James E. Hillman, "The History of Teacher Training," *North Carolina Education* 2 (Feb. 1936), 224–225, Lanier Papers; *Biennial Report of the Superintendent of Public Instruction of North Carolina, for the Scholastic Years 1901–1901 and 1901–1902* (Raleigh: Edwards & Broughton, State Printers, 1902), xxvi–xxix, https://digital.ncdcr.gov/Documents/Detail/biennial-report-of-the-superintendent-of-public-instruction-of-north-carolina-for-the-scholastic-years-...-1900-1902/3969794.
50. Lanier, 46–47; *Raleigh Post*, 15 Feb. 1903.
51. "The Death of M.C.S. Noble," *The Chapel Hill Weekly* (Chapel Hill, NC), 5 June 1942; https://ed.unc/about/ history/.
52. Van Noppen and Van Noppen, 167.
53. Van Noppen and Van Noppen, 170.
54. Lanier, 20. Lanier notes that the letter was written 4 May 1901.
55. Bingham, 81 (quoting from the Report of Superintendent of Public Instruction, J.Y. Joyner, 1900, III), AppState Closed Archives.
56. Lanier, 43.
57. Van Noppen and Van Noppen, 168–69.
58. Lanier, 41; Van Noppen and Van Noppen, 169–70.
59. Lanier, 38–43. Lanier cites several letters between J.Y. Joyner and Wallace Buttrick from December 1902.
60. D.J. Whitener, *History of Watauga County*, 78.
61. Lanier, 43. See Dougherty to Joyner, 7 Jan. 1903, S.P.I. Correspondence.
62. Lanier, 43. See *Biennial Report of the S.P.I., 1901–1902*, pp. lxii–lxiii.
63. Lanier, 44.
64. Lanier, 44.
65. Lanier, 44.
66. Brown, *B.B. Dougherty*, 61.
67. Brown, *B.B. Dougherty*, 61–62; Curtis, "Memories of Watauga Academy and Appalachian," 9, 19–11. Jesse Curtis established *The Lewiston News* and Curtis Printing Company in Lewiston, Idaho. From there he wrote, at the request of Dr. B.B. Dougherty, his "Memories of Watauga Academy" and sent them to Dr. Dougherty in December of 1937.
68. Brown, *B.B. Dougherty*, 61–62; Curtis, "Memories of Watauga Academy and Appalachian," 19–11.
69. B.B. Dougherty, interview by Wade Brown, 29 Nov. 1956, ASU Oral History Collection.
70. Richard D. Howe, "Edward F. Lovill," in Gaffney, ed., 268.
71. https://www.ncpedia.org/biography/lovill-edward-francis. Elected to the General Assembly, E.F. Lovill served in the Senate in 1883 and in the House in 1885. He was again elected to the House in 1893 and to the Senate for terms in 1907–08 and

1919-20. During his final term he had the distinction of being the last Confederate veteran to serve in the North Carolina General Assembly, and it has often been observed that he was among the minority of legislators who supported women's suffrage. Among Lovill's other public services he was for a time director of the Masonic Orphanage at Oxford by appointment of Governor Charles B. Aycock. As commissioner to the Chippewa Indians (1893-97), by appointment of President Grover Cleveland, he was involved in classifying lands ceded by the Indians to the U.S. government. For many years Lovill was chairman of the board of trustees of the Appalachian Training School, where a building on the campus now bears his name. As a community leader, he was responsible for the establishment of a tobacco warehouse in Boone.

72. Brown, *B.B. Dougherty*, 62-63; Whitener, *History of Watauga County*, 65; Lillie Veach, "Autographs," a memento book of personal messages and autographs, in possession of the family. Lillie Veach attended the Normal School in Boone in 1888.

73. B.B. Dougherty, interview by Wade Brown, 29 Nov. 1956, ASU Oral History Collection. The acquisition of a typewriter for Lovill's law office in July 1902 was itself considered newsworthy. *Watauga Democrat*, 17 July 1902.

74. B.B. Dougherty, interview by Wade Brown, 29 Nov. 1956, ASU Oral History Collection.

75. B.B. Dougherty, interview by Wade Brown, 29 Nov. 1956, ASU Oral History Collection.

76. Brown, *B.B. Dougherty*, 98.

77. Brown, handwritten sketches and notes used for his biography of B.B. Dougherty, Stam Collection.

78. Vance Howell, "In Memoriam of Dauphin Disco Dougherty," *The Handbook Edition of the Rhododendron 1929*, vol. 7 (Boone, NC: Published by Faculty and Students of Appalachian State Teachers College, 1929), 11, UA.47: Doris Stam Collection, University Archives, Special Collections Research Center, Appalachian State University, Boone, N.C.

79. Rev. W.R. Bradshaw, "Life and Character of D.D. Dougherty," delivered at the memorial service for D.D. Dougherty, 26 Oct. 1929, Stam Collection.

80. B.B. Dougherty, interview by Wade Brown, 29 Nov. 1956, ASU Oral History Collection.

81. DeWeese, 36; McLeod, 202-03.

82. B.B. Dougherty, interview by Wade Brown, 29 Nov. 1956, ASU Oral History Collection.

83. Brown, *BB. Dougherty*, 63.

84. Brown, *B.B. Dougherty*, 63-64; *Time Magazine*, 25 March 1940.

85. Lanier, 48.

Chapter 14

1. B.B. Dougherty, interview by Wade Brown, 29 Nov. 1956, ASU Oral History Collection.

2. Brown, *B.B. Dougherty*, 62, 64. Brown notes in parenthesis that this dictated account from B.B. Dougherty took place with his nephew, Edwin Dougherty, in November 1955.

3. Lanier, 45; North Carolina House Bill 379, *Journal of the House of Representatives, 1903*, 186.

4. Lanier, 45.

5. Brown, *B.B. Dougherty*, 64.

6. Brown, *B.B. Dougherty*, 65.

7. B.B. Dougherty, interview by Wade Brown, 29 Nov. 1956, ASU Oral History Collection.

8. Brown, *B.B. Dougherty*, 65.

9. Brown, *B.B. Dougherty*, 65-66.

10. Brown, *B.B. Dougherty*, 65-66.

11. Brown, *B.B. Dougherty*, 66.

12. Lanier, 46.

13. Lanier, 47. See *Raleigh Post*, 15 Feb. 1903.

14. Lanier, 45.

15. Lanier, 47.

16. UA 45: Elizabeth Brown Scoggins Collection, Special Collections Research Center, Appalachian State University, Boone, NC. See Lanier, 45-46.

17. Lanier, 46-47.

18. Brown, *B.B. Dougherty*, 66; Lanier, 47-48; *Watauga Democrat*, 15 Feb. 1903. Lanier cites the *Watauga Democrat* for the information and not the *News and Observer*, however, the *Democrat* was reprinting the article from the *Observer*, as was their common practice.

19. D.J. Whitener, *History of Watauga County*, 77-78.

20. *Watauga Democrat*, 19 Feb. 1903, 3.

21. Brown, *B.B. Dougherty*, 64.

22. Lanier, 48, citing *News and Observer*, 5 March 1903, and *Raleigh Post*, 5 March 1903.

23. Lanier, 48, citing *Raleigh Post*, 5 March 1903. (Ruby Lanier's meticulous research corrects the progression in Lester Brown's book.)

24. Brown, *B.B. Dougherty*, 49; *Raleigh News and Observer*, 5 Mar. 1903.

25. Henry C. Ferrell, Jr., *No Time for Ivy: East Carolina University: 1907-2007* (Greenville, NC: East Carolina University, 2006), 4; Lanier, 49.

26. Ferrell, *No Time for Ivy*, 4-5; Brown, *B.B. Dougherty*, 67; Lanier, 49.

27. B.B Dougherty, "Founders' Day 1945."

28. D.J. Whitener, *History of Watauga County*, 78.

29. D.J. Whitener, *History of Watauga County*, 78. See Brown, *B.B. Dougherty*, 67; *The Mountain Times*, 27 May 1999, by Jim Thompson. Brown was unclear as to the exact order of events leading to the one-vote passage of the bill.

30. Brown, *B.B. Dougherty*, 67; Van Noppen and Van Noppen, 180; *Watauga Democrat*, 26 Feb. 1903. Lester Brown and the Van Noppens place Blan's hour-long speech as happening before the joint session. But *Watauga Democrat* reports that Blan was in Boone, having returned before February 21. It seems that folklore has expanded the facts.

31. Lanier, 50.

32. *Watauga Democrat*, 9 April 1903.
33. Brown, *B.B. Dougherty*, 68. When Moses H. Cone died in 1908, his widow was elected to replace him on the board. She remained a trustee for several years and continued his philanthropic work in support of education and of health care in Greensboro—unusual for a woman at that time. See Appalachian "Hall of Fame," brochure for the event held by the Alumni Association on May 5, 1962, in the Fine Arts Auditorium at Appalachian State Teachers College, Boone, North Carolina, Stam Collection (given to Doris Perry Stam by Reba Smith Moretz). See list of trustees in *The Greensboro Patriot*, 9 Dec. 1908.
34. Lanier, 51, quoting *Public Laws of North Carolina, 1903*, c. 798; *Watauga Democrat*, 12 Mar. 1903, 3.
35. Lanier, 52, citing *Watauga Democrat*, 16 Apr 1903.
36. *Watauga Democrat*, 16 Apr. 1903.
37. Lanier, 52.
38. Alfred Adams personal recorded interview by Doris Perry Stam, Aug. 2001, Stam Collection; Barry M. Buxton, *A Village Tapestry: The History of Blowing Rock* (Boone, NC: Appalachian Consortium Press, 1989), 116; B.B. Dougherty interviewed by Wade Brown, Nov. 29, 1956. UA. 33, University Archives Oral History Collection, University Archives, Special Collections Research Center, Appalachian State University, Boone, NC; Lanier, 53. The group of leaders had also met on May 2, 1903, and again on May 14, 1903, in Boone.
39. *Watauga Democrat*, 21 May 1903, 3. See also D.D. Dougherty, interview by Wade Brown, 29 Nov. 1956, ASU Oral History Collection.
40. Brown, *B.B. Dougherty*, 71; Lanier, 53; *Watauga Democrat*, 21 May 1903. Lanier also cites William H. Plemmons, "A History of the Office of President," n.d., unpublished typewritten copy, in the possession of the writer (Dr. Ruby Lanier).
41. Lanier, 53; *Watauga Democrat*, 11 and 18 June, 2-25 July, 6-27 Aug., 3-24 Sept., 1-8 Oct. 1903.
42. https://www.in2013dollars.com/us/inflation/1903?amount=1.
43. UA 02.01, Office of the President. Blanford Barnard Dougherty Records, University Archives, Special Collections, Appalachian State University, Boone, N.C.
44. Lanier, 54.
45. UA 02.01, Office of the President. Blanford Barnard Dougherty Records, University Archives, Special Collections, Appalachian State University, Boone, NC.
46. UA 02.01, Office of the President. Blanford Barnard Dougherty Records, University Archives, Special Collections, Appalachian State University, Boone, NC.
47. Curtis, "Memories of Watauga Academy," 16.
48. *Watauga Democrat*, 10 Sept. 1903, 3.
49. *Watauga Democrat*, 10 Sept. 1903, 3.
50. Brown, *B.B. Dougherty*, 76.
51. https://www.ncpedia.org/biography/linney-romulus-zachariah.
52. John Preston Arthur, 327-328.
53. John Preston Arthur, 254. Romulus Zachariah Linney is the great-grandfather of the playwright of the same name and the ancestor to the actress Laura Linney.
54. Hyatt, 97; *Watauga Democrat*, 10 Sept., 1 Oct. 1903.
55. *The Dew Drop* (Boone, NC: Appalachian Training School, Dec. 1917), Stam Collection.
56. *The Dew Drop* (Boone, NC: Appalachian Training School, Dec. 1917), Stam Collection.
57. Lanier, 54.
58. Lanier, 54, citing B.B. Dougherty to Joyner, 18 July 1903, S.P.I. Correspondence.
59. Eggers, 13-14.
60. *Watauga Democrat*, 10 Sept. 1903.
61. *Watauga Democrat*, 10 Sept. 1903, 2.
62. *Watauga Democrat*, 10 Sept. 1903, 3.
63. Curtis, "Memories of Watauga Academy," 18.

Chapter 15

1. *Watauga Democrat*, 1 Jan. 1903.
2. *Watauga Democrat*, 8 Jan. 1903.
3. Diane Cook Barefoot, *The Dougherty House: Appalachian State University Buildings Survey Project* (Boone, NC: Appalachian State University, Department of History, Jan. 1987), 8-13.
4. Diane Cook Barefoot, *The Dougherty House: Appalachian State University Buildings Survey Project* (Boone, NC: Appalachian State University, Department of History, Jan. 1987), 8-13; J. Daniel Pezzoni, ed.; based on the work of Tony N. VanWinkle, Elizabeth C. Stevens, and Deborah J. Thompson, *The Architectural History of Watauga County North Carolina* (Boone, NC: Watauga County Historical Society, 2009), 122-123.
5. Barefoot, 9.
6. Barefoot, 13.
7. Brown, *B.B. Dougherty*, 119, 202-204.
8. *Watauga Democrat*, 23 Apr. 1903.
9. *Watauga Democrat*, 23 Apr. 1903, 3.
10. The Doughertys owned a pedal pump organ, which Bartlett and Dianne Dougherty donated to the current location for the relocated Dougherty House, Appalachian Heritage Museum at Mystery Hill on te Blowing Rock Road near Boone.
11. *Watauga Democrat*, 23 Apr. 1903, 3.
12. *Watauga Democrat*, 23 Apr. 1903, 3.
13. Brown, notes and sketches for his biography of B.B. Dougherty, Stam Collection.
14. D.D. Dougherty's milking stool is a treasured family heirloom.
15. Brown, *B.B. Dougherty*, 119.
16. "October Marks First Official Registration on Present Campus," *Watauga Democrat*, 3 Oct. 1963, 2. From Early Files, in the 60th Anniversary of A.S.T.C. (no name given for author of article).
17. D.J. Whitener, *History of Watauga County*,

Notes—Chapter 15

80. This total number and division of students is slightly different than that reported by B.B. Dougherty in "A Circular of Information" from 1904.

18. D.J. Whitener, *History of Watauga County*, 80.

19. Norris and Boatmon, 21; D.J. Whitener, *History of Watauga County*, 82.

20. M.T. Neal, *Edgar Tufts*, 40.

21. Jerry Wilson, interview by Doris Perry Stam, 9 Aug. 2007, recorded, Stam Collection.

22. Curtis, "Memories of Watauga Academy," 17-18.

23. D.J. Whitener, *History of Watauga County*, 80. D.J. Whitener describes this land as being "in the suburbs," which is misleading, for the location was two blocks from the village of Boone on farmland between the Watauga Academy building and Boone. No housing developments sprouted until the 1920s. Interestingly the new total of land for A.T.S. was listed as being seven acres. The original gift of land in 1899 had been six acres from John F. Hardin and Daniel Baker Dougherty. Some adjustments must have been made when donating the building to the state or the total would be 10 acres.

24. Lester Brown, interview with Clyde Eggers, 1965, notes for B.B. Dougherty biography, O.L. Brown files, Stam Collection.

25. Carl Day, interview with Doris Stam, Aug. 2002, recorded, Stam Collection; Brown, notes and sketches for his biography of B.B. Dougherty, Stam Collection.

26. Brown, *B.B. Dougherty*, 73.

27. Curtis, "Memories of Watauga Academy," 18.

28. B.B. Dougherty, "A Circular of Information" from the Trustees of Appalachian Training School, 1904, Stam Collection. B.B. Dougherty's calculation of 301 students is slightly different than the number and division of students D.J. Whitener quotes in his research for *The History of Watauga County*, 80.

29. B.B. Dougherty, "A Circular of Information" from the Trustees of Appalachian Training School, 1904, Stam Collection.

30. Lanier, 5.

31. J.P. Arthur, *History of Watauga County*, 252.

32. *Watauga Democrat*, 6 June 1957, quoting the *Charlotte Observer*.

33. Ed Hutchins and Nita Howard, "Found Doughertys Had a Dry Humor," *Watauga Democrat*, 11 July 1974, 4C.

34. Curtis, "Memories of Watauga Academy," 18-19.

35. Brown, *B.B. Dougherty*, 75.

36. *Raleigh Morning Post*, March 5, 1905.

37. Lanier, 55.

38. Lanier, 56; *Watauga Democrat*, 2 and 9 March 1905.

39. Rupert Gillett, "Leaders in the Carolinas," *Charlotte Observer*, 26 April 1953.

40. Dr. Harvey Durham interviewed by Doris Perry Stam, 26 June 2021; *The Morning Post* (Raleigh, NC), 2 March 1905.

41. *The Raleigh Post*, 5 March 1905, in Lanier, 56.

42. D.J. Whitener, *History of Watauga County*, 81.

43. Lanier, 55.

44. Lanier, 57; Joyner to Buttrick, *Letter Book of the North Carolina Superintendent of Public Instruction, 23 Aug 1905 to 15 Nov 1905* (Raleigh, NC: Department of Archives and History, 4 Sept. 1905); B.B. Dougherty to Joyner, 13 Jan. 1906; Buttrick to Joyner, 22 Dec. 1905. The Van Noppens incorrectly use the spelling "Buttruch" for Wallace Buttrick, S.P.I. Correspondence. The General Education Board also helped modernize farming practices in the South. It helped eradicate hookworm and created the county agent system in American agriculture, linking research as state agricultural experiment stations with actual practices in the field. https://en.wikipedia.org/wiki/General_Education_Board#.

45. *Raleigh Post* (Raleigh, NC), 5 March 1905, in Lanier, 56.

46. Lanier, 56-57; *Watauga Democrat*, 25 May, 31 Aug. 1903. See also Brown, *B.B. Dougherty*, 76-77, and *Dew Drop* 1906-1907.

47. *Dew Drop* 1905-1906. Later *Dew Drops* would describe Lovill Home as accommodating 85 students, not 100.

48. *Dew Drop* 1914-1915, 11.

49. Richard Howe, "Edward Francis Lovill," in Gaffney, ed., 268.

50. Curtis, "Memories of Watauga Academy," 6.

51. *Dew Drop Catalogue Edition, Second Year 1904-1905, Appalachian Training School* (Sparta, NC: The Star Publishing Co., 1905). Online *The Dew Drop, Catalogue Edition 1905*, 1-30. https://lib.digitalnc.org/record/34738?ln=en#?xywh=-3382%2C-1%2C10914%2C4634&cv=2.

52. Norris and Boatmon, 28.

53. *Dew Drop* 1905-1906.

54. Robert L. Patton, IV, email exchange with Doris Perry Stam, 28 June 2023.

55. Lanier, 56-57; *Watauga Democrat*, 1 and 18 Jan. and 22 Feb. 1906.

56. Lanier, 56-57; *Watauga Democrat*, 1 and 18 Jan. and 22 Feb. 1906.

57. G.W. Paschal to D.D. Dougherty, 19 Feb. 1906, Stam Collection.

58. *Dew Drop* 1906-1907, 13. The first record in *The Dew Drop* of these scholarships is noted in the August 1907 edition. It is possible that the offering of scholarships began before 1907.

59. *The Dew Drop, Catalogue Edition, Seventh Year, 1909-1910, Appalachian Training School* 8, no. 1 (Boone, NC: n.p., Aug. 1910). Online *The Dew Drop, Catalogue Edition 1906-1918*, 31-75. https://lib.digitalnc.org/record/34758?ln=en#?xywh=1306%-2C-20%2C4245%2C1802&cv=34.

60. A fire in 1946 destroyed the Watauga Academy and science and music buildings, and a fire in 1966 destroyed the second administration building and most of the school's records.

61. Van Noppen and Van Noppen, 176-178.

62. Van Noppen and Van Noppen, 176–178.
63. Van Noppen and Van Noppen, 176–178.
64. *Watauga Academy Alumni Association, 38th Annual Session* (Butler, NC: Butler Baptist Church, 13 Aug. 2000), from the booklet for that event, Stam Collection, Box 3, Folder 36. Announced in this program booklet was the opening of the Butler and Watauga Valley Heritage Association Butler Museum. See also the article from *The Tomahawk* (Mountain City, TN), 5 Apr. 2000, about the opening of the museum.
65. Curtis, "Memories of Watauga Academy," 5.
66. Brown, *B.B. Dougherty*, 55–56; Curtis, "Memories of Watauga Academy," 3–4.
67. *Program of Dedication and Naming: Lillie Shull Dougherty Hall*, Appalachian State Teachers College, Boone, North Carolina, Sunday, two-thirty in the afternoon, 5 Dec. 1965, "Mrs. Lillie Shull Dougherty," 2, Stam Collection.
68. Brown, *B.B. Dougherty*, 55. (This piano is still in the Brown-Dougherty family.)
69. Curtis, "Memories of Watauga Academy," 6–7.
70. Curtis, "Memories of Watauga Academy," 6–7; Gaffney, ed., 33–34; Lanier, 68–69.
71. Lanier, 68.
72. https://www.appalachianhistory.net/2019/08/lost-provinces.html.

Chapter 16

1. Lanier, 58. It is significant to note the designation by the state of "White" in the school name, barring the enrollment of "Negro" students who were assigned to one of the state normal schools for African Americans. Appalachian's hands were also tied, such that they could not admit non-white students without jeopardizing state funding.
2. John Allen Tucker and Arthur Carlson, *East Carolina University: The Campus History Series* (Charleston, SC: Arcadia, 2013), 11, 13; Ferrell, *No Time for Ivy*, 6; https://www.carolana.com/NC/Towns/Greenville_NC.html; https://www.uptowngreenville.com/about/history-of-greenville/.
3. Ferrell, *No Time for Ivy*, 4.
4. Ferrell, *No Time for Ivy*, 6.
5. Ferrell, *No Time for Ivy*, 6.
6. Lanier, 58.
7. Ferrell, *No Time for Ivy*, 6.
8. Ferrell, *No Time for Ivy*, 7–8.
9. Lanier, 58.
10. *Watauga Democrat*, 21 Feb. 1907; Lanier, 57–58.
11. *Watauga Democrat*, 23 May 1907; LeVerne Fox, interview by Doris Perry Stam, 9 Aug. 2007, recorded, Stam Collection. The current football stadium is located on what was the T.S. Coffey farm.
12. *Dew Drop* 1906–1907; Brown, *Biography Notes*, Scoggins Collection.
13. Lanier, 58, citing *Watauga Democrat*, 25 June, 3 Sept., 12 Nov. 1908; *Dew Drop* 1909–1910, 9.
14. Pezzoni, 47. "The original wooden building was rolled back a few rods and for years was not used, but during World War II it was renovated and was in use until being replaced. Its occupants affectionately call it 'The Barn.'"
15. https://en.wikipedia.org/wiki/William_C._Newland; Ruby Lanier Papers. Newland had lost a close race for Congress in 1904 to Republican E. Spencer Blackburn, whose brother, Manly Blackburn, was a trustee of Watauga Academy, presumably, and later of Appalachian Training School (1907–1921).
16. *Dew Drop* 1906–1907.
17. Bob Rivers, "King Street: Old Horses … Like Old People," *Watauga Democrat*, 24 May 1962; Lester Brown writings, Stam Collection. Prior to Bob, a horse named Gunpowder attended the superintendent, according to Rivers.
18. I.G. Greer, "Old Bob," in *The Handbook Edition of The Rhododendron 1929*, vol. 7, 23. My dad, Dr. Johnnie Perry, recalled seeing the pair during the mid-1920s when my dad was a young boy in Boone.
19. I.G. Greer, "Old Bob," in *The Handbook Edition of The Rhododendron 1929*, vol. 7, 23. See also Brian Haines, "More to the Story: Cars Put an End to Livery Stables, Trains," *Hutchinson Leader*, 3 Nov. 2021, updated 8 Dec. 2022, https://www.crowrivermedia.com/hutchinsonleader/news/opinion/columnists/more-to-the-story-cars-put-an-end-to-livery-stables-trains/article_92ca4c38-35cd-11ec-a846-471f5a09c8bb.html; and Le Vern Fox, interview with Doris Perry Stam, Aug. 2007, Stam Collection.
20. *Dew Drop* 1906–1907. Mrs. Moore told an interviewer that she came in 1906, but the school records indicate it was not until 1907. The *Dew Drop* for 1906–1907 listed only Gabriella Blair as a matron of Lovill Home for the school year but included Mrs. Emma Moore for the summer term of 1907. Dr. B.B. Dougherty's remarks in 1949 verify the years of service of several employees, including Mrs. Emma Moore beginning her work in 1907.
21. Pam Mitchem, "Emma Horton Moore: Launching into an Unknown Sea," a presentation given at the Founders' Day events of Sept. 2022. Emma Horton married Louis P. Moore (of High Point, North Carolina) in 1895, in Georgia.
22. Leonard Eury, "Emma Horton Moore," Gaffney, ed., 196–197.
23. "Musings—Mrs. Emma Moore," UA 30.026, Ruby Lanier Papers, University Archives and Records Management Services, Special Collections Research Center, Appalachian State University, Boone, NC.
24. "Musings—Mrs. Emma Moore," UA 30.026, Ruby Lanier Papers, University Archives and Records Management Services, Special Collections Research Center, Appalachian State University, Boone, NC.
25. "Musings—Mrs. Emma Moore," UA 30.026,

Ruby Lanier Papers, University Archives and Records Management Services, Special Collections Research Center, Appalachian State University, Boone, NC. Mrs. Moore told her interviewer that "Dr. Dougherty" purchased the food. Blan was given an honorary doctorate in 1926. Dauph functioned as the treasurer and business manager, overseeing the purchase of food until his death in 1929.

26. "Musings—Mrs. Emma Moore," UA 30.026, Ruby Lanier Papers, University Archives and Records Management Services, Special Collections Research Center, Appalachian State University, Boone, NC.

27. *Dew Drop* 1906–1907, 10.

28. Norris and Boatmon, 34.

29. Wood and Blethen, 48. Cullowhee Normal and Industrial School had another name change in 1925 and was renamed Cullowhee State Normal School. In 1953 the school became Western Carolina College, and in 1967 it became Western Carolina University.

30. Ferrell, *No Time for Ivy*, 9.

31. Annie Dougherty Rufty, speech notes, Stam Collection. The quote is taken from handwritten notes by Annie Dougherty Rufty for a speech she gave at Appalachian, probably given at a gathering in the 1960s, but which specific event has not yet been determined.

32. Eggers, 11, 21.

33. *The Dew Drop, Catalogue Edition, Ninth Year 1911-1912, Appalachian Training School* 10, no. 1 (Raleigh, NC: Edwards & Broughton Printing Company, Aug. 1912). Online *The Dew Drop, Catalogue Edition 1905*, 34–90. https://lib.digitalnc.org/record/34738?ln=en#?xywh=-2780%2C0%2C11559%2C4907&cv=33; *The Dew Drop, Catalogue Edition, Eleventh Year, 1913-1914, Appalachian Training School* 12, no. 1 (Raleigh, NC: Edwards & Broughton Printing Co., Aug. 1914). Online *The Dew Drop, Catalogue Edition 1906-1918*, 130–184. https://lib.digitalnc.org/record/34758?ln=en#?xywh=-2014%2C-1%2C8490%2C3605&cv=130. After high school commencement Edgar continued another year taking classes and was also listed among the graduates for 1909, with the note that he had been hired by Southern Railway.

34. J.P. Arthur, *A History of Watauga County*, 252.

35. *Dew Drop* 1914–1915. State Farm Road in Boone is named for this property.

36. Brown, *B.B. Dougherty*, 120.

37. Alice Shull Smith to Lillie Shull Dougherty, 14 Sept. 1908, in possession of the family.

38. Nettie (Virginia) Shull Sherwood to Lillie Shull Dougherty, 14 Sept. 1908, in possession of the family.

39. Vinnie (Victoria) Shull Campbell to Lillie Shull Dougherty, 14 Sept. 1908, in possession of the family.

40. https://www.mayoclinic.org/diseases-conditions/typhoid-fever/symptoms-causes/syc-20378661.

41. Brown, *B.B. Dougherty*, 120. See the novel *Christy*, by Catherine Marshall (1967), pages 418 and following, for more on typhoid in the mountains.

42. *Watauga Democrat*, 3 Sept. 1908, 3.

43. Lanier, 59; Board of Trustees of Appalachian Training School, *Report of the Officials of the Appalachian Training School, Boone, North Carolina, to Governor W.W. Kitchen, 1903 to 1908* (Boone, NC: Appalachian Training School for Teachers, 1908), 3–5.

44. https://www.ncpedia.org/public-education-part-4-expansion.

45. *The Evening Times* (Raleigh, NC), 16 Feb. 1909, 8. No name is given for the author of the article but the content contains quotes from the report by Board of Trustees Chairman E.F. Lovill.

46. Appalachian Training School, Official Report 1903 to 1908, 3–5.

47. *Evening Times*, 16 Feb. 1909, 8.

48. *Evening Times*, 16 Feb. 1909, 8.

49. *Evening Times*, 16 Feb. 1909, 8.

50. *Public Laws of North Carolina*, 1909, 449.

51. *Dew Drop* 1909–1910. See Bird, 53–54.

52. Barnard worked as assistant business manager 1929–38 during the years when his mother was business manager. When she retired, Barnard became business manager under his uncle, President B.B. Dougherty, and worked as comptroller 1955–65. Barnard died March 26, 1965.

53. Lester Brown, who clearly remembered seeing the comet and who later became part of the Dougherty family, lived to see the comet's return in 1986.

54. Lanier, 59–60.

55. Pezzoni, 47.

56. Pezzoni, 47.

57. J.P. Arthur, *A History of Watauga County*, 252.

58. Wood and Blethen, 36.

59. Lanier, 60–61.

60. Lanier, 61, citing the governor's speech printed in the Raleigh *News and Observer*, 6 Jan. 1911.

61. Lanier, 60–61.

62. Lanier, 61–62.

63. Wood and Blethen, 36, 38.

64. Wood and Blethen, 38.

65. D.J. Whitener, *History of Watauga County*, 82–83.

66. Frank A. Linney, *Speech: 1911*, Stam Collection. Regionally well-known Hon. Romulus Z. Linney was the father of Frank Linney. Their descendent is the actress Laura Linney.

67. DeWeese, 59.

68. Altmayer, 63.

69. *Watauga Democrat*, 12 Oct. 1911, 2.

70. *Watauga Democrat*, 3 Aug. and 28 Oct. 1911; Martha Shull to Lillie Dougherty, 14 Nov. 1911. In possession of the author.

71. Lanier, 62–63, citing Dougherty to Joyner, 15 Oct. 1911, S.P.I. Correspondence. A major extension of Appalachian State University in

Caldwell County near Lenoir, North Carolina, was opened in 2023.

72. Lanier, 63.

73. Lanier, 63, quoting from the Raleigh *News and Observer*, 17 Oct. 1911.

74. Lanier, 63.

75. Brown, *B.B. Dougherty*, 208. Appalachian State University opened a campus in Hickory, Catawba County, near Caldwell County, North Carolina, in the year 2023. The new campus is 45 miles south of Boone.

Chapter 17

1. Wood and Blethen, 38, 41.

2. Wood and Blethen, 38, 41. William Ernest Bird, *The History of Western Carolina College: The Progress of an Idea* (Chapel Hill: he University of North Carolina Press, 1963), 30–31. Prof. Bird taught at Cullowhee for 37 years.

3. Bird, 71; Wood and Blethen, 37, 40–41. This theory was mentioned to me by the staff at the Western Carolina University archives.

4. William Ernest Bird, *The History of Western Carolina College: The Progress of an Idea* (Chapel Hill: University of North Carolina Press, 1963), 30–31; Wood and Blethen, 38, 41. Madison would later be reinstated as president for the years 1920–1923.

5. Bird, 71.

6. Isaac Newton Carr, *History of Carson-Newman College 1, Survey History, 1851–1959* (Jefferson City, TN: Carson-Newman College, 1959), 96–101.

7. Ferrell, *No Time for Ivy*, 51, 68–72.

8. Rebecca Greene Ragan, "Memories of Rebecca Greene Ragan, 1902–2001," unpublished manuscript, UA 47, Box 3, Folder 8, Doris Perry Stam Collection, University Archives, Special Collections Research Center, Appalachian State University, Boone, NC.

9. Brown, *Elopers*.

10. Brown, *Elopers*, 10–11.

11. Brown, *Elopers*, 11.

12. Brown, *Elopers*, 11.

13. Brown, *Elopers*, 13.

14. Lester Brown, "Clara Bartlett Dougherty Brown," in Gaffney, ed., 115–116.

15. Brown, *Elopers*, 13.

16. *Watauga Democrat*, 17 Oct. 1912, 3.

17. *Watauga Democrat*, 17 Oct. 1912, 3.

18. *Watauga Democrat*, 7 Nov. 1912.

19. Martha Sousanna Lewis Shull, born 1841, married September 1865, died November 24, 1913. Her parents were Mary Polly Goodwin and William Lafayette Lewis.

20. *Greensboro Patriot* (Greensboro, NC), 5 Dec. 1912.

21. D.J. Whitener, "Education for the People," 190. See Cratis Williams, "The Appalachian Experience: Historical Sketches of Southwest Virginia," 1977, Ruby Lanier Papers, University Archives, Special Collections Research Center, Appalachian State University, Boone, NC.

22. *The Evening Chronicle* (Charlotte, NC), taken from "'Pauper' Counties: Sentiment Strong Against a Continuance of Present Conditions," *Winston-Salem Sentinel*, 21 Dec. 1912.

23. *The Evening Chronicle* (Charlotte, NC), 20 Mar. 1912.

24. *The Charlotte Daily Observer*, 24 Dec. 1912.

25. *Watauga Democrat*, 23 June 1949, reprinting a letter by B.B. Dougherty from 20 Dec. 1912.

26. Brown, *B.B. Dougherty*, 141; Lanier, 143–155.

27. E.F. Lovill, "Report of the Chairman of the Trustees," in the *Report to the Governor and the General Assembly of the Officers of the Appalachian Training School, January 1911–January 1913*. UA 43, Box 1, Folder 18, Appalachian Training School Collection, Special Collections Research Center, Appalachian State University, Boone, NC.

28. Lanier, 61.

29. E.F. Lovill, "Report of the Chairman of the Trustees," *Report to the Governor and the General Assembly … January 1911–January 1913*.

30. E.F. Lovill, "Report of the Chairman of the Trustees," *Report to the Governor and the General Assembly … January 1911–January 1913*.

31. B.B. Dougherty, "Report of the Treasurer," *Report to the Governor and the General Assembly … January 1911–January 1913*.

32. J.Y. Joyner, "Report of North Carolina Superintendent of Public Instruction," *Report to the Governor and the General Assembly … January 1911–January 1913*.

33. Col. Harris, "The Appalachian Training School, as Seen by Distinguished Editor," *Watauga Democrat*, 18 Sept. 1913, printed an editorial from the *Charlotte Observer*.

34. Lanier, 64.

35. Brown, *Elopers*, 13.

36. *The Dew Drop, Catalogue Edition, Eleventh Year 1913–1914, Appalachian Training School*, Vol. XII, No. 1, Aug. 14, 1914, Boone, NC.

37. Annie Dougherty Rufty, interview by Lib Brown Scoggins, Boone, NC, 20 Sept., 4 Oct. 1999, recorded, Stam Collection.

38. *The Dew Drop, Catalogue Edition, Eleventh Year 1913–1914, Appalachian Training School*, Vol. XII, No. 1, Aug. 14, 1914, Boone, NC.

39. Brown, *Elopers*, 14; Brown, "John Preston Arthur Early Boone Resident Plagued by Loneliness, Want," *Watauga Democrat*, 3 Jan. 1963; Brown, "John Preston Arthur Came From SC, as NY Lawyer," *Watauga Democrat*, 10 Jan. 1963; Brown, "John Preston Arthur Finished At VMI; Wasn't Good Student," *Watauga Democrat*, 17 Jan. 1963.

40. Brown, *Elopers*, 15.

41. Boone Creek was known as Kraut Creek from the 1930s until after the year 2000. When the vats were rinsed at the Kraut Factory, the water released into the creek had a strong odor which lingered nearby in Boone and downstream through

the lower school campus. See article by Val Maiewskij-Hay, "Mountain Made Kraut: The Rise and Fall of Cabbage in the High Country," *High Country Magazine*, Oct. 2009.

42. Edwin Powell, "When Wilkesboro was a Major Excursion," *Watauga Democrat*, 29 Aug. 1990.

43. Alfred and Daisy Adams, interview by Doris Perry Stam, 8 Aug. 2000, recorded, Stam Collection; Edwin Powell, "When Wilkesboro was a Major Excursion," *Watauga Democrat*, 29 Aug. 1990.

44. E.T. Campbell, *Tweetsie Tales: A Collection of Reminiscences* 1, 50.

45. https://www.collectorsweekly.com/tools-and-hardware/sad-and-flat-irons. (Sad irons, also called flat irons or smoothing irons, are thick, triangular pieces of metal that are flat and polished on one side and have a handle attached to the other. "Sad" is an Old English word for "solid," and the term "sad iron" is often used to distinguish the largest and heaviest of flat irons, usually five to nine pounds. The forebears to modern electric irons, these flat irons are often triangular or come to a point to make it easier to iron around buttons. The heft of a sad iron would help it hold heat, as well as to press the fabric flat.)

46. Ragan, "Memories," excerpts, Stam Collection.

47. *Dew Drop* 1914–1915; Lanier, 67.

48. Lester Brown, "Some Little Known Incidents in the Life of the Late Dr. Blanford Barnard Dougherty," in possession of the family; McLeod, 183–184.

49. Brown, *Elopers*, 15.

50. Brown, *Elopers*, 16. See also Oral History, Floretta Lyon, "Appalachian State University: Appalachian Training School," AC.111, Tape #318, Box 49, Folder 32, transcription, 12–13, University Archives, Special Collections Research Center, Appalachian State University, Boone, NC.

51. *Dew Drop* 1914–1915.

52. Brown, *Elopers*, 17.

53. Ragan, "Memoirs," Stam Collection.

54. Brown, *Elopers*, 16–19.

55. Brown, *Elopers*, 18–19.

56. Brown, *Elopers*, 18–19.

57. Brown, *Elopers*, 18–19. Lester and Clara long marriage was filled with a remarkable affection and dedication to each other, as can be affirmed by their many descendants, myself included.

58. Brown, *Elopers*, 18–19.

59. Brown, *B.B. Dougherty*, 77.

60. Herb Wey, interview by Ruth Currie, not dated (1970s?), transcript sent to Ruby Lanier by Ruth Currie on 18 March 1997, Lanier Papers.

61. *Dew Drop* 1913–1914, 20.

62. "Greene Diaries," 11 Aug. 1906; Richard D. Howe, "Andrew Jackson 'Jack' Greene," in Curtis Smalling, *Heritage of Watauga County North Carolina 2* (Winston-Salem, NC: Southern Appalachian Historical Association with Hunter Publishing Company, 1987), 78. Jack kept a personal diary from 1906 to 1942, with "a wealth of information," which was given to the Appalachian State University Library.

63. "Greene Diaries," 27 July 1906.

64. Emma H. Moore, "Educational Progress at Boone Since 1900," written in 1918, in E.H. Moore Scrapbook.

65. Bird, 87.

66. Bird, 84.

67. Bird, 84.

68. *News and Observer*, 8 Jan. 1915.

69. D. Hiden Ramsey to Rev. O.L. Brown, 9 Aug. 1962, Stam Collection.

70. Brown, *B.B. Dougherty*, 83–85.

71. Green Diaries, 23 Feb. 1915; Lanier, 64–65.

72. Tom Corbitt, ed., compiled by a Bicentennial Committee: Reka W. Shoemake, Chairman, Maxie G. Edmisten, Lucy G. Luther, Kate Peterson, and Beatrice C. Winkler, "Development of Public Education in Watauga County North Carolina" (Boone, NC: Appalachian State University, 1976), 14.

73. Van Noppen and Van Noppen, 108.

74. Brown, *B.B. Dougherty*, 85. See also Bird, 90.

75. Pezzoni, 122–124.

76. Ragan, "Memoirs," Stam Collection.

77. *Watauga Democrat*, 4 Mar. 1915; "Greene Diaries," 23 Feb. 1915.

78. Ferrell, *No Time for Ivy*, 31.

79. Curtis, 3.

80. McLeod, 227.

81. *Dew Drop Catalogue, 1904–1905* (Sparta, NC: Appalachian Training School for Teachers with The Star Publishing Co., 1905), 10.

82. McLeod, 219; Wood and Blethen, 120.

83. Gaffney, ed., 166.

84. *Watauga Democrat*, 4 Mar. 1915.

85. *Watauga Democrat*, 4 Mar. 1915.

86. Greene Diaries, 7 and 15 Sept. 1916; *Watauga Democrat*, 10 Oct. 1918.

87. *Watauga Democrat*, 4 Mar. 1915.

88. https://www.history.com/news/how-the-sinking-of-lusitania-changed-wwi; https://www.loc.gov/collections/world-war-i-rotogravures/articles-and-essays/the-lusitania-disaster/.

89. https://www.history.com/news/how-the-sinking-of-lusitania-changed-wwi.

Chapter 18

1. Lanier, 35–36; "Greene Diaries," 6 July 1915; *Watauga Democrat*, 15 July 1915.

2. *Dew Drop* 1914–1915, 11. The large dormitory was called "New Dormitory" in the 1916 and 1921 *Dew Drop*, but the same building is called "Lovill Hall" in a 1924 photo pamphlet. It was the second dorm to be named Lovill Home, the original being a wood frame structure from 11906.

3. Miriam Glovier, "Alumni Secretary Recalls Early Days of Lees-McRae," *Watauga Democrat*, 21 Jan. 1937; M.T. Neal, *Edgar Tufts*, 36.

4. Eliot Wigginton, ed., *Foxfire 6* (Garden City,

NJ: Anchor Press/Doubleday,1980), 324–326. The major portion of this volume of *Foxfire* is devoted to Ben Ward, his interesting life, craftsmanship and inventions. Ward later joined the Navy, with Blan's encouragement. After World War I Ben Ward experienced prolonged mental health issues.

5. Ray and Virginia Ward, interview with Doris Perry Stam, Oct. 2018, recorded, Stam Collection.

6. Brown, *B.B. Dougherty*, 80; Val Maiewskij-Hay, "Boone Ablaze with Beautiful Lights," *Carolina Mountain Life* (Summer 2009), 29.

7. Brown, *B.B. Dougherty*, 80–81.

8. https://nrlp.appstate.edu/about/history. See Brown.

9. Brown, *B.B. Dougherty*, 80; Maiewskij-Hay, "Beautiful Lights," 29.

10. "Greene Diaries," 18 Aug. 1915.

11. Ruth Currie, *Appalachian State University: The First Hundred Years* (Louisville, KY: Harmony House Publishers, 1998), 33. The "new Lovill Home" was brick, and also called Lovill Hall, to designate its difference from the wood frame Lovill Home of 1906.

12. Jeni Gray, "Satie Hunt: Appalachian Celebrating 90th Birthdays," *Watauga Democrat*, 12 July 1988.

13. Jeni Gray, "Satie Hunt: Appalachian Celebrating 90th Birthdays," *Watauga Democrat*, 12 July 1988.

14. *Watauga Democrat*, 11 July 1974.

15. Dianne Dougherty interviewed by Doris Perry Stam, 14. Feb. 2024; Lanier 136; "Education: Hillbilly's School System," *Time Magazine*, 25 Mar. 1940, https://content.time.com/time/subscriber/printout/0,8816,763741,00.html.

16. *Watauga Democrat*, 11 July 1974. See also Lanier, 136–138, and "Oldest Living Wataugan Ed Culler Dies at 97," *The Mountain Times*, April 30, 1998.

17. *Dew Drop Catalogue*, Aug. 1916 and Aug. 1917.

18. Annie Dougherty Rufty, interview by Doris Perry Stam, 9 Aug. 2009, Stam Collection.

19. *Watauga Democrat*, 22 July 1915.

20. Barefoot, 13.

21. Brown, *Elopers*, 20. During March of 1915 Clara worked on a tapestry for hours every day. The subject was Hagar and Ishmael and the wilderness, a greatly enlarged study of a small print that depicted the original by the artist Taylor.

22. Annie Dougherty Rufty, interview by Doris Perry Stam, Aug. 1995, Stam Collection.

23. Jeni Gray, "Satie Broyhill, Appalachian Celebrating 90th Birthdays"; "Satie Hunt Broyhill, ASU Celebrate Together" and "Dedication: Triple Celebration Planned," ASU News Bureau, *Watauga Democrat*, 13 July 1981, or ASU communications with Broyhill descendants Annie Broyhill Hsu and James Edgar Broyhill, 2023. See also Mitchem, 29.

24. William Stevens, *Anvil of Adversity: Biography of a Furniture Pioneer* (Kingsport, TN: Kingsport Press, 1968), 6, 24–28, 61, 76–79, 85–86, 119, 126–127, 195.

25. ASU News Bureau, "Satie Broyhill, ASU Celebrate Together," *Watauga Democrat*, 12 July 1988.

26. ASU News Bureau, "Satie Broyhill, ASU Celebrate Together," *Watauga Democrat*, 12 July 1988.

27. ASU News Bureau, "Satie Broyhill, ASU Celebrate Together," *Watauga Democrat*, 12 July 1988.

28. William Stevens, *Anvil of Adversity: Biography of a Furniture Pioneer* (Kingsport, TN: Kingsport Press, 1968), 6, 24–28, 61, 76–79, 85–86, 119, 126–127, 195.

29. William Stevens, *Anvil of Adversity: Biography of a Furniture Pioneer* (Kingsport, TN: Kingsport Press, 1968), 6, 24–28, 61, 76–79, 85–86, 119, 126–127, 195.

30. John L. Bell, "Broyhill Furniture," *Encyclopedia of North Carolina,* edited by William S. Powell (Chapel Hill: University of North Carolina Press, 2006), https://www.ncpedia.org/broyhill-furniture.

31. Stevens, 6, 24–28, 61, 76–79, 85–86, 119, 126–127, 195. The Broyhill company in Lenoir faced hard times during the 1930s–1940s. Bolstered by the post World War I economic boom, Broyhill Furniture Industries grew into one of the largest employers in North Carolina during the 1950s–1970s.

32. "Greene Diaries," 17 and 24 Jan. 1916; O. Lester Brown, *Tales from the Tall Hills* (Charlotte, NC: privately published, 1977), 37, Scoggins Collection.

33. "Greene Diaries," 10 July 1916.

34. "Greene Diaries," 17 and 24 Jan. 1916, 19 Mar. 1916.

35. "Greene Diaries," 30 Jan. 1916

36. "Greene Diaries," 24 Jan. 1916.

37. Lanier, 69.

38. Lester Brown, notes and sketches, handwritten notes, Stam Collection.

39. Lanier, 70; *Dew Drop* 13, no. 4 (Boone, NC: Appalachian Training School, Feb. 1916). In possession of the author.

40. Brown, *B.B. Dougherty*, 205; Lanier, 70–71.

41. "Greene Diaries," 20–29 Feb. 1916.

42. Brown, *B.B. Dougherty*, 101.

43. "Greene Diaries," 19 and 24 Apr 1916.

44. "Greene Diaries," 18 Mar. 1916.

45. Altmayer, 121. As noted in an earlier chapter, there must have been a reason that Arthur gave so little space in his book to A.T.S. and neglected to mention Watauga Academy. Lester Brown indicated that Arthur's snub may have been purposeful.

46. Brown, *Elopers*, 14; Brown, "John Preston Arthur Early Boone Resident Plagued by Loneliness, Want," *Watauga Democrat*, 3 Jan. 1963; Brown, "John Preston Arthur Came from SC, Was NY Lawyer," *Watauga Democrat*, 10 Jan. 1963; Brown, "John Preston Arthur Finished at VMI; Wasn't Good Student," *Watauga Democrat*, 17 Jan. 1963.

47. "Greene Diaries," 7 Dec. 1916.
48. "Greene Diaries," 19 and 17 Apr., 15 July 1916.
49. *Dew Drop* 1916–1917.
50. "Greene Diaries," 21 July 1916.
51. "The Great Flood of 1916," *Blue Heron Whitewater*, online, copyright 2007–2018 (Marshall, NC), https://www.blueheronwhitewater.com/blog/great-flood-1916; Pamela Whitener, "Flood of '16 Worst Ever to Hit Area," *Hickory Daily Record* (Hickory, NC), 6 June 1970.
52. Howell Cook, recorded interview by Doris Perry Stam, Valle Crucis, NC, July 2022, in possession of the author; Pamela Whitener, "Flood of '16 Worst Ever to Hit Area," *Hickory Daily Record* (Hickory, NC), 6 June 1970.
53. Maiewskij-Hay, "Beautiful Lights," 29.
54. Lanier, 79.
55. Pamela Whitener, "Flood of '16 Worst Ever to Hit Area," *Hickory Daily Record* (Hickory, NC), 6 June 1970.
56. C.D. Neal, *Miss Chessie*, 17. Train service in Jefferson began in 1915, four years before Boone finally got passenger train service in 1919. Tweetsie began transporting cargo in and out of Boone in late 1918.

Chapter 19

1. "Greene Diaries," 2 Jan. 1917.
2. "Greene Diaries," 29 and 30 May 1917.
3. "Greene Diaries," 23 Feb. 1916.
4. Lanier, 73; *Public Laws of North Carolina, 1917*, 154, 193.
5. "Greene Diaries," 30 May 1017.
6. "Greene Diaries," 4 June 1917.
7. "Greene Diaries," 4 May 1917.
8. "Greene Diaries," 4 May 1917; Annie Dougherty Rufty, speech notes, Stam Collection. The quote is taken from handwritten notes by Annie Dougherty Rufty for a speech she gave at Appalachian, probably at the dedication of the Lillie Shull Dougherty building in the 1960s.
9. Lanier, 118–119; McFarland, 4–6; *Watauga Democrat*, 8 Nov. 1973. From 1926 to 1930 the hotel had a live orchestra for dancing on Friday nights led by Jennie Blackburn Critcher's niece, Lillian Hopkins, joined on mandolin played by Mrs. Dewitt Barnett (Nell Smith) and others on saxophone and tenor banjo. See also Julia MacFarland, "The Critcher Hotel: A Glimpse of Boone's Beginning," 3, University Archives, Special Collections Research Center, Appalachian State University, Boone, NC.
10. https://onboarding.ncsu.edu/univnamehistory/. The original name of North Carolina College of Agriculture and Mechanic Arts, given in 1887 at the establishment of the land grant college, was changed in 1917 to North Carolina State College of Agriculture and Engineering, "to reflect the increasing emphasis on the professional and theoretical aspects of technical education." By 1930 the school was being referred to as "State College," and officially became North Carolina State University in 1965.
11. Dauph Dougherty to Lillie Shull Dougherty, 12 July 1917, Stam Collection; *Dew Drop, Catalogue Edition, Fifteenth Year, 1917–1918*, Appalachian Training School 16, no. 1 (Boone, NC: n.p., Sept. 1918). See the online *The Dew Drop, Catalogue Editions 1906–1918*, 375–409. https://lib.digitalnc.org/record/34758.
12. Dauph Dougherty to Lillie Shull Dougherty, 12 July 1917, Stam Collection.
13. *Watauga Democrat*, 7 Aug. 1919.
14. "Greene Diaries," 12 Sept. 1917; *Watauga Democrat*, 21 Aug. 1917. *Dew Drop Catalogues* for most years are available online, with student names and enrollment numbers.
15. "Greene Diaries," 12 Sept. 1917.
16. Lanier, 72–73; *Watauga Democrat*, 22 Nov. 1917.
17. "Greene Diaries," 21 and 23 Aug., 12 Sept., 1 Oct. 1917; Brown, *B.B. Dougherty*, 81; *Watauga Democrat*, 1 Mar. 1917.
18. *Dew Drop* (Boone, NC: Appalachian Training School, June 1921).
19. *Dew Drop*, Feb. 1916, 4; the Dew Drop (Boone, NC: Appalachian Training School, May 1924). The first women's dorm on the campus was a wood frame structure, Lovill Home, completed in 1906.
20. "Greene Diaries," 21 and 23 Aug., 12 Sept., 1 Oct. 1917; Brown, *B.B. Dougherty*, 81.
21. *Dew Drop* 1916–1917.
22. https://axaem.archives.ncdcr.gov/findingaids/WWI_8_U_S__Food_Administration__.html; https://medium.com/nc-stories-of-service/food-administration-in-n-c-during-wwi-a248d7513d1c.
23. *Watauga Democrat*, 4 July 1918.
24. "Greene Diaries," 17 Jan. 1918.
25. *Watauga Democrat*, 28 Mar. 1918.
26. "Greene Diaries," 2 May 1918.
27. "Greene Diaries," 24 June 1918.
28. "Greene Diaries," 27 July 1918; *Watauga Democrat*, 4 and 13 July 1918, 3.
29. *Watauga Democrat*, 11 July 1918.
30. *Greensboro Daily News* (Greensboro, NC), 29 Aug. 1918, 4.
31. Lanier, 72, citing "Greene Diaries," 10 and 15 Oct. 1918.
32. "Greene Diaries," 12 Sept. 1918.
33. "Greene Diaries," 13 July 1918.
34. "Greene Diaries," 14 July 1918.
35. *Watauga Democrat*, 26 July 1918.
36. H.B. Perry, Jr., "The Dr. Henry Baker Perry Family," in Gaffney, ed., 307.
37. Doris Taylor Perry, handwritten notes on the life of her husband, Dr. H.B. Perry, Sr., written during the early 1950s. Stam Collection.
38. *Greensboro Daily News* (Greensboro, NC), 29 Aug. 1918, 4.
39. Brown, *Elopers*, 23–24.
40. https://www.ncmuseumofhistory.org/

learn/in-the-classroom/timelines/twentieth-century-north-carolina.
  41. https://www.ncmuseumofhistory.org/blog/flu-pandemic-of-1918-1920.
  42. "Greene Diaries," 10 and 15 Oct. 1918.
  43. Norris and Boatmon, 49.
  44. Morley, 26, from an article about Mrs. Will Walker titled "An Oldster Remembers Butler."
  45. https://www.ncmuseumofhistory.org/learn/in-the-classroom/timelines/twentieth-century-north-carolina.
  46. "The War Is Not Over," *Watauga Democrat*, 11 Nov. 1918.
  47. Lanier, 73, citing Greene, "Record of Events," 11 Nov. 1918.
  48. E.T. Campbell, 49.
  49. Plaag, 25.
  50. Susan E. Keefe with assistance from the Junaluska Heritage Association, *Junaluska: Oral Histories of a Black Appalachian Community*. Contributions to Southern Appalachian Studies 48 (Jefferson, NC: McFarland, 2020), 49–50.
  51. Lanier, 83, citing economist Cecil Kenneth Brown, *The State Highway System of North Carolina, Its Evolution and Present Status* (Chapel Hill: University of North Carolina Press, 1931), 15, 43, 53.
  52. E.T. Campbell, 2.
  53. E.T. Campbell, 51.
  54. *Watauga Democrat*, 7 Dec. 1918.
  55. Lanier, 81.
  56. Eric W. Plaag, *Images of America: Remembering Boone* (Charleston, SC: Arcadia, 2021), 25.
  57. Ragan, "Memories."
  58. Brown, *B.B. Dougherty*, 96. When Blan died, his wallet revealed several Greyhound and Queen City bus passes, which he used in 1937–1940. The passes were gifts from Glen Wilcox. Stam Collection.
  59. Alfred Adams, "Some History About the Banks of Watauga County," in *Watauga County Times...Past* (Boone, NC: Watauga County Historical Society, June 1992), 4, Caldwell County Historical Society and Heritage Museum in Lenoir, NC; Robert Shipley, interview by Doris Perry Stam, recorded, January 2005, Stam Collection. Bynum Taylor sometimes rode his horse from Valle Crucis to Boone to sell cars. Taylor co-owned a car dealership in Valle Crucis before opening one in Boone.
  60. "Greene Diaries," Jan. 5, 7 and 15 Feb. 1919.
  61. Wood and Blethen, 58.
  62. "Greene Diaries," 26 Apr 1919.
  63. *Watauga Democrat*, 3 and 10 July 1919.
  64. Powell, *North Carolina: A History*, 181, 185.
  65. Ferrell, *No Time for Ivy*, 19.
  66. https://www.ncmuseumofhistory.org/learn/in-the-classroom/timelines/twentieth-century-north-carolina.
  67. https://www.ncmuseumofhistory.org/learn/in-the-classroom/timelines/twentieth-century-north-carolina.
  68. *Lenoir News-Topic* (Lenoir, NC), 23 May 1888.

  69. John Crouch, "Historical Sketches of Wilkes County," Wilkes Genealogical Society, Inc., 1902. "This copy was made from the 50th anniversary issue of the *Journal Patriot* (North Wilkesboro, NC), 27 June 1940, by special permission of the author. Mr. Crouch was on the staff of the *Chronicle* in Wilkesboro when he wrote, printed and bound the history."
  70. Spainhour, "The Dougherty Brothers," 13.
  71. Fox, Stam Collection.
  72. Sloop, 110, 188.
  73. Nannie Greene and Catherine Stokes Sheppard, *Community and Change in the North Carolina Mountains: Oral Histories and Profiles of People from Western Watauga County*, Contributions to Southern Appalachian Studies 13 (Jefferson, NC: McFarland, 2006), 262–63.
  74. Ed Culler, interview by Ed Hutchins for the *Watauga Democrat*, 11 July 1974, 9C.
  75. "Greene Diaries," 11, 14 and 27 Feb. 1920.
  76. "Greene Diaries," 13 Mar. 1920; *Watauga Democrat*, 18 Mar. 1920, 4.
  77. *Watauga Democrat*, 18 Mar. 1920, 4.
  78. My mother, Lillie Alene Brown, married Dr. Henry Baker Perry, Jr., on 9 Aug. 1943.

Chapter 20

  1. "Greene Diaries," 9 July 1919; Lanier, 241; Van Noppen and Van Noppen, 181–182.
  2. Ferrell, *No Time for Ivy*, 21.
  3. Ferrell, *No Time for Ivy*, 21.
  4. Lanier, 88.
  5. Lanier, 88.
  6. Ferrell, *No Time for Ivy*, 28; Lanier, 88–91.
  7. Van Noppen and Van Noppen, 181–182.
  8. Lanier, 88–89; Van Noppen and Van Noppen, 182.
  9. Lanier, 89–90, citing A.J. Greene, "Record of Events," 29 Sept. 1920; *Watauga Democrat*, 5 Oct. 1920. Lanier cites numerous newspaper articles, letters between Brooks and B.B. Dougherty, and the events recorded by A.J. Greene.
  10. Lanier, 89–90.
  11. Photocopy of letter to Eugene Clyde Brooks, 7 Oct. 1920, Eugene Clyde Brooks Papers, David M. Rubenstein Rare Book & Manuscript Library, Duke University, Ruby Lanier Papers, W.L. Eury Appalachian Collection, Special Collections Research Center, Appalachian State University, Boone, NC. The letter is more than 100 years old and it is not available to the general public. The name of the writer is withheld here, as originally requested.
  12. D.J. Whitener, *History of Watauga County*, 82.
  13. D.D. Dougherty to Annie Dougherty, 27 Feb. 1922, Box 3, Folder 7, Stam Collection.
  14. Lanier, 90.
  15. Lanier, 89.
  16. D.J. Whitener, *History of Watauga County*, 82.

17. Lanier, 90–91.
18. *Dew Drop*, 1921; Lanier, 91; *Watauga Democrat*, 19 May 1921.
19. *Watauga Democrat*, 19 May 1921.
20. Lanier, 91.
21. Lanier, 92.
22. D.J. Whitener, *History of Watauga County*, 81–82; Lanier, 91–92; *Watauga Democrat*, 19 May 1921.
23. "Greene Diaries," 5 and 6 Apr 1921; *Watauga Democrat*, 14 Apr. 1921.
24. Lanier, 93.
25. *The Dew Drop, Annual Catalogue, Year 1920-1921*, Appalachian Training School (Boone, NC: n.p., July 1921). Online *The Dew Drop, Catalogue Edition 1919-1924*, 20–52. https://lib.digitalnc.org/record/34760?ln=en#?xywh=-671%2C0%2C5831%2C3382&cv=20.
26. *Dew Drop* 1920–1921; *The Dew Drop* 15, no. 3 (Boone, NC: Appalachian Training School, Dec. 1917). In possession of the author.
27. "Greene Diaries," 22 Sept. 1919.
28. *Dew Drop* 1920–1921, 19; *Watauga Democrat*, 15 Nov. 1921.
29. Xerox of the 1921 contract for the sale of land from the Doughertys to the state, Scoggins Collection. The boundaries of the Dougherty property being sold to the state were indicated as "on the east by the Lovill Home tract and also by the main tract of the Appalachian Training School, on the south by the Blowing Rock and Boone Turnpike Rd and on the north by North Street of the school property, and on the west by the lands of E.S. Coffey, and also on the west by the school lot, known as E.S. Coffey's lot, said land to include all of the buildings owned by the parties of the first part between the property of the Appalachian Training School on the west and on the south Blowing Rock and Boone Turnpike roads, posing to contain by estimation 6 acres of land more or less."
30. "Greene Diaries," 4 Jan. 1922; Lanier, 92.
31. B.B. Dougherty, "Manly B. Blackburn," *The Rhododendron 1922*, vol. 1 (Boone, NC: Senior Class of the Appalachian Training School, 1922), 4, University Archives, Special Collections Research Center, Appalachian State University, Boone, NC. Professor B.B. Dougherty's remarks from the funeral were printed in the yearbook.
32. "Greene Diaries," 31 Jan., 21 Feb. 1922.
33. *Charlotte Observer*, 9 Mar. 1922.
34. D.D. Dougherty to Annie Dougherty, 27 Feb. 1922, Box 3, Folder 7, Stam Collection. Alene, mentioned in the letter, refers to Lillie Alene Brown, born October of 1920.
35. Emily Spivack, "The History of the Flapper: Part 4: Emboldened by the Bob," *Smithsonian Magazine*, 26 Feb. 2013, https://www.smithsonianmag.com/arts-culture/the-history-of-the-flapper-part-4-emboldened-by-the-bob-27361862/.
36. Ferrell, *No Time for Ivy*, 31–32.
37. Zetta Barker Hamby, 75.
38. Zetta Barker Hamby, 89–97, 118–119.
39. Zetta Barker Hamby, 89.
40. Zetta Barker Hamby, 89.
41. Zetta Barker Hamby, 97–99.
42. Ira T. Johnson, "Appalachian in 1907," *Watauga Democrat*, 11 July 1974. See also Virginia Dare Strother, Appalachian Oral History Project, "Appalachian State University: Appalachian Training School," AC.111, Tape #138, Box 45, Folder 18, transcription, 4, University Archives, Special Collections Research Center, Appalachian State University, Boone, NC.
43. D.J. Whitener, *History of Watauga County*, 83.
44. D.D. Dougherty, "Educational Needs of Children in Rural Sections," Scoggins Collection. The digital version of the original newspaper has not been located. A xerox copy was found in the Scoggins Collection and in family documents, but the original newspaper identification heading is missing.
45. D.D. Dougherty, "Educational Needs of Children in Rural Sections," Scoggins Collection. The digital version of the original newspaper has not been located. A xerox copy was found in the Scoggins Collection and in family documents, but the original newspaper identification heading is missing.
46. *Watauga Democrat*, 27 Apr., 11 May 1922, 3
47. *Watauga Democrat*, 21 June 1923, reprinted 21 June 1963. See also Le Verne Fox interview.
48. *The Dew Drop, Annual Catalogue, 1923-1924*, Appalachian Training School 22, no 1 (Boone, NC: n.p., July 1924).
49. *Dew Drop* 1923–1924.
50. *Dew Drop* 1923–1924.
51. Ned Trivette, interviews with Doris Perry Stam, 2012–2014.
52. "Administration Building Burns," *Appalachian Alumnus* (Boone, NC: Appalachian State University Alumni Office, Jan. 1967), Stam Collection. The building was slated to be torn down in 1967. The fire happened on December 29, 1966, as I was visiting great aunt Annie Dougherty. Annie's nephew David Dougherty ran into the house to tell us the Administration Building was on fire, and Annie screamed, "The portraits! The portraits! David, run and try to save the portraits!" My aunt Gertrude Perry quickly took us back to her home in Boone, with the dark smoke filling the air across the road from the Dougherty house. The image of the event is strong in my mind, even though I was only 12 years old.
53. https://nrlp.appstate.edu/about/history; *Watauga Democrat*, 16 Mar. 1922, 3. In 1922 the Watauga Academy was underpinned with rock so that it could be heated from the Science Building. New River Light and Power (NRLP) has been providing electric power to App State and the Boone community since 1915.
54. D.J. Whitener, *History of Watauga County*, 82.
55. Wood and Blethen, 88.
56. Wood and Blethen, 92.
57. Ferrell, *No Time for Ivy*, 15.

58. Ferrell, *No Time for Ivy*, 34.
59. Sloop, 228–29. The Crossnore and Linville areas had no high school until the Sloops convinced the community and the state to create one in 1919. The Sloops attributed the success of their work to prayer.
60. David Golann, Librarian, Vanderbilt University, Nashville, TN, to Doris Perry Stam, email 19 July 2021,.
61. Richard D. Howe, "Chapell Wilson," Gaffney, ed., 385. Prof. Wilson led the Demonstration School until 1957. He served as the inaugural dean of the Graduate School from 1948 to 1957, director of Summer Sessions, and chairman of the Department of Education.
62. Brown, *Elopers*, 24–26.
63. Brown, *Elopers*, 25–26.
64. "Secretary Back to 1924 Starting Point," *Watauga Democrat*, 16 May 1968.
65. "Mrs. Redman Recalls That First Cold Day," *Watauga Democrat*, 11 July 1974, 4C.

Chapter 21

1. *Public Laws of North Carolina, 1925*, 204.
2. Lanier, 97; *Dew Drop* 1925–1926.
3. Ruby Lanier Papers, draft for a chapter titled "Appalachian State Normal School," unpublished materials, unprocessed as of 2022, Ruby Lanier Papers, W.L. Eury Appalachian Collection, Special Collections Research Center, Appalachian State University, Boone, NC.
4. Corbitt, 31.
5. Lanier, 101–102.
6. Lanier, 97–98.
7. Bird, 130.
8. "Dr. Dougherty to Faculty: Head of Appalachian State Normal Addresses Summer School Teachers" (Boone, NC), 11 June 1927. Special to the *Sentinel*.
9. Lanier, 96–97, citing *Private Laws of North Carolina, 1925*, c. 204.
10. Brown, *B.B. Dougherty*, 208–09. The vast majority of his assets were given to the college at his death, according to the family.
11. Wade Edward Brown, *Wade Edward Brown: Recollections and Reflections* (Boone, NC: Parkway, 1997), 117.
12. Anna Boyce [Winkler] Phillips, "Gordon Henry Winkler," Gaffney, ed., 389.
13. Anna Boyce [Winkler] Phillips, interviewed by Doris Perry Stam, 16 Oct. 2021.
14. Mark Trivette, interview 15 Oct. 2021. Also, interviews with Ned Trivette, 2012–2013, and communications that followed those visits.
15. Jim Thompson, "Looking Back: 1925," *Mountain Times* (Boone, NC), 15 May 1997, Stam Collection.
16. Lanier, 99; *Watauga Democrat*, 14 May 1925.
17. *Watauga Democrat*, 24 May 1917.
18. *Watauga Democrat*, 24 Sept. 1924, 7 Jan., 12 and 26 Feb., 9 April, 9 July 1925.
19. Dr. Henry Baker Perry, Jr., interviewed by Doris Perry Stam, Aug. 1999, Stam Collection.
20. Dr. Henry Baker Perry, Jr., interview with Doris Perry Stam, Aug. 1999, Stam Collection.
21. Powell, *North Carolina: A History*, 196.
22. Powell, *North Carolina: A History*, 196.
23. Ferrell, *No Time for Ivy*, 35.
24. Lanier, 99.
25. *Watauga Democrat*, 6 Jan. 1921; 30 Sept., 7 Oct. 1926.
26. Brown, *B.B. Dougherty*, 161.
27. Alfred Adams, "Some History About the Banks of Watauga County," in *Watauga County Times ... Past* (Boone, NC: Watauga County Historical Society, June 1992), 4, found in the Caldwell County Historical Society and Heritage Museum in Lenoir, NC.
28. Brown, *B.B. Dougherty*, 166. See also the Ruby Lanier book.
29. Lanier, 157–58; 163–81. Dr. Ruby Lanier devotes over half her biography, *Blanford Barnard Dougherty: Mountain Educator*, to the fight for equalizing public school funding.
30. Lanier, 149.
31. Lanier, 150–51, citing *Charlotte Observer*, 13 July 1926, and *Watauga Democrat*, 15 July 1926.
32. Ferrell, *No Time for Ivy*, 31–32.
33. "Doughton Gets Some Advice," *Watauga Democrat*, 8 Jan. 1925.
34. Mary Moretz, interview by Doris Stam, 7 June 2021, in possession of author.
35. Plaque in Alumni Hall of the Reich School of Education, Appalachian State University, Boone, NC.
36. Dr. Richard D. Howe, "Dean Maxie Greene Edmisten," *The Heritage of Watauga County, Volume II*, Curtis Smalling, ed. (Winston-Salem, NC: Southern Appalachian Historical Association, in cooperation with The History Division, Hunter Publishing Company, 1987), 64–65. After teaching in the Watauga County public schools for many years, and working on her M.A. in elementary education, Maxie did post-graduate work in counseling before becoming dean of women at Appalachian.
37. Cubbage and Moore, 17–18; LeVerne Fox, interview with Doris Perry Stam, 9 Aug. 2007, recorded, Stam Collection. LeVerne quit school in 1929 and began to work for the college.
38. Cubbage and Moore, 11.
39. Cubbage and Moore, 11.
40. Lanier, 100; "Greene Diaries," 15 and 16 Feb. 1928.
41. *Watauga Democrat*, 17 Nov. 1928.
42. Lanier, 102–103, citing B.B. Dougherty, "Report to the Joint Committee on Appropriations," 28 Jan. 1929, S.P.I. Correspondence.
43. Lanier, 99.
44. "Greene Diaries," 28 March 1928.
45. Lanier, 102.
46. Lanier, 125.
47. D.J. Whitener, *History of Watauga County*, 84–85. See also *Greensboro Daily News*, 25 Mar. 1929; Lanier, 104.

48. Wood and Blethen, 82.
49. Lanier, 127.
50. Wood and Blethen, 146.
51. Brown, *B..B. Dougherty*, 127.
52. O. Lester Brown, "Blanford Barnard Dougherty," *Dictionary of North Carolina Biography* (Chapel Hill: University of North Carolina Press, 1986). "From 1943 to 1950 B.B. Dougherty was on the Board of Trustees of the North Carolina Baptist Hospital, Winston Salem. In 1946 he was named President of the Northwestern Bank, serving eleven years. In 1950, the North Carolina Citizens Association, Inc., commended him as the number-one man in the state." https://www.ncpedia.org/printpdf/5151.
53. Lanier, 147.
54. Lanier, 147–155.
55. Lanier, 155–181, 251–253; Brown, *B.B. Dougherty, 125–141*.
56. Brown, *B.B. Dougherty*, 140; Lanier, 251–253. "Education: Hillbilly's School System," *Time Magazine*, Monday, 25 Mar. 1940, https://content.time.com/time/subscriber/printout/0,8816,763741,00.html. Wake Forest College conferred the doctor of education on B.B. Dougherty in 1936.
57. Brown, *B.B. Dougherty*, 127; "Education: Hillbilly's School System," *Time Magazine*, Monday, 25 Mar. 1940, https://content.time.com/time/subscriber/printout/0,8816,763741,00.html.
58. B.B. Dougherty to A.T. Allen, 15 Mar. 1929; Lanier, 177. On April 23, 1929, superintendents and board chairman from 98 counties descended upon Raleigh to attend the "School of Economy" meetings.
59. B.B. Dougherty to A.T. Allen, 23 Apr., 14 May 1929, S.P.I. Correspondence; Lanier, 179.
60. B.B. Dougherty to A.T. Allen, 14 May 1929, S.P.I. Correspondence.
61. *Statesville Record and Landmark* (Statesville, NC), 8 Apr. 1929, 1.
62. *Winston-Salem Journal*, 10 June 1929.
63. "Appalachian State Teachers College," Lanier Papers, preliminary work on the history of ASU.
64. *Winston-Salem Journal*, 10 June 1929.

Chapter 22

1. Ruth Barker later married, continuing as secretary at Appalachian for decades as Mrs. Ruth Redman.
2. Lanier, 105.
3. Ellen Brown Surratt Otterbourg, interviewed by Doris Perry Stam, 22 June 2019, Stam Collection.
4. Herb Wey, interview in Tom Corbitt and William Dunlap, *Remembrances: Seventy-Five Years* (Boone, NC: Appalachian State University, 1976) (no page numbers are printed in this book which was published in celebration of Appalachian's 75th Anniversary); Reba Smith Moretz, interviewed by Doris Perry Stam, 7 June 2021, Stam Collection.
5. "Secretary Back to 1924 Starting Point," *Watauga Democrat*, 16 May 1968. Comment made by Dauph's secretary, Ruth Barker Redman. See also Ferrell, *No Time for Ivy*, 29.
6. Reba Smith Moretz, interview with Doris Perry Stam, 27 July 2021, recorded, Stam Collection.
7. Lanier, 136–138.
8. Carl Day, interview with Doris Perry Stam, 7 Aug. 2001, recorded, Stam Collection.
9. Lanier, 137.
10. Dr. Henry Baker "Johnnie" Perry, Jr., interview with Doris Perry Stam, May 1998, recorded, Stam Collection.
11. Brown, *B.B. Dougherty*, 211; Lanier, 137.
12. Brown, 54–55, 120–123.
13. McLeod, 203; https://sbhla.org/wp-content/uploads/631-3.pdf.
14. Burd, 153; Wood and Blethen, 97.
15. Tucker and Carlson, 64.
16. Brown, 206; Lanier, 120–124.
17. Stam, *Mountain Educators*, 194, quoting from Karl E. Campbell, "B.B. and D.D. Dougherty," *North Carolina Century: Tar Heels Who Made a Difference, 1900–2000*, edited by Howard E. Covington and Marion A. Ellis (Charlotte, NC: Levine Museum of the New South, 2002), 221–224.
18. Lanier, 138–139.
19. Dianne Dougherty, interview by Doris Perry Stam, 19 Mar. 2021, recorded, Stam Collection
20. Lanier, 136–137.
21. Lanier, 102. The recommended amounts from the State Budget Bureau, for maintenance of the following state-supported schools in 1929, according to Blan Dougherty's calculations, was the following appropriation per capita: University of North Carolina, $338; State College, Raleigh, $330; North Carolina College for Women, Greensboro, $388; Eastern Carolina Teachers College, $225; Cullowhee, $315; Appalachian, $142.
22. Lanier, 108–109. North Carolina proposed appropriations for 1931–1933 ranged from a high distribution of $189 per capita at Chapel Hill, with Western Carolina Teachers College close to most schools at $121, and three of the ten other schools between $59 and $77 per student. The *proposed* appropriation for Appalachian was $40 per capita.
23. Lanier, 108.
24. Lanier, 103.
25. Ferrell, *No Time for Ivy*, 42–43; Lanier, 108–109; Wood and Blethen, 97–99.
26. Ferrell, *No Time for Ivy*, 48–49.
27. Ferrell, *No Time for Ivy*, 31–32, 48. In a chapel address on March 20, 1934, President Wright announced to the students: "We simply can't give you that privilege, of having off campus boyfriends come on campus for dates. I want you to thoroughly understand this morning that your college is ready and waiting to remove a lot of rules and regulations now in the handbook, if you can stand it, but you must demonstrate that you are ready for it. I heard the other day that two students were lying down on campus. You may think that

was all right, but I don't and the general public that goes by our college doesn't think so."

28. Brown, *B.B. Dougherty*, 123.
29. Brown, *B.B. Dougherty*, 119, 123.
30. Lanier, 106. (Lanier took this information from interviews with family members. I learned about Blan's eating habits from an interview with my cousin, Bartlett Dougherty, in 2018.)
31. Brown, *B.B. Dougherty*, 119.
32. Gaffney, ed., 165–167; J.P. Whitener, *History of Watauga County*, 84.
33. M.T. Neal, *Edgar Tufts*, 98–99.
34. M.T. Neal, *Edgar Tufts*, 22, 32–33, 90–91, 98–99. Edgar Tufts' death is attributed to prolonged exposure to cold while riding his horse from Banner Elk to Blowing Rock to make a pastoral call on some elderly women.
35. Bird, 32.
36. Kay Reita Dickson, *Glade Valley School: 1909–1985* (Raleigh, NC: Pentland Press, 1998), 29, 89, 141, 158–159.
37. McCleod, 169–170.
38. I am indebted to Timothy McKeown for helping me with this concept. Prof. Lori Lake Edwards, UNC Greensboro English Department, encouraged me to think about how ladies' clubs, particularly garden clubs, were often a means of great benefit for communities.
39. Brown, *B.B. Dougherty*, 119 and 123; Gaffney, ed., 166; *Watauga Democrat*, 11 May 1922. Family photographs.
40. Jeff L. Norris and Ellis G. Boatman, *Fair Star: A Centennial History of Lenoir-Rhyne College* (Virginia Beach, VA: The Donning Co. Publishers, 1990), 36.
41. Annie Dougherty Rufty and the five Dougherty granddaughters, interviews by Doris Perry Stam, recorded, Stam Collection; "Greene Diaries," 1916–1940.
42. *Watauga Democrat*, 27 April, 11 May 1922.
43. Lillie Brown Perry and Ellen Brown Surratt Otterbourg, interviews by Doris Perry Stam, 28 Dec. 2007, 14 July, 25 and 26 Jan. 2017; 22 June 2019, recorded, Stam Collection.
44. Curtis, 5; https://en.wikipedia.org/wiki/Literary_society, accessed 31 Oct. 2021. ("There was a specialized form of the literary society which existed at American colleges and universities in the 19th century. The college literary societies were a part of virtually all academic institutions. Usually, they existed in pairs at a particular campus, and would compete for members and prestige, and supplemented the classical studies of the curriculum with modern literature and current events…. These are Latin-named and -themed organizations whose purposes vary from society to society. Activities include but are not limited to: The weekly presentation of papers written by society members, and a debate on its merits; Readings of members work and others', followed by discussion; literary Productions, which are practices in oratory skill; intramural sports teams; service events; and social gatherings. Meetings were often ended with snacks, such as peanuts or sardines.")
45. Dianne and Bartlett Dougherty, interview by Doris Perry Stam, 21 and 30 July 2021, recorded, Stam Collection; Ellen Brown Surratt Otterbourg, interview by Doris Perry Stam, Sept. 2021, phone conversation, Stam Collection. Boone Junaluska native Lynn Patterson did not know where John Adams was from or why he came to Boone.
46. Nadine Brozan, "Role of College Presidents' Wives: From Helpmate to Colleague," *New York Times*, 19 Dec. 1987; *Watauga Democrat*, 30 Mar. 1911; Dr. and Mrs. Harvey and Susan Durham, interview with Doris Perry Stam, 5 July 2023.
47. Brown, *B.B. Dougherty*, 122.
48. Brown, *B.B. Dougherty*, 122.
49. Rev. J.C. Canipe, Pastor of First Baptist Church of Boone, NC, message given at the funeral service of Lillie Shull Dougherty, 22 Jan. 1945, in Boone, NC, Stam Collection.
50. Annie Dougherty Rufty, Virginia Brown Brown and Lib Brown Scoggins. Interview by Dr. Ruth Currie, Boone, NC, 21 and 31 Oct. 1995. Videotape recorded. Scoggins Collection.
51. Brown, *B.B. Dougherty*, 56.
52. Lillie Shull Dougherty to Clara Dougherty Brown, 1939, Stam Collection.
53. LeVerne Fox, interview by Doris Perry Stam, 3 Aug. 2007, recorded, Stam Collection; Lillie Brown Perry, interview by Doris Perry Stam, 26 Jan. 2017, recorded, Stam Collection.
54. Elizabeth "Lib" Brown Scoggins, interview by Doris Perry Stam, Jan. 2005, recorded, Stam Collection.
55. Edwin Dougherty to Lester Brown, 27 May 1942, Stam Collection.
56. Lillie Dougherty to Mrs. Lillie Belle Hardin, May 1944, Stam Collection.
57. Rev. F.M. Huggins to Mrs. [Clara] Brown, 27 Jan. 1945, Stam Collection.
58. *Charlotte Observer* (Charlotte, NC), 22 Jan. 1945, 2.
59. Brown, *B.B. Dougherty*, 119, 181–82.
60. Brown, *B.B. Dougherty*, 119, 181–82.
61. *Watauga Democrat*, 14 July 1949.
62. Brown, *B.B. Dougherty*, 183.
63. Brown, *B.B. Dougherty*, 98
64. Brown, *B.B. Dougherty*, 122–123.

Chapter 23

1. J.F. Spainhour, "The Dougherty Brothers," *The Handbook Edition of The Rhododendron 1929*, vol. 7, 13.
2. "D.D. Dougherty, Co-Founder of Normal College, Succumbs," *Watauga Democrat*, 13 June 1929.
3. "Greene Diaries," 21 Nov.1915; 29 Jan. 1916.
4. Spainhour, "The Dougherty Brothers."
5. Brown, *B.B. Dougherty*, 176.
6. Hutchins and Howard, "Dry Humor," *Watauga Democrat*, 11 July 1974, 4C.

7. Brown, *B.B. Dougherty*, 105–106.
8. F.P. Moore to B.B. Dougherty, 19 July 1899; Hutchins and Howard, "Dry Humor," *Watauga Democrat*, 11 July 1974, 4C.
9. Lanier, 106.
10. Smith Hagaman, "A Tribute," *Watauga Democrat*, 13 June 1929. See also Brown, *B.B. Dougherty*, 104.
11. Eggers, 36; Smith Hagaman, "A Tribute," *Watauga Democrat*, 13 June 1929. See also Brown, *B.B. Dougherty*, 104.
12. Eggers 36, 48; Gaffney, ed., 163–64; Lanier, 106–07.
13. Eggers, 23, 27, 29, 32.
14. "D.D. Dougherty, Co-Founder of Normal College, Succumbs," *Watauga Democrat*, 13 June 1929. See Eggers, *The First Baptist Church at Boone, North Carolina: A History* (1969).
15. W.G. Sink, "The Story of Chemistry at Appalachian State Teachers College," Academic Affairs, Long-Range Planning, Departmental and Office Histories File, 1963, Ruby Lanier Papers, W.L. Eury Appalachian Collection, Special Collections Research Center, Appalachian State University, Boone, NC.
16. "Mathematics in the History of Appalachian State Teachers College," Academic Affairs, Long-Range Planning, Departmental and Office Histories File, 1963, Ruby Lanier Papers, W.L. Eury Appalachian Collection, Special Collections Research Center, Appalachian State University, Boone, NC. See the *Dew Drop Catalogues*.
17. "The Appalachian State Teachers College Library," Academic Affairs, Long-Range Planning, Departmental and Office Histories File, 1963, Ruby Lanier Papers, W.L. Eury Appalachian Collection, Special Collections Research Center, Appalachian State University, Boone, NC; *Dew Drop Catalogue, 1904-1905* (Sparta, NC: Star Publishing Co., for Appalachian Training School, Boone, NC, 1905), 10.
18. Annie Dougherty Rufty, "Dauphin Disco Dougherty," Gaffney, ed., 164. See also the speech notes of Annie Dougherty Rufty, and the interview by Dr. Ruth Currie.
19. Brown, *B.B. Dougherty*, 100–101; Gaffney, ed., 164, 165.
20. Brown, *B.B. Dougherty*, 99.
21. Brown, *B.B. Dougherty*, 100.
22. Brown, notes for his biography of B.B. Dougherty, Stam Collection.
23. Annie Dougherty Rufty, interview by Elizabeth "Lib" Brown Scoggins, Boone, NC, 20 Sept., 4 Oct. 1999, Scoggins Collection. Dianne Dougherty reported in 2024 that some of the species Dauph collected exist today by the Duck Pond on the Appalachian campus.
24. "Forestry Preservation," letter to the editor, *Watauga Democrat*, 1 Feb. 1923.
25. Annie Dougherty Rufty, speech given for an unknown event at Appalachian, probably during the 1970s. Notes for her speech in her longhand. UA 47, Doris Perry Stam Collection, University Archives, Special Collections Research Center, Appalachian State University, Boone, NC; Annie Dougherty Rufty, Virginia Brown Brown and Lib Brown Scoggins, interview by Dr. Ruth Currie, Boone, NC, 21 and 31 Oct. 1995. Videotape recorded. UA 45: Elizabeth Brown Scoggins Collection, Special Collections Research Center, Appalachian State University, Boone, NC.
26. Brown, *B.B. Dougherty*, 100.
27. E.H. Moore, "Tribute to D.D. Dougherty." Elijah Dougherty contributed to J.B. Killebrew's book on grasses in Tennessee. See Hyatt, 4, and https://www.biodiversitylibrary.org/bibliography/33590.
28. ASU News Bureau, "Satie Broyhill"; Jeni Gray, "Satie Hunt."
29. Cubbage and Moore, 7-9; LeVerne Fox, interview by Doris Perry Stam. Filmore Fox, father of LeVerne, was the campus plumber and handyman. "There were two different Doughertys.... One was just as smart in his way, and the other in his ... brilliant people. They were wonderful people—loved by everyone. While they were completely different in their actions, they shared a common dream of better education for everyone. He was a brilliant man and was always busy thinking. He did not think like you or I, though. He thought between other people," remarked LeVerne Fox.
30. Cubbage and Moore, 7-9; LeVerne Fox interview with Doris Perry Stam, Boone, NC, 9 Aug. 2007, Stam Collection.
31. R.C. Rivers, "D.D. Dougherty," *Watauga Democrat*, 13 June 1929, 3.
32. Brown, *B.B. Dougherty*, 101.
33. Brown, *B.B. Dougherty*, 100.
34. Rebecca Henderson, "Nobody Like Us," *Forever Alive: Mountain People, Mountain Land* (Boone, NC: Appalachian State University, 1978), 9-13.
35. Brown, *B.B. Dougherty*, 101–102.
36. Edwin Powell, "'Mr. Ed,' 99 going on 100: When Wilkesboro Was a Major Excursion," *Watauga Democrat*, 29 Aug. 1990, Stam Collection.
37. Ed Culler, interview by Wade Brown, "Ed Culler: Reminiscences," videotaped, 15 Nov. 1988, in possession of the author.
38. *History of North Carolina 4: North Carolina Biography by Special Staff of Writers* (Chicago: Lewis Publishing Co., 1919), 342–345.
39. See *Dew Drop Catalogues*, found online at https://lib.digitalnc.org/.
40. Brown, *B.B. Dougherty*, 181; *The Alleghany Times*, 23 Aug. 1934.
41. *History of North Carolina 4: North Carolina Biography by Special Staff of Writers* (Chicago: Lewis Publishing Co., 1919), 342–345.
42. Brown, *B.B. Dougherty*, 100.
43. Brown, notes for his biography of B.B. Dougherty, Box 3 Folder, Stam Collection.
44. Brown, *B.B. Dougherty*, 100.
45. Brown, *B.B. Dougherty*, 86.
46. Gaddy, "Recollections of the Man," *Watauga Democrat*, 28 June 1962, 14. Barnard Dougherty

began his career as assistant business manager to his mother in 1929 after his father's death. In 1938 Barnard became the business manager, and later vice president and comptroller of Appalachian. Edwin Dougherty became a professor of history at Appalachian after earning his master's and having taught at another school.

47. Brown, *B.B. Dougherty*, 99.
48. Carrie Smith, "North Carolina First Southern State to Help Train Teachers," *The Alleghany Times*, 23 Aug. 1934.
49. Bradshaw, "Tribute Paid Benefactor," special to *Charlotte Observer*, 26 Oct. 1929. Also see *Watauga Democrat*, 31 Oct. 1929. Rufus Bradshaw had been a college classmate to Dauph, and as a well-respected pastor and preacher, had come to Boone many times through the years for speaking engagements and as a guest in the Dougherty home.
50. Brown, *B.B. Dougherty*, 86–106.
51. Brown, *B.B. Dougherty*, 105.
52. E.H. Moore, "Tribute to D.D. Dougherty."
53. Dale Gaddy, "Died at ASTC in June 1929: A Rainy Day, and Recollections of the Man Who Brought Higher Education to This Area," *Watauga Democrat*, 28 June 1962.
54. Brown, *B.B. Dougherty*, 101.
55. Bradshaw, "Tribute Paid Benefactor," special to *Charlotte Observer*, 26 Oct. 1929.
56. J. Bahnson Greenwood, "Dauphin Disco Dougherty: Scholar, Thinker, Christian," 1937. *Appalachian Alumni*, photocopy of this page, without indication from the printed volume from which it was taken, was found in Scoggins Files, Scoggins Collection.
57. Brown, notes for his biography of B.B. Dougherty, Box 3 Folder, Stam Collection.
58. *Watauga Democrat*, taken from the *Winston-Salem Journal*, 20 June 1929.
59. Carrie S. Smith, "North Carolina First Southern State to Help Train Teachers," *The Alleghany Times*, 23 Aug. *1934*.
60. Brown, *B.B. Dougherty*, 103.
61. Spainhour, "The Dougherty Brothers," 13.
62. "Educator of Fine Record," *Watauga Democrat*, quoting the *Charlotte Observer*, 20 June 1929.
63. O. Lester Brown, "Blanford Barnard Dougherty," *Dictionary of North Carolina Biography* (Chapel Hill: University of North Carolina Press, 1986).
64. Brown, *B.B. Dougherty*, 183–199.
65. Brown, *B.B. Dougherty*, 108.
66. Lanier, 228.
67. Brown, *B.B. Dougherty*, 106–09; Lanier, 128; "Education: Hillbilly's School System," *Time Magazine*, Monday, 25 Mar. 1940, https://content.time.com/time/subscriber/printout/0,8816,763741,00.html.
68. Brown, *B.B. Dougherty*, 99, 103.
69. Elizabeth Brown Scoggins, interview by Doris Perry Stam, recorded, Boone, NC, Jan. 2005, Stam Collection.
70. Annie Dougherty Rufty, Virginia Brown Brown and Lib Brown Scoggins, interview by Dr. Ruth Currie, Boone, NC, 21 and 31 Oct. 1995. Videotape recorded. UA 45: Elizabeth Brown Scoggins Collection, Special Collections Research Center, Appalachian State University, Boone, NC.
71. Brown, *B.B. Dougherty*, 100.
72. Brown, *B.B. Dougherty*, 98–106.
73. Brown, *B.B. Dougherty*, 99.
74. "Greene Diaries," 21 Nov. 1915; 29 Jan. 1916.
75. Gaddy, "Recollections of the Man," *Watauga Democrat*, 28 June 1962, 14.
76. Gaddy, "Recollections of the Man," *Watauga Democrat*, 28 June 1962.
77. Lillie Shull Dougherty's portrait was stolen from the building named for her, probably for the value of the frame. Clara painted two replicas of her mother's professional portrait. These are the only portraits of the Doughertys. These amateur paintings are on display in the B.B. Dougherty Administration Building, and another copy, by Clara D. Brown of her father, hangs in the D.D. Dougherty Library entrance.
78. Brown, *B.B. Dougherty*, 109.
79. Spainhour, "The Dougherty Brothers," 13.
80. Brown, *B.B. Dougherty*, 98.
81. Downum, "An Appreciation for a Friend (to Prof. D.D. Dougherty)," written 25 Nov. 1934, E.H. Moore Scrapbook. In 1920 Downum had written a letter to the state superintendent which was critical of B.B. Dougherty and complementary of D.D. Dougherty's leadership.
82. Hagaman, Smith, "A Tribute," *Watauga Democrat*, 13 June 1929. See also H.C. Moore, *Patton*, 70.
83. Bradshaw, "Tribute Paid Benefactor," special to *Charlotte Observer*, 26 Oct. 1929. See also *Watauga Democrat*, 31 Oct. 1929.
84. "Greene Diaries," 10 June 1929.
85. Spainhour, "The Dougherty Brothers," 13.
86. "Educator of Fine Record," *Watauga Democrat*, quoting *Charlotte Observer*, 20 June 1929.
87. *Watauga Democrat*, 31 Oct. 1929.
88. *The Rhododendron*, 1931, dedicated to the memory of D.D. Dougherty.
89. Rufty, "Dauphin Disco Dougherty," in Gaffney, ed., 164.
90. D.D. Dougherty, written 31 Dec. 1890, saved among family documents, UA 47: Doris Stam Collection, University Archives, Special Collections Research Center, Appalachian State University, Boone, NC.

Bibliography

Primary

Abrams, Dr. Amos. "Well Do I Remember." *60th Anniversary Special Edition of the Appalachian Alumnus*. Boone, NC: Appalachian State Teachers College, 8 Nov. 1963.

Adams, Alfred T. "The T.P. Adams Family." *The Heritage of Watauga County, North Carolina, Volume 1*, edited by Sanna Ross Gaffney and others, Watauga County Historical Society, 89. Winston-Salem, NC: Heritage of Watauga County Book Committee in cooperation with the History Division of Hunter Publishing Co., 1984.

Anthony, Maud Patton. "Historical Sketch of First Baptist Church Morganton, North Carolina and Personal Reminiscences." Morganton, NC: First Baptist Church Morganton, 1956, reprint 1995.

Ashe County Court, Minute Book (MS.). 10 Aug., 9 Nov. 1807.

Ballard, Sandra L., and Leila E. Weinstein. *Neighbor to Neighbor: A Memoir of Family, Community, and Civil War in Appalachian North Carolina*. Boone, NC: Center for Appalachian Studies, Appalachian State University, 2007.

Barden, Milton B. *I Can't Call Your Name But Your Face Sure Looks Common: A Collection of Boyhood Memories of Boone and Watauga County, NC*. Asheboro, NC: M & M Communications, 1995.

Barr, Basil Duke. *Jefferson, North Carolina: My Boyhood Town at the Turn of the Century*. Jefferson, NC: privately published, 1975.

Biennial Report of the Superintendent of Public Instruction of North Carolina, for the Scholastic Years 1887 and 1888. Raleigh, NC: North Carolina Department of Public Instruction, 30 Nov. 1888. https://digital.ncdcr.gov/Documents/Detail/biennial-report-of-the-superintendent-of-public-instruction-of-north-carolina-for-the-scholastic-years-...-1887–1888/4720646?item=472 4154.

Biennial Report of the Superintendent of Public Instruction of North Carolina, for the Scholastic Years 1898–'99 and 1899–1900. Raleigh: Edwards & Broughton and E.M. Uzzell, State Printers, Presses of Edward & Broughton, 1900. https://docsouth.unc.edu/nc/ncinstruction1898/ncinstruction1898.html.

Biennial Report of the Superintendent of Public Instruction of North Carolina, for the Scholastic Years 1900–1901 and 1901–1902. Raleigh: Edwards & Broughton, State Printers, 1902. https://digital.ncdcr.gov/Documents/Detail/biennial-report-of-the-superintendent-of-public-instruction-of-north-carolina-for-the-scholastic-years-...-1900-1902/3969794.

Bradshaw, Rev. W.R. "Life and Character of D.D. Dougherty." Delivered at the memorial service for D.D. Dougherty, 26 Oct. 1929. UA 47: Doris Perry Stam Collection, University Archives, Special Collections Research Center, Appalachian State University, Boone, NC.

Brown, O. Lester. *Blanford Barnard Dougherty: A Man to Match His Mountains*. Charlotte, NC: privately published, 1963.

Brown, O. Lester. *The Browns in a Delightful Mountain County*. Greensboro, NC: Piedmont Press, O. Lester Brown, 1972. UA 47, Doris Perry Stam Collection, University Archives, Special Collections Research Center, Appalachian State University, Boone, NC.

Brown, O. Lester. Notes, sketches and drafts for various writings he did about the Dougherty family and other Watauga and Ashe County people and events. Unpublished manuscripts. UA 47: Doris Perry Stam Collection, University Archives, Special Collections Research Center, Appalachian State University, Boone, NC.

Brown, O. Lester. "Obituary at Funeral of Blanford Barnard Dougherty." Unpublished manuscript, 1957. UA 45: Elizabeth Brown Scoggins Collection, Special Collections Research Center, Appalachian State University, Boone, NC.

Brown, O. Lester. *On the Trail of the Elopers: The Brunette and the Redhead*. Charlotte, NC: O. Lester Brown, 1975. UA 45: Elizabeth Brown Scoggins Collection, Special Collections Research Center, Appalachian State University, Boone, NC.

Brown, O. Lester. *Tales from the Tall Hills*. Charlotte, NC: O. Lester Brown, 1977, 37. UA 45: Elizabeth Brown Scoggins Collection, Special Collections Research Center, Appalachian State University, Boone, NC.

Brown, Wade Edward. *Wade Edward Brown: Recollections and Reflections*. Boone, NC: Parkway, 1997.

Bibliography

Canipe, Rev. J.C., Pastor of First Baptist Church of Boone, NC. "Lillie Shull Dougherty." Message given at the funeral service of Lillie Shull Dougherty. Unpublished manuscript, 22 Jan. 1945. UA 47: Doris Perry Stam Collection, University Archives, Special Collections Research Center, Appalachian State University, Boone, NC.

Carter County, Tennessee, Board of Education Minutes. Elizabethton, TN: Board of Education, 1890s.

Cullom, W.R. "Wayside Heroism: The Dougherty Brothers." *Charity & Children* (periodical of Baptist Children's Homes of North Carolina), 1 Feb. 1945. UA 47, Doris Perry Stam Collection, University Archives, Special Collections Research Center, Appalachian State University, Boone, NC.

Curtis, Jesse W. "Memories of Watauga Academy and Appalachian." Lewiston, ID, March 1, 1938, University Archives, Special Collections Research Center, Appalachian State University, Boone, NC.

Dew Drop 1904–1905, 1906–1907. Sparta, NC: Appalachian Training School for Teachers with The Star Publishing Co., 1905 & Aug. 1907. https://lib.digitalnc.org/search?ln=en&p=dew+drop&f=&sf=&so=d&rg=10&fti=1.

Dew Drop 1909–1924. Boone, NC: Appalachian Training School for Teachers, 1909–1924. https://lib.digitalnc.org/search?ln=en&p=dew+drop&f=&sf=&so=d&rg=10&fti=1.

Dew Drop 1925–1927. Boone, NC: Appalachian State Normal School, 1925–1927. https://lib.digitalnc.org/search?ln=en&p=dew+drop&f=&sf=&so=d&rg=10&fti=1.

Dougherty, B.B. "Appalachian State Teachers College Founders' Day 1945," event program. Boone, NC: Appalachian State Teachers College, 8 May 1945. UA 47: Doris Perry Stam Collection, University Archives, Special Collections Research Center, Appalachian State University, Boone, NC.

Dougherty, D.D. "Day Ledger." Unpublished manuscript, 1899–1903. UA 47, Doris Perry Stam Collection, University Archives, Special Collections Research Center, Appalachian State University, Boone, NC.

Dougherty, D.D. "Holly Spring College." *Baptist Reflector*. Nashville, TN: Tennessee Baptist Convention, 2 Dec. 1897.

Dougherty, D.D. "Ledger Book from Newland Hall." Unpublished manuscript, 1913–1915. UA 47, Doris Perry Stam Collection, University Archives, Special Collections Research Center, Appalachian State University, Boone, NC.

Dougherty, Edwin. "Diary." Unpublished manuscript, 1929. UA 47, Doris Perry Stam Collection, University Archives, Special Collections Research Center, Appalachian State University, Boone, NC.

Dougherty Family Bible. University Archives, Special Collections Research Center, Appalachian State University, Boone, NC.

Fontaine, Harry E. *I Remember "Old" Butler*. Butler, TN: Harry E. Fontaine, 1984.

Greene, A. Jackson. "Greene Diaries." Unpublished manuscripts, 1906–1942. AC 105, Andrew Jackson Greene Collection. W.L. Eury Appalachian Collection, Special Collections Research Center, Appalachian State University, Boone, NC. https://omeka.library.appstate.edu/items/browse?collection=39.

Greene, Ivery C. *A Disastrous Flood: A True and Fascinating Story*, 4th ed. Lenoir, NC: Smith Printing Co., 1941, reprint 1976.

Greene, Nannie, and Catherine Stokes Sheppard. *Community and Change in the North Carolina Mountains: Oral Histories and Profiles of People from Western Watauga County*. Contributions to Southern Appalachian Studies 13. Jefferson, NC: McFarland, 2006.

Hamby, Zetta Barker. *Memoirs of Grassy Creek: Growing Up in the Mountains on the Virginia-North Carolina Line*. Contributions to Southern Appalachian Studies 1. Jefferson, NC: McFarland, 1998.

Hardin, Alene. "Private Papers." Unpublished manuscripts. UA 47: Doris Perry Stam Collection, University Archives, Special Collections Research Center, Appalachian State University, Boone, NC.

Holly Spring College. "Teacher's Report to Parents." For L.B. Shull, signed by J.H. Smith. Unpublished manuscript, 10 May 1893. UA 47, Doris Perry Stam Collection, University Archives, Special Collections Research Center, Appalachian State University, Boone, NC.

Horton, Ben. *Glimpses of Yesteryears in Watauga County*. Boone, NC: privately published, Dec. 1975.

Hughes, I. Harding, Jr. *My Valle Crucis: The 1930s*. Valle Crucis, NC: I. Harding Hughes, Jr., 2002.

Hutchins, Ed, and Nita Howard. "Found Dougherty's Had a Dry Humor." *Watauga Democrat* (Boone, NC), 11 July 1974.

Hyatt, Rebecca Dougherty. *The Dougherty Family in America: 1744–1965*. Ann Arbor: Edwards Brothers, 1965.

Idol, John Lane, Jr. *Blue Ridge Heritage: An Informal History of Three Generations of the Family of John Nicholson Idol*. Boone, NC: Parkway, 2005.

Keefe, Susan E., with assistance from the Junaluska Heritage Association. *Junaluska: Oral Histories of a Black Appalachian Community*. Contributions to Southern Appalachian Studies 48. Jefferson, NC: McFarland, 2020.

Lyon, Floretta, Appalachian Oral History Project, "Appalachian State University: Appalachian Training School," AC.111, Tape #318, Box 49, Folder 32, transcription, University Archives, Special Collections Research Center, Appalachian State University, Boone, NC.

Memories of Davenport. Lenoir, NC: Caldwell Historical Society and Heritage Museum, c. 1900.

Minute Book "A" of Watauga County Board of Education. UA 30.026, Ruby Lanier Papers, W.L.

Eury Appalachian Collection, Special Collections Research Center, Appalachian State University, Boone, NC.

Moore, Emma Horton. "Emma Horton Moore Scrapbook." Boone, NC: unpublished manuscript. UA 30.024, Emma Horton Moore Scrapbook, University Archives, Special Collections Research Center, Appalachian State University, Boone, NC.

Moore, Hight C. "The Editor's Tribute to a Great Teacher: Robert Logan Patton." *Biblical Recorder: Journal of the Baptist State Convention of North Carolina*. Raleigh: Biblical Recorder, Incorporated, Feb. 1942.

Moore, Hight C. "Globe Academy: Founded 1882: Flood-Destroyed 1916." *Biblical Recorder: Journal of the Baptist State Convention of North Carolina*. Raleigh, NC: Baptist State Convention of North Carolina, 11 Oct. 1952.

Moore, Hight C. "Globe Academy: Memories by Hight C. Moore." *Biblical Recorder: Journal of the Baptist State Convention of North Carolina*. Raleigh, NC: Baptist State Convention of North Carolina, 11 Oct. 1952.

Moore, Hight C. *Patton: Southern Highlander: A Biography of Rev. Robert Logan Patton*. Morganton, NC: privately published, 1964. UA 47, Doris Perry Stam Collection, University Archives, Special Collections Research Center, Appalachian State University, Boone, NC.

Moore, W.M. "Globe Academy Towers with Majestic Greatness in Garden of Fond and Inspiring Memories." *Lenoir News-Topic* (Lenoir, NC), Sept. 1941.

Neal, Margaret Tufts. *And Set Aglow a Sacred Flame: History of the Edgar Tufts Memorial Association 1895–1942*. Banner Elk, NC: Pudding Stone Press, Lees-McRae College, 1983.

Neal, Mrs. C.D. *Miss Chessie's Memories: Interesting People, Places and Stories in Ashe County History Recounted*. Ronda, NC: privately published by Elizabeth Parks Neal, 1982.

Patton, Robert L. Autobiography, "My Struggle for an Education." *Carter's Weekly* (North Wilkesboro, NC), 26 July 1919, and *North Carolina Education*, Feb 1920. In possession of the author.

Patton, Robert L. "A Ten Years' Drive Financing One College Diploma." *North Carolina Education*, Feb. 1920. https://digital.ncdcr.gov/Documents/Detail/north-carolina-education-1920-february/408378?item=416657.

Perry, Doris Taylor. "The Life of Dr. Henry Baker Perry, Sr." Boone, NC: unpublished manuscript, 1954. UA 47, Doris Perry Stam Collection, University Archives, Special Collections Research Center, Appalachian State University, Boone, NC.

"Population of North Carolina by Counties and Minor Civil Divisions." *United States Bureau of the Census, Twelfth Census of the United States: 1900. Census Bulletin* no. 39. Washington, D.C.: Government Printing Office, 22 Jan 1901, 12. https://www2.census.gov/library/publications/decennial/1900/bulletins/demographic/39-population-nc.pdf.

Program of Dedication and Naming: Lillie Shull Dougherty Hall. Boone, NC: Appalachian State Teachers College, 5 Dec. 1965. UA 47, Doris Perry Stam Collection, University Archives, Special Collections Research Center, Appalachian State University, Boone, NC.

Ragan, Rebecca Greene. "Memories of Rebecca Greene Ragan, 1902–2001." Unpublished manuscript. UA 47, Box 3, Folder 8, Doris Perry Stam Collection, University Archives, Special Collections Research Center, Appalachian State University, Boone, NC. Mrs. Ragan, interviewed by her son, Claude Ragan, during the years 1995–1997. A partial transcript was sent to Doris Perry Stam by Mrs. Ragan's nephew, Bob Greene, c. 2013.

Report to the Governor and the General Assembly of the Officers of the Appalachian Training School, January 1911–January 1913. UA 43, Box 1, Folder 18, Appalachian Training School Collection, Special Collections Research Center, Appalachian State University, Boone, NC.

The Rhododendron 1922, vol. 1. Boone, NC: Appalachian Training School for Teachers, 1922. University Archives, Special Collections Research Center, Appalachian State University, Boone, NC.

The Rhododendron, 1929, vol. 7. Boone, NC: Published by Faculty and Students of Appalachian State Teachers College, 1929. University Archives, Special Collections Research Center, Appalachian State University, Boone, NC.

Rufty, Annie Dougherty. Speech given for an unknown event at Appalachian, probably during the 1970s. Notes for her speech in her longhand. UA 47, Doris Perry Stam Collection, University Archives, Special Collections Research Center, Appalachian State University, Boone, NC.

Scoggins, Lib, with the help of Annie Dougherty Rufty and Virginia Brown. "A Brief Biography of Lillie Shull Dougherty." Boone, NC: unpublished typed manuscript, 1989. UA 47, Doris Perry Stam Collection, University Archives, Special Collections Research Center, Appalachian State University, Boone, NC.

Sherwood, A.C., and D.D. Dougherty. *The Holly Leaf 1*. Butler, TN: Holly Spring College, 19 Dec. 1896. UA 47: Doris Perry Stam Collection, University Archives, Special Collections Research Center, Appalachian State University, Boone, NC.

Sloop, Mary T., with Legette Blyth. *Miracle in the Hills: The Lively Personal Story of a Woman Doctor's Forty-Year Crusade in the Mountains of North Carolina*. New York: McGraw-Hill, 1953.

Smith, James H. "David Harrison Shull," Obituary, 1926. UA 47, Doris Perry Stam Collection, University Archives, Special Collections Research Center, Appalachian State University, Boone, NC.

Smith, James H., and D.D. Dougherty. *Annual Catalogue of Holly Spring College 1895–96, Butler,*

Tennessee. Elizabethton, TN: News Job Office, 1895. UA 47: Doris Perry Stam Collection, University Archives, Special Collections Research Center, Appalachian State University, Boone, NC.

Strother, Virginia Dare. Appalachian Oral History Project, "Appalachian State University: Appalachian Training School," AC.111, Tape #138, Box 45, Folder 18, transcription, 4, University Archives, Special Collections Research Center, Appalachian State University, Boone, NC.

Tester, Herman. *Butler: Old, New and Carderview, A Story of Butler, Johnson County, Tennessee 1768–2006*. Johnson City, TN: C.H. Tester, 2007.

Tullos, Allen. *Habits of Industry: White Culture and the Transformation of the Carolina Piedmont*. Chapel Hill: University of North Carolina Press, 1989.

UA 30.026, Ruby Lanier Papers, W.L. Eury Appalachian Collection, Special Collections Research Center, Appalachian State University, Boone, NC.

U.S. Department of Commerce Bureau of Census. *Thirteenth Census of the United States Taken in the Year 1910: Statistics for North Carolina: North Carolina Population of Minor Civil Divisions: 1910, 1900, and 1890 for Boone, NC*. Reprint of the Supplement for North Carolina Published in Connection with the Abstract of the Census. Washington, D.C.: Washington Government Printing Office, 1914, 584. http://www.townofboone.net/DocumentCenter/View/1195/13th-Census-for-United-States-NC-Population-1890-1900-1910-PDF.

Watauga County, North Carolina, Old Deed Books, Book D, 638.

Watauga County, North Carolina, Old Deed Book, Book F, 301.

Watauga County, North Carolina, Old Deed Book, Book J, 488.

Watauga County, North Carolina, Old Deed Books, Book L, 530.

Watauga County, North Carolina, Old Deed Books, Book M, 248.

Wigginton, Eliot, ed. *Foxfire 6*. Garden City, NJ: Anchor Press/Doubleday, 1980.

Williams, Cratis. *I Become a Teacher: A Memoir of One-Room School Life in Eastern Kentucky*. Ashland, KY: The Jesse Stuart Foundation, 1995.

Wilson, Walter W. *Johnson County Tennessee: 1860 Census*. Los Alamos, NM: Custom Printing, 1979.

Secondary

Abrahamson, Rudy, and Jean Haskell. *Encyclopedia of Appalachia*. Knoxville: University of Tennessee Press, 2006.

Ackers, Donna Gayle, and Brian Lambeth. *Images of America: Watauga County*. Charleston, SC: Arcadia, 2008.

Altmayer, Bud. *A Family History of Watauga County*. Boone, NC: Minor's Printing Co., 1996.

Anderson, E. Carl, Jr., ed. *The Heritage of Caldwell County: North Carolina* 1. Lenoir, NC: Caldwell County Heritage Book Community; Winston-Salem, NC: Hunter Publishing Company, 1983.

"The Appalachian Spirit." 62-page advertisement and solicitation for private funding of public education as part of "The 8 [Million] by '78 Campaign," a publication of the Office of Development, Ruby Lanier Papers, W.L. Eury Appalachian Collection, Special Collections Research Center, Appalachian State University, Boone, NC.

Arthur, John Preston. *A History of Watauga County North Carolina: With Sketches of Prominent Families*, 2nd ed. Johnson City, TN: The Overmountain Press, 1992.

Ashe County Historical Society. *Images of America: Ashe County Revisited*. Charleston, SC: Arcadia, 2002.

Barefoot, Diane Cook. *The Dougherty House: Appalachian State University Buildings Survey Project*. Boone, NC: Appalachian State University, Department of History, Jan. 1987.

Bealer, Alex W. *The Art of Blacksmithing*. New York: Castle Books, 1995.

Beaver, Patricia Duane. *Rural Community in the Appalachian South*. Lexington: University Press of Kentucky, 1986.

Bell. John L. "Broyhill Furniture." *Encyclopedia of North Carolina*, edited by William S. Powell. Chapel Hill: University of North Carolina Press, 2006.

Biennial Report of the Superintendent of Public Instruction of North Carolina, for the Scholastic Years 1896–'97 and 1897–'98. Raleigh: Guy V. Barnes, Printer to Council of State, 1898. https://archive.org/details/biennialreportofspi1896nort/mode/2up.

Bingham, Paul W. "The Growth and Development of Education in Watauga County." Master's Thesis, Appalachian State Teachers College, Aug. 1950. Appalachian State Teachers College, University Archives, Special Collections Research Center, Appalachian State University, Boone, NC.

Bird, William Ernest. *The History of Western Carolina College: The Progress of an Idea*. Chapel Hill: University of North Carolina Press, 1963.

"The Blair Education Bill: A Lost Opportunity in American Public Education." *Studies in American Political Development* 35, no. 1, Apr. 2021. https://bpb-us-e1.wpmucdn.com/sites.usc.edu/dist/2/77/files/2018/01/Blair_bill-15u43mp.pdf.

Boggess, Carol. *James Still: A Life*. Lexington: University Press of Kentucky, 2017.

Brozan, Nadine. "Role of College Presidents' Wives: From Helpmate to Colleague." *New York Times*, 19 Dec. 1987.

Burns, A.M., III. "A Pioneer in Educating Blacks." *Discovering North Carolina: A Tar Heel Reader*, edited by Jack Claiborne and William Price. Chapel Hill: University of North Carolina Press, 1991.

Buxton, Barry M. *A Village Tapestry: The History of Blowing Rock*. Boone, NC: Appalachian Consortium Press, 1989.

Campbell, E.T. *Tweetsie Tales: A Collection of Reminiscences* 1. Blowing Rock, NC: New River Publishing Co., 1989.

Campbell, Karl E. "B.B. and D.D. Dougherty." *North Carolina Century: Tar Heels Who Made a Difference, 1900–2000*, edited by Howard E. Covington and Marion A. Ellis. Charlotte, NC: Levine Museum of the New South, 2002.

Cappon, Lester J. "Iron-Making—A Forgotten Industry of North Carolina." *The North Carolina Historical Review 9, no. 4*. Raleigh, NC: North Carolina Historical Commission, Oct. 1932, 331–348. https://archive.org/details/sim_north-carolina-historical-review_1932-10_9_4_0/page/331/mode/1up.

Carrier, Ernest Edward. "Chapter 2: Let's Build a Church." *Pilgrims in Paradise: The Story of Baptist Pioneers of Upper East Tennessee*. Jefferson City, TN: Carson-Newman College, 1976. https://www.jctcuzins.org/pilgrims-in-paradise-page-2.

Carrier, Ernest Edward. *The Story of Baptist Pioneers of Upper East Tennessee*. Jefferson City, TN: Carson-Newman College, 1976. Mildred L. Iddins Special Collections, Stephens-Burnett Memorial Library, Carson-Newman University, https://www.jctcuzins.org/pilgrims-in-paradise.

Christensen, Rob. *The Paradox of Tar Heel Politics: The Personalities, Elections, and Events that Shaped Modern North Carolina*. Chapel Hill: University of North Carolina Press, 2008.

Connelly, Thomas L. *Civil War Tennessee: Battles and Leaders*, 7th ed. Knoxville: University of Tennessee Press: Nashville: The Tennessee Historical Commission, 1996.

Connelly, Thomas L., with the Tennessee Historical Commission. *Civil War Tennessee: Battles and Leaders*. Knoxville: University of Tennessee Press, 1979.

Corbitt, Tom, ed., Bicentennial committee, Reka W. Shoemake, chairman, Maxie G. Edmisten, et al. *Development of Public Education in Watauga County, North Carolina*. Boone: Appalachian State University, 1976. University Archives, Special Collections Research Center, Appalachian State University, Boone, NC.

Crouch, John. *Historical Sketches of Wilkes County*. North Wilkesboro, NC: Wilkes Genealogical Society, Inc., 1902.

Crowe, Dan. *Old Butler and Watauga Academy*. Butler, TN: privately published,1983.

Cubbage, Susan C., and Jan E. Moore. "Changes in an Era: 1924–1940: Recollections of LeVerne Smith Fox." A paper presented to Dr. Ruby Lanier, History, Section 101. Unpublished manuscript, 7 Dec. 1982. University Archives, Special Collections Research Center, Appalachian State University, Boone, NC.

Currie, Ruth Douglas. *Appalachian State University: The First One Hundred Years*. Louisville, KY: Harmony House, 1998.

Davenport Female College Catalogue, 1891–1892. Lenoir, Caldwell County, NC: Davenport College, 1891–1892.

Davenport, David. "Why So Many Presidents Burn Out." *Christian Science Monitor*, 21 July 1992. https://www.csmonitor.com/1992/0721/21182.html.

Davenport Female College Handbook. Lenoir, NC: Davenport Female College, 1859.

Depew, Michael, and Lanette Depew, with the Butler Museum. *Images of America: Old Butler*. Charleston, SC: Arcadia, 2005.

Deweese, Charles W. *Baptist Mountain Mission Schools: Featuring A.E. Brown and Mars Hill University*. Mars Hill, NC: Mars Hill University, 2016.

Dickson, Kay Reita. *Glade Valley School: 1909–1985*. Raleigh: Pentland Press, 1998.

Drummond, Henry. "I Corinthians 13." *The Greatest Thing in the World*. Grand Rapids: Fleming H. Revell Company, 2011 reprint of 1874 original.

Duffus, R.L. *The Valley and Its People: A Portrait of TVA*. New York: Alfred A. Knopf, 1946.

Dunlap, Bill, and Tom Corbitt. *Remembrances: Seventy-Five Years*. Boone, NC: Appalachian State University, 1974.

Duvall, John A. "A View of Ashe County in the Twentieth Century." Bernard Goss, chairman, Ruth Weaver Shepherd and the Ashe County Historical Society, eds., *The Heritage of Ashe County, North Carolina, Vol. 1, 1799–1984*. Winston-Salem, NC: Hunter Publishing Company and Ashe County Historical Society, 1984.

"Education: Hillbilly's School System." *Time Magazine*, Monday, March 25, 1940. https://content.time.com/time/subscriber/printout/0,8816,763741,00.html.

Eggers, Herman R. *The First Baptist Church at Boone, North Carolina: A History*. Boone, NC: privately published, Dec. 1969.

Etheridge, Bob. *The History of Education in North Carolina*. Raleigh, NC: North Carolina Department of Public Instruction, 1993.

Ferrell, Henry C., Jr. *No Time for Ivy: East Carolina University, 1907–2007*. Greenville, NC: East Carolina University, 2006.

Ferrell, Henry C., Jr. *Promises Kept: East Carolina University, 1980–2007*. Durham, NC: BW&A Books, 2007.

Fletcher, Arthur Lloyd. *Ashe County: A History; A New Edition*. Contributions to Southern Appalachian Studies 14. Jefferson, NC: McFarland, 2006.

Gaffney, Sanna Ross, ed., and the Heritage of Watauga County Book Committee. *The Heritage of Watauga County North Carolina Volume 1*. Winston- Salem, NC: Heritage of Watauga County Book Committee in cooperation with the History Division of Hunter Publishing Co., 1984.

Gatewood, Willard B., Jr. "North Carolina and Federal Aid to Education: Public Reaction to the Blair Bill 1881–1890." *North Carolina Historical Review* 40, no. 4. Raleigh, NC: North Carolina Historical Commission, Oct. 1963, 465–488. https://archive.org/details/northcarolinahis1963nort/page/464/mode/2up?q=gatewood.

Glenn, Alfonso. "A Survey of Public Education in Watauga County, North Carolina." Master's Thesis, U.N.C. Chapel Hill, NC, 1932. University Archives, Special Collections Research Center, Appalachian State University, Boone, NC.

Goss, Bernard, chairman, Ruth Weaver Shepherd, and the Ashe County Historical Society, eds. *The Heritage of Ashe County North Carolina Vol. 1, 1799-1984*. Winston-Salem, NC: Hunter Publishing Company and Ashe County Historical Society,1984.

Graybeal, Johnny. *Along the ET & WNC: Volume III: The Depots*. Hickory, NC: Tarheel Press, LLC, 2002.

Hamby, Robert P. *Brief Baptist Biographies 1707–1982* 2: Selected Baptist Historians and Associations in North Carolina, Georgia, South Carolina, Pennsylvania, Tennessee, and Virginia. Hendersonville, NC: Robert P. Hamby, 24 June 1982.

Hardy, Michael C. *Images of America: Avery County*. Charleston, SC: Arcadia, 2005.

Hardy, Michael C. *Images of America: Caldwell County*. Charleston, SC: Arcadia, 2006.

Hardy, Michael C. *A Short History of Watauga County*. Boone, NC: Parkway, 2005.

Harmon, Terry. *Images of America: Watauga County Revisited*. Charleston, SC: Arcadia, 2016.

Hawkins, John O. *The Most American Thing: A History of Education in Caldwell County, North Carolina*. Lenoir, NC: John O. Hawkins, privately published, 2001.

Hillman, James. E. "The History of Teacher Training." *North Carolina Education* 2, Feb. 1936. Ruby Lanier Papers, W.L. Eury Appalachian Collection, Special Collections Research Center, Appalachian State University, Boone, North Carolina.

History of North Carolina 4: North Carolina Biography by Special Staff of Writers. Chicago: Lewis Publishing Co., 1919. Located in Ruby Lanier Papers, Box 2, Dougherty folder, Appalachian Collection, Special Collections Research Center, Appalachian State University, Boone, North Carolina.

Horton, James H., Theda Perdue, and James Gifford. *Our Mountain Heritage: Essays on the Natural and Cultural History of Western North Carolina*. Franklin, NC: The North Carolina Humanities Committee and Mountain Heritage Center, Western Carolina University, 1979.

Houck, John, Clarice Weaver, and Carol Williams. *Ashe County Historical Society, Images of America: Ashe County*. Charleston, SC: Arcadia, 2000.

Hughes, I. Harding, Jr. *Valle Crucis: A History of an Uncommon Place*. Valle Crucis, NC: I. Harding Hughes, Jr., 1995.

Hyle, Edward A. *Appalachian State University Maps*. "Edward Hyle Map Collection." 7 Dec. 2020.

Jenkins, George. "The History of Watauga Academy of Butler, Tennessee." Master's Thesis, Appalachian State Teachers College. Boone, NC: unpublished manuscript, presented to the Faculty of the Department of Education 23 Aug. 1950. UA 30.026, Ruby Lanier Papers, W.L. Eury Appalachian Collection, Special Collections Research Center, Appalachian State University, Boone, NC.

The Johnson City Staff. "L.L. Maples Preacher of 60 Years in the Baptist Church." *The Journal and Tribune*, 14 Jan. 1917.

King, Arnold K. *The Multicampus University of North Carolina Comes of Age, 1956-1986*. Chapel Hill: University of North Carolina, 1987.

Lanier, Ruby. *Blanford Barnard Dougherty, Mountain Educator*. Durham: Duke University Press, 1974.

Lefler, Hugh Talmadge. *History of North Carolina 2*. New York: Lewis Publishing Company, Inc, 1956.

Lefler, Hugh Talmadge, and Albert Ray Newsome. *The History of a Southern State: North Carolina*. Chapel Hill: University of North Carolina Press, 1954.

LeLoudis, James L. *Schooling in the New South: Pedagogy, Self, and Society in North Carolina 1880-1920*. Chapel Hill: University of North Carolina Press, 1996.

Link, William A. *William Friday: Power, Purpose, and American Higher Education*. Chapel Hill: University of North Carolina Press, 1995.

Maiewskij-Hay, Val. "Boone Ablaze with Beautiful Lights." *Carolina Mountain Life*, Summer 2009.

Maiewskij-Hay, Val. "Mountain Made Kraut: The Rise and Fall of Cabbage in the High Country." *High Country Magazine*, Oct. 2009.

Mast, Clyde A. *History of Watauga County, North Carolina*. Boone, NC: self-published, c. 1976. In possession of the author.

McFarland, Julia. "The Critcher Hotel: A Glimpse of Boone's Beginnings." *Watauga County Times ... Past*, no. 16, Mar. 1985, 2–9. University Archives, Special Collections Research Center, Appalachian State University, Boone, NC.

McKinney, Gordon B. "Southern Mountain Republicans and the Negro, 1865-1900." *Journal of Southern History* 41, no. 4, Nov. 1975.

McLeod, John Angus. *From These Stones: Mars Hill College, the First Hundred Years*. Mars Hill, NC: Mars Hill College, 1955.

Mitchem, Pamela Price. *Appalachian State University: The Campus History Series*. Charleston, SC: Arcadia, 2014.

Morley, Freddie C., staff coordinator. *The History*

of Johnson County 1986: Sesquicentennial Edition. Waynesville, NC: County Heritage, Inc., sixth printing, 2008.

Morris, Margaret W. "The Completion of the Western North Carolina Railroad: Politics of Concealment." *North Carolina Historical Review* 52, no. 3. Raleigh, NC: North Carolina Division of Archives and History, July 1975.

Nathans, Sydney. *The Quest for Progress: The Way We Lived in North Carolina, 1870-1920*. Chapel Hill: University of North Carolina Press, 1983.

Noble, Marcus C.S. *The History of Public Schools of North Carolina*. Chapel Hill: University of North Carolina Press, 1930, reprint 2013.

Norris, Jeff L., and Ellis G. Boatman. *Fair Star: A Centennial History of Lenoir-Rhyne College*. Virginia Beach: The Donning Co. Publishers, 1990.

North Carolina Retired School Personnel. *So Proudly We Taught: Retired Tar Heel Teachers*. Charlotte: Heritage Printers, 1976.

North Carolina Troops: 1861-1865 Vol II. Raleigh NC: NC Department of Archives and History, 1968 & 1989, various pages.

Painter, Jacqueline B., and Appalachian Consortium Press. *The Seasons of Dorland-Bell: History of an Appalachian Mission School*. Asheville, NC: Biltmore Press, 1996.

Paschal, George W. *History of Wake Forest College*, Vol II. Raleigh: Edwards & Broughton Company, 1943.

Paschal, George Washington. "Baptist Academies in North Carolina." *North Carolina Historical Review* 28, no. 1. Raleigh, NC: North Carolina Historical Commission, Jan. 1951, 47-62. https://archive.org/details/northcarolinahis1951nort/page/46/mode/2up?q=Paschal.

Pezzoni, J. Daniel, ed.; based on the work of Tony N. VanWinkle, Elizabeth C. Stevens, and Deborah J. Thompson. *The Architectural History of Watauga: County North Carolina*. Boone, NC: Watauga County Historical Society, 2009.

Plaag, Eric. W. *Images of America: Remembering Boone*. Charleston, SC: Arcadia, 2021.

Powell, William S. *North Carolina: A History*, 2nd ed. Chapel Hill: University of North Carolina Press, 1977, paperback edition 1988. https://tnsla.ent.sirsi.net/client/en_US/search/asset/127565/0.

Powell, William S. *North Carolina Through Four Centuries*. Chapel Hill: University of North Carolina Press, 1989.

Ready, Milton. *Tar Heel State: A History of North Carolina*. Columbia: University of South Carolina Press, 2005.

Ruby Lanier Papers. Draft for a chapter titled "Appalachian State Normal School," unpublished materials, unprocessed as of 2022, Ruby Lanier Papers, W.L. Eury Appalachian Collection, Special Collections Research Center, Appalachian State University, Boone, North Carolina.

Ruscin, Terry. *A History of Transportation in Western North Carolina: Trails, Roads, Rails, & Air*. Charleston, SC: The History Press, 2016.

Saunders, Donald B. *For His Cause a Little House: A Hundred Year History of Rumple Memorial Presbyterian Church*. Boone, NC: Appalachian Consortium Press, 1988.

Sheffield, Betty Jane. *Barbering Under King Street: 67 Years, Jerry Wilson's World, Friends*. Boone, NC: privately published, Creative Printing, Inc., 2006.

Shepherd, Ruth Weaver, Project Director, and the Ashe County Historical Society, eds. *The Heritage of Ashe County North Carolina, Vol. 2, 1799-1984*. West Jefferson, NC: Hunter Publishing Company and Ashe County Historical Society, 1994.

Smalling, Curtis, ed. *The Heritage of Watauga County North Carolina*, Vol. II, 1987. Winston-Salem, NC: Southern Appalachian Historical Society, Hunter Publishing Co., 1987.

Sorrell, Robert. *Historic Homes of Northeast Tennessee*. Charleston, SC: Arcadia, 2016.

Stam, Doris Perry. *Mountain Educators: The Dougherty Family and the First Fifty Years of Appalachian*. Boone, NC: Watauga Press, 2010.

Stanbury, Dosi Elaine Cook. *Mountain Echoes: Beech Mountain, North Carolina*. Boone, NC: Parkway, 2005.

Stevens, William. *Anvil of Adversity: Biography of a Furniture Pioneer*. Kingsport, TN: Kingsport Press, 1968.

Sudderth, Steve. *Trails Through Time: A History of the Blowing Rock Area 1400-1900*, ed. Jessica Cook. Sparta, NC: Imaging Specialists, Inc./Steve Sudderth, 2020.

Toomey, Glenn A. *Watauga Baptist Association Tennessee, 1868-1978*. From Carson-Newman College, sent to Doris Perry Stam, Nov. 2021.

Tucker, John Allen, and Arthur Carlson. *Images of America: East Carolina University*. Charleston, SC: Arcadia, 2013.

Van Noppen, Ina W., and John J. Van Noppen. *Western North Carolina Since the Civil War*. Boone, NC: Appalachian Consortium Press, 1976.

Warmuth, Donna Ackers. *Images of America: Blowing Rock*. Charleston, SC: Arcadia, 2004.

Warmuth, Donna Ackers. *Images of America: Boone*. Charleston, SC: Arcadia, 2003.

Warren, Jule B. "New Economic Empire Blossoms from Educational Vision of Doughertys." *We The People 3*, Aug.–Sept. 1949, Appalachian State Teachers College, 1903-1954. Boone, NC: Appalachian State Teachers College News Bureau, 1949. UA 02.01. Office of the President. Blanford Barnard Dougherty Records, University Archives, Special Collections Research Center, Appalachian State University, Boone, North Carolina.

Whisnant, David E. *All That Is Native and Fine: The Politics of Culture in an American Region*. Chapel Hill: University of North Carolina Press, 1983.

Whitener, Daniel J. "Education for the People." *North Carolina Historical Review* 36, no. 2.

Raleigh, NC: North Carolina Historical Commission, Apr. 1959, 188. https://archive.org/details/northcarolinahis1959nort/page/186/mode/2up?q=WHITENER.

Whitener, Daniel J. *History of Watauga County: A Souvenir of Watauga Centennial, Boone, NC.* Boone, NC: privately published, 1949. UA 47, Doris Perry Stam Collection, University Archives, Special Collections Research Center, Appalachian State University, Boone, NC.

Whitener, Daniel J. "The Republican Party and Public Education in North Carolina, 1867–1900." *North Carolina Historical Review* 37, no. 3. Raleigh, NC: North Carolina Historical Commission, July 1960, 382–396. https://archive.org/details/northcarolinahis1960nort/page/n429/mode/2up?q=whitener.

Wikipedia, The Free Encyclopedia, s.v. "Henry W. Blair." Last modified 15 July 2023. https://en.wikipedia.org/wiki/Henry_W._Blair.

Williams, Cratis. "The Appalachian Experience: Historical Sketches of Southwest Virginia," 1977. Ruby Lanier Papers, University Archives, Special Collections Research Center, Appalachian State University, Boone, NC.

Wilson, Dell B. *The Grandfather and the Globe.* Banner Elk, NC: Pudding Stone Press, 1969.

Wood, Curtis W., and H. Tyler Blethen. *A Mountain Heritage: The Illustrated History of Western Carolina University.* Charlotte, NC: The Delmar Company, 1989.

Interviews

Adams, Alfred, and Daisy Adams. Interview by Doris Perry Stam. Recorded. Boone, NC, 8 Aug. 2001. UA 47, Doris Perry Stam Collection, University Archives, Special Collections Research Center, Appalachian State University, Boone, NC.

Brown, Wade. Interview by Doris Perry Stam. Recorded. Boone, NC, Aug. 2000, 8–9 Aug. 2001. UA 47, Doris Perry Stam Collection, University Archives, Special Collections Research Center, Appalachian State University, Boone, NC.

Cook, Howell. Interview by Doris Perry Stam. Recorded. Valle Crucis, NC, 9 and 10 June, 26 July, 14 Aug., 8 and 18 Oct. 2022. In possession of the author.

Councill, Johnny. Interview by Doris Perry Stam. Recorded. Boone, NC, 8 Nov. 2018; 22 July 2020. In possession of the author.

Culler, Ed. Interview by Edwin Dougherty. Recorded, 1960s; re-recorded, 11 Nov. 2021. UA 47, Doris Perry Stam Collection, University Archives, Special Collections Research Center, Appalachian State University, Boone, NC.

Culler, Ed. Interview by Wade Brown. "Ed Culler: Reminiscences." Recorded, 15 Nov. 1988; re-recorded by Doris Perry Stam, Aug. 2000. UA 47, Doris Perry Stam Collection, University Archives, Special Collections Research Center, Appalachian State University, Boone, NC.

Daughtry, Ralph. Interview by Doris Perry Stam. Unrecorded. Valle Crucis, NC, 9 June 2022. In possession of the author.

Day, Carl. Interview by Doris Perry Stam, 7 Aug. 2001. Recorded. Stam Collection.

Day, Carl, and Iva Day. Interview by Doris Perry Stam. Recorded. Boone, NC, Aug. 2002. UA 47, Doris Perry Stam Collection, University Archives, Special Collections Research Center, Appalachian State University, Boone, NC.

Durham, Dr. Harvey. Interview by Doris Perry Stam. Recorded. Boone, NC. 23 and 26 June, 10 July 2021; unrecorded 22 July 2022. In possession of the author.

Durham, Harvey, and Bobby Snead. Interview by Doris Perry Stam. Recorded. Boone, NC, 10 July 2021. In possession of the author.

Farthing, Glen. Interview by Doris Perry Stam. Unrecorded. Greensboro, NC, 1996.

Fox, LeVerne. Interview by Doris Perry Stam. Recorded. Boone, NC, 9 Aug 2007. UA 47, Doris Perry Stam Collection, University Archives, Special Collections Research Center, Appalachian State University, Boone, NC.

Greene, Perry, and Theresa. Interview by Doris Perry Stam. Unrecorded. Boone, NC, 1996.

Hardy, Michael C. Interview by Doris Perry Stam. Recorded. Boone, NC, 28 July 2021. In possession of the author.

Horton, David "Strawberry." Interview by Doris Perry Stam. Recorded. Blowing Rock, NC, 31 July 2009; 4 Aug. 2019. UA 47, Doris Perry Stam Collection, University Archives, Special Collections Research Center, Appalachian State University, Boone, NC.

Horton, Irene. Interviewed by Doris Perry Stam. Phone call. Philadelphia, 7 Aug. 2009.

Larrimore, Mr. A.C. Interview by Doris Perry Stam. Recorded. Boone, NC, 10 June 2022; Winston-Salem, NC, 21 July 2022. In possession of author.

Mast, "H" and Mary Hazel. Interview by Doris Perry Stam. Recorded. Valle Crucis, NC, 8–9 Aug. 2001. UA 47, Doris Perry Stam Collection, University Archives, Special Collections Research Center, Appalachian State University, Boone, NC.

Mast, Mary Hazel. Interview by Doris Perry Stam. Recorded. Valle Crucis, NC, 2018, 2021. In possession of author.

Moretz, Mary. Interview by Doris Perry Stam. Recorded. Boone, NC, 7 June 2021. In possession of author.

Moretz, Reba Smith. Interview by Doris Perry Stam. Recorded. Boone, NC, 27 July 2021. In possession of author.

Patterson, Lynn (worked multiple years in the Belk Library, ASU). Interview by Doris Perry Stam. Unrecorded. Boone, NC.

Patton, Robert L., IV. Interview by Doris Perry

Stam. Unrecorded phone interview and email correspondence. 3 Oct. 2021; 24 Jan. 2022; 28 June and 1 July 2023. Notes in possession of author.

Presnell, Perry. Interview by Doris Perry Stam. Recorded. Bethel, NC, 8 June 2019. In possession of author.

Shipley, Agnus. Interview by Doris Perry Stam. Vilas, NC, 6 Sept. 2018. In possession of author.

Shipley, Robert. Interview by Doris Perry Stam. Recorded. Boone, NC, Jan. 2005, Oct. 2010. UA 47, Doris Perry Stam Collection, University Archives, Special Collections Research Center, Appalachian State University, Boone, NC.

Shook, Mrs. Zeb "Nurse." Interview by Doris Perry Stam. Recorded. Boone, NC, Aug. 2002. UA 47, Doris Perry Stam Collection, University Archives, Special Collections Research Center, Appalachian State University, Boone, NC.

Shores, Katy Bentley. Interview by Doris Perry Stam. Recorded. Valle Crucis, NC, 30 June 2017. In possession of author.

Spencer, Sarah Blair. Interview by Doris Perry Stam. Unrecorded. Boone, NC, 1996 and 2010. In possession of author.

Taylor, Gail. Interview by Doris Perry Stam. Recorded. Valle Crucis, NC, 24 July, 18 Oct., 12 Nov. 2022. In possession of author.

Taylor, Michael. Interview by Doris Perry Stam. Recorded. Valle Crucis, NC, 14 Aug. 2022. n possession of author.

Taylor, Nina Church. Interview by Doris Perry Stam. Recorded. Valle Crucis, NC, 8–9 Aug. 2001. UA 47, Doris Perry Stam Collection, University Archives, Special Collections Research Center, Appalachian State University, Boone, NC.

Tester, Herman. Interview by Doris Perry Stam. Recorded. Butler, TN, 27 July 2017. UA 47, Doris Perry Stam Collection, University Archives, Special Collections Research Center, Appalachian State University, Boone, NC.

Trivette, Ned. Interview by Doris Perry Stam. Recorded. Bethel, NC, 2014. UA 47, Doris Perry Stam Collection, University Archives, Special Collections Research Center, Appalachian State University, Boone, NC.

Underwood, Wayne (owner of Mystery Hill). Interview by Doris Perry Stam. Phone interview. Blowing Rock, NC, 2009. Notes from interview in possession of author.

Ward, Ray, and Virginia Ward. Interview by Doris Perry Stam. Recorded. Cove Creek, NC, 20 Oct. 2018. UA 47, Doris Perry Stam Collection, University Archives, Special Collections Research Center, Appalachian State University, Boone, NC. In possession of author.

Watson, Jan. Interview by Doris Perry Stam. Recorded. Boone, NC, 6 Sept. 2022. In possession of author.

Whitener, Janice. Interview by Doris Perry Stam. Recorded. Boone, NC, 31 July 2009. UA 47, Doris Perry Stam Collection, University Archives, Special Collections Research Center, Appalachian State University, Boone, NC.

Whittington, Buster, Lenny Whittington, and Marcella Whittington. Recorded. Interview by Doris Perry Stam. Junaluska, Boone, NC, July 2009. UA 47, Doris Perry Stam Collection, University Archives, Special Collections Research Center, Appalachian State University, Boone, NC.

Wilcox, Glenn. Interview by Doris Perry Stam. Recorded. Boone, NC, 5 Sept. 2018. In possession of author.

Wilson, Jerry, and Marie Wilson. Interview by Doris Perry Stam. Recorded. Boone, NC, 9 Aug. 2007. UA 47, Doris Perry Stam Collection, University Archives, Special Collections Research Center, Appalachian State University, Boone, NC.

Winkler, Anna Boyce (Phillips). Interview by Doris Perry Stam. Recorded. Boone, NC, 16 Oct. 2021. In possession of author.

Winkler, Bea Culler. Interview by Doris Perry Stam. Recorded. Boone, NC, Aug. 2002. UA 47, Doris Perry Stam Collection, University Archives, Special Collections Research Center, Appalachian State University, Boone, NC.

Winkler, Iva Dean (Appalachian Brian Estates). Interview by Doris Perry Stam. Recorded. Boone, NC, Jan. 2005. UA 47, Doris Perry Stam Collection, University Archives, Special Collections Research Center, Appalachian State University, Boone, NC.

Yates, Herbert Hoover. Interview by Doris Perry Stam. Recorded. Summer 2001. UA 47, Doris Perry Stam Collection, University Archives, Special Collections Research Center, Appalachian State University, Boone, NC.

Clara Dougherty Brown Children

Brown, Thomas, and Susanne Brown Talbott. Interview by Doris Perry Stam. Recorded. Boone, NC, 6 Sept. 2022. In possession of the author.

Otterbourg, Ellen Brown Surrratt. Interview by Doris Perry Stam. Recorded. Charlotte. NC, 22 June 2019; Boone, NC, 23 Feb. 2022. In possession of the author.

Otterbourg, Ellen Brown Surrratt. Interview by Doris Perry Stam. Unrecorded phone interview. Charlotte, NC, Sept. 2021, 6 Oct. 2021, Jan. 2023. UA 47, Doris Perry Stam Collection, University Archives, Special Collections Research Center, Appalachian State University, Boone, NC.

Perry, Lillie Brown. Interview by Doris Perry Stam. Recorded. Greensboro, NC, 1994; 28 Dec. 2007; 30 Dec. 2014; 25 and 26 Jan. 2017; 14 and 15 July 2017; 30 Dec 2017. UA 47, Doris Perry Stam Collection, University Archives, Special Collections Research Center, Appalachian State University, Boone, NC.

Perry, Lillie Brown, Ellen Brown Surratt Otterbourg, and Becky Brown Fanelty. Interview by

Doris Perry Stam. Recorded. Greensboro, NC, 26 Nov. 2017. UA 47, Doris Perry Stam Collection, University Archives, Special Collections Research Center, Appalachian State University, Boone, NC.

Perry, Lillie Brown, Lib Brown Scoggins, Ellen Brown Surratt Otterbourg and Becky Brown Fanelty. Interview by Doris Perry Stam. Recorded. Greensboro, NC, 2005; Archdale, NC, 15 July 2017. UA 47, Doris Perry Stam Collection, University Archives, Special Collections Research Center, Appalachian State University, Boone, NC.

Scoggins, Elizabeth "Lib" Brown. Interview by Doris Perry Stam. Recorded. Boone, NC, Jan 2005. UA 47, Doris Perry Stam Collection, University Archives, Special Collections Research Center, Appalachian State University, Boone, NC.

Dougherty Family

Dougherty, Bartlett. Interview by Doris Perry Stam. Recorded. Boone, NC, 22 July 2020. In possession of the author.

Dougherty, Bartlett. Interview by Doris Perry Stam. Recorded. Durham, NC, 27 Nov. 2018. UA 47, Doris Perry Stam Collection, University Archives, Special Collections Research Center, Appalachian State University, Boone, NC.

Dougherty, Bartlett, and Diane Dougherty. Interview by Doris Perry Stam. Recorded. Vilas, NC, 23 July, 29 and 30 Aug. 2021. In possession of the author.

Dougherty, B.B. Interview by Wade Brown. Boone, NC, 29 Nov. 1956. UA 33 University Archives Oral History Collection, Special Collections Research Center, Appalachian State University, Boone, NC.

Dougherty, David. Interview by Doris Perry Stam. Recorded. Greensboro, NC, 2007. UA. 47, Doris Perry Stam Collection, University Archives, Special Collections Research Center, Appalachian State University, Boone, NC.

Dougherty, Dianne. Interview by Doris Perry Stam. Recorded. Durham, NC, 19 Mar. 2022. In possession of the author.

Dougherty, Eddie. Interview by Doris Perry Stam. Recorded. Boone, NC, 8 June, 10 July, 16 Sept., 31 Oct., 9 and 10 Nov. 2021; 23 Feb. 2022. In possession of the author.

Dougherty, Eddie, and Kathleen Dougherty. Recorded. Interview by Doris Perry Stam. Boone, NC, 17 July 2009; 9 Mar. 2017; 23 May 2017. In possession of the author.

Rufty, Annie Dougherty. Interview by Doris Perry Stam. Recorded. Boone, NC, Aug. 1995; 9 Aug. 1999; 13 Aug. 2000. UA 47, Doris Perry Stam Collection, University Archives, Special Collections Research Center, Appalachian State University, Boone, NC.

Rufty, Annie Dougherty. Interview by Lib Brown Scoggins. Boone, NC, 20 Sept., 4 Oct. 1999. Scoggins Collection. UA 45: Elizabeth Brown Scoggins Collection, Special Collections Research Center, Appalachian State University, Boone, NC.

Rufty, Annie Dougherty, Virginia Brown Brown, and Lib Brown Scoggins. Interview by Dr. Ruth Currie. Boone, NC, 21 and 31 Oct 1995. Videotape recorded. UA 45: Elizabeth Brown Scoggins Collection, Special Collections Research Center, Appalachian State University, Boone, NC.

Wilson, Jane Dougherty. Interview by Doris Perry Stam. Unrecorded. Rock Hill, SC, 2005; 23 Feb 2022. In possession of the author.

Perry Family

Bradford, Madeline Edmisten. Interview by Doris Perry Stam. Recorded. Boone, NC, 2001. UA 47, Doris Perry Stam Collection, University Archives, Special Collections Research Center, Appalachian State University, Boone, NC.

Edmisten, Leta Mae. Interview by Doris Perry Stam. Recorded. Bethel, NC, 8 Mar. 2017; 6 Sept. 2018. In possession of author.

Lineberry, Susan Perry, and Donna Perry Vandiver. Interview by Doris Perry Stam. Recorded. Morehead City, NC, 30 Sept. 2022. In possession of author.

Love, Addie Mae Edmisten. Interview by Doris Perry Stam. Recorded. Bethel, NC, 2001. UA 47, Doris Perry Stam Collection, University Archives, Special Collections Research Center, Appalachian State University, Boone, NC.

Perry, Baker. Interview by Doris Perry Stam. Recorded. Lake Junaluska, NC, 4 Sept. 2022. In possession of author.

Perry, Dr. Henry Baker, Jr. Interview by Doris Perry Stam. Recorded. Boone, NC, 31 Aug. 1995. UA 47, Doris Perry Stam Collection, University Archives, Special Collections Research Center, Appalachian State University, Boone, NC.

Perry, Dr. Henry Baker, Jr. Interview by Doris Perry Stam. Recorded. Greensboro, NC, Aug. 1999; Dec. 1999. UA 47, Doris Perry Stam Collection, University Archives, Special Collections Research Center, Appalachian State University, Boone, NC.

Perry, Dr. Henry Baker, III. Recorded. Interview by Doris Perry Stam. Lake Junaluska, NC, 4 Sept. 2022. In possession of author.

Stanley, Marilyn Edmisten, cousin Eileen, and Marilyn Edmisten. Interview by Doris Perry Stam. Recorded. Bethel, NC, 27 July 2021. In possession of author.

Vandiver, Donna Perry. Interview by Doris Perry Stam. Recorded. Anderson, SC, 17 Aug. 2020. In possession of author.

Vandiver, Donna Perry, and Dr. Henry Baker Perry III. Interview by Doris Perry Stam. Recorded. Lake Junaluska, 6 Sept. 2022. In possession of author.

Ward, Lou Iva Edmisten. Interview by Doris Perry Stam. Recorded. Bethel, NC, 2001. UA 47, Doris Perry Stam Collection, University Archives,

Letters

Dougherty, Adam
Adam Dougherty to B.B. Dougherty, 18 Sept. 1916, Stam Collection.

Dougherty, B.B.
B.B. Dougherty to D.D. Dougherty, 12 Oct. 1888, Stam Collection. B.B. Dougherty to D.D. Dougherty, 23 Nov. 1888, Stam Collection. B.B. Dougherty to D.D. Dougherty, 1 Dec. 1888, Stam Collection. B.B. Dougherty to D.D. Dougherty, 10 Dec. 1888, Stam Collection. B.B. Dougherty to D.D. Dougherty, 1891, Stam Collection. B.B. Dougherty to D.D. Dougherty, 31 Oct. 1891, Stam Collection. B.B. Dougherty to D.D. Dougherty, Dec. 1891, Stam Collection. B.B. Dougherty to D.D. Dougherty, 7 Jan. 1892, Stam Collection. B.B. Dougherty to Dr. Charles Taylor, c. 7 Jan. 1892, Stam Collection. B.B. Dougherty to D.D. Dougherty, 27 Apr. 1897, Stam Collection. B.B. Dougherty to D.D. Dougherty, 10 Feb. 1899, Stam Collection. B.B. Dougherty to D.D. Dougherty, 21 Apr. 1899.

Dougherty, Daniel Baker
Daniel Baker Dougherty to D.D. Dougherty, 21 Aug. 1888, Stam Collection. Daniel Baker Dougherty to D.D. Dougherty, 9 Sept. 1888, Stam Collection. Daniel Baker Dougherty to D.D. Dougherty, 21 Sept. 1888, Stam Collection. Daniel Baker Dougherty to D.D. Dougherty, 23 Nov. 1888, Stam Collection. Daniel Baker Dougherty to D.D. Dougherty, 10 Dec. 1888, Stam Collection. Daniel Baker Dougherty to D.D. Dougherty, 15 Dec. 1888, Stam Collection. Daniel Baker Dougherty to D.D. Dougherty, prior to Nov. 1891, Stam Collection. Daniel Baker Dougherty to D.D. Dougherty, 10 Nov. 1891, Stam Collection. Daniel Baker Dougherty to D.D. Dougherty, 22 Mar. 1897, Stam Collection. Daniel Baker Dougherty to D.D. Dougherty, 10 Apr. 1899, Stam Collection.

Dougherty, D.D.
D.D. Dougherty to B.B. Dougherty, 30 Oct. 1891, Stam Collection. D.D. Dougherty to B.B. Dougherty, 1 or 2 Jan. 1892, Stam Collection. D.D. Dougherty to Lillie Shull, 11 Oct. 1894, Stam Collection. D.D. Dougherty to Lillie Shull, 8 Dec. 1894, Stam Collection. D.D. Dougherty to Lillie Shull, 9 Dec. 1894, Stam Collection. D.D. Dougherty to Lillie Shull, after 10 Dec. 1894, Stam Collection. D.D. Dougherty to Lillie Shull, 9 Feb. 1895, Stam Collection. D.D. Dougherty to Lillie Shull, Spring 1895, Stam Collection. D.D. Dougherty to Lillie Shull, 14 June 1896, Stam Collection.

Dougherty, Lillie Shull
Lillie Shull to D.D. Dougherty, 26 Nov. 1895, Stam Collection. Lillie Dougherty to Mrs. Lillie Belle Hardin, May 1944, Stam Collection.

Family Letters
11 Oct., 8 and 9 Dec. 1894; 9 Feb., 26 Nov. 1895; 14 and 17 June, 13 Sept. 1896, Stam Collection.

Memos
D.D. Dougherty, memo from 31 Dec. 1890/1 Jan. 1891, Stam Collection. L.R. Mills, written from Wake Forest College for D.D. Dougherty, June 1891, Stam Collection.

Moore, Bob
Bob Moore to D.D. Dougherty, 31 May, 4 July 1888, Stam Collection. Bob Moore to D.D. Dougherty, 4 July 1888, Stam Collection. Bob Moore to D.D. Dougherty, 10 Aug. 1888, Stam Collection. Bob Moore to D.D. Dougherty, 17 Aug. 1888. Stam Collection.

Paschal, G.W.
G.W. Paschal to D.D. Dougherty, 19 Feb. 1906, Stam Collection.

Archives

Amherst College Archives
Appalachian State University Archives
Berea College Archives
Carson-Newman College Archives
Carson-Newman University, Stephens-Burnett Memorial Library, Mildred L. Iddins Special Collections,
Harvard University Archives
Lees-McRae College Archives
Mars Hill University Archives
Milligan University, Holloway Archives
Mount Holyoke University Archives
North Carolina Archives and History
Peabody University Archives and Special Collections
Southeastern Seminary Archives
Tennessee State Library Archives
University of North Carolina Archives; Wilson Library, North Carolina Collection U.S. Library of Congress
Vanderbilt University Archives
Wake Forest University Archives
Western Carolina University Archives
Western North Carolina Archives and History

Newspapers

Alleghany Times (Sparta, NC)
Carter's Weekly (North Wilkesboro, NC)
The Chapel Hill Weekly (Chapel Hill, NC)
Charlotte Observer (Charlotte, NC)
The Daily Free Press (Kinston, NC)
Greensboro Daily News (Greensboro, NC)
Hickory Daily Record (Hickory, NC)
Journal and Tribune (Knoxville, TN)

Special Collections Research Center, Appalachian State University, Boone, NC.

Journal Patriot (North Wilkesboro, NC)
Lenoir News-Topic (Lenoir, NC)
The Morning Post (Raleigh, NC)
News & Observer (Raleigh, NC)
Raleigh Post (Raleigh, NC)
Statesville Record and Landmark (Statesville, NC)
Winston-Salem Journal (Winston-Salem, NC)

Index

academic freedom 41, 206
Adams, John 223
Adams, Sarah 21, 55, 70
Adams, Tarlton Pulaski ("Doc Adams"; "T. P.") 55, 67, 72, 124, 136, 140
African Americans 62–64, 79, 87, 92–93, 101, 104, 106, 132, 179, 188, 262
Aenon Seminary 25–26, 48
Agricultural and Mechanical College for the Colored Race *see* North Carolina A & T University
Alderman, Edward A. 62, 101, 105
Alleghany County 105, 107–8, 113, 115, 125, 130
Allen, Arch T. 34, 212–14
American Association of Teachers Colleges and Normal Schools 211
Amherst College 32
Anglo-Saxonism 99–100
Appalachia 17, 25, 32, 100, 109
Appalachian Elementary 200
Appalachian High School 200
Appalachian Mountains 66, 139
Appalachian Normal School 1, 75
Appalachian State Normal School 201–2, 204, 210–12
Appalachian State University 1, 19, 74, 97, 114, 164, 210, 239
Appalachian State Teachers College 1, 103, 166, 189, 207, 209, 210–11, 214, 216, 229, 239–40; accredited 158, 211–12; administration building 189, 198–99, 124, 235, 237–38, 240, 241; appropriations 211–13, 219; athletics 211–12; campus 202–3; charter 214; and the Depression 177, 216–18; enrollment 210, 212, 218; president's home 119; state farm 210, 217; strict rules and regulations 210, 222; summer school 210–11, 214, 219; teacher training 219
Appalachian Training School (ATS) 94, 99–205, 233; administration building (first) 123, 125, 127, 132, 139, 142, 147; administration building (second) 189, 198–99, 124, 235, 237–38, 240, 241; appropriations for 104, 112, 114, 116, 123–26, 132–33, 138–41, 191, 199, 211–15, 219; athletics 150, 170, 179, 193, 194–96, 211–12; becomes a normal school 202–4, 210; begins 118; bill for establishing 107–114; board of trustees 114–118, 124, 126, 133–134, 136, 138, 147, 161, 170, 179, 190, 191; boarding students 120, 122, 138, 147, 164; campus 191; chapel 199–200; commencement 148–50, 154, 170, 172–73, 196, 220, 225; construction at 119, 123–25, 133, 140, 161, 179, 193, 198, 218; contributions to 115–118, 124; correspondence courses 203; dancing 177; delayed opening 117; demonstration school 200, 207; discipline problems, rowdy students 169–70; efforts to establish 109–119, 124–25, 131–33, 138–39; electricity 162, 164, 199; enrollment 121, 127, 139, 144, 150, 155, 159, 176, 184, 197; existence in jeopardy 140–41, 144, 149; faculty 131, 141, 143; farm-to-table 159–60; farms 133–34 136–37, 160, 170, 191, 240; fires at 2, 128, 155, 189, 198–99, 238; gymnasium 179, 193; high school 119–20, 122, 126, 128, 132, 138, 141, 143–45, 150, 154–55, 164, 168–169, 172, 179, 188–89, 191, 196–97, 200, 202–4, 210; in loco parentis 185–86; junior college 159, 189, 200, 202; Justice Hall 114, 179, 187, 198–200; library 134, 151, 158–59, 230–31; literary societies 195; location 114–15, 117; Lovill Home, Loville Hall 95, 125, 132, 132, 134, 139, 147, 164, 179, 205–6; music (choir) 177; Newland Hall 114, 133–34, 140, 145, 164, 169–70; normal department 193, 194, 200, 202; reorganization 188–201; required matching funds 118, 124–25; rules and regulations, strict, 134, 145, 151–52, 154, 169, 186, 196; sanitation, toilets, bathrooms 138–39, 157, 193, 198; scholarships to UNC and Trinity College (Duke) 97, 127; Science Hall 140, 198, 240; standard, substandard high school 141, 189; State Normal School 210; student protest 154; summer school, summer session, summer term 122, 124, 126, 131, 134, 143, 150, 154, 166, 171, 173, 177, 180–81, 196–97, 200, 204–5, 235; training teachers 1, 28, 130, 133, 139, 141, 144, 149, 170, 188, 192, 204; trustees 114–16; tuition 121–22; White Hall 114, 179; World War I 160, 175–87
Arthur, John Preston 19, 117, 140, 151, 171, 173
Ashe County 12, 14–16, 34, 49, 107–108, 115, 125, 130, 139, 175, 196, 223
Asheville 34, 56, 66–67, 103–4, 140–45, 147–49, 151, 155–56, 173, 218
Asheville Farm School 66
Asheville Normal College 218
Avery County 107–8, 115, 134, 183, 209

Index

Aycock, Charles Brantley 1, 92–93, 98–102, 104–5, 113
Ayers, Mrs. McKinley 79

Banner Elk 66, 122, 161, 183, 220
Baptist Conference Center, Ridge Crest 166
Baptist State Convention 224
Baptists 11, 18, 22, 25, 31, 34–35, 42, 48, 52, 55–56, 60, 65–67, 71, 74, 79, 81, 99, 109, 118, 128–29, 136, 166, 171, 177, 207, 218, 224; Home Mission Board 218; Woman's Missionary Union 224, 230; *see also* Baptist State Convention; Boone Baptist Church; Butler Baptist Church; Southern Baptist Convention; Three Forks Baptist Institute
Barker, Ruth (Mrs. Ruth B. Redmond) 201, 216, 234, 237
Barker, Zetta 196–97
bartering *see* Watauga Academy
Bartlett, Edwin Clinton 15–18, 245, 254, 260
Bartlett, Caroline *see* Dougherty, Ellen Bartlett
Beaver Dams, Watauga County 28, 39, 83; *see also* Bethel, Watauga County
Beckwith, Kate R. 136
Berea College 216
Bernhardt, John Mathias 115
Bethel, Watauga County 28, 246
Bickett, Thomas W. 188
Bingham, Robert Knox (R. K.) 205
Blackburn, Manly B. 74, 83, 88–89, 116, 194
Blacks *see* African Americans
Blair Hotel 90, 151
Blowing Rock 90–91, 110, 112, 115, 120, 126, 145, 179, 232, 238, 240
boarding 31, 35, 42, 47, 54, 200; *see also* Appalachian Training School; Watauga Academy
Bob 134–35
Boone 2–3, 10, 13–21, 25, 27–31, 24, 37–40, 42, 46, 55, 60, 66–105, 107–9, 111–29, 132–41, 143–59, 162–64, 166–73, 177, 180–93, 198, 200, 204–6, 214, 218–19, 223–25, 231, 236, 239–42
Boone Academy 39, 71, 79, 85, 255
Boone Baptist Church 71, 79, 214, 224, 230–31

Boone Cemetery 21, 79, 214, 226, 240
Boone Creek 28, 98, 151, 247, 264
Boone Episcopal Church 230
Boone Methodist Church 74, 81, 99, 204
Boone (Watauga County) Courthouse 21, 29, 79, 98–99, 130, 171, 180, 245, 255
Bostwick Loan Fund 42, 127
Bower, Absolum 12
Bower, Eve 12, 244
Bower, George 12
Bower, Sarah 12
Bower, W.H. "Hort" 129
Bowie, Thomas Contee (T.C.) 115, 256
Bradshaw, the Rev. William Rufus 5, 34, 37, 42, 96, 171, 185, 235, 238–39
Brooks, Eugene Clyde 189–91
Brown, Elizabeth ("Lib") 198, 224–25, 235, 277, 282–83
Brown, Ellen (Mrs. Ellen Surratt Otterbourg) 224
Brown, Lillie Alene (Mrs. H. B. Perry, Jr.) 187, 206
Brown, Lillie Belle 139
Brown, O. Lester 5, 42, 139, 145, 150–51, 153–55, 162–63, 166, 168, 170–71, 181, 187, 194, 198–201, 226, 232–36
Brown, Mrs. O. Lester *see* Dougherty, Clara
Brown, Pauline 178, 186–87
Brown, Virginia (Emma Virginia) 168, 178, 187, 198, 223
Brown, Wade 72, 81, 109
Broyhill, James Edgar ("Ed"), 170–71, 176, 228
Broyhill, Mrs. Satie *see* Hunt, Satie
Buncombe County 140–41, 144, 157, 189
Burke County 31–32, 125
Butler, Tennessee 22, 25–27, 46–70, 84, 96–97, 109, 120, 128, 136, 138, 154, 166, 176, 181
Butler Baptist Church 52, 56, 60

Caldwell County 74, 85, 96, 103, 108, 115, 125, 139, 142–43, 175
Campbell, Lillie Belle 145, 154, 172
Carson-Newman College, Tennessee 48, 55, 59, 93, 144, 194
Chapel Hill 36, 60–61, 67, 94, 98, 101, 104, 105–6, 127–28, 156, 188–89

Chautauqua 106
Cherokee Indian State Normal School (UNC-Pembroke) 191
Civil War 1, 10–14, 19–20, 24–26, 29, 40–41, 53, 59–63, 65–66, 72, 75, 77, 93, 100, 125, 185, 244–45
Cleveland Panic of 1893 67
coal mining 87
Coffey, E.S. ("Ed") 37, 108
Coffey, W.C. 115–16
Coffey Hotel 90, 177
colored race *see* African Americans
Common School, public 81, 84, 247
Cone, Moses H. 90–91, 115, 117, 260
Councill, Alice 20, 28, 83
Councill, Benjamin 12
Councill, Jordan, Jr. 12, 14, 19, 20
Councill, Sally 20
Councill, William Bower (W.B., Sr.) 20, 83
Councill's Store 19
court days 24, 29, 117, 129–30
Cove Creek 8, 55, 70, 84
Cove Creek Academy 84
Craig, Locke 97, 141, 144, 147, 149, 155–57, 170
Cranberry 183
Creston, Ashe County 145, 153
Critcher Hotel, 177
Crossnore School 75, 87, 186, 200
Culler, Ed 83, 151, 165–66, 186, 217, 233
Cullom, W.R., 43
Cullowhee 103–4
Cullowhee High School 102–4, 112–13, 128, 133, 135–36, 140, 149, 155–57, 188–91, 200, 203–4, 212, 220;
Currie, Ruth 164
Curtis, Jesse 89, 107, 110, 128

Daniel Boone Restaurant (Dan'l Boone Inn) 205
Daniels, Josephus 100, 113
Darby 173
Darwin, Charles 41
Davenport, June 179
Davenport Female College 66
Davidson College 97
Day, Carl 218
Democratic Party 1, 53, 56, 63, 92–93, 97, 117, 134
depression of 1880s, 1890s 62, 66, 71, 75
depression, the Great Depression (1929, 1930s) 177, 216–18

Index

The Dew Drop Catalogue 85, 90, 117, 125–27, 135, 139, 141, 150, 152, 155, 161, 166, 191, 198
Dodd, Monroe 66
Dorland-Bell School 66
Dougherty, Adam 10, 117
Dougherty, Annie Lewis (Annie Rufty, Mrs. Roy Rufty) 120–21, 136, 138–39, 140, 145, 149–50, 154, 166–67, 173, 178, 194, 196–97, 201, 214, 224–26, 231, 237
Dougherty, Barnard (David Barnard) 139, 145, 149, 150–51, 178, 214, 216, 220–221, 224–26, 234
Dougherty, Blanford Barnard (B.B., Blan): ancestry 2–21; appeals for appropriations 104, 112, 114, 116, 123–26, 132–33, 138–41, 191, 199, 211–15, 219; attends Carson-Newman College, Tennessee 55; attends Globe Academy 42–43; attends Holly Spring College 49; attends University of North Carolina 61, 67; attends Wake Forest College 43–45; awarded honorary degrees 39, 207; bachelor 43, 56, 59, 72–73, 180, 231; Baptist 230; banks 218, 236; birth 20; businessman 236; and Caldwell County proposition 142–43; campaigns for donations to Appalachian Training School 115–18, 124; campaigns for donations to Watauga Academy 77–78, 91; caring for sick 213–14; ciphering on sole of shoe 123, 133, 165, 236; conducts teachers' institutes 93, 98, 102, 104, 106; considered a school alignment with Baptists 71–72; considered other jobs 93, 109; co-principal of Watauga Academy 97; courtship of Clara Powell 56, 59, 72–73; criticized 190; death of Lillie Shull Dougherty 226; death of mother 20–21; debater 55, 94–95; differences between brothers 107–8, 228–30, 233–35; discouraging letter from F. . Moore 74–75; donations to Watauga Academy 78; drama production about 180; driving a car 184; early education 28–34; establishes endowment fund 204; financial hardship 67–68; first teaching job 43; frugal 123, 164, 237; and the Hancock Bill 213, 230, 236; on horseback as Superintendent 72, 79, 83, 94, 101, 134–35, 161; horses and wagon teams 28, 40; in loco parentis 185–86; known state-wide 213, 234; learning about state support for teacher training in NC 102–4; manually helping construct Watauga Academy 77–78, 85; and pauper counties 146, 213; and politics 236–237; president of Appalachian State Teachers College 229; president of Appalachian Training School (ATS) 191; prohibitionist, temperance 185; proposal to relocate ATS; and railroads, trains 43, 107, 110, 112, 143, 146–47, 149, 173; recruiting adult students 77, 94; salary 72, 85, 157; speech giver 95, 111–12, 145; State Board of Education 233, 236; State Committee on Teacher Salaries 213; State Committee on Textbooks 231; State Equalization Board 208, 213, 211, 230, 236; and State Legislature 109–114, 124–25, 131–33, 138–39; State Textbook Committee 211, 233; superintendent of Appalachian Training School 115; superintendent of Watauga County Public School 72, 79, 83, 94, 101, 134–35, 161; teacher at ATS 55; teacher at Globe Academy 49–50, 55, 58; teacher at Holly Spring College 59–60; teacher at Hamilton Institute, Ashe County 49; teacher at Watauga Academy 81, 85, 107, 110; teacher in Watauga County Public Schools 42–43, 49; as teenager 38–39; in *Time Magazine* 213; tutored by brother D.D. 43; *see also* Allen, Arch T.; Aycock, Charles B.; Cone, Moses H.; Craig, Locke; Joyner, James Y.; McIver, Charles D.
Dougherty, Clara (Clara D. Brown, Mrs. O. L. Brown) 59–60, 73, 89, 96, 119–121, 137–38, 145, 150–55, 166–68, 186–87, 194, 198–200, 214, 224–26, 232, 238
Dougherty, Daniel Disco 127, 137, 187
Dougherty, Dauphin Disco (D.D., Dauph): ancestry 2–21; attends Globe Academy 30–34; attends New River Academy 30; attends Peabody College 194; attends Wake Forest College 35–47; baptism 41–42; birth 18, 20; building boarding houses, 75, 91, 101;business manager and treasurer 201, 191, 194, 231; considering a school alignment with Baptists 71–72, 109–110; co-principal of Watauga Academy 1, 97; courtship 22, 50–57; death and funeral 214–15, 228–29, 236, 239; death of child, grandchild 137, 145–46; death of mother 20–21; differences between brothers 107–8, 228–30, 233–35; early education 28–34; establishing departments at ATS 159, 230–31; farmer, gardener 96, 103, 121, 141; frugal 123, 164, 237; illness, heart condition 194, 200–1, 213–16; in loco parentis 185–86; leger 85, 276; and legislature 131–33; library 158–59; manually helping construct Watauga Academy 77–78, 85; name (Dauphin Disco, Dolf) 7, 18–19, 28; and pauper counties 146, 197–98; principal of Appalachian Training School 190, 198, 233; and Prof. Robert L. Patton 31–37, 40, 42, 50, 66, 88, 185; religious call to teach 66; romance with Lillie Shull, 24, 51–58; and rural schools 197; salary 72, 85, 157; scholar 39, 42, 44–45, 235–36; as a speaker 179, 231; strict 149–150, 154, 158, 170; Sunday School superintendent and teacher 228, 230; teacher, professor at ATS 115, 119–22, 126–27, 131–32, 138–39, 142, 144–45, 149–51, 166, 170–71, 176–80, 185–91, 230; teacher, professor at Holly Spring College 45–69; teacher, professor at Watauga Academy 81–92, 93–98, 104, 107, 108–9, 111, 230; tutors his brother B.B. 39, 43
Dougherty, Daniel Baker (D.B.) 7, 10, 14–21, 29–30, 38, 67, 80, 82, 85, 96, 100, 117,

123, 127, 151, 230; Baptist 18; birth 10; blacksmith 21, 38, 96; courtship and marriage 15–18; death 96–97; donating land 29, 73; farmer 28–29, 38, 69, 73, 84, 98, 103, 119; and Farmers' Alliance 62–63, 96; frugal 164, 218, 236; home on King Street 73, 84–85, 122; justice of the peace 38, 96; land surveyor 14, 20–21, 29; land transactions 14, 19; mayor 38, 96; miller 38, 73, 96; miner 38; nickname was "Boone" 18–19; postmaster in Boone 38, 96; promoting public education 29, 30; urges sons move back to Boone and start a school 67–70, 80, 96; views on soil conservation 231; and *The Watauga Democrat* 19, 38, 63, 96–97; widowed 28; wife *see* Dougherty, Ellen Bartlett
Dougherty, Edwin Shull 148–49, 166–67
Dougherty, Elijah 7–15, 29, 46, 231
Dougherty, Ellen Caroline Bartlett (Mrs. Daniel Baker Dougherty) 10, 16–29, 59, 230
Dougherty, Etta Mae (Lura Etta Mae, Mrs. Richard M. Greene) 15, 20–21, 49, 55, 70, 73, 77, 83, 85, 110, 117, 122–23, 146, 151, 154, 193
Dougherty, Eve 8–15
Dougherty, Grace Stacy Boyd 224–26
Dougherty, Lillie Shull: background 22–27; birth 22; boarding students 86, 89, 96, 98, 119–20, 151–52, 157–58; and Boone Baptist Church 129, 224; business manager and treasurer 1, 216, 220; care of her brother-in-law 219–20; children (*see also* Brown, Clara Dougherty; Dougherty, Daniel Disco; Dougherty, David Barnard; Dougherty, Edwin Shull; Rufty, Annie Dougherty); courtship and marriage 22, 50–58, 73; death and funeral of 225–226; death of child, grandchild, sisters 137, 145–46, 187; Dougherty house 119–20, 138, 157–58, 237; establishing departments at ATS 159, 230–31; extended family in the home 89, 136, 117, 155, 168, 178; faculty club 171, 220; Faculty Dames 223; Friday Afternoon Club 198, 223; gardener 225; hospitality 171, 216, 220, 223–24, 237; hostess for Appalachian 220, 224, 227; illness 224–25; Meadow View 89, 98, 119, 168; music performances 27, 91, 96, 128–29, 224; music training for 26–27; salary 85, 216; stabilizing force 227; strain upon 138; student at Holly Spring College 47–49, 50–51; teacher at Holly Spring College 54–56; teacher at Watauga Academy 81, 84–85, 89; teacher in Carter County, Tennessee 50–53; teaching music and art 91, 128–130
Dougherty, Sarah 20–21, 28, 83, 97
Doughton, Rufus Alexander (R.A.) 113–14, 117
Downum, James Monroe 131, 238–39
Duke University *see* Trinity College

East Carolina Teachers' College 200, 203, 207–8, 211
East Carolina Teachers Training School 131, 133, 189
Edmisten, Maxie Greene 210
Edmisten Farm 133–34, 136–37
education: academic freedom 41, 206–7; attendance problems 75, 77; attitude of rural Southerners 1, 11–12, 41, 53, 77; compulsory 28–29, 75; Farmers' Alliance promoting education 69; illiteracy 75, 77, 188; movement in the South 60–63, 65, 77, 93, 125; opportunity through 64, 90, 94, 204, 213; private verses public school 65–66, 71; purposes of Christian private schools 65; revival 101; Southern Board of Education (Southern Education Board) 1, 98, 101; standardized 43, 188; state supported free public education 64 (*see also* Hancock Bill); universal education 64, 105
Eggers, Graydon 236
Eggers, Stacy, Jr. 141
Elizabeth City, N.C. 107, 192
Elizabeth City State Normal School 192
Elizabethton, Tennessee 26, 226
Elon College 39
Episcopal Church 230
Exeter Academy, New Hampshire 32

Farmers' Alliance 61–64, 69, 96
Farmers' Legislature 64
Farthing, Dudley 12
Farthing, James 180
Fayetteville State Normal School 63, 191
Finger, Sidney M. 43
flood(s) 31, 59, 75, 173, 174, 183
flu 59, 176, 180–81, 186, 193–94
Ford cars 181, 184
Forsyth County 125, 208
Founders Hall 205
Fox, LeVerne 5, 210, 232
Freedmen's Bureau *see* African Americans

General Assembly (North Carolina) 108, 115–16, 124, 133, 140, 147, 156, 188, 190–91, 206, 209; House 12, 62, 111, 113, 126, 141; House Committee on Education 111–12; Joint Appropriations Committee 141; Legislature 63–64, 101, 103, 105–6, 108–13, 124–45, 130–34, 139, 148–50, 156–67, 176, 191, 199, 202, 211, 213, 215, 219, 233; Senate 62, 113–14, 126, 141
General Education Board 103, 106, 125
Glade Valley School 220
Globe 30–32, 49–50, 56, 59, 74–75, 173–174
Globe Academy 30–35, 37, 40, 42–43, 47, 49–50, 55–59, 67, 74, 88, 91, 93, 96, 173
Graham, Edward Kitter 181
Graham, William Kidder 182
Grandfather Mountain, 175
Greene, Andrew Jackson ("Jack") 155, 164, 169–71, 173, 178, 180, 186, 193–94, 210, 228, 237, 239
Greene, Etta Dougherty *see* Dougherty, Etta Mae
Greene, Mrs. Richard Greene *see* Dougherty, Etta Mae
Greene, Rebecca (Mrs. Rebecca G. Ragan) 151, 157
Greene, Richard Manly 55, 73, 122, 146
The Greene Inn 122–23, 151, 226
Greensboro 90, 101, 104–6, 111, 112, 115, 128, 132–33, 140, 146, 169, 188–89, 213, 225
Greensboro College 221
Greenway Trail 162

Index

Hagaman, Smith 230, 238
Haley's Comet 139
Hancock Education Bill (School Equalization Bill) 213, 230, 236
Hardin, Alene 16, 20
Hardin, John F. 73, 82–83, 89, 136, 142
Hardin, Mary Lillington (Mrs. Edgar Shull) 136, 139, 142
Hatton, Morris 93
Henderson, John T. 55
Hicks, P.A. 214, 230
Highland Academy 66; *see also* Lenoir-Rhyne College
highways *see* roads
Hillman, James E. 193, 200, 203
Hillsborough Academy, Hillsborough, Illinois 32
Hoey, Clyde R. 114
Hoey Hall 114
Holly Spring College 26 27, 46–69, 128, 136
Holmes Convention Center 28
Home Guard 13
horse(s), horseback 29, 43, 76, 79, 83, 86, 94, 97, 102–3, 110, 121, 134–135, 145, 154, 166, 168, 175, 180–81, 184, 191
Horton, Emma *see* Moore, Emma Horton
Horton, Frazier 93
Horton, Ronda 90
Horton, W.P. 115
Horton family 91
hospital 205–206
The House *see* General Assembly
House Education Committee *see* General Assembly
Howard's Creek 161
Howard's Knob 78, 98, 132, 149, 154, 182, 242
Howell, Vance 5
Hunt, Satie 168–69, 174, 231
Hunter, Hiram T. 212, 225

illiteracy 75, 77, 188

Jefferson 12, 15–20
Jim Crow 100; *see also* African Americans
Johns River 30–31, 59, 75, 173
Johnson City, Tennessee 226
Johnson County, Tennessee 13–14, 25
Jones, John Walter (Jones House, Boone) 205
Joyner, James, Y. 101–7, 113, 188, 132–33, 140–43, 148
Junaluska, (Boone) 90, 93
Justice, E.J. 114, 139

Justice Hall 114, 179, 187, 198–200

Kitchin, William W. 41, 140, 147

Lanier, Ruby 78, 114, 233
Lees-McRae College 66, 122, 161, 220
Legislature *see* General Assembly
Lenoir 31, 37, 40, 44, 59, 73–74, 76, 85, 101, 110–11, 126, 129, 135, 143, 151, 168, 170, 177, 181, 193, 201, 220
Lenoir College 66, 126
Lenoir-Rhyne College 66, 85, 135, 220
Linney, Frank 141, 226
Linney, Romulus Z. 116–17, 129–30, 179
Linville 75, 115, 183
literary societies 27, 48, 94–95, 195, 210
Lovill, Edward Francis 107–8, 111, 114–16, 124–27, 138, 147, 235
Lovill, Will 108, 235
lumber 33, 75, 78, 85, 97, 119, 122, 182–83
lumbering/logging 10, 25, 61, 87, 94, 182–83, 231
Lutheran 66, 85
Lyon, Mary 32

Mabel 173
Madison, Ella Richards (Mrs. R. L. Madison) 220
Madison, Robert Lee (R.L.) 102–4, 128, 141, 144, 220
Maples, the Rev. L.L. 27–28
Mars Hill College 33–34, 36, 56, 65, 67, 93, 102, 104, 144, 149, 220
Marshall, William Furney 34–35, 50
Martin, Julius C. 147
Martin, LeRoy 229
Martin, Santford 229
Mast, Eve *see* Dougherty, Eve Mast
Mast, Eve Bower *see* Bower, Eve
Mast, Jacob 21, 55, 70
Mast, Ruben 12
Mast Store 97, 180
McIver, Charles Duncan 62, 64, 101, 105–6, 111–12, 132–33
McLean, Angus 213
Meadow View 89, 98, 119, 168
Meadows, Leon Renfroe 144, 218
Meat Camp 55

Mebane, Charles H. 64
Methodist 18, 66, 74, 86, 200
Methodist Church (Boone) 81, 99, 204
Milligan College 26
Mitchell County 96, 98, 103, 107–8, 115
Montezuma 115
Moore, Billy 37
Moore, Emma Horton 4, 113, 134, 225, 234
Moore, F.P. 74–75, 115, 230
Moore, Hight 37
Moore, Mrs. R.L. ("Edna") 220
Moore, Robert L. "Bob" 33–37, 41–42, 56, 67, 95
Morganton 71, 91–92, 238
Mt. Holyoke Seminary/Mt. Holyoke College 32

Nashville, Tennessee *see* Tennessee Centennial Exposition
Neal, "Miss Chessie" 175
Negro *see* African Americans
New River Academy 30, 39, 49, 91, 134
New River 7, 162, 164
New River Light and Power Company 161–66, 173
Newland 115
Newland, William C. 111, 113–14, 133–34, 139, 179
The Newland Bill 113–14, 179
Noble, Marcus C. S. 60, 105
Normal and Industrial Institute, Elizabeth City, NC 104
The Normal and Industrial School for White Women *see* University of North Carolina at Greensboro (UNCG)
Normal courses/departments, 68, 106, 110
Normal Institute (in NC counties/regions), 95, 100, 109–110
Normal School, 64, 66, 86, 107, 110, 119, 190, 192
North Carolina A & T University 64, 104
North Carolina Board of Education 190–91, 213, 228
North Carolina Board of Equalization 208, 213, 230
North Carolina College for Women *see* University of North Carolina at Greensboro (UNCG)
North Carolina General Assembly *see* General Assembly

Index

North Carolina Medical College 97, 180
North Carolina State Agricultural and Mechanical College 63, 106, 140
North Carolina State Agricultural and Technological University at Greensboro, *see also* A & T
North Carolina State Superintendent of Public Education 34, 43, 64, 102–9, 118, 132–33, 140–41, 148, 189–90, 212–13, 220
North Carolina Teachers Assembly 64, 184

Oak Hill Academy 30

Paschal, George W. 41, 66, 127
Patton, Robert Logan 31–37, 40, 42, 50, 66, 88, 185
Payne, Bruce L. 34
Peabody, George 62
Peabody College 34, 194, 200
Peabody Education Fund 61–62
People's Party 63
Perry, Gertrude 205
Perry, Henry Baker, Jr. "Johnnie," 206–7
Perry, Henry Baker, Sr. 83, 97, 180–81, 205–7
Perry, Mrs. H.B. Perry, Jr. *see* Brown, Lillie
Perry, Mrs. Henry Baker, Sr. (Doris Taylor) 206
Perry, Sarah Dougherty *see* Dougherty, Sarah
Polk, Leonidas L. 63, 97
population of Boone 83, 124, 191; *see also* Boone
Populist Political Party 1, 63–64
Poteat, William Lewis 41, 206–7, 231
Powell, Clara 55–56, 59, 73
Presbyterians 65–66
Prohibition, temperance 41, 117, 184–85

racism 93, 100–1; *see also* African American
Radford College 186
railroads 2, 25, 37, 39, 59, 61, 97, 104, 106–7, 112, 132, 140, 143, 146–49, 157, 173–76, 182–84, 205, 218
Raleigh 1, 16, 37, 45–46, 63, 97, 100, 104, 106, 109–14, 118, 121, 124–25, 132, 138, 140–42, 149, 156, 170, 176–78, 181, 190, 218, 237
Reconstruction *see* Civil War

Red Cross 59, 180, 201
Redmond, Mrs. Ruth (Ruth Barker) 201, 235, 238
Republicans 53, 56, 93, 117
Revolutionary War 7
Reynolds, Alonzo C. 144, 155
Reynolds Tobacco Company (R.J. Reynolds) 208
The Rhododendron 194, 196, 228
Rich Mountain 98, 117
Rivers, Robert Campbell (R.C.) 19, 39, 63, 70, 92, 96, 107
Rivers Street 90
R.J. Reynolds Tobacco Company 207
roads 2, 25, 31, 39, 50, 63, 65, 79, 97, 99, 100, 103, 105, 112, 130, 136, 168–70, 174, 183–4, 206–8, 235
Roan Creek 7, 9, 11, 24–25
Rockefeller, John D., Jr. 100, 125
Royall, W.B. 42
Rufty, Roy 224, 226

Scoggins, Elizabeth Brown *see* Brown, Elizabeth ("Lib")
Scopes Trial 206
Senate *see* General Assembly
Sherwood, A.C. "James" 52, 146
Sherwood, Martha 146, 178
Shipley, Anna Mae 180
Shull, Addie 84
Shull, Alice (Mrs. Lawson W. Campbell) 47, 137, 154, 226
Shull, David Harrison 22, 24–25
Shull, Edgar L. 142–43, 145, 148, 174, 222
Shull, Lillie *see* Dougherty, Lillie Shull
Shull, Martha Sousanna Lewis 22, 24–25, 142
Shull, Minnie 84
Shull, Mollie (Mrs. James H. Smith) 27, 47, 120
Shull, Mrs. Edgar *see* Hardin, Mary Lillington
Shull, Sarah (Mrs. David Shull) 24
Shull, Victoria (Vinnie; Mrs. Lawson W. Campbell) 47, 137, 178
Shull, Virginia (Nettie; Mrs. A. C. Sherwood) 120, 137, 142, 145–46, 178
Shulls Mill 24, 115, 183–84
Silverstone 117
Slater State Normal School (Winston-Salem State) 192
slaves (slavery) 11–12, 19, 26, 93, 101
Sloop, Eustace 75, 87, 186

Sloop, Mary 75, 87, 186
Smith, James Hamilton 26–27, 46–47, 49, 54, 60
Smith, Mollie Shull (Mrs. James H. Smith) *see* Shull, Mollie
Smith, Wiley 216, 218
Southern Appalachia 66
Southern Association of Colleges and Secondary Schools (SACSS) 158, 212
Southern Baptist Convention 218; *see also* Baptist
Southern Education Board/ Southern Board of Education 1, 101
Spainhour, Joseph Felix 30, 33–35, 38–39, 50, 71, 91, 96, 101, 185, 228, 236, 239
Spainhour, W.R. 30
Spanish-American War 61
Spanish Influenza *see* flu
Sparta 105, 220
Stanbury, W.A. 86
Stapp, Charles Patrick 144
Stedman, W. W. 177–178
Stone Mountain (Watauga County, North Carolina/ Johnson County, Tennessee) 8, 9, 12, 14, 25, 97
Sylva 103

Tater Hill 117
Taylor, Adolphus 155
Taylor, Charles E. 37, 38, 40–41, 44, 65
Taylor, Doris *see* Perry, Mrs. Henry Baker, Sr.
Taylor House 180
Taylor-Mast Store *see* Mast Store
Taylorsville 116–17, 129 145
teacher certification, certificates 72, 84, 86, 98, 102–3, 188, 196–97, 203, 205, 211
teacher training 1, 62–63, 84, 97, 102–12, 128, 130, 132–33, 134, 141, 143–44, 149, 170, 186, 188, 191–92, 197, 204, 219
teacher training institutes 63, 102, 104–6
temperance *see* prohibition
Tennessee Centennial Exposition 60–61, 87–88
Tennessee Valley Authority (TVA) 25
textile mills/manufacturers 87, 90, 112, 146, 186
Thompson, Betty 209–10
Thompson, Lola 209–10
Three Forks Baptist Institute 29, 70, 79, 230, 232
Time Magazine 110, 213

Index

tobacco 41, 87, 112, 132, 146, 178, 185, 208
Trade, Tennessee 25
trains *see* railroads
Trinity College 86, 97, 127, 150
Trivette, Ned 205
Tufts, Bessie 66, 161, 220
Tufts, Edgar 66, 161, 220
Tweetsie Railroad 176, 182–84, 205, 218, 226

United States 6–7, 13, 26, 37, 40, 61–62, 65, 100, 106, 112, 160, 176, 180, 206
U.S. Census 13, 83, 101
U.S. Congressional Committee on Education and Labor 61
United States Constitution: 18th Amendment 185; 19th Amendment 186
University of North Carolina at Chapel Hill 35, 60–61, 94, 104, 133, 140, 150, 156, 180–81
University of North Carolina at Greensboro (UNCG) 64–65, 101, 104, 111–12, 132–33; *see also* Normal and Industrial College, Greensboro; Normal and Industrial School for White Women; North Carolina College for Women
University of South Carolina 217

Valle Crucis 12, 24, 97, 115, 180–81, 184, 205–6
Vance, Zebulon B. 63
Venable, Francis P. 106
virgin forest 24
Virginia 7, 25, 30, 87, 130, 187, 196

wage labor 13, 43, 67, 87, 151, 166
Wake Forest College 3, 30, 34–49, 64–65, 79, 127, 150, 155, 206, 231
The War Between the States *see* Civil War
Ward, Ben 161

Warren Wilson College 66
Washington, D.C. 103, 106, 181
Watauga Academy 1, 74–120, 123–35, 129, 131–32, 137, 141, 152–53, 162, 180, 185, 188, 191–92, 198, 240; bartering for tuition 83; begins 81; boarding at 73–75, 86, 89, 96, 99, 119; Commencement 91–97, 120, 123, 257; Common School, Public School classes 81, 84, 247; a community effort 77; construction 77–78, 83, 91; contributions, donations for 77–78, 91; debates 94–95; *Dew Drop Catalogue* 91; enrollment 83, 85–86, 88, 96; fires 2, 128, 162, 238; land donated 73, 78; library 94; literary societies 91, 94–95, 128; name 74; a new Watauga Academy in Butler, Tennessee 128; Subscription school 79, 83, 85, 90; summer school 97; trustees 73, 90; tuition cost 85; working for tuition credit (work-study) 83
Watauga Baptist Association of Tennessee 60, 128
Watauga Club 63
Watauga County 1–2, 4, 8, 11–12, 14, 18–19, 28–29, 38–39, 42–43, 49, 55, 62–63, 67, 69, 70–72, 77, 79, 83, 85, 87, 91, 93, 96–97, 101–4, 107–8, 115, 117, 125–26, 130, 140, 143, 146, 151, 155, 161, 171, 173, 175, 179, 182–84, 186, 199, 205, 208, 218, 226, 228
Watauga County Board of Education 70, 72, 85, 140, 161
Watauga County Public Schools 72, 74–75, 77, 96, 101, 134, 230
The Watauga Democrat 38–39, 57, 63, 70–71, 73–75, 78–79, 81, 91–94, 96–97, 99, 107, 112, 115, 118, 156, 207, 225, 228, 231–32, 237
Watauga Lake 25

Watauga River 22, 24–2, 50, 128, 161, 182
Western Carolina Teachers College, 218, 218, 225
Western Carolina Teachers Training School 140, 212; *see also* Cullowhee High School; Western Carolina Teachers College; Western Carolina University
Western Carolina University 220
Wey, Herb 155, 217
White, R.B. 114
White Hall 114, 179
white supremacy 92–93, 100–1; grandfather clause 95 *see also* African Americans
Whitener, Daniel J. 75, 103
whites 1, 62–63, 77, 92, 100–1, 104, 125–26, 132, 188; *see also* African Americans
Wilkes County 32, 101, 115, 125
Wilkesboro 96, 117–18, 143, 151, 173, 185
Wilmington Massacre 92
Wilson, Chapell 200
Wilson, Woodrow 100
Winkler, Gordon 204–5
Winkler's Creek 145
Winston, George T. 140, 156
Winston-Salem State Normal School (Winston-Salem State University) 191
Women's Normal and Industrial College, Greensboro *see* University of North Carolina at Greensboro
women's suffrage 126, 184
World War I 159–60, 174–88, 208
World War II 212
Wright, Robert Herring 208

Yancey County 107–8, 115

Zionville 43